Curriculum Auditing

Curriculum Auditing

FENWICK W. ENGLISH, Ph.D.

PROFESSOR and HEAD
DEPARTMENT OF EDUCATIONAL ADMINISTRATION
COLLEGE OF EDUCATION
UNIVERSITY OF CINCINNATI
CINCINNATI, OHIO

LANCASTER · BASEL

Published in the Western Hemisphere by
Technomic Publishing Company, Inc.
851 New Holland Avenue
Box 3535
Lancaster, Pennsylvania 17604 U.S.A.

Distributed in the Rest of the World by
Technomic Publishing AG

Printed in the United States of America
10 9 8 7 6 5 4 3 2

Main entry under title:
Curriculum Auditing

A Technomic Publishing Company book
Bibliography: p. 353
Includes index p. 357

Library of Congress Card No. 88-050463
ISBN No. 87762-592-1

/ TABLE OF CONTENTS

/ INTRODUCTION

CURRICULUM AUDITING IS not a new concept in education. Decades ago, county superintendents rode on horseback and walked hundreds of miles to visit and inspect the schools. Their observations and thoughts have been recorded in their annual reports to the state superintendent.

Consider the following example of County Superintendent Samuel P. Bates of Crawford County, Pennsylvania, in *Pennsylvania Common Schools Report of the Superintendent of Common Schools*, June 4, 1860 (p. 43):

> The schools in all the districts have been kept open four months during the year, though the duplicates were recalled, and the tax reduced, in a few instances, after the destructive frosts of June. Most of the districts had six months, and a few had eight and ten months' terms. The schools were, generally, well managed, and the people were well satisfied with the results. A good system of classification was observed in every school in the county, and a liberal supply of black-boards is in constant use. About three-fourths of the schools are provided with large maps of North America, and in a few others Pelton's and Mitchell's outline maps have been supplied. A few schools have used Johnson's Philosophical charts with much profit. History of United States, physiology, philosophy, and algebra, are taught in a large number of schools; and geometry, chemistry, descriptive astronomy, and the rudiments of the languages, in a few of them. I have visited, during the year, about two hundred and thirty schools, and the district superintendents, in many districts, have visited their schools once a month.

As this report indicates, the forerunner of the curriculum audit found itself rooted in the same data base as today: visitations, interviews, observations, and document review. Then, as now, the impact of the observations was grounded in their "publicness" and general visibility, not to mention the capability of the observer to forcefully articulate the meaning and impact of the review itself.

The difference between the auditing function then and now lies in the implications of the record revealed. Schools have historically been accountable for teaching and the quality of teaching. Only recently have they been specifically accountable for learning. The rise of pupil measurement and the increased precision of the measurement process have provided a base for discussing "results." So successful has the *accountability movement* been, that no one seriously challenges the idea that schools should be judged on their *learning effectiveness*, not solely on their teaching capabilities.

Of course, there are, and continue to be, serious challenges to the validity of measurement and what some instruments in fact assess, and a continuing debate about the criteria and assumptions utilized in the selection and rejection of the actual content of school curriculum.

I learned about curriculum audits by doing them. The first was a programmatic audit of the Title I thrust in the Hartford (Connecticut) Public Schools in the late 1970s. As a result of a career change from the superintendency to an eventual partnership in the Big 8 accounting and consulting firm of Peat, Marwick, Mitchell (now Peat, Marwick, Main), I ended up managing the first programmatic audit of a complete curriculum in a large urban system in Columbus, Ohio, in 1979.

The Columbus engagement taught me much about the process of programmatic auditing. I learned from this experience the power of human observation as expressed in language and how what might be a deadly dull report can be made lively and emotional. I learned about how human systems do and do not make tangible messages from the policy actions to operational actions. Mostly, I learned how school systems continually "co-opt" power at the apex of the organization and dilute it, so that in schools and classrooms almost no policy decision makes much difference. Thus, do superintendents ensure that they "run" the schools instead of the respective boards of education.

And in the midst of what otherwise might be a rather pessimistic message about whether public education is or can be more responsive to the public, I learned how the *linkages* can be created within school systems to enable them to become so.

That experience and subsequent audits in six other states have convinced me that school systems are possible. Any real observer of American public education has to conclude that most school systems are not really systems at all, but confederations. The advantage of a system is to enable the client to partake functionally of a structured series of experiences embodied in a curriculum that minimizes disruptions in learning caused by a disjointed and uncoordinated series of teachers "each doing his/her own thing," however interesting that might be. Complex learning requires a very systematic effort over many years. In short, it requires focus.

Working in real school systems struggling to conquer coordination problems, financial difficulties, debilitating internal and external squabbles, lack of solid leadership, ignorance of sound managerial principals, and rampant romanticism about "reform," have established for me an internalized view of how school systems can be created to replace collections of schools. The *curriculum audit* is a very powerful process and product to build synergistic muscles, tissue, and bone for acquiring a new form of organizational effectiveness and efficiency in public education.

So, I'm very impatient with critics of public education who in essence want to dismantle it further with plans for "empowerment," which would be a giant step backward.

If "empowerment" means that every individual teacher decides what's best and creates his or her own curriculum, there can be no system to teaching whatsoever. It means some children will receive four years of dinosaurs and others will know nothing of them at all. It will mean some children will be learning critical thinking skills and others will be doing only rote work. And ultimately it will mean that boards of education cannot be accountable for anything to do with learning or teaching because their election or appointment will have nothing to do with what goes on in the schools. A good deal of the lack of responsiveness of school systems currently is the direct result of ineffective curriculum management.

The curriculum audit is *system oriented*, though the audit technology is capable of being used to track a non-system, if that is what the planners have in mind. Auditing is a technology and it can be employed to ascertain how well system-wide goals/objectives are being reached or how well initiated change at the sub-system level is being pursued by relatively autonomous units that make up the whole.

To those who have never engaged in an audit, never examined the power it contains, or never seen the changes which occur as a result of engaging in one, the process is more than the "technicization of education." Educational philosophers, particularly those with little or no administrative experience, rapidly dismiss such ideas as mechanical and minor adjustments in an otherwise mindless machine. They vastly oversimplify the efforts of many practitioners because they often lack direct familiarity with what practitioners do, and are openly hostile to the function of administration in public education. Very few have produced a workable model of education that operates on assumptions credible in the real world.

I view this book as an effort to explain curriculum audits and how I've done them. There is certainly much more to learn. The process is one of continual refinement.

Chapter I of the book deals with the question, "Why audit?" Broadly conceptualized, auditing is a very old human activity. It has many manifestations and forms. In this chapter the criteria for determining if an audit is warranted are presented. There are at least three basic types of audits, and they are described in this chapter as well.

Chapter II is a comprehensive chapter regarding standards of the audit. It fleshes out data sources and shows how the three primary activities of document review, interviews, and site visitations yield answers to the questions inherent in each audit standard.

Chapter III of the book deals with writing the audit and the guidelines in creating the final document, including the use of photographs.

Chapter IV is an exposé of the *hidden curriculum* as revealed through the medium of still photographs. This facet of auditing is perhaps the most fertile for further development. It also is one of the most creative elements within the auditing concept.

The next four chapters (V–VIII) present case studies. All of them were actual audits conducted in the time period 1986–1987. Originally I wanted to reproduce all of them with the actual district names and photographs. However, I finally decided to use pseudonyms. While two of the districts consented to their use, one did not. One is involved with litigation and may end up in the U.S. Supreme Court. I was advised against using the audit in print without the permission of the district, which I deemed impossible to obtain under the circumstances.

One option open to me would have been to drop the two and use audits obtained prior to 1986. I decided against this because the two audits presented some of the most difficult situations I've encountered in doing auditing during the last eight years. The reader deserves to see the most challenging cases.

To prevent identification of the districts, I've therefore omitted descriptive references that could pinpoint their exact geographical location, and detail is missing where I believed it would reveal the actual school district.

It should be noted, however, that all of the audits were paid for with public funds and that they are public documents. All but one have been reported in the public press. The one that was not was subject to an intensive cross-examination in a public forum. So while there is nothing secretive about the actual case studies, there is some sensitivity about exposing them to a larger national audience via this book. I can say that the audits were conducted in urban, suburban, and semi-rural settings in widely different regions in the U.S.

The reader will also note that I have not spent a lot of detail on explaining "how to" handle collating data or attacking certain data generative situations. The purpose of the case studies is to demonstrate just how data is utilized, including the use of quotations. In this sense the case studies speak for themselves. They also illustrate the shortcomings of the audit as opposed to, say, conventional research reporting.

But I've noted in the text in several places that curriculum audits are not products of conventional research methods, though some of the techniques are the same. An audit is a problem-solving tool. It dares to tread where research would only describe or modestly hypothesize. The audit accepts standards that research may only moderately support or even contradict. The world of action in which board members, administrators, and teachers function each day is still a mystery to many researchers and the research activity itself. The audit is simply more assertive on some points than I suspect most researchers would feel comfortable with.

Chapter IX deals with pre- and post-auditing activities. These are the tangible linkages that fully connect the audit to practice and to the promise of salutary change.

Chapter X is devoted to considering the audit in a non-rational school system.

I felt compelled to deal with this topic because of the important work in organizational theory by Karl Weick at the University of Texas and David Clark at the University of Virginia. These two professors are pushing conventional organizational thinking very hard and, in many ways, issuing severe challenges to our notions of what makes a "good" organization.

Throughout the book I also reference some of the important thought of the leftists in curriculum and education. While they have largely been ignored in the popular "main line" curriculum journals, they have much to offer practitioners by the way of reflective critique. Specifically, the works of Michael Apple, Henry Giroux, and Stanley Aronowitz are cited in the text. While I find their ideas challenging, I've also indicated where they cease to have much relevance for practitioners, as I know them, in the forty-nine states and several hundred school districts where I've worked in the last twenty years. But, at least for me, they have been instrumental in forcing a re-examination of more than a few of my own assumptions. The restatement of the working assumptions of the audit has therefore been far more malleable and tentative because of their writings. While certainty is a great asset in undertaking most ventures, it ought to be secured through nothing less than a continual criticism of one's own beliefs and methods. Henry Giroux exemplifies this outlook better than anyone else I've read.

And what of the millions of school children daily laboring in our schools? Walking through the hallways and corridors has left me with a myriad of impressions. Some days I have felt overcome with optimism and been positively reinforced. Amid some of the most terrible working conditions one could imagine, serious learning occurs which is reflective and meaningful. Other times I've felt decidedly pessimistic. Some schools lobotomize the brains and eviscerate the human spirit from the children they are supposed to be helping. Instead of helping children become independent, we make them addicts of the worst kind of social trivia imaginable, lifelong victims of TV sitcoms and numbing game show glitz. Social realities are explained away in ritualized myths that are perpetuated as knowledge worth learning.

This criticism of schools is not new. One of the most famous American courtroom lawyers, orators, thinkers and iconoclasts of all time, wrote of his boyhood in school in Kinsman, Ohio, in the mid-nineteenth century:

> As I look back at my days at the district school and the academy, I cannot avoid a feeling of the appalling waste of time. . . .
>
> For my part, I never could learn grammar, at either the primary or the high school. I have used language extensively all my life, and no doubt have misused it too; in a way, I have made a living from its use, but I am convinced that I was rather hindered than helped in this direction by the public schools. . . .
>
> Memorizing history is likewise of no avail. We learned the names of presidents and kings, of the generals, of the chief wars . . . but none of it had any relation to our lives. . . . As well might Caesar and Hannibal and Napoleon have inhibited Mars, so far as we students were concerned. To us they meant nothing but dry and musty dates and proper names.
>
> Schools were not established to teach and encourage the pupil to think; beyond furnishing a place for keeping the children out of the way, their effort was to cement the minds of pupils according to certain moulds.[1]

The writer was the defender of Eugene V. Debs, John T. Scopes, and many others, the ultimate cross-examiner, Clarence Darrow, who was right and lost both cases, Debs and Scopes.

And there is both the promise and potential pitfall of auditing. Audit the wrong thing and it is done better next time. We have to be sure we are going in the right direction before we audit. No amount of auditing can excuse us from the ultimate responsibility of defining and shaping purposeful activity towards ends which are enobling and emancipatory.

Having been a party to some twenty audits and witnessed the power of the activity, it is with the greatest sensitivity that its application is

[1]Clarence Darrow (1932). *The Story of My Life*. New York: Grosset & Dunlap. pp. 22–25.

passed on in this book to the larger audience who may use it. I hope that its wider utilization will enable schools to become more socially responsible by changing society wherever prejudice, injustice, and poverty may be excused or perpetuated, and wherever a teacher teaches the truth, no matter how unpopular. That is the challenge, not so much for the audit, but for the people who use it.

Fenwick W. English
Cincinnati, Ohio

/ I / *Why Audit?*

AUDITING HAS A time-honored function in human affairs. The broadest definition of *auditing* is simply an objective, external review of a record, event, process, product, act, belief, or motivation to commit an act. Consider these contemporary examples:

- The U.S. Supreme Court reviews the decision of a lower court and rejects its findings (Mirga, 1987, p. 1).
- A National Investigation Board is convened to delve into the reasons for the Challenger debacle (Recer, 1986, p. 5).
- A routine financial audit of a student activity account at a New Jersey high school shows a discrepancy of more than $16,000 and leads to the indictment and conviction of the accounting teacher and the high school principal (Wharton, 1987, p. 1).
- A university convenes a special panel of professors to check the accuracy of a colleague suspected of faking his research data (Wheller, 1987, pp. 1, 7).
- An accreditation visitation committee files a report regarding whether a high school should receive formal approval to be certified.
- The President of the United States forms a special review board (Tower, Muskie, and Scowcroft, 1987) to examine the conduct of members of his administrative team in matters of foreign policy and affairs.
- The FAA conducts a formal inquiry to review the reasons for a jetliner plane crash.
- A special review of ballots cast in an election reveals some were improperly marked.

The origins of auditing can be traced back to the palace of Nestor in ancient Greece, where records have been found of the work of accountants (Stevens, 1981, p. 3). In the conduct of human activities, reviews, inquiries, investigations, studies, and reports are so common, we don't often think of them as anything special.

When people want to know why a disaster occurred so as to establish culpability and determine liability, determine possible cause and effect relationships, and prevent a similar occurrence from happening again, an audit-type activity is employed.

When President John F. Kennedy was assassinated in Dallas, Texas, newly installed chief executive Lyndon Johnson felt a Lone Star State inquiry would be nothing but a whitewash (Manchester, 1963, p. 630). Johnson therefore pressed Chief Justice Earl Warren into heading a commission that heard ninety-four witnesses over six months and questioned 395 other people through investigative activities.

The final report established that a single assassin had been responsible, and that there was not a larger plot involved. Yet many of the other findings were downplayed when it came to formulating recommendations regarding Presidential security, particularly as it pertained to the FBI and the Secret Service (Manchester, 1963, p. 631).

When the New York brokerage firm of E. F. Hutton got involved in a check-kiting scheme in which the actions of its management led to bilking banks of millions in interest earned due to deliberate overdrafting, the scandal drew several federal inquiries resulting in a $2 million fine from the Justice Department.

Yet Hutton went further. It independently contracted with former U.S. Attorney General Griffin B. Bell to conduct his own investigation. Bell issued a 183-page report, which was based on the work of fourteen lawyers, who interviewed more than 370 current and former employees. The report, a stringent example of an audit, recommended disciplining fourteen high-level executives with substantial fines and letters of reprimand (Koepp and Constable, 1985, p. 54).

An educational example of an equally profound and violent conflict is illustrated in the National Education Association's Inquiry Panel of the textbook rebellion in Kanawha County, West Virginia in the late 1970s (NEA, 1975).

The Kanawha County conflict involved flaming rhetoric and bombings, carried out by self-appointed fundamentalist groups who opposed certain textbooks which had been adopted by the Board of Education. The NEA Inquiry Panel held open hearings in Charleston, West Virginia, for four days. They listened to over seventy witnesses from a variety of groups and as individuals. An eighty-six-page report was generated which noted:

> The storm . . . has left in its wake . . . a Board of Education whose elected majority has been intimidated; a superintendent who has been driven out; teachers who are frustrated, angry, and fearful; and students who have had a lesson in demagoguery that undoubtedly has had a

> more depressing and negative effect than any textbook words . . . could have (NEA, 1975, p. 54).

The NEA Panel concluded:

> There was a failure on the part of school officials to anticipate an adverse reaction to the adoption of these language arts materials (p. 59).
>
> There was a failure to prepare in advance for the possibility of protest (p. 60).
>
> There was a failure to respond promptly and effectively to the first challenge (p. 61).

The audits reported in this book, like those that comprise the bulk of auditing activity, are considerably less traumatically induced than those provoked by national calamities or media events. They are more routine and conducted with less fanfare than those just portrayed. Indeed, the power of an audit is that it reflects standard operating procedure rather than something extraordinary in the way of good practice.

THE MANAGEMENT AUDIT

A curriculum audit is a type of management audit. Sayle (1981) has defined a *management audit* as:

> an independent examination of objective evidence, performed by trained personnel, to determine whether integrated management systems, which are required to fulfill the contractual and legal obligations . . . are being effectively implemented (p. 4).

Historically, the audit function in schools was performed by the county superintendent and before that by individual members of the board of education. Records of the observations of county superintendents still exist in state archives and some public libraries.

One is cited here as evidence that the management audit function has been around schools for a very long time as standard operating procedure and in curriculum specifically for just as long.

In the 1866 *Report of the Superintendent of Common Schools of Pennsylvania*, Bedford County Superintendent John W. Dickerson reported on curricular matters. In those days, curriculum was reported as *courses of study* (a term still used today). Wrote Dickerson:

> It is also clearly the spirit and intention of the school laws that directors (board members) shall prescribe the course of study to be pursued in the schools; that is, that they shall determine what branches the pupils shall pursue, and when they shall begin them. This is always done in the union and graded schools. . . . In our ungraded country schools . . . it is seldom done. Parents prescribe the studies, or pupils select them, and take only such as they fancy they will like.

The result is, there is no such thing as a regular course of study, no system or regularity. One pupil studies one branch, another studies a different branch. In one school all study mental arithmetic; in another they all neglect it, and so with the other branches.

. . . The following statement of ten schools is a fair illustration of the whole county in this respect:

School	Reading in 3d, 4th & 5th Readers	Studying mental arith-metic	Studying written arith-metic	Studying geogra-phy	Studying grammar
First school	17	3	12	0	11
Second school	5	0	0	11	0
Third school	21	24	11	0	0
Fourth school	11	3	11	0	0
Fifth school	8	0	5	12	1
Sixth school	13	0	6	0	1
Seventh school	12	3	7	0	2
Eighth school	11	7	0	0	0
Ninth school	31	14	14	2	1
Tenth school	14	17	2	0	0

Dickerson then noted that, with respect to 100 schools in his county, 1,271 pupils were reading 3d, 4th, or 5th readers, 811 were studying mental arithmetic, 735 were studying written arithmetic, 398 geography, and 167 grammar. He commented:

These statements seem to me to disclose a most lamentable condition of things. The excuses given by parents and pupils, and sometimes by teachers are that "the higher branches are of no use," or that "if pupils study so many branches, they will make no progress in any" (p. 56).

The county superintendent then rejoined with these arguments:

Pupils who at the proper time take up and study all of the branches, are most proficient in each and every one of them; and pupils who study a few branches, and neglect the rest, are most deficient even in the few branches they study (p. 57).

The problem of school to school curricular variability still exists in many school systems today. That variability plays havoc with system responsiveness to state testing mandates which require a tight curriculum and low variability within schools and across schools.

County Superintendent Dickerson had performed a kind of *curriculum mapping* exercise (English, 1978) in which he was focusing on the lack of the ability of the system to provide for a desired level of consistency and continuity in what students were being taught. Without that consistency being present in real terms, a common curriculum was an impossibility. In this case, there was no common school.

Management audits or *operations audits* can be performed on most any function within a school or school district. The personnel system can be examined or payroll or the automated data systems. This book is focused on the curriculum.

Management audits are most often performed to seek answers to the following questions:

(1) Does the system or sub-system being audited know the proper content and scope of its functions or services?

(2) How has the system or sub-system being audited determined that its existing content and scope of functions/services is correct?

(3) Is the system or sub-system being audited in control of the necessary resources and decisions regarding functions/services in order to shape and deploy them effectively?

(4) Have data been gathered regarding the functions/services being performed?

(5) Have the data been used as feedback to improve the functions/services?

(6) Has the use of feedback resulted in an improved level of functions/services being delivered? Consistently?

(7) Have an improved array of functions/services resulted in lowering the costs of the same functions/services?

(8) What recommendations can be formulated to improve the quantity, quality, configuration, scope and cost-effectiveness of those functions/services?

(9) What steps must the district officials take to implement the recommendations?

(10) What is a reasonable period of time for all of the above to occur?

CONTEMPORARY PRESSURES TO CONSIDER AUDITING

The contemporary educational scene is littered with provocations and pressures to consider auditing as a rational response.

The National Reports

Beginning with Secretary T. H. Bell's National Commission on Excellence in Education's *Open Letter to the American People* (U.S. Department of Education, 1983), there was a flood of urgent calls for changes and reforms in the schools.

The tone of the report was best embodied in its title *A Nation at*

Risk. The report sent a chill down the collective national spine with its opening clarion, "Our once unchallenged preeminence in commerce, industry, science, and technological innovation is being overtaken by competitors throughout the world" (p. 5).

Calling the state of the schools "an act of unthinking, unilateral educational disarmament," the commission's view was that "the educational foundations of our society are presently being eroded by a rising tide of mediocrity" (p. 5).

A Nation at Risk was a kind of national educational audit in and of itself. The National Commission's findings began with the perceived shortcomings in curriculum. They noted that:

- Secondary school curricula have been homogenized, diluted, and diffused to the point that they no longer have a central purpose . . . we have a cafeteria-style curriculum in which . . . appetizers and desserts can easily be mistaken for the main courses (p. 18).
- This curricular smorgasboard, combined with extensive student choice, explains a great deal about where we find ourselves today (p. 18).
- Twenty-five percent of the credits earned by general track high-school students are in physical and health education, work experience outside the school, remedial English and mathematics, and personal service and development courses (p. 19).
- In thirteen states, 50 percent or more of the units required for high school graduation may be electives chosen by the student (p. 20).
- "Minimum competency" examinations (now required in thirty-seven states) fall short of what is needed, as the "minimum" tends to become the "maximum," thus lowering educational standards for all (p. 20).

When it came to formulating recommendations, the authors of *A Nation at Risk*, chaired by David P. Gardner, president of the University of California, stipulated:

(1) Strengthening graduation requirements in the "new basics" which included four years of English, three years of mathematics, three years of science, three years of social studies, one-half year of computer science, and for the college-bound, two years of foreign language

(2) The adoption of more rigorous and measurable standards and higher expectations for students

(3) Significantly more time to the "new basics," more effective use of the school day, a longer school day and an increased school year

(4) Improving teacher preparation by requiring higher standards and improved academic competence

(5) That citizens hold educators and elected officials responsible for providing the leadership to achieve the proposed reforms

The commission spoke to parents directly when it said, "You have the right to demand for your children the best our schools and colleges can provide. Your vigilance and your refusal to be satisfied with less than the best are the imperative first step" (p. 35).

It was in the matter of assurance that the necessity for an audit and the auditing process was generated. Assurance is the basis for trust and confidence. Those factors are the foundation for public support.

The same condition prompted the growth of the role of accountants in the private sector. The business panic of 1907 witnessed the failure of banks and business enterprises in sufficiently large numbers to prompt J. P. Morgan to invite Marwick and Mitchell (now Peat, Marwick, Main) to assess publicly the strength of one of his main banks, the Knickerbocker Trust Company. That work is credited with helping to end the panic of 1907 by restoring public trust and confidence in the banking industry (Stevens, 1981, p. 4).

Trust is not engendered by calling for "trust," rather it is fostered by a visible, tangible record of operations and improvement. Trust is results- or outcome-based. It is rooted in openness, not secrecy. Its main referent is visibility. The auditing process is a matter of public record. There is the clear expectation that the audit will be made public no matter what it discloses. The actual "ground zero" revealed becomes the base upon which to build for an improved future. The political power of an audit always rests upon its full disclosure, its publicness. No matter how technically brilliant an audit may be, it will not generate improved public support for schools unless it is a public document.

The national reports of the 1980s heightened public expectation of education and helped foster an increased militancy on the part of parents and their representatives in the fifty state capitals for a larger role in the schools and significantly upgraded technical and testing mandates. These efforts have vastly increased the acceleration of recasting the curriculum that had already begun prior to the national reports' being issued.

State Initiatives

As the myriad of reports (see Griesemer and Butler, 1983) cascaded into the national press and rippled into the respective state capitals, legislation began to pour forth to give muscle to the recommendations contained within them.

A flurry of legislative mandates implemented expanded state testing, state-developed curriculum and curriculum standards, teacher career ladders, and changed licensing procedures for educational professionals. Some even began developing proposals to put failing school districts in bankruptcy, most notably, several in New Jersey (McCoy, 1987, pp. 1, 5-B).

At a meeting of the Republican governors in 1986, U.S. Education Secretary William Bennett said, "If a school is failing, I think the state has a responsibility to the parents and the children in that school to give them an alternative" (Seglem, 1986, p. 9-A).

Tennessee Governor Lamar Alexander similarly agreed, "There are some schools doing such a poor job that probably we ought to take them over and reorganize them the way we do a failing business" (Seglem, 1986).

New Mexico Governor Garrey Carruthers enjoined, ". . . if you're going to have accountability, then you must call in the accounts on someone" (Seglem, 1986).

The chief state school officers agreed to seek the funds to develop a common testing instrument that would be utilized in all fifty states and become the basis for state by state comparisons of achievement in the future (Olson, 1986, pp. 1, 14).

Governor Bill Clinton of Arkansas was responsible for pumping $32 million new dollars into higher education. "This country is in a period of profound economic change. To have real economic growth, we're going to have to produce more better-educated people" (Jaschik, 1986, p. 25).

Clinton issued a warning about how to approach the issue of more state funds for education. Cautioning against "the motherhood-and-apple-pie approach," he noted that some of those using this popular slogan don't follow through on what happens to the dollars. Clinton made it clear that he saw increasing financial support tied to increased demands on the educational system for results, specifically higher education, which was "notoriously resistant to change" (Jaschik, 1986, p. 25).

Local Pressures and Problems

As the costs of education have steadily risen at both the state and local levels, taxpayers have steadily resisted the increased demands for more funding. "The early 1980s have brought a period of disillusionment with professionals in general and educators in particular. Distrust has grown as more claimants at the local level squabble over a limited resource base of support for the public schools" (Kirst, 1984, p. 12).

Proposition 13 in California and Proposition 2½ in Massachusetts were popular expressions of taxpayer rage and frustration which took on referendum form. The impact upon schools in both states has been devastating, particularly in the scope of the services offered and the numbers of professional staff employed.

Where local taxpayers still retain the power to deal with costs, the results can be frustrating. Take the case of the Palmyra public schools in New Jersey. In 1987, Palmyra voters defeated a bond issue for the sixth time in ten years. "Senior citizens . . . were lined up 15 deep when the polls opened at 2 p.m." (Ottaviano, 1987, p. B-1).

The results of the defeat will be serious penalties imposed upon the school district by the state education department, and the possible loss of accreditation. With these facts known, the bond issue still went down.

In November of 1979 the Chicago public schools teetered on the verge of bankruptcy. The system's superintendent and assistant superintendent for business had resigned amid revelations that funds had been improperly transferred from building/bond accounts to the general fund to support current expenses (Cronin, 1980, p. 5).

As representatives of the state of Illinois, the city of Chicago, and the board of education met to resolve the financial problems, it became apparent that to do so would require massive system-wide cuts. Under the direction of a top manager from the Inland Steel Company, four task forces were organized involving eighty-three loaned executives from the ranks of big businesses and corporations in Chicago.

The four task forces filed a report (*Special Task Force on Education*, 1981) which began, "Chicago's schools are in trouble. Everybody knows it. Everybody deplores it." The report then reeled off the problems:

- years of top-level conflict between the general superintendents and the board of education
- serious inbreeding which has curbed outside influence
- overcentralization
- declining employee morale
- neighborhood groups with special agendas which conflict with system-wide needs
- resources spent on retaining unneeded school buildings which should be closed

- labor unions desiring privileges not common to most labor management agreements
- too few parents involved in the schools
- declining student population

After examining the functions of instructional management, administration and support, personnel management, and overall organization design, the task forces developed 253 recommendations of which 65 percent could be implemented by the school administration and which would annually save the Chicago Board of Education $18,063,000 and the city of Chicago $440,000.

In the area of curriculum the task forces revealed that four departments within the Chicago public schools shared responsibility for curriculum planning and development. The major Department of Curriculum consisted of thirteen bureaus and had a fiscal 1981 budget of $2.8 million.

The recommendations developed to improve curriculum planning and implementation in Chicago were as follows:

(1) Reaffirm effective education as the school system's first priority with other activities structured to support this goal.

(2) Establish measurable goals, objectives and priorities against which to measure system performance and the general superintendent.

(3) Communicate short- and long-range goals for the school system to the public.

(4) Have key personnel develop annual plans to achieve board objectives.

(5) Mandate the use of the objectives and sequential content of the system's approved curriculum as minimum learning goals for students.

(6) Establish closer coordinating relationships between the units responsible for curriculum design and implementation.

(7) Consolidate the Departments of Curriculum and Instruction Services.

(8) Include computer education within the Department of Curriculum or the proposed Department of Curriculum and Instruction Services.

(9) Integrate the Bureau of Computer-Assisted Instruction (CAI) into related bureaus such as Language Arts and transfer other functions presently done by CAI such as mathematics, to the appropriate bureau within the Department of Curriculum.

(10) Increase coordinators in special program areas to facilitate local

participation in curriculum development and to assist in curriculum implementation.

(11) Improve the local school's ability to provide effective instructional programs.

(12) Give principals full responsibility for all operations in their schools.

(13) Assign an assistant principal to each elementary school.

(14) Strengthen the ability of the district offices to implement more effective instructional programs.

(15) Increase staff in the Departments of Curriculum and Instruction Services.

(16) Provide pertinent, timely management data to enhance the instruction program.

(17) Institute a system-wide plan to ensure instructional continuity.

(18) Combine the Bureau of Special Education with the Division of Programs for the Gifted.

(19) Ensure that vocational education programs provide students with current entry-level skills.

(20) Provide in-service vocational education training for high school principals, counselors and program schedulers.

(21) Conduct orientation sessions whenever special programs are introduced into a school.

(22) Develop a comprehensive mission statement and implementation plan for carrying out the system's evaluation function.

(23) Contract for an annual audit of the city-wide testing program and placement and exiting procedures for students enrolled in special programs.

(24) Increase the professional staff.

(25) Establish a communications system to serve operating units responsible for data collection, program planning and evaluation and development of funding proposals.

(26) Extend the use of textbooks to a five-year cycle.

(27) Develop a computerized inventory for textbooks and vocational education equipment.

(28) Develop a shortened list of standard texts for each subject area.

(29) Transfer responsibility for the selection, approval, and storage of standard texts from the Bureau of Instruction Materials to the Department of Curriculum.

(30) Require publishers to demonstrate a minimum 80 percent correlation between their texts and curriculum objectives.

(31) Establish centralized distribution for textbooks.
(32) Establish a maximum for administrative services charged to the Free Textbook Fund.
(33) Include audio-visual equipment repairs in the authorized uses for monies from the Free Textbook Fund.
(34) Establish a program to rebind usable books.
(35) Define the role of the school system's library program.
(36) Improve communications between the Bureau of Libraries and other areas in the school system.
(37) Consolidate responsibility for the film collection in the Bureau of Visual Education.
(38) Designate one person at each school as media coordinator (pp. 18–39).

The Chicago task force had really performed a curriculum audit as we now know it. The examination involved not only the function of curriculum in a school system, which was "to attain adherence to basic curricula" (p. 18), but had to confront the obvious organizational problems involved. The way the system had organized itself to carry out its functions became an obstacle to the goal for which it was created in the first place. These had to be resolved before its job within the system could be successfully performed.

A curriculum audit means examining curriculum within an operational context and not in an ivory tower. Too many professors of curriculum in colleges and universities are little more than armchair theorists about curricular matters and problems because they have had no real administrative experience with curriculum in functional schools and school systems.

The Chicago audit is a startling and expansive sweep of the problems of curriculum and school administration (English, 1986–87) confronting curriculum professionals today. It is not only the creation of curriculum per se, but its evaluation and measurement, textbook adoption, and library and audio-visual support that must be considered. All of these must be coordinated and integrated around specific objectives in order to configure the system's resources effectively and efficiently.

The Chicago audit closed with these comments that could fit many local school districts just as aptly:

> There is much to be done. So many of the necessary ingredients of a successful organization have been missing: strong leadership; board-management trust; planning; accountability; training; employee morale; merit reward and punishment; and a strong sense of direction (p. xi).

Dealing with the Cost-Quality Relationship

It was assumed in the Chicago audit that if the school system followed the recommendations that it would become increasingly capable of delivering improved services and thereby foster greater pupil achievement. It would also engender greater public support in terms of financial backing. This is based on the idea that with improvements, more money will bring about upgraded (i.e., "better") services (Burrup and Brimley, 1982, p. 23).

The relationship between costs and quality are far from obvious in education, particularly as it pertains to the various state efforts to define and mandate quality for schools (Wise, 1979). Yet it remains the central thesis when anyone is concerned about improving the schools.

Perhaps one example might be supplied in the case of Hampton University. Historically, Hampton was a black university and for the last fifteen years was not able to balance its budget. A new president, William R. Harvey, was elected and tackled the cost-quality relationship head on.

In his first year, Mr. Harvey wiped out Hampton's $500,000 debt and ended the year with a $44,000 surplus. Since then, enrollment spurted up 57 percent to 4,300; endowment increased by 145 percent to $71 million; corporate contributions increased by 190 percent to $994,000; foundation gifts by 767 percent to $2.1 million; and federal grants by 152 percent to $9.7 million. In 1985 there were 5,000 applications for 800 places in the freshman class.

"We have emphasized management and budget as a means of achieving high-quality education," muses Harvey." People like to buy into quality and success" (Evans, 1986, p. 16).

Harvey's success may be based on more image than substance, yet it is hard to ignore the message that is there: continually poor mouthing education and citing poor pupil performance do not lead to confidence in providing more money for schools. Turning the corner means putting one's own ship in order and showing that one is getting the most from what one has.

It is that motivation that probably led the New York City Board of Education president to suspend members of a local board in upper Manhattan after a ten-month grand jury investigation showed that "sleazy politics . . . emphasized favors for personal friends and political club colleagues over the needs of Bronx children" (Prial, 1987, p. 33).

Said the president, "Our sending in the team to District 6 is all part of an effort to show the districts we are going to hold them accountable to education" (Perlez, 1987).

Tuition Tax Credits

Public disaffection with the schools has led to a variety of proposals to create alternatives. Legislative proposals to permit tax credits that parents could use in sending their children to non-public schools have been introduced at the federal or state level since 1967. During the period 1967–77, six tuition tax credit proposals were approved by the U.S. Senate. In the 95th Congress tuition tax credit bills were introduced in both the House and the Senate. At the state level, over twelve legislatures have considered tuition tax credit proposals. The state of Minnesota introduced such a law which has been subsequently upheld by the U.S. Supreme Court (Mueller v. Allen, 1983).

Seccombe (1987) examined a sample of families in Connecticut to determine how many would take advantage of a $300.00 tuition tax credit if it were made available to them. She found that approximately 25 percent of the parents would use the tax credit in sending their children to a private/parochial school.

Seccombe's study matched other studies of parental attitudes. Gratiot (1979) found that income levels between public and private school parents were not significant factors in shifting children to private schools. Gratiot discerned that dissatisfaction with public schools was the crucial variable in selecting non-public schools.

The issues for which parents selected private schools were primarily lack of achievement in the public schools, concerns with classroom discipline, academic standards, class size, and lack of religious instruction (Edwards and Richardson, 1981; and Frechtling and Frankel, 1982).

If approximately one-quarter of the students would be moved from the public to a non-public school with a modest (under $1,000) tax credit at the state or federal level, that portends a rather significant shift in overall pupil population.

If approximately 45 million students are in elementary and secondary schools with 5 million already in non-public schools (Seccombe, 1987), a 25 percent movement would mean losing 10 million children. The impact upon the public schools would be enormous and costly.

It also seems apparent that the reason parents move their children from a public to a non-public school is not for curricular innovations, popular fads, electives, more creativity, or openness in schools, but because the public schools are perceived as too lax, too open, too permissive, with too many electives. The message behind both the tuition tax credit legislation and the surveys of why parents moved their children to non-public schools, or would move them to non-public schools, is to obtain solid, directed, basic academic instruction. The overwhelming reasons appear to be conservative rather than liberal.

What parents want, at least those who would move or strongly consider moving their children from the public schools, are the perceived essential cultural transmission curriculum content (Miller and Seller, 1985, pp. 37–60).

International Concerns and Problems

Once the world's leading exporter of steel, in recent decades the U.S. has become the world's largest importer. The problems of the steel industry in the U.S. have been graphically described by John Strohmeyer in *Crisis in Bethlehem* (1986).

Strohmeyer chronicles the rise of the second leading U.S. producer of steel, Bethlehem, that built the Golden Gate and George Washington bridges, the Waldorf Astoria Hotel in New York City, the Merchandise Mart in Chicago, and the National Gallery in Washington. Today, Bethlehem Steel is only a ghost of a company.

Writes Strohmeyer:

> Now, forty years later, steel industry statistics portray an image of national debilitation—more than 250,000 jobs lost forever, more than 30 million tons of capacity wiped out as aging facilities are shut down never to reopen, and one-fourth of the domestic market captured by aggressive foreign nations with newer plants and lower wage rates (1987, p. 21).

Domestic industries are struggling to meet the tide of international competition. The restoration of U.S. world-wide "competitiveness" has become a political slogan.

Yet it isn't only high labor costs and antiquated plants that trouble U.S. industry. It's a basic attitude of the U.S. work force. Consider the case of General Motors, once the undisputed flagship automaker in the world, now struggling to hold on to a diminishing percentage of the U.S. auto market.

An article in the *Detroit News* (Sorge, 1987, p. E.1) indicated that an average of 33,440 hourly GM employees failed to come to work each day in the previous year. The cost to the company was $1 billion! These "controllable" job "no-shows" are quite different from employees who are sick or who are taking approved leaves. The rate of employees who fail to come to work is increasing, from 8.6 percent in 1985 to 8.8 percent in 1986.

The U.S. has become the world's largest debtor nation. In 1986 the U.S. owed the rest of the world $263.6 billion, more than twice what it owed at the end of 1985 (Associated Press, *Philadelphia Inquirer*, 1987, p. 1). Foreign debt grew by 135 percent in 1986, surpassing the combined debts of Brazil, Mexico, and Argentina.

The U.S. has not been a debtor nation since 1911. In 1982 the U.S.

was the world's largest creditor country and posted a $137 billion investment surplus. The economic gongs were sounding over the U.S. plunge into debt. The Committee for Economic Development comprised of the nation's 200 biggest companies developed a report which showed that by early 2000, the U.S. foreign debt would surpass $2 trillion, "a legacy that no previous U.S. generation has passed onto its children since the Civil War" (Associated Press, *Philadelphia Inquirer*, 1987, p. 12-A).

The cries over the loss of U.S. economic punch center on the notion of productivity. In simple terms productivity is concerned with the amount of inputs vs. outputs assessed in a unit of time such as per hour (see Walberg, 1982).

American productivity has been slowing up for some time. Baumol (1987) points out that a nation's productivity growth is related to: (1) its savings investment record and (2) its performance with innovation. It is in the area of innovation that Baumol, a Princeton economist, centers his concerns on education.

In order for a nation to have a high innovation rate, it must possess a highly educated, technically literate, and trained labor force. But, Baumol notes:

> Here two trends are disquieting: first, the inadequate effort devoted to education of children from the very minority groups whose educational attainments are lowest and who simultaneously constitute a rapidly rising proportion of the population, and second, the lagging role of education in the sciences and mathematics. Both of these are matters of high priority for the longrun position of the economy (p. B.2).

As one looks at the U.S. to ascertain how well the schools are doing in preparing such a workforce, the statistics are not encouraging. A current U.S. Assistant Secretary of Labor noted in *The Chronicle for Higher Education* (Fields, 1986):

> We're appalled by the fact that we are graduating 750,000 to a million kids from high school a year who are functionally illiterate, and an equal number are dropping out or are being pushed out of our school system (p. 39).

The U.S. school system has been compared to the Japanese and found wanting. Japanese test scores on international standardized batteries in math and science have led the Western world for years.

An international study of mathematics conducted by a team of researchers from the University of Illinois at Champaign-Urbana found U.S. student achievement behind those of other nations. The U.S.'s best calculus students "were at or near the average level of achievement for students in the other countries which included France, England,

Nigeria, and Canada. In algebra the performance of average U.S. students fell near the average of those from other countries" (*Kappan*, 1987, p. 559).

The U.S. math curriculum appears to lack focus, challenge, and vitality according to Illinois professor and study director Kenneth Travers: "In school mathematics the United States is an underachieving nation and our curriculum is helping to create a nation of underachievers" (Associated Press, *Burlington County Times*, 1987, p. 9).

As the curriculum becomes the problem, so it has to become the solution. If a state's testing program is not assessing the curriculum, it must be aligned (English, 1986). This is particularly true if teachers are to be paid on the basis of pupil scores on a test (Rothman, 1987, p. 1).

It is no wonder that curriculum matters have become a major concern of school superintendents as disclosed in a recent survey of chief executive officers conducted by the University of Texas at Austin and the American Association of School Administrators (AASA, 1987, p. 36).

HOW TO KNOW IF YOU REQUIRE AN AUDIT

A curriculum audit is one kind of management tool. It is not an appropriate response to every situation confronting a school administrator or a board of education. An audit best suits a situation when the following conditions pertain.

1. When the Stakes Are High

While audits can be a routine matter, it is the non-routine that seems to prompt them. When it is important enough to get an objective view, meet some state mandate, find out what really happened, stop problems from cropping up, or establish a new practice upon a firm foundation, an audit will appear as a necessary or appropriate response.

2. When the Status Quo Is Not Acceptable

When the set of current school or organizational responses are clearly not adequate, even after they have been tried and refined, an audit may be a viable way of fostering improved understanding of what is not appropriate in the old responses and recommending more appropriate ones.

3. When Objectivity Is Necessary

When the first two conditions pertain, it usually means that a new and innovative organizational response is required. That will mean, in turn, readjustments inside the organization in roles and resource allocation and flow. That in turn alters jobs, responsibilities, and relationships. That portends significant change. Such change can be quite threatening.

Under such circumstances, those inside the organization may know what to do, but their motivations are suspect because they may have a stake in the outcome. Thus, their position of influence can be damaged if they enter the fray and become partisans. To avoid such internal politics and the possible deleterious fallout, an outsider is sought to ensure that the analysis and recommendations are more detached than if the consultant/auditor were part of the internal, ongoing staff.

4. When Enhanced Expertise Is Required

The auditor should bring to an engagement recognized technical and political expertise. In some cases, that expertise may be significantly beyond that possessed by those inside a school or school district. Such expertise may see problems better and help those internal to the organization see possible solutions they did not imagine before the audit.

5. When the Past and Present Are Not Well Understood

An audit documents where a school, program, or district has been and is at the time of the audit. The audit fixes and defines the context of operations. Details of the operational context may elude those in it because they have become insensitive to various stimuli over a long period of time.

Also, through interviewing and observation, the auditor can help an organization acquire an understanding as to why it responded as it did in the past. This is because some organizations act first and plan later. They can't know where to go in the future until they see where they have been in the past (Weick, 1985). What happens in such organizations is a kind of retroactive "fitting" of behavior to an appropriate rationale.

Administrators do not always know all the reasons they act in some decision-making situations. One reason is that they often do not have time to acquire all of the data to clearly identify the options and alternatives. Then, too, they are limited by their own knowledge and biases.

More than once the most beneficial aspect of an audit has been to provide the decision makers with another view of what they did in the past. This helps them "link" current responses to past ones. It helps them make sense of their own behavior "in context."

6. When Public Confidence and Trust Must Be Re-established or Retained

Public trust is a constantly required ingredient for any organization serving the public. Without it, the necessary resources needed to keep the organization operative may not be forthcoming:

> Today's reality is that the public schools must stand in line with the other public institutions and plead for their share of tax revenue. Taxpayers have become more skeptical of the educational establishment and, whether directly or through elected officials, demand clear answers to such questions as (1) what are you going to do with the money? and (2) what did you do with the money we gave you last year? (Hoyle, English, Steffy, 1985, p. 41).

Public trust is directly related to knowing what the organization is doing, how it is functioning, and whether it is doing its perceived job in the larger social context.

Often an audit is used to dispel myths about rumored shortcomings in school operations, curriculum, or pupil achievement. The truth, even if there may be some surprises, is always more comforting than ignorance. Besides, after performing many audits, I can testify that there are very few things the public doesn't know or suspect that are truly a secret in most school systems. The only ones who may be surprised are school officials, normally ones in top-level management who have shut themselves off from the day-to-day realities of organizational life.

Public support and public knowledge go hand in hand with one another. Trust is never a permanent condition. It must be earned and maintained over time.

7. When Results Count

Are kids really learning? What are they learning? How well are they really learning? These questions deal with the outcome of the schooling process. Schools are supposed to be places for the young to learn what is socially important within a culture.

When it is important to know whether kids are learning and, more critically, if what they are learning is important enough to learn, an audit can probe both dimensions simultaneously.

Knowing the validity of results means asking questions which puncture the overt and subtle mechanisms of cultural transmission in the schools. It means probing beneath the surface to discern the values and assumptions that are embodied in learning goals and objectives. The audit asks, "How does the system (being audited) know if the values, assumptions, and goals it says it wants students to learn are the right ones? How does it determine what is right?"

The problem with mass culture today is that it is overwhelmingly visually oriented, often at the expense of hard and critical thinking and the use of abstract concepts not rooted in empirical validation. "In short, reality is dissolved into objecthood, whose particular existence defines its boundaries" (Aronowitz and Giroux, 1985, p. 49).

Objective tests objectify knowledge and provide a false kind of security about the world. If "results" are always and only defined and measured within one stream of knowing and thinking, other alternative streams will appear very difficult or not important. In the rush to objectify and measure, many educators sense something has been lost which is much more important and perhaps elusive to capture, i.e., the real intellectual inheritance of western civilization as it exists in the arts and literature, and not as much as in the sciences.

8. When Cost Is Important

When it is important to know whether costs are worth the effort, and school system officials have not been able to approach the equation with anything less than platitudes or hopes, an audit is called for.

For a long time, costs were not questioned in education. It was considered "crass" to try to deal with costs and outcomes. Those times have changed. A publication by the U.S. Chamber of Commerce in the early 1970s was one of many blistering attacks on public education for the failure to deal with cost effectiveness, productivity, and accountability. The Chamber noted:

> . . . the largest portion of state and local expenditures—education, has grown from 6.5 billion in 1947 to approximately 68 billion in 1969. This is more than a 1000 percent increase in expenditures for education in a time when the gross national product went from 234.3 billion to 931.4 billion, an increase of 400 percent.
>
> In terms of resources allocated, the American school system is the most expensive in the world. But what about its productivity? Its effectiveness? What has the American public received for its money (U.S. Chamber of Commerce, 1971, p. 1).

Educators, most notably professors, are reluctant to come to terms with the cost issues. That attitude still prevails in many colleges of education. A criticism of the current debate in the Holmes Group on reforming teacher education is that such changes "have usually been debated solely on their educational merits, even though such changes would be extremely costly" (Jaschik, 1987, p. 17).

Measuring costs in education is difficult. Garms, Guthrie, and Pierce (1978) note that in approaching the matter of the proper educational amount one can either look at it from the view of the amount of knowledge or schooling a given student receives or as the extent of opportunity a student is provided to become educated (p. 64).

Johns, Morphet, and Alexander (1983) indicate there are three ways to approach the cost-benefit question in education:

- the net-present-value notion
- the internal rate-of-return (IROR) idea
- the benefit-cost ratio

The *net-present-value* index is simply the "sum of the benefits minus the sum of the costs" (p. 48). Both sums are discounted at an appropriate rate.

The *internal rate-of-return* does not take into account the total value of costs or benefits of education. If costs and benefits were graphed, the internal rate-of-return is the place were the curve for costs and benefits intersects (p. 49).

The *benefit-cost ratio* utilizes the mathematical principle of unity. If the contemporary value of benefits divided by the contemporary value of costs exceeds one (unity), a program may be considered worthwhile (p. 49).

None of the above deal with the issue of quality in schools. If by quality it is meant the degree of excellence or superiority of the schooling process, then quality might be a matter of amount or degree. This reduces the process of determining it to the process of measurement and, in crudest terms, to knowledge and facts of things or processes.

So there is much talk about educational quality but very little hard data about it. Even if quality is reduced to measures of quantity, the matter is not made much more manipulatable in front-line school operations.

Most audits tackle quantity. While quality is approached, it is never addressed directly, but only indirectly and usually within the framework of how the entity being audited defines it or is forced to deal with it by the extant regulatory agencies to which it must be responsive. For schools this ranges from policy directives of the local board of education, regional accreditation agencies, state departments of education, legislative requirements in statute, state board directives, or U.S. Department of Education requirements/rules. Some districts involved with school integration may also face judicial fiats as well.

TYPES OF AUDITS

There are three basic types of audits: functional, operational, or programmatic. Within each type, there are three issues that can be dealt with, singly or comprehensively. They are scope, compliance, and optimization. All of these are influenced by the location of the auditor, whether the person or persons is internal or external to the entity undergoing the audit.

Graphically, all of the variations just described are shcwn in Exhibit 1 below.

A *functional audit* is concerned with the activities of a school or school district as they are typically represented in a traditional line-item budget. The functions are personnel, administration, curriculum, transportation, maintenance and operations, school plant, instruction, etc.

An *operational audit* is centered on specific activities, normally within functions, for example, curriculum development with the curriculum function or staff development in the area of personnel.

A *programmatic audit* closely parallels the traditional concept of

Exhibit 1
Variations on Basic Audit Types

Types of Curriculum Audits

Location of Auditor	Functional			Operational			Programmatic		
	Scope	Compliance	Optimization	Scope	Optimization	Compliance	Scope	Compliance	Optimization
Internal	A	B	C	D	E	F	G	H	I
External	J	K	L	M	N	O	P	Q	R

subject matter disciplines such as mathematics, health, English, or social studies.

Then there are the issues of whether the auditor is internal to the school or district, or external.

The *scope of the audit* refers to how much of a function, operation, or program is to be included. *Compliance* refers to whether or not the auditor is expected to determine how closely a function, operation, or program is adhering to guidelines, laws, policies, or regulations, no matter what their source. *Optimization* refers to the charge to the auditor to examine a function, operation, or program with respect to whether or not resources (inputs) have been maximized in obtaining a given range of results (outputs).

Compliance issues may differ from *optimization* issues when the former are not concerned with the relationship between inputs and outputs, but only with propriety as embodied in statute, policy, regulation, or guidelines. Auditing the personnel function to determine adherence to Affirmative Action would be an example of a *compliance* review without a concern as to whether *optimization* in that function had occurred. A state's regulation for twenty minutes of physical education per day at any cost, irrespective of whether objectives in PE had been attained, would be another. An accreditation regulation that there be ten books per child in the school library, no matter how the library or books are used, is still another.

A curriculum audit, as performed by the auditor–author, typically involves cells L, K, and J in Exhibit 1. All of the audits reported in this book involved all grade levels of the districts (full scope) and all subjects in the curriculum. The audits examined if the curricular activities, as totally operational, attained the results desired (however defined) within the existing state-legal-policy framework (compliance).

If, however, the auditor–author had examined only the subject area of junior high school language arts, that would be an example of cells P and Q in Exhibit 1. P would be grades 7–9 only (narrow scope). And if the auditing activity were confined only to adherence to state law, regulation, and local policy requirements, it would be a *compliance review* only. *Optimization* would not be examined unless, of course, it were contained in board policy or state law-regulation as a requirement.

The *functional audit* is typically the most broad-based because it normally includes all of the operations within the function being examined, and all of the programs as well. The distinctions made in Exhibit 1 are not always so neatly delineated because the nature of the work of activity being reviewed may overlap and be somewhat ambiguous, particularly to those working inside the schools. As such, the audit is always contextually anchored for a final determination of the content and scope to be examined.

DETERMINING READINESS FOR AN AUDIT

Unlike the financial audit, a school district has a choice about engaging in a curriculum audit. The decision about whether or not to undertake an audit are closely related to knowing when an audit may be required. For example, if the board of education and superintendent believe that the credibility of a program is at stake, they may determine that an audit is one way to affirm its excellence.

However, the risk is always there that the audit may disclose something that will damage program credibility and weaken public confidence. The downside of the auditing process is the political risks inherent in the act of disclosure.

Once the auditing process has begun, it is extremely difficult to stop or even change it. It gains a momentum of its own. The auditor–author can only recall one in over twenty audits where school district officials became afraid of the results they saw in a draft copy of an audit. They then issued a check in the final amount and insisted that no final copy of the audit be sent to the school board offices, realizing that as a public document paid for with public funds, it would be picked up by the local press.

That audit brought about changes in curricular practices and staffing in the curriculum division of the same school system, something it was designed to do. However, the "publicness" of the audit was effectively squelched.

This is in contrast to the manner in which Robert Janson, superintendent of the Mt. Pleasant (Michigan) public schools handled his public relations after a curriculum audit was performed in that district in 1985.

The thirty-two page audit included fifteen findings and eight recommendations (English, 1985). Janson noted in a newsletter mailed to the entire community in which the findings of the audit were publicized, "We did not invest tax dollars and countless staff hours to receive a perfunctory pat on the back. These recommendations . . . will go a long way toward making us an exemplary system" (*Mt. Pleasant Public Schools Newsletter*, 1985, p. 1, see Chapter 9).

The proactive posture by Superintendent Janson neutralized any negative political fallout from the discrepancies about the curriculum management system in Mt. Pleasant. The act of disclosure was used instead to build public support for the changes recommended in the audit.

It takes courage to engage in a review of past decisions and practices that will be made public regardless of what is said. Of course, the district officials have the opportunity to affirm or deny the audit's findings as they would have the right to comment on the findings and recommendations of a financial audit. In most cases, however, in-house comments are considered "defensive" remarks by those external to the system and are not given the same weight as those findings and recommendations of the auditor.

Perhaps the major advantage to the curriculum audit is the enhanced leverage it provides to the key organizational decision makers. The leverage is gained via disclosure of important issues and problems discovered. Whereas in some circumstances organizational leaders may have been at a point of stalemate in efforts to make internal changes, the weight of the audit, under the guise of a fair and impartial analysis of the situation, strengthens the hand of the leaders to make political and technical alterations by minimizing their own political vulnerability.

This is because all human organizations are more than collections of individuals with technical skills. Organizational life is first and foremost political in the best sense of the word. Politics is the art of influence. Organizations may be thought of as coalitions of groups existing in a kind of dynamic tension with one another.

Various groups within an organization advocate changes which enhance their ability to influence and control their own destinies. So, as Mintzberg (1979) points out, managers at strategic positions in an organization promote changes which promote the aggregation of power wherever they may be located. Those of the support staff promote *horizontal decentralization*. Line managers favor *vertical decentralization* to their position and *horizontal centralization* to solidify their authority. And so it goes (p. 291).

A curriculum audit conducted from the perspective of the total school system will inevitably formulate findings and recommendations that enhance the capability of the organization to function more effectively and efficiently as a system. This means that system level officials will have fresh ammunition in their fight to create system (rather than unit) responses. Audits normally lead to improved centralization of power because they are system focused. They tend to be favored, therefore, by boards of education and top-level line officers for that reason.

Readiness and timing are also intimately related. The time for an audit is not in the middle of a pitched battle between community control advocates and those of central power. Likewise, an audit would not fare well during a teacher's strike or even immediately after one.

Nor should an audit be used as a ploy to avoid impending change, such as a tactic to avoid being dismissed as a superintendent or prior to a grand jury investigation into system corruption. "Let's wait until the results of the audit are in" is nothing more than a deliberate ruse to forestall other action. The public looks at such excuses as "one more study" to confirm what is already known, rather than as an honest attempt taken in time to develop thoughtful interventions.

The best time for an audit is in the beginning of a new superintendent's tenure or about three to four years after a superintendent has been on the job. As a tool, the audit can establish a firm base for the new superintendent to act boldly on long-standing organizational problems. It also frees the new superintendent from the sins of past administrations by establishing a definite line of accountability and responsibility for who did what to whom and when.

An audit after a superintendent has been on the job three or four years can help the CEO break a logjam and get on with the business of change and development.

The highest risks with a curriculum audit are for the long-tenured CEO. Questions will inevitably be raised about "why" he or she didn't do something about the problems uncovered "before" the audit disclosed them. Such findings tend to make the superintendent look stupid or inept or both. However, there are some courageous superintendents who still take the step, believing that the results will be salutary for them and the system. The cited case of the district which backed out of the curriculum audit involved a long-tenured superintendent. That superintendent had engaged in a long-standing public relations blitz that portrayed the "excellence" of the system in self-congratulatory and glowing terms. The findings of the audit would have provided contradictory evidence to the district's own rhetoric. Such districts often paint themselves into a public relations corner where they are "too good for an audit," or for any activity that would contrast with the super-puff image they have created for themselves.

As one can tell, the readiness factors described in this section are not technical, but political. Technical shortcomings within a school system are rarely the reason for not pursuing an audit. The real reason is the political vulnerability of the board and/or superintendent to take a hard look at their actual practice and the results obtained for their energy, time, money, and sweat. It is a rather uncommon board or superintendent who wants to invite a probing look at his or her or the group's labors after having to do battle with the usual lines of naysayers, kooks, and doubting Thomases along the way. To take the risk of having the data in an independent audit being used against them after they have prevailed politically is simply asking too much. The invitation is to reopen old wounds and jeopardize the extant balance, no matter how tenuous it might be.

For this reason, unlike common financial audits required by law, voluntary curriculum audits will be reserved for uncommon school districts, boards of education, and chief school officers, despite the fact that in most cases audit disclosures, even when negative, reaffirm political power and often remove the opposition's agenda and momentum. In this sense an audit can be a form of organizational karate in which the force of an opponent is used to disarm him or her in the process. Within the fulcrum of full disclosure, political motion can be redirected. While an audit mainly examines technical processes, the real test and power of it lies in the political acumen of the educational leadership of a school system. The employment of an audit is therefore a test of the political skills, sensitivities, and strength of that leadership, collectively and individually.

CHECKPOINTS

Common Questions Asked the Author–Auditor

Question 1: *What are the most influential forces in fostering the development of a curriculum audit?*

Answer: Probably state-wide testing programs that result in a lot of publicity for those districts and schools that consistently perform poorly. Popham (1987, p. 681) has called this thrust "high-stakes testing." Such testing programs are forcing functions for school leaders to re-examine traditional methods of linking teaching, learning, and measurement together.

Another force has been expanded state level curricular requirements that have led to "curricular compression," most notably at the secondary level. Lots of curricular areas are being squeezed, some right out of the curriculum. The crunch at the local level has prompted local educators to begin to review the role of curriculum and broach questions that deal with curriculum balance.

Question 2: *What are the precedents for a curriculum audit?*

Answer: The precedents are, of course, the long-standing perceived success of the financial audit, its objectivity, integrity, and visibility. It was these features that attracted early advocates like Leon Lessinger to write about them in his book *Every Kid a Winner* (New York: Simon and Schuster, 1970).

Lessinger desired a public report centered on results as measured by achievement tests of students. Lessinger conceptualized this report as an *educational audit* which included more than the curriculum per se. Leon served as my external advisor when I managed the Columbus, Ohio, educational performance audit for Peat, Marwick, Mitchell

& Co. (now Peat, Marwick, Main) in 1979. I remember his comment after looking over the draft final audit document. He said that when he wrote about it as a concept he knew it was a powerful idea, but he had no idea how really powerful it was until he reviewed the Columbus audit.

Question 3: *How does an auditor get around the problem of simply assessing efficiency (cost) and never questioning effectiveness (results)?*

Answer: It is easy to stop at where the entity being audited considers its boundaries and focusing only on what it has allowed or been forced to accept as the proper content of its activities. Were an auditor only to perform this function, the risk is run that the audit would seek to improve an obsolete function.

The auditor must go further by trying to determine how the entity knows what is proper for its work content. The auditor seeks to discern the *metacriteria* that the entity has used to select the content of its activities or work. Sometimes such *metacriteria* are not stated. They simply "float" around, and people seem to know what they are but don't put them into any kind of formal statement. For such cases, I have cited a district marked by their absence and made it clear that such standards should be explicated.

I'm troubled by the ambiguity of the values that support many of the functions of the public schools. Serving as an auditor, I've found very large value differences among people working at all levels in a school district. There is a lot of substituting of values and redefining of them as one travels down the chain of command. This means that what a board of education desired is not always what is delivered in a classroom. Somewhere the message was reconstituted and repackaged in the process of moving from intention to real work activities, or from policy to operations. It is a problem not unique to schools.

Question 4: *What are the most serious objections to the idea of a curriculum audit?*

Answer: I would classify the objections or concerns about curriculum into two areas, those concerned with technical issues and those dealing with ideological issues. The technical issues pertain to whether a curriculum can (or should) be considered like a financial matter. I think a financial accountant uses many assumptions that are quite similar. But the two processes are not equivalent. I don't think they have to be to apply the auditing concept to curriculum. The other technical issues pertain to measurement of results and assumptions that deal with linkages between values and work, policy and operations, particularly in organizations with the characteristics like schools.

The ideological issues are belief matters. They pertain to what schools should be about in a society. If one does not subscribe to the current role of schools in our capitalistic society, he or she would definitely not support the idea of an audit which may be designed to improve its effectiveness within that society. Auditing would be seen as a means to refine what is viewed as an improper, even vulgar, activity.

Also, if one believes that any activity that would further centralize authority in school system governance "is bad" overall for schools and/or teachers, auditing would be objectionable on the grounds that it would lead to increased centralization. Too often, the objectors criticize an idea but don't really reveal their own agenda in the critique. Thus, some leftist criticism of practices in school administration takes the form of "false scientism," when the actual agenda is a near or total rejection of the current form of schooling and those in authority who have the responsibility of maintaining that form.

Question 5: *In your experience what seems to be the major motivation for a school district to desire a curriculum audit?*

Answer: The most obvious motivator has been the desire of the school district to enhance or improve pupil learning, largely as assessed by a variety of tests. I can't recall any of the districts where I engaged in an audit where the overwhelming concern was cost, i.e., *efficiency*. The primary motivator was *effectiveness*. I didn't bump into anybody that wanted "cheaper education." I did encounter a lot of people who wanted "better education."

Question 6: *Why did you spend so much time talking about the superintendent's place in the curriculum audit process?*

Answer: Because the audit as designed examines the management system from the point of view of the total school district. The person with the administrative responsibility for the total district is the superintendent. Most superintendents are quite vulnerable politically. Therefore the superintendent will pay the ultimate price for what may be revealed in a curriculum audit.

The same would be true if an audit were completed at the school building level. In this case it would be the school principal who would bear the brunt of the findings and recommendations. Whoever occupies the position of authority and responsibility of the function or program being audited will be the person whose performance and practices are directly or indirectly reviewed as well.

Question 7: *What about the board of education? Aren't they also on the line with a curriculum audit?*

Answer: Most definitely. It is the board that has the policy responsibility to define and monitor the process of management itself. Kuhn and Beam (1982) call this *metamanagement*: "It does not manage the organization; it manages the process of management" (p. 326). This is the role of the board. What I've found is that boards don't perform this function at all. Instead they abrogate their policy role and engage in *micromanagement,* i.e., administrative matters. One result is that no one is doing any *metamanagement* at all. The process by which the organization does business is not governed at all. Instead, individual actions are scrutinized or critized. Everyone becomes an administrator but no one is managing anything. Most boards I've worked with on audits do not understand the role of policy development as *metamanagement.*

Question 8: *What are the major determinants of knowing whether an auditor should be external or internal to a school district?*

Answer: If the problem is purely technical in nature and a person inside the system has as much or more expertise as any outsider, the auditor most likely should be an insider. However, if the problem also involves (and it usually does) political considerations, insiders are often at a considerable disadvantage in formulating "hard" recommendations that will require changes in the school district.

It is important that the auditor's stance be considered as uninvolved and impartial in formulating recommendations to the people inside the system, as well as the larger community who may be called upon to allocate additional resources to pay for the changes.

The characteristics of credibility and objectivity are most often attributed to an outsider, rather than an insider, as an auditor. This point will be explored in more detail in the section dealing with standards for the auditor (see Chapter II).

/ II / *Audit Standards*

AN AUDIT IS both a process and a product. It is an activity and an event. At the heart of the process is the act of comparison. There are at least two ways most things, processes, events, services, persons, or entities can be compared and analyzed.

The first way of comparing is to classify the process, service, event, or entity to others like it and note similarities and differences. For example, if the reader wanted to buy a certain type of automobile, he or she might purchase a recent issue of a trade magazine and study the mileage performance, maintenance and safety records, etc., as well as price, in order to make a decision regarding purchase.

Some consumers of schools often do that. Parents may want to make a choice of neighborhoods or of private schools and examine a variety of data to determine what school appears to be most advantageous for their children.

The second method for comparison involves not an analysis of similar things, events, processes, or entities, but a set of standards or indices by which that aspect of what is being audited is subsequently scrutinized.

Thus a financial auditor doesn't compare the records of monetary transactions of one bank to another inasmuch as both may be bad. Instead, the comparison is of one bank's financial records to a series of accepted benchmarks which represent what is believed to be "good" or "best" practice about how such records ought to be kept and what ought to be in them.

The accounting profession has spent much time and money trying to secure agreement on terms and methods for performing a financial audit. The codification is called GAAP (Generally Accepted Accounting Principles). GAAP represents the way most CPAs would go about examining the financial records of a school system or any human organization's fudiciary transactions.

To determine whether an accountant did a credible job, another reviewing accountant (an auditor) would determine whether the first accountant followed certain agreed upon conventions given the evidence presented by the client organization. Legal liability of the accountant also hinges upon similar considerations.

Educational research as an activity follows similar practices. Most researchers follow conventions derived over time which are believed to attain the "best" results. In some cases such results can be empirically validated, and in other cases the agreement about methods or approaches is more arbitrary (Selltiz, Wrightsman, and Cook, 1976, pp. 200–249).

Audit standards are the judgmental criteria against which the data or evidence gathered in the auditing process are collected, weighed, and culled into a final report. In turn, such standards rest upon assumptions about human organizations, management practices, schooling, teaching, curriculum, and how they ought to relate one to the other. In a number of cases, the relationships have been empirically validated as in some of the "effective schools" research. In other cases the relationships appear to be logical derivatives. Still others represent little more than qualified opinions by those with some expertise in one or more aspects of what is included in an audit.

And those doing a curriculum audit do not have the advantage of agreement within the profession about standards or methods as do accountants. For example, in November of 1987, some 225,000 members of the American Institute of Certified Public Accountants voted on ten new auditing standards. Among those standards was one which would compel an auditor to disclose whether or not a company or firm might fail based on "substantial doubt" in the mind of the auditor (Paschal, 1987, p. H-1).

There is not now in the education profession agreement as to what constitutes anything that could be construed as GAAP for accountants. In fact, the education profession, at least academically, is embroiled in extended debate about the meaning and purpose of schooling in a capitalistic society (Shor, 1986).

So, a curriculum audit is on less concrete ground than its financial cousin. This situation is reflected in the curriculum audit standards themselves. They are certainly less precise and "hard" than those of the financial realm.

To determine whether or not the standards and supporting assumptions should be utilized in the reader's situation, they are explicated here for review. The reader is invited to determine his or her support for them as used in the curriculum audits and others reported or referenced in this book.

THE CULTURAL MILIEUX OF AN AUDIT

A *curriculum audit* is a process of examining documents and practices that exist within a peculiar institution normally called a "school" in a given time, culture, and society.

Depending upon how those in positions of authority define the role of the school within that time, culture, and society, the audit (which is a determination of compliance) will be influenced.

Suppose that one is assigned to audit a school that trains social change agents. The goal of the school is founded on the premise (explicit or implicit) that certain social functions are wrong and ought to be altered. The school's curriculum is designed to prepare social change agents to go out in that society and engage in activities that will lead to such changes (Alinsky, 1969).

A *curriculum auditor* would examine documents that define the school's mission; interview staff to determine whether or not the people working in the school translated its purpose into specific activities that led to the acquisition of the skills, knowledges, and attitudes of its students to become social change agents; and decide whether the data the school had collected indicated if it had been successful in attaining its mission.

An audit always takes place in a political climate. The participants of the audit are always political actors. They represent persons in authority positions. Those positions are attached to institutions which have specific purposes within society.

So if a school is viewed as a conserving agent of a society, as most schools are, then an audit would attempt to discern the extent to which those curricular objectives and activities, which do in fact conserve and preserve the dominant values of that society, are perpetuated and advanced in its respective classrooms.

What any audit does is determined by who authorized it and the time frame and value system in which it was conducted. Audits are therefore highly situational. They are like individual case studies of a particular curriculum, and one does not generalize from specific results easily, if at all.

STANDARDS AND ASSUMPTIONS OF THE CURRICULUM AUDIT

There are five standards of the curriculum audit utilized by the author since 1979. They are:

- The school district is able to demonstrate its control of resources, programs, and personnel.

- The school district has established clear and valid objectives for students.
- The school district has documentation explaining how its programs have been developed, implemented, and conducted.
- The school district uses the results from the district designed or adopted assessments to adjust, improve, or terminate ineffective practices.
- The school district has been able to improve productivity.

Standard 1: Control of Resources, Programs, and Personnel

What is meant by control in a curriculum audit is the direction of organizational energy and resources towards specific ends. It is assumed that a school district can select a direction and change its resource allocation practices over time to attain what it set out to do. That, of course, means that school district officials have options. Even if they appear not to have them, there is always the option of doing nothing.

At least some organizational theorists (Weick, 1976) have posited the idea that a school district's organizational structure is not "tight." Weick called school systems "loosely coupled." What this means is that there is not a neat chain of command with a sliding scale of authority which overlaps one office to the next.

Hasenfeld (1983) has indicated that there are good reasons as to why schools are probably "loosely coupled" (p. 152). The first is that schools often function in volatile environments where competing groups place contradictory pressures on them. In order to be responsive, schools "de-couple" themselves internally in order not to cause undue internal friction.

Hasenfeld is also sanguine about what happens to the quality of human services when loose coupling is dominant. The result is ". . . a fragmented and disjointed service delivery system" (p. 158).

The control standard of the curriculum audit assumes that a "loosely coupled" organization is dysfunctional, particularly in an environment of increasing central accountability thrust upon schools by state legislatures. In order to be responsive, school systems have to become "tighter," not looser, in building close connections among and between offices hierarchically and laterally.

Human organizations are not "natural," insofar as they are special kinds of artificial constructs. And as constructs, they can be changed. So as a curriculum auditor, I have never accepted the "loosely coupled" description as an optimal or desired condition.

Some curriculum administrators and professors have trouble with the word "control." For them the word conjures up some dastardly Machiavellian world where cunning superintendents manipulate the masses of teachers. "Control" means no such thing within the confines of a curriculum audit. Without the capability of directing itself towards alternative ends by altering its internal means, school districts are not in control of themselves as organizations. So there has to be a chain of command from those who are legally accountable and responsible for the system to those who are to do the work of the system.

The presence of the "chain of command" is simply the ability of the system to be internally "connected" from some central source to its respective parts. In a school system this means that the board of education as the official and legal body of record sets the policy framework into which the administrative hierarchy headed by a superintendent functions to carry out its policies. The control audit standard simply determines if the machinery is in place and if it is working.

This means that the school system has to function as a system, i.e., an integrated, holistic body, rather than a confederation of smaller self-contained units.

The control standard implicitly assumes that the major directions regarding final decisions about mission or purpose flow from the accountable and responsible body (the elected or appointed board of education) TO those who must carry out that mission.

There is currently a good deal of discussion about "teacher empowerment" (Darling-Hammond, 1986). While the terms are vague they seem to imply that teachers will decide what to do. If this is the meaning of teacher empowerment, it runs counter to established legal and organizational precedents.

The control standard does not relegate teachers to the status of mindless bureaucrats. There is nothing inherent in it that precludes their active involvement and participation in the decision-making process. But it does preclude them from having the "final say" about "what goes." A school board may be run democratically, but the school system is not. Teachers don't vote on whether to accept or reject a board policy. They are employed to follow board policy.

And the role of the board of education is to engage in *metamanagement* (Kuhn and Beam, 1982). The board establishes the processes and the structure by which individual decisions are made by the administrative staff. When the administration engages in decisions *within* board policy, it is engaged in *micromanagement*.

What the Curriculum Auditor Looks For

In approaching a school district to determine if it is in control, the curriculum auditor looks for the following things and may ask the questions listed as examples in order to answer them.

DOCUMENTS

The key to effective board control is sound policy development. That means that the policies <u>are used</u> by administrators in actual decision making, specifically in curriculum evaluation and development, testing, textbook adoption, and course construction. The actual use of the policies is normally determined from interview data. However, the review of documents will reveal the extent to which the policies exist and are capable of being translated, i.e., they are unambiguous and consistent.

Board policies in the curriculum area are notoriously vague. There is the usual "philosophy of education" which is a near useless statement to direct actual curriculum practice. They are usually grandiose prose and pious platitudes. I simply call them the "we believes" because they are filled with such phrases.

The auditor's framework for examining the efficacy of board policy centers around the relationship shown in Exhibit 2.

Exhibit 2
A Conceptual Framework for Board Policy

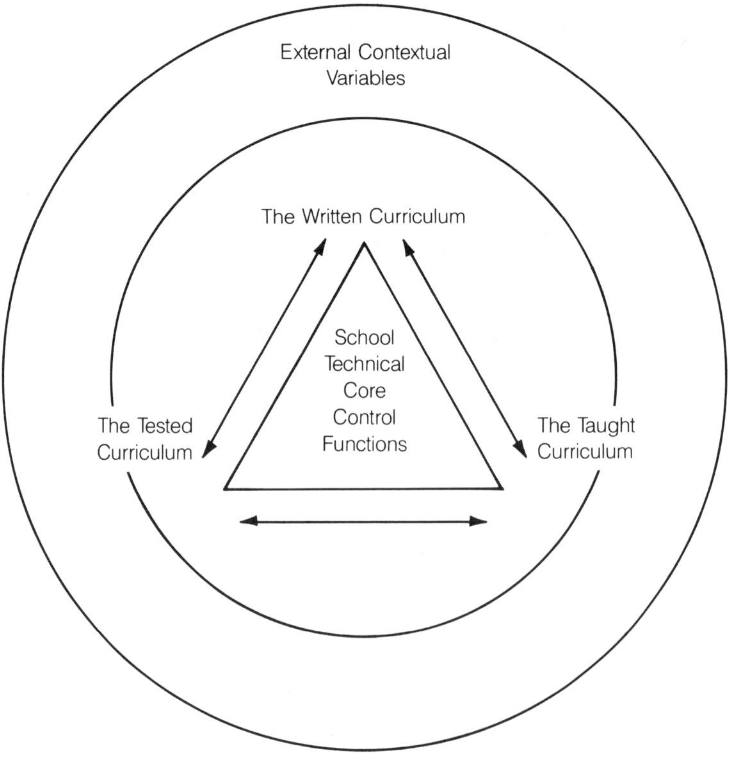

The framework was developed by English (1987) for the New York State Education Department to assist them in their efforts to improve achievement scores in chronically low scoring schools on the state testing program.

An effective board policy for sound curriculum management and control should include a planned relationship between the written, taught, and tested curricula. The relationship should exist at all levels and be transactional, i.e., mutually interactive. It should ensure that the written curriculum has planned relationships to the taught curriculum, and that the taught curriculum and written curriculum are related to the tested curriculum. This is the essence of *quality control* (English, 1977).

Board policy(ies) should also specify that test and textbook adoption should be based on validated curriculum approved by the board of education after that curriculum has been officially adopted. In this sequence, local curriculum adoption drives textbook and test adoption, rather than the contrary practice.

As a further explication of the standards will reveal, the auditor also looks for policies that indicate that budget development follows and is linked to curriculum development. This sequence ensures that the budget is shaped by the curriculum and not vice versa.

Data pertaining to the control standard in a curriculum audit are also derived from *interviews*.

INTERVIEWS

Interview questions relate to determining how extant board policy is followed or referenced by both the board and the professional staff. Questions pertaining to policy ambiguities are also related to both groups.

Some sample questions regarding control are listed with some discussion from the author–auditor about their meaning and typical findings.

Questions for Board Members

(1) "What does the board mean when it says in policy #2390 that 'only those courses that contribute to a sound basic understanding of contemporary society should be offered as electives at the high school'?"

(2) "Your policy states that 'each child should be educated to his or her full potential.' How does the board or the staff know or determine a child's full potential?"

(3) "What evidence or data does the administration present to the board to show that its policies are being followed?"
(4) "Does the board of education ever formally review the district's curriculum and candidly seek data regarding its strengths and weaknesses?"
(5) "How does the board determine if the district's curriculum is adequate?"
(6) "Approximately what percentage of time does the board spend on curricular affairs stipulated in policy?"
(7) "What is your impression of the district's curriculum? How have you arrived at these impressions? In what way do these impressions reflect the board's intent as it pertains to curricular matters?"
(8) "How does the board evaluate the superintendent's curricular leadership? the principal's?"

Board members' knowledge of curriculum is rarely technical. Board members too often feel intimidated by the professional staff when it comes to the curriculum. They may receive the unstated but plain message from the professionals that they are not "experts" in curricular decisions.

Yet board members always deal with curriculum priorities, normally through budget development. The budget is the mirror side of the curriculum. Few board members feel intimidated about fiscal priorities. So their curricular biases permeate the school budget. This practice means that on a day-to-day basis, budgets shape curriculum, rather than being the product of conscious and public curricular priorities.

I blame superintendents for much of this problem. Too many want to keep the board ignorant of curricular matters, believing that the curriculum is politically sacrosanct. They are incredibly naive. The board is always in curriculum one way or another. Their influence is often disguised by the fact that curricular affairs are not publicly discussed. However, boards who do not get into curricular matters "on the front end" usually get into curriculum through the budget back door.

Even if this were not the case, curriculum is more than a series of technological issues such as scheduling, format, scope and sequence, alignment, etc. It is first and foremost a political arena.

Superintendents really don't like political discussions. One reason is that such discussions threaten the role of the superintendency, given that the position is still far from secure and certainly not conflict-free. Engaging in political discussions opens the way for possible undesired "influences" and some superintendents work hard to keep the board away from such dialogue.

Yet one of the most serious problems facing the schools today is purely political. It concerns the question of priorities and the inability of school boards to come to agreement on them. The result is that everything winds up in the curriculum and there is too much of it for the actual teaching time available. Professionals who consistently work on this problem as a technical problem of format or design are usually defeated. There is no solution as long as the problem is conceptualized as a technical one.

A school superintendent who believes that the board's role is merely advisory in curricular affairs blunts the capacity of the school system to resolve a question of priorities in the overall curriculum.

Questions for Superintendents

(1) "Of all the actions taken by the administration regarding curriculum, how does the administration know if they are the right ones?"
(2) "What systematic evidence has been gathered about the strengths or weaknesses of the district's curriculum?"
(3) "In what way do board policies guide your actions about curriculum?"
(4) "Can you describe a recent decision you made about curriculum that was referenced to a board policy?"
(5) "How are curriculum decisions made at the building level influenced by overall curricular priorities of the district?"
(6) "In what ways has curricular consistency across and among schools been determined?"
(7) "What types of curricular complaints have you received from board members or parents in the last year or two?"
(8) "How do you deal with problems of curricular coordination and articulation? What are the most serious areas of the curriculum in which coordination or articulation as a problem has surfaced?"
(9) "How do you or have you assessed overall district curricular quality?"
(10) "Has the district ever done a comprehensive needs assessment?"
(11) "Does the district have a long-range curriculum plan?"
(12) "How does the board systematically set curricular priorities?"

(13) "How has the board translated curricular complaints from the community into specific curricular priorities?"
(14) "What have been the major determinants pushing for curricular changes in the district?"
(15) "What data indicate to you that the curriculum is adequate?"

Superintendents I've interviewed are normally quite uncomfortable with these questions. First, they realize they don't know as much about curriculum as perhaps they should. Secondly, the questions reveal almost instantly their lack of control and direction of the curriculum in their own district. With the exception of brand new superintendents or seasoned and very secure veterans, most superintendents simply can't take the heat.

In one audit mentioned earlier, the findings were so contradictory to the press releases pumped out by the superintendent's office that I was handed a check in the amount of $17,000 and told the audit "was over." The superintendent's top level staff did not even want a completed audit after they reviewed the draft audit copy, since that would have become a public document. At the same time the administrators could not cite one flaw or error in the documents reviewed or the findings. They simply "bailed out."

It is an unusual superintendent who can answer the questions posed with any assurance or specificity. Rarely can they supply specific instances when occasions require a response to such questions.

This *gap* is revealing. The problem of curricular change and leadership is firmly rooted in the expertise of the superintendent in dealing with matters unique to that office. Only the superintendent has the total view of the district and the power to change it. If the person in that role is not knowledgeable or is unwilling to engage in planning or thinking seriously and deeply about curricular affairs, it is unlikely the district can improve its overall curriculum, even though important building level changes occur in the latitude provided to school principals. A strong K–12 curriculum is usually the result of a vigorous, knowledgeable, and supportive school superintendent.

Questions for School Principals

Questions to school principals often focus on the link between the policies and directives of the central administration and how they are translated and extended at the school building. Principals have a good deal of latitude in most school systems. Because of the extended spans of control of a central supervisor or the superintendent, there is not normally "close supervision." Therefore, principals enjoy much autonomy.

If there are not difficult learning standards to attain that require tight coordination across the system, central administrators do not have to worry about creating and maintaining close connections among separate building programs (referred to as "curriculum articulation") within a school system. However, the more strenuous the standards, the greater are the pressures exerted upon the system to bring the decision-making focus of the principal into line with a centrally defined and monitored curriculum.

The curriculum auditor looks for the extent of close supervision of the central office of the buildings. The auditor also looks for ways principals respond and bring various programs into line with centrally defined guidelines. The major question is how much centralization is really required. If the school system is located in a state that does not require minimum competency testing, then a much lower degree of coordination is required within a school system. That means that greater deviations would be found and that would be operationally sound. The question is not "What does the auditor want?" Rather, it is "What do the system's goals require?"

(1) "How are board policies influential in your work as a principal in dealing with building level curriculum problems?"
(2) "Are there administrative regulations concerning curriculum that accompany board policy you have found useful in resolving curriculum issues? Which ones? How often?"
(3) "What kinds of internal curricular problems dealing with consistency do you or have you faced? How were they resolved?"
(4) "Have you or your teachers noticed problems of curricular articulation in terms of children coming to your school from one or more 'feeder' schools? What kind? Are they continuing? How have you confronted them?"
(5) "In what ways do you know how good or 'adequate' your school's curriculum may be?"
(6) "What are the major forces that drive your curriculum? How many do you feel are anticipated and planned for? Which ones?"
(7) "How does the district set overall curriculum priorities? If you don't agree with them, in what ways can you voice your concerns? Do they or have they made a difference?"
(8) "Have you received any parental complaints about the curriculum? If so, what have they been?"
(9) "Do you require teachers to submit lesson plans? If yes, how do

you know the content they delineate is appropriate? If not, do you know as principal what the curriculum is?"

Elementary principals are normally much more comfortable than secondary principals in responding to these types of questions. Many elementary principals feel more at home with curriculum and instructional issues than secondary principals. The career ladder of secondary principals has something to do with it. Many secondary principals came into the job from coaching with physical education backgrounds. While this is usually very adequate to deal with human relations and public relations issues, it has not been a good route to secure instructional or curricular expertise.

Secondary principals confront a larger and more complex school environment with a curriculum which is departmentalized and more specialized than that of their elementary colleagues. The department chair plays a crucial "middle role" in providing subject area curricular leadership. For this reason, department chairs may be interviewed in a curriculum audit, particularly if they have exercised strong curriculum leadership in the past. In this case they are asked many of the same questions addressed to principals.

Questions for Classroom Teachers

(1) "What are the most influential determinants when you make decisions about teaching content?"
(2) "If you have a question regarding curriculum content propriety, what source do you normally reference?"
(3) "Have you noticed problems of curricular articulation or coordination? Can you provide specific examples?"
(4) "How does your principal help insure curricular consistency in your school?"
(5) "What steps has the district taken to create curricular consistency in your subject across and among schools?"
(6) "How much latitude do you have to ignore the district's curriculum?"
(7) "Has anybody asked you about curriculum in your classroom? When? What was the nature of the question?"
(8) "Have you ever consulted a board policy or administrative regulation regarding content or methods in your classroom? How often do you do this? What was the result? If there was a conflict, how was it resolved?"
(9) "What channels are present in the district for you to voice your concerns about curriculum?"

(10) "What do you think are the board of education's major concerns with curriculum in the schools?"

(11) "What changes in the curriculum have you found yourself making to improve its effectiveness with students? Has anybody ever asked you about those adjustments?"

(12) "Do you believe the district's curriculum is adequate? If yes, how so? If not, why not?"

Teachers look at curriculum with mixed feelings. Based on the author's interviews with many of them in a curriculum audit, they appear to want curriculum consistency in teaching and content up to "their place" in the curriculum. Having students at the proper place when they first encounter them helps them do a better job.

However, as individuals, they are often reluctant to accept strictures regarding their unfettered authority to make curriculum decisions apart from the formal command structure of the school district. Most teachers do not see these perceptions as contradictory, i.e., they can't allow all of their colleagues "to do their own thing, the system be damned," and pretend to have an articulated, coordinated curriculum. Wide variations in student responses are partly caused by a very uneven curriculum being delivered in classrooms every day.

The answer lies in the fact that a curriculum should provide guidance and the basis for consistency <u>without</u> becoming <u>standardized</u>. Standardization drives out all possibility of unique responses when they are actually called for in classrooms.

The question of preshaping teacher responses about content selection varies by subject matter, since some content areas appear to demand more congruence to a logical curricular sequence than others.

Also, basic courses require more consistency than advanced courses or electives. The variety of curricular content will vary by the types of requirements present, the level of the school system, the characteristics of the students, and the subject area under consideration. No "standard" answer will suffice and be equally viable in all situations.

Teachers are much more apt to be critical about the lack of curricular consistency than to put forth proposals to solve the problem. However, their perceptions of the *gaps* in the curriculum are usually quite accurate since they are the ones who deliver it on a day-to-day basis. But the curriculum auditor should not believe that their criticisms of the curriculum will provide fertile ground for changes, particularly when such changes may portend the development of guidelines which require some adherence by the faculty where none existed previously. Teachers may desire the <u>result</u> of good coordination, but resist the controlling procedures necessary to attain it.

Questions for Students

Interviews of school students have been customarily confined to the secondary level (grades 9–12) where the maturity of the audience is such as to reflect on the curriculum.

Students can provide some poignant insights to several facets of curriculum implementation in a school district. Students can make observations about:

- how well a given curricular sequence holds together and is connected from course to course as they experienced it
- whether course offerings are available to match their ability and interest levels
- whether courses taken prepared them well for exams and national tests
- individual proclivities of specific teachers in emphasizing specific curricular content

Of course, students can and usually do comment about how they "liked" their teachers, or whether their teachers were inspirational or effective. These are instructional areas of information and not curricular, so they are not usually reported in a curriculum audit.

Students can also be excellent sources of data regarding curricular support functions, for example, whether the guidance function is working to help them select the proper courses and be prepared for college or a vocation. They also offer insights into the grading procedures, school morale, the general expectations for achievement by the faculty, accessibility of the administration and counseling staffs, and community perceptions of a school's program.

Occasionally a student will question the actual curriculum content of a school. However, most student perceptions center around delivery of the curriculum and not its design. It is for the auditor to separate student responses that deal with curriculum design or delivery.

These are some questions asked of students in a curriculum audit:

(1) "Does the curriculum appear to you to be adequately connected from year to year, especially in the required courses?"

(2) "Have you felt that the courses you took here prepared you for the college entrance exams or other required tests?"

(3) "Who sets the curricular expectations in this school or district? Have you ever been involved in a discussion of this type?"

(4) "Are support services adequate?"

(5) "What is your perception of the relationship (balance) between required and elective courses here?"

(6) "What do you wish were in the school's curriculum that is not?"

(7) "What things that are now in the curriculum have the least value to you? Why?"

(8) "If you believed that a particular course or chunk of the curriculum was of no value, to whom would you protest?"

Under the best of circumstances the curriculum auditor will interview all kinds of students: college-bound, job-bound, misfits, and hard-core types who resist everything school stands for. It is good if the auditor doesn't know ahead of time who is who. Some of the most articulate students with the most insightful views of the school and the inadequacies of the curriculum are the ones who have been less than "successful" in them. Some are painfully aware of a school's shortcomings and can express them well.

Questions for Parents and Citizens

If parents or citizens have been close to the school district over an extended period of time, they can offer consumer-oriented opinions about the curriculum. Normally, parental views of the curriculum constitute secondary sources of data which are largely "hearsay" in nature, i.e., parents learn about school through the eyes of their children. Few parents or citizens have direct, firsthand contact with a school's curriculum unless they happen to be in the school in a volunteer or paid capacity as an aide or teacher's assistant.

Parental input is therefore less reliable than student perceptions, though no less important. Parents may also have personal axes to grind against or for certain teachers depending upon their children's experiences with them. The auditor should be aware of this phenomenon when interviewing parents. A negative opinion about a particular curriculum is often really a "vote" against a teacher in that area rather than the curriculum per se.

Like students, parents cannot easily separate curriculum design issues from curricular delivery issues. "Good curriculum" is therefore intimately linked to "good teachers." As consumers they cannot normally make a distinction between a sound curriculum design and abysmal delivery of that curriculum. The auditor, however, has to make such distinctions. Parental input, therefore, has to be treated with sensitivity and some skepticism.

Below are listed some questions asked of parents or citizens in the context of a curriculum audit:

(1) "Have you ever seen a copy of the district's curriculum?"

(2) "Do you know how curricular priorities are established in the district?"

(3) "Do you have children currently in school? Based on their experiences, what appears to be a strength as it pertains to consistency? weaknesses on the same criterion?"

(4) "Do you think the proper curriculum content is being stressed in the schools?"

(5) "What information do you wish were available to you or your children about the district's curriculum?"

The author–auditor has encountered some very perceptive parental comments over the past decade. For example, one parent said, "If I ask the principal for a copy of the curriculum for math, she can give me one. However, if I asked her for a copy of the third-grade curriculum, she would have to give me a stack of books I couldn't carry to the car."

This parent was commenting upon the habit of school officials to develop curriculum within existing disciplines and always vertically. Most districts have not given proper attention to lateral views of the curriculum. It was a perceptive comment by this parent which led to a recommendation being formulated to give attention to this facet of curriculum development.

Another area where parents may offer unusually perceptive views is the lack of cohesion or articulation among and across schools in a school district. Many parents are acutely aware of discrepancies in programs, standards, books, and expectations from one school to the next. They are often at a loss to explain them, believing that the district is neglectful of its responsibilities to ensure equity if such gaps persist. Much of the gossip in school support groups and PTAs centers around cross-checking for such discrepancies. As such, they are usually easily mentioned in interviews with parents.

ON-SITE SCHOOL VISITATIONS

On-site visitations to schools are essential, though for probably not the reason most teachers and administrators fear the most. Such visitations are not inspections and they are not evaluations of personnel. Rather, they are context determiners. The curriculum auditor wants to know the situation outside and inside a school.

For example, consider the two photographs of different schools on p. 47. The picture on the top was taken in a posh suburban school system. The grounds were superbly kept. Flowers bloomed in neat beds beside the windows. Now examine the second picture. It is of an inner-city school located next to a vacant lot littered with debris from a torn down apartment complex. An abandoned sofa lies overturned facing the windows. The lawn next to this school has not been cut in

Two views of the external environs of two schools, the top one of a surburban school. The bottom perspective is from an inner-city school situated next to a junk-filled and rat-infested vacant lot. There were no flowers next to the inner-city school, only long dried out grass that had not been cut in many months.

months. It is a far different sort of environment that faces these school windows than the colorful flowers and shady streets of the first school.

Consider the internal environment. The next two photographs (p. 49) show two gymnasiums that differ in age and location. The first gym was built in the 1930s in a small eastern suburb. The second was built in the West in the 1970s in a mushrooming suburb. It is immediately apparent that the physical arrangement of a school is of great importance in setting a tone for it. The atmosphere or "climate" of a school is an important indicator of its ability to effectively deliver a curriculum (Rowan, Bossart, and Dwyer, 1983).

The next pair of pictures (p. 50) provides another contrast in the "mood" in a school, once again between city and suburb. The top photograph was taken in a suburban elementary school, the bottom in an inner-city elementary school. The bottom shot shows a burned out classroom caused by arson. It had been vacant for some time in the condition shown. The effect of such rooms creates a "chilling" effect on a school population.

The on-site visitation reveals to the curriculum auditor the environment for learning and the special problems, barriers, impediments, and facilitators that may be present within a district's schools. Of course, the exact impact of facilities upon instruction is hard to calculate. Leaving those questions aside for the moment, the "atmosphere" is different.

Occasionally, site visitations produce data which contradict that obtained from other sources. For example, as the author–auditor was touring a district elementary school reading lab, he queried the lab teacher about the use of test data. The director of research and testing for the district had insisted test data had been used to modify instruction.

"Oh yes," said the teacher, "we do get the data from the county office, however, it doesn't come until three weeks prior to the end of the year. No one can use it then. It's really useless."

DATA TRIANGULATION

As with the case of the control audit standard, and with every audit standard, the curriculum auditor follows some well-worked procedures used in the social sciences. One of these practices is called data triangulation (Denzin, 1978, p. 295). This practice refers to the use of multiple data sources that bear upon any single point of view, i.e., in this case a single audit standard. Practically speaking, it means that an auditor will not cite a fact or a finding unless it can be substantiated from at least two different sources, preferably more.

Instructional usage varies within spatial arrangements. Two different gymnasiums on the two U.S. coasts, East and West. The smaller gym in the top photo is in a 1930s elementary school. The bottom is a more modern high school. Is a gym a gym a gym?

Burned out classrooms such as shown in the bottom picture are an ugly scene in any school. Contrast the environs with a class in session in the top picture. The curriculum auditor must have a "feel" for the schools in which the curriculum is being delivered.

For example, suppose that in an interview it is revealed that the reason the school district has failed to hire a math supervisor for several years is that the previous incumbent is still under indictment for trying to retain his job by bribing a board member.

This would be classified as strictly "hearsay," a rumor until it can be verified. Suppose that the auditor also finds an account of the grand jury indictment in the paper by going back through several years of microfiche. The indictment has now been verified. Legal records can be procured from the grand jury's offices. When the auditor cites the fact that a curriculum supervisor was indicted, there are several sources to substantiate the finding. The finding was verified by data triangulation.

The author–auditor has encountered plenty of "vanishing trails" in performing audits. Sometimes an internal document is referenced in one source, and subsequent interviews reveal no one knows or knew about it. It is impossible to know if people are "fudging" on answers or they really don't know about something.

In another actual example, the author–auditor found an external review of the personnel function in a school district completed by an external consulting firm some years before. This report was highly critical of certain board hiring practices, namely, the board not taking minutes when personnel were hired, in order to avoid tracing the placement of political friends or party hacks on the payroll. The external consulting report referenced an internal audit report critical of the same practices.

I wanted to review that internal audit report, but I was not sure who had it or if the system would admit to doing it. The reason is that the system would have to acknowledge the same problems the external consultant noted. I was looking for data triangulation.

First, I interviewed the superintendent about the external consultant's report. He said, "The board buried it. It never saw the light of day." However, when I asked the same question of the assistant superintendent, he said, "Oh, that report, it was on the front page of the paper the night it was reported to the board." I fixed the date and searched back through library microfiche. Sure enough, the assistant superintendent was correct. The report had "seen the light of day." And there in the story was the information about the other missing internal report. That led me back to ask the assistant superintendent for the internal audit. He said he couldn't let me see it without the permission of the superintendent. When permission was asked of the superintendent, he said I could see the report but could not copy it. And he added that if I wanted to interview the assistant superintendent, he would have to be present. I agreed to the first condition and declined the second.

Triangulation had done the following:

(1) Confirmed that such a document existed
(2) Led to questions about the document being developed, which
(3) Resulted in the original document being produced, which
(4) Led to inclusion of the final report

THE RUMOR MILL GRINDS ON: DATA EXCLUSION

It is not unusual for the auditor to pick up innuendos, gossip, and rumors that would rival the front page stories in the *National Enquirer*. Confidential interviews and the shield of anonymity are temptations for tongues to waggle. At the end of two full days of interviews, it is customary to know or be exposed to office love affairs, the sexual exploits or appetites of high-ranking officials, drinking habits of board members, and other human twaddle. Unless such stories involve stealing, misuse of funds, or an actual crime, the auditor doesn't normally even record such information. The audit is about curriculum and how it is delivered. While people are people, the inclusion of such tidbits would move the audit from one plane to the status of a tabloid, better left unrecorded and uncited. In this sense an audit is not a research document. A researcher might be tempted to include such data to fully expose the problems in the working environment. The auditor does not, since to include them would invite lawsuits and controversy that would eclipse the findings of the audit itself. The purpose of the audit is ultimately to improve the operations of the district. A research report is in and of itself the only justifiable end required in a research study.

Standard 2: Clear and Valid Objectives

The second curriculum audit standard pertains to the ability of the school system to develop clear and valid objectives for itself. Many school systems have no precise set of outcome standards towards the accomplishment of which they direct their resources (people, time, materials). This has a direct impact on budgetary practices and so is related to Standard 5 as well.

Lack of precision in outcomes also denies to school officials any means of answering such questions as:

- "Do we have too many electives in our program?"
- "What constitutes a core curriculum?"

- "If we can't have all our programs, which ones should be considered essential and which ones optional?"
- "What educational activities in social studies are considered primary and which ones are ancillary?"
- "How can our courses in the humanities be re-configured more effectively?"

DOCUMENTS

Documents are of critical importance in determining the adherence of the school system to Audit Standard 2. Documents represent the "products" of school system efforts to define its mission. Documents which may include the "mission" of a school district are:

- board policies and minutes
- administrative regulations
- official reports to intermediate or state education agencies
- curriculum guides or scope and sequence charts
- accreditation documents
- long-range plans
- budget documents

Typical board documents are very nebulous and ill-defined. For example, consider this mission statement from a school district in Florida:

> The mission of the school system is to help all students become productive, responsible citizens who will adapt and grow intellectually, socially, emotionally and physically in a changing world. This will be accomplished by providing lifelong learning opportunities in an environment which reflects community, culture, values, and needs (Sarasota, Florida, 1987).

Questions which could be asked in an audit:

- "What data would indicate that this mission statement had been accomplished?"
- "What exactly is 'help' in "help all students"?
- "How will the school system officials know lifelong learning has been accomplished?"
- "Whose culture and values are to be reflected in lifelong learning?"

Typically one obtains a different answer from as many different people as may be interviewed. Often such answers conflict with one another. If this is the case, the "mission" statement is an example of "mission impossible." Interpreting such statements is like trying to read tea leaves—very subjective. As such, the "mission" does not guide; it sanctions almost any action that might be taken on its behalf. This is the weakness in the typical "philosophy of education" statement found in most board policies.

Now the Sarasota statement includes some "we believes." These, too, are not measurable. For example, "We believe that education must result in the development of both creative and critical thinking skills." What evidence or data would indicate that creative skills had been developed? And exactly what is "critical thinking"? How would the district resolve an argument that hinged on whether or not it had met this "belief"?

Such statements are not intended to be operational statements that influence practice. They are, rather, symbolic statements which often shield the "hidden curriculum" from public view (Apple, 1979).

The auditor can expose the shallowness of such statements with a few probing and deft questions. The major aim of the questions is to discern what effect such statements have on the real operations and day-to-day political decisions regarding choice and allocation of resources and power within the school system. Almost without exception, such high sounding statements are never referenced in such decisions and are never used to change the internal organization and distribution of power within a school district. What they do do is sanctify existing power relationships.

INTERVIEWS

The following questions have been used by the author–auditor in the conduct of curriculum audits as they relate to Standard 2.

For Board Members

(1) "What is the purpose of the district's schools?"
(2) "What is the paramount objective of the school system?"
(3) "Where could I find a concise statement of the overall mission of the school system?"
(4) "How do you know if the school's mission is being accomplished?"
(5) "Does the district have a current long-range plan? May I see it?"
(6) "How would I know as a taxpayer if my money was being spent on attaining the district's top priorities?"

For Superintendents

(1) "How does the district set overall priorities? What are they?"
(2) "What's the main mission of the district? Has it changed during your tenure?"
(3) "How have district priorities changed over the years? Why?"
(4) "Tell me about goal setting in the district."
(5) "How are operational objectives derived from goals?"
(6) "How do you know when to change your goal focus in the district?"

For School Principals

(1) "How do you tell teachers about the district's goals? How often have they changed?"
(2) "How do you account for the district's goals in the formulation of this building's goals?"
(3) "How much independence do you have in shaping goals that are not district goals?"
(4) "How is your job performance assessed relative to district priorities?"
(5) "What do you reference to help you understand district priorities?"

For Classroom Teachers

(1) "How do you know what the district's goals are for your area?"
(2) "How much flexibility do you have in shaping educational outcomes?"
(3) "How is the district's curriculum monitored?"
(4) "How do you know if your own classroom planning extends the district's goals?"

For Parents

(1) "Do you know how overall curricular priorities are established?"
(2) "What problems have you discerned (if any) with the focus of the school's curriculum?"
(3) "Have you ever tried to obtain answers to any questions about the district's curriculum? What was your experience?"

ON-SITE VISITATIONS

On-site visitations can reveal the presence of goal statements that are visible to personnel in the field and referenced in their daily activities. For example, central district goal statements may be displayed in school principals' offices or in school hallways. Some have even been found posted near teachers' boxes.

Once, I asked for the long-range plan in a large school district. Everyone interviewed said it contained goal statements. However, no one knew where the plan was. Finally, I spoke to a veteran teacher who confessed that the long-range plan was probably a scope and sequence chart published some eight years before. When I asked to see a copy of it, he produced one from a basement closet. If ever such a document was referenced, it had long since ceased to be useful to decision making. Except for this veteran teacher, it was all but lost to the collective memory of the organization.

Standard 3: Documentation Explaining How Programs Have Been Developed, Implemented, and Conducted

This standard represents how programs have been developed. Programs are organizing points for configurations of resources and activities within schools. The standard assumes that there are logical relationships in the creation of programs and that these relationships can be understood in light of a review of documents which demonstrate rational thought processes at work in schools.

There are at least some organizational theorists (Weick, 1985) who would question this conventional organizational logic, believing that school officials more likely act first and invent reasons for their actions second. "Thus," notes Weick, "trappings of rationality such as strategic plans are important largely as binding mechanisms," i.e., they reinforce actions rather than trigger them (p. 127).

Weick's ideas, however, cut against the grain of a large body of organizational literature, though there is certainly plenty of evidence that organizations must make room for the creative hunch and intuition in selecting program choices.

Once the author–auditor was doing a programmatic audit of ten years of Chapter 1 funding in an eastern city. A simple bar graph was constructed showing the total amount of dollars funded by grade level over the decade. It revealed that those grades receiving the most money were grades 7-8-9. That fact contradicted prevalent notions that the money should be spent earlier in a child's school career because it was more likely to produce greater effects. When school system officials were confronted with the bar graph, most simply shrugged their shoulders and said, "That's because in the beginning the junior high school principals were the most aggressive in going after fed funds. It just stayed that way after that."

Here is an example of dollar flow set by the idiosyncracies of the system and perpetuated by tradition. There was no rational decision made in the beginning about where the funds should be spent based on need, and no plan or criteria developed to correct a spending pattern once established. The lack of such mechanisms meant that the system probably used the funds unwisely and did not obtain the maximum benefit from them. Even more damaging was the lack of any procedure to correct an initial mistake in program development.

DOCUMENTS

The documents most useful in examining this curriculum audit standard are board policies which shape resource flow, from textbook adoption to budget development. Long-range plans, annual reports, initial grant proposals, interim reports, and in-house memoranda are also important sources of program description, need, and priorities.

INTERVIEWS

Questions for Board Members

(1) "What are generally considered the strongest and weakest programs in the district? How did they get that way?"
(2) "How does the board evaluate its programs? What actions have been taken based on an evaluation?"
(3) "In what ways have dollar resources been directed to shore up weak programs and/or maintain strong ones?"

Board members are most often frustrated at their inability to penetrate to the program level in school organizations, except in the rarest of circumstances. When it occurs, it is usually centered around extracurricular functions such as athletics.

When queried, most board members usually attribute "strong" programs to "good" teachers and "weak" programs to "poor" teachers. Most board members have only the most cursory idea of how any action they might take as a board member could improve educational programs. Thus, they do not normally connect policy decisions or even budget decisions to program effectiveness. Many administrators are not much clearer about the "connections" either.

This "grey area" is most perplexing. It is a kind of "no-man's land" between decisions on one level and operations on another. The "brokers" between policy and operations are administrators, which in part explains their great power. But to be truly powerful, the real criteria are mostly hidden from view because to make them public would diminish the authority of the persons occupying the offices.

Seasoned school principals are perhaps the most adept at internal organizational politics and knowing the unwritten rules of influencing the resource flow of the organization. They "milk" the real power structure by knowing how much latitude central office administrators have and who the "right people" are. The reason administrators themselves are not clear about these matters is that, especially in large systems, much of the authority is decentralized and hidden from one another. It is like a large game of organizational poker where the players are not at a table, but occupy boxes somewhere in the organizational chart.

The auditor should understand but not necessarily "accept" these conditions as inevitable. At this point some curriculum audits include a study of the formal organizational relationships among and between central administrative officers. Often, audits point up the weaknesses in organizational charts and the confusion that may exist in a school system about who does what to whom and under what conditions.

Questions for Superintendents

(1) "How do you ensure that educational programs are balanced and reinforce the overall goals of the district?"
(2) "How do you assess the requirements for the establishment of new programs?"
(3) "Have any programs in this district ever been terminated based upon poor performance? If so, which ones? What criteria did you use to make this decision?"

Questions for Principals

(1) "What programs are strongest and weakest at your school? How did they come to be in this condition?"
(2) "What actions have you taken to improve weak programs?"
(3) "What barriers stand in your way to improve or terminate weak programs?"
(4) "In what ways do you know if all of your programs result in a sound, overall program for your students?"

Questions for Teachers

(1) "What do you think are the strongest or weakest programs in this school? Why are they so?"
(2) "What actions has the principal taken to improve weak programs?"
(3) "What do you think would improve weak programs?"

There is a tendency for personnel interviewed to "waffle" on many of these questions. At such times, the auditor presses for specifics, clarifies contradictions, rephrases questions, and follows up on ambiguities. It is done as a reporter would conduct a good interview and not as a lawyer would cross-examine a stubborn witness. The auditor has no legal power to compel responses. In order to illustrate how this is done, a "mock" interview is highlighted.

A MOCK INTERVIEW WITH GERALD JONES, SCHOOL PRINCIPAL

Auditor: "What do you think are your programs of greatest strength and weakness here at Brevard School?"
Jones: "Oh, my, it's easier to talk about our strengths. I'm not sure we have any weaknesses, really."
Auditor: "OK, let's say programs that need improvement."
Jones: "That's better. What do you want first?"
Auditor: "Whatever you want to talk about first."
Jones: "Well, our reading program is strong. Art is super. I would say math is strong, too."
Auditor: "Why do you think these programs are so strong?"
Jones: "The teachers. The art teacher, Sue Spreck, she is a dynamo. Her room is just alive with kids doing things. She gets involvement."
Auditor: "What kind of basal do you use in reading?"
Jones: "Oh, that's it. Five years ago we went to *Open Court* in the early grades. Our reading scores on the district test at the third grade are phenomenal. The teachers are committed."
Auditor: "All the teachers?"
Jones: "Well, the primary teachers are. The upper grade teachers are not as sold on it. In fact from fourth on, we use another series—the Scott-Foresman set."
Auditor: "Tell me about that decision."
Jones: "Well, we got some parental complaints about *Open Court*. Yes, and some board members asked questions about it at a meeting."

Auditor: "Isn't that unusual, I mean, for a board to ask questions about a specific reading program?"

Jones: "Well, yes, but a couple of our board members are ex-teachers. I don't think some like *Open Court*. I don't know."

Auditor: "What were their objections?"

Jones: "It was centered on test scores, really. The scores dropped after third grade."

Auditor: "Was it on the basis of test scores that the program was dropped after third grade?"

Jones: "Well, not solely. Maybe it was. Anyway, we tried out the Scott-Foresman at some other grade levels and our teachers liked it better."

Auditor: "What happened to the test scores?"

Jones: "I think they were better with the Scott-Foresman. Anyway, that made the teachers on the board happier, I guess."

Auditor: "Have you seen any test data?"

Jones: "I don't recall. You'd have to ask the superintendent about that."

Auditor: "You mentioned the math program."

Jones: ""Yes, there we use Harcourt-Brace. We use it at every grade level. It has given us a solid program. Parents like it, too."

Auditor: "And the test scores?"

Jones: "Very consistent. Good. We're pleased. We don't have the same kinds of problems with the textbook business as in reading."

Auditor: "And the programs that need improvement?"

Jones: "Science is not strong. I'd say we are not happy with our writing. And recently we've been made aware of certain deficiencies in geography. I guess we don't teach it at all."

Auditor: "What about science particularly?"

Jones: "Well, you know most elementary teachers feel uncomfortable with doing experiments. If we do science, it's textbook science and not hands-on science. Science, here, if it is taught at all, is just facts. It's pretty boring for a lot of kids."

Auditor: "How is it that when you think of math or reading, the textbook is a strength, but in science it's not?"

Jones: "Because if any subject should be taught inductively it's science. You know, the scientific method and all."

Auditor: "But aren't some parts of math inductive?"

Jones: "Perhaps. But the state test is driving our program, and it's mostly didactic stuff they want."

Auditor: "And writing?"

Jones: "We don't teach writing here. We teach grammar. I've asked the superintendent for funds to train our staff in holistic writing and scoring for two years. I'm not a specialist in that area. I was a P.E. teacher at the middle school for seven years. What do I know about writing?"

Auditor: "What is it that is really desired, creative or expository writing?"

Jones: "Our teachers do a lot of creative stuff. But when it comes to writing a decent paragraph at the upper grades, many are at a loss to know what to do."

Auditor: "Why do you think the holistic writing is the answer?"

Jones: "One of our teachers took a course at State Tech and she said that all of the tests are going in that direction."

Auditor: "You mentioned geography."

Jones: "I don't have any hard data on this. But you know the recent national reports on assessment of students show they don't know even the basics about where mountains and oceans are. I'm afraid to ask around here. My observation of the classes here show me no time is spent on geography."

Auditor: "Do you look for this in teacher plan books?

Jones: "We don't have a policy about that. I look at some of them. But I don't see any geography at all."

Auditor: "What policy? Yours or the district's?"

Jones: "The district has no policy about plan books. I let the teachers decide. I do ask our new teachers to keep them."

Auditor: "What about other areas of the curriculum? Like music, literature, physical education, social studies?"

Jones: "I think our programs are good there, but they aren't in the same league as the ones I mentioned to you as our strengths."

Auditor: "What have you done as principal to improve your weak areas?"

Jones: "I've written requests to the superintendent. I've tried to get the teachers to conferences. I call meetings and talk about it. But you know, with a bunch of old dogs like I've got, they've been here longer than I have. Some are now teaching the kids of kids they had earlier. It's hard to change them."

Auditor: "What about budget development? Have you requested funds there?"

Jones: "Not really. We only get a small piddly amount for materials but nothing big at all."

Auditor: "Do you see any way to improve those programs?"

Jones: "You tell me. I've tried everything I know. That's what we hope to find out in the audit. That's why you're here."

Auditor: "Thanks. Let's take our tour."

The interview, while a composite of many conducted, is fairly typical of what is encountered in some schools. The problem is the lack of leadership of the principal. The auditor is gentle but firm, open, warm, and understanding.

The early facade of defensiveness is broken down. The principal is frank. The interview reveals many dimensions of what the auditor is looking for. The reader should not believe that answers to interview questions are one-dimensional in nature. Rarely are questions answered simply "yes" or "no." Many questions are broad such as "tell me about that." The tack taken by the auditor is determined by such factors as the defensiveness of the person being interviewed, whether the information can be verified from other sources (triangulation), and a subjective determination that a person simply doesn't know, and it is not in the interests of the auditor to embarrass or humilate anyone. After an interview a person should not feel browbeaten or criticized. They should feel that someone who understands their situation has sympathetically listened to them and they have really been "heard."

ON-SITE VISITATIONS

Strong programs leave many clues in schools. Evidence of strong programs are high pupil enrollment, vibrant classrooms, abundant displays of student work, and excellent attendance records. Classrooms reveal good supplies of equipment and tangible traces of adherence to achievement indicators such as posted test results, displays of commendations, certificates of merit, newspaper clippings of students, etc.

Weak programs assume properties which are the opposite. Poor attendance, dull and monotonous instruction, poor discipline, lack of learner attentiveness, few displays of outstanding pupil work, antiquated materials, and a paucity of supplies; in short, a kind of institutional "barrenness" prevails.

Standard 4: The School District Uses the Results from District-Designed and/or Adopted Instruments to Adjust, Improve, or Terminate Ineffective Practices or Programs

This curriculum audit standard focuses on results, however defined, obtained by the district. The data gathered deals with how decisions using results have been determined, analyzed, and fed back through the system to make changes in organizational functions.

Typically, school district officials make very poor use of feedback in the form of standardized test data. There are a variety of reasons for this. For one, such tests are usually adopted independently of any consideration of the curriculum in a district. What that means is that the data provided "floats" around a school system with no specific anchor to classroom instruction.

When that is the case, and the test feedback is distributed to teachers (it is rarely explained), they make very little use of it to change anything in their own work places. The data are considered about children and not about teachers or the curriculum.

It is this breakdown in the application of test data that is an integral part of the audit. The assumption is that test data should serve the purpose of providing feedback about instruction. For it to legitimately do so, it must be an accurate reflection of the curriculum in the district.

This assumption will undoubtedly anger some test publishers or those who see such instruments as performing some function regarding learner classification. The purpose of testing is to provide feedback so teaching can be re-configured. To the extent some tests help in this process, they would be considered functional.

Too often, however, standardized tests provide nothing but a false barometer of anything but socio-economic status, the one variable to which they are most positively correlated. Even if one could accept the speculative premise that such tests show that rich people are smarter, of what good would that be in going about improving learning in schools?

DOCUMENTS

The documents most often reviewed by the curriculum auditor are reports on testing and test results given to the board of education, trend analyses the district officials have done to know whether certain weaknesses have been spotted and corrected over time, and memoranda from instructional supervisors and/or principals as to what to change in the curriculum (content emphasis, time, or sequence) or what to alter in teaching so as to improve pupil performance as assessed.

The curriculum auditor is looking for something called *linkage documents*. These documents are system-created interstitial records that point out specific places which connect test data to organizational functions (curriculum and/or teaching) and call for changes in the existing work patterns. If test data are really functional, such *linkage documents* are almost "natural" creations. They make a lot of sense.

As such test data should be examined *transactionally*, i.e., to determine if someone has created the functional connections between feedback and operations (testing and teaching), and then interviews indicate whether or not there has been any "action" as a result of the creation of the *linkages*.

INTERVIEWS

Questions for Board Members

(1) "What kinds of decisions has the board ever made with test data?"
(2) "How often do you receive reports about testing? Have you understood what the data meant?"
(3) "What kinds of decisions do you think the professionals make with the data? How do you know they do it well?"
(4) "How are areas of the curriculum not tested assessed?"
(5) "Do you believe every area of the curriculum is adequately assessed? If not, why not?"

Questions for Superintendents

(1) "What criteria served as the basis for the adoption of the existing test batteries?"
(2) "How are test data used by principals to improve instruction?"
(3) "What percentage of the curriculum locally is assessed by the existing test batteries?"
(4) "How are areas of the curriculum not included in the test assessed?"
(5) "If you utilize different batteries, on what basis was compatibility (alignment) determined?"
(6) "Could you indicate any specific instructional/curricular decisions made in the system as the result of using test feedback in the last two–three years?"

Questions for School Principals

(1) "Do you receive test data in a usable format?"
(2) "How do you expect teachers to use test data (specifically)?"
(3) "How well do your teachers use test data to improve instruction? Provide some examples."
(4) "What decisions have you or the staff at your building made as the result of testing trends?"
(5) "How are areas of the curriculum not tested assessed?"
(6) "Have you noticed any curricular distortion caused by testing? If so, how and where?"

Questions for Classroom Teachers

(1) "How useful has test data been to you in knowing what to change in the curriculum you teach?"
(2) "Could you provide specific examples of ways test data has been applied to change your teaching or the curriculum?"
(3) "What kinds of decisions has your principal made with the data? your district?
(4) "What have been your observations about the impact of testing on your teaching?"
(5) "How do you assess areas of the curriculum not tested?"

Questions for Parents

(1) "What do test scores mean to you?"
(2) "Do you understand the curricular implications of test data?"
(3) "Do you know what part of the curriculum is assessed with any specific test and what part is not? If not, why not?"

ON-SITE VISITATIONS

On-site visitations can reveal the extent to which students and teachers are using test data to make decisions. In schools where test data are visible, it is not unusual to see simple bar graphs about school-wide performance displayed in various places, from the principal's office to the faculty room.

One school had organized "the test busters." This was an effort to get everyone focused on the state test and to do their best. Other districts have developed charts which display test scores and smaller measures administered on a weekly or monthly basis. In one school the principal required a prepost test to be used as the basis for shaping lesson plans. The test results were kept in the back of each teacher's plan book for reference.

On-site visitations can reveal the extent to which the presence of testing has been made aware to all concerned. Schools that are seriously trying to improve test scores create a heightened awareness of the importance of doing well. Such awareness efforts most often take on tangible (visible) form.

Standard 5: The School District Has Improved Productivity

This standard deals with results and costs. It is important that it is the last standard, too. It makes little sense to talk about costs or reducing costs until one knows if the required results are being obtained (effectiveness).

The first thing the auditor looks for is a structured relationship between the curriculum and the budget. That relationship is most often portrayed or specified in the annual budget document itself.

The auditor assumes in this standard that there must be a logical relationship between the curriculum and the budget. Furthermore, this relationship ought to take on a programmatic form so that it is possible to ultimately link costs and results.

Of course, school districts can't control directly all of their costs and budgets don't really control anything, they reflect costs. For example, personnel costs, which comprise 70–80 percent of most school budgets, are controlled not in budgets but in contract negotiations. Contract settlements are then reflected in the budget but not "controlled" by it.

The sequential relationship is also important. Most school systems adopt the budget first and then shove as much curriculum into it as possible. This scenario produces a *budget-driven curriculum*. To reverse this relationship, curriculum decisions ought to come first and the budget developed to support them. This would result in a *curriculum-driven budget*. However, this rarely occurs because:

- Curriculum and budget are not formally connected.
- The board does not usually adopt curriculum priorities which shape the budget.
- Financial decisions are made independently of curricular ones and referenced to separate political "winds."

One solution would be a detailed program budget. However, that is not necessary. Programmed budgeting was a fad in the 1960s that died because it led, not to improved control and rationality, but to acres of paperwork and tedium.

What the curriculum auditor is looking for are tangible, visible, and logical relationships between curricular priorities and financial priorities.

Without these linkages it is impossible to determine productivity gains. For purposes of the audit, productivity is simply the relationship between all of the inputs and the cost of obtaining any given level of outputs. Productivity occurs when the same or improved outputs are procured with the same or less inputs.

In actual school operations, productivity remains elusive, partly because labor costs rise no matter what, and school systems have not been able to trade off labor-intensive operations to technical improvements such as computers. Not that that would necessarily be a good thing. It is simply to note that conventional analyses of school operations do not equate to industrial models without some adaptation.

It is possible, however, to impact outputs with changes which are internal and do not necessarily add to costs. One practice that illustrates this is *curriculum alignment*, i.e., linking curriculum and testing to produce focused teaching (English, 1986–87).

So the curriculum auditor approaches the productivity standard gingerly. The key dimension is whether the auditor can find systematic linkages between budget practices and curricular priorities.

DOCUMENTS

The most obvious document involved with this standard is the annual school budget and the work papers which go into the budget formulation. Such work papers are the forms completed by administrators and teachers to do specific activities in the budget development process. Thus, the curriculum auditor can trace the evolution of the budget and where it is connected to the curriculum.

Other documents of value are external financial audits of the district completed by an accounting firm. Often, these documents contain clues regarding impending fiscal problems that ultimately will have or have had a curricular impact. For example, if the external audit reveals that certain areas of the budget have been chronically exceeded, it may be caused by sloppy, decentralized requisition procedures. Such procedures may result in dollars spent on duplicating the same textbooks, computer programs, workbooks, and other teacher ordered materials among the schools. This creates shortages of materials in some areas and oversupply in others.

Most CPA (certified public accounting) firms submit their financial audits with a *management letter*. While much of the management letter is standard boiler plate verbiage, usually sandwiched into this document are descriptive statements that may point to fiscal problems or control problems that will have an impact on overall operations. It is important that the curriculum auditor know how to read such documents, what they say, and what they really mean. Some CPA firms are bolder about this than others.

It ought to be noted again that the budget is the "mirror side" of the curriculum. The budget is a curriculum configuration expressed in dollars instead of with content or program objectives.

Other documents useful with this standard are any output data such as test scores that the district has related to its inputs. The budget alone ought to be a linkage document by illustrating how inputs are connected to outputs via programs.

INTERVIEWS

Questions for Board Members

(1) "How are budget priorities established?"
(2) "By what criteria do you make decisions as a board about budget reductions?"
(3) "In what ways has the budgeting process been used to improve identified weak areas of the curriculum? What have been the results?"
(4) "How do you know as a board member that funds spent on priorities are effective? What are your data sources?"
(5) "What curricular areas have been reshaped or terminated based on obtaining poor results over time after funding has been systematically applied?"
(6) "How are test scores (or other assessment or feedback data) used to guide budget development?"

Questions for Superintendents

(1) "What types of guidelines do you use in preparing the budget?"
(2) "How are such guidelines influenced by curricular priorities?"
(3) "How are the curricular priorities established?"
(4) "On what basis is increased budgetary support justified?"
(5) "Have you ever recommended decreasing support or terminating support based upon a review of any output data? If yes, cite specifics."
(6) "How much latitude do principals have in shaping local fiscal/programmatic priorities that differ from the district's?"

Questions for Principals

(1) "How are budget priorities established in your school?
(2) "Are your curricular priorities at your building reflected in the school's budget or the district's budget?"

(3) "Describe your input and its weight in the development of the district's budget."
(4) "In what ways has your input made (or not made) a difference?"

Questions for Teachers

(1) "Do you feel your resources are adequate in your school?"
(2) "In what ways do you see the budget development process as supporting your efforts? or not supporting?
(3) "Has your principal made a difference in helping you secure needed curricular modifications?
(4) "What changes in financial priorities are required to make this program of which you are a part more effective with children?"

The curriculum audit as described in this book does not assume that there is some "ideal" configuration regarding involvement in budget development. Some school systems are quite centralized but manage to involve a lot of people. Others are also centralized and exclude any local building shaping of the budget.

Decentralized budgeting is not necessarily any more effective. Too often, such building-based management represents nothing less than an abrogation of any responsibility to be accountable for system-wide results. Whenever questions are asked about results, the buck is passed to the principals. The problem is that tests assess school work in more than one building. Most state competency tests are batteries aimed at assessing cumulative skills. Such skills are to be learned in sequences that stretch across many buildings and involve many teachers. Such a situation requires central coordination and direction. Decentralization is an answer to some issues, but not all. Decentralization works best when there are very loose measures employed of system-wide performance that do not require "tight coupling" of internal units. If that is not the case, centralization is the better response.

There isn't any magic pattern. The bottom line is always, "Are we getting better results?"

SITE VISITATIONS

Beyond those characteristics of effective schools that dot the literature, productivity per se is dependent upon measures of learning. Learning is the result of schooling. Productivity is something that is felt more than it is seen in on-site visitations.

CHECKPOINTS

Common Questions Asked the Author–Auditor

Question 1: *Is the curriculum audit atheoretical? Does it possess a good theoretical framework?*

Answer: If I had to select a framework that I thought best suited the curriculum audit, it would be Ludwig von Bertalanffy's *General System Theory: Foundations, Development, Applications.* Bertalanffy was a biologist and looked at organizations as extensions of biological functions.

Question 2: *But what about curriculum theory?*

Answer: The last book dealing with curriculum theory as most practitioners envision it was George Beauchamp's *Curriculum Theory* published in 1975. Since that time a number of academics have pushed the frontiers very hard, primarily using Marxian constructs. I am thinking of the work of Michael Apple at Wisconsin. Other thinkers are Stanley Aronowitz and Henry Giroux. All are very concerned with the "hidden curriculum."

Question 3: *Aren't there other constructs or ideas that could become standards in a curriculum audit?*

Answer: Of course. For example, if one believed in the concept of "teacher empowerment," then an audit standard could be developed which captured this idea and made it obligatory to be considered "on target." The five standards used in the curriculum audits since 1979 and which form the data base for this book are more generic to the literature of organizational theory and management. As such, a major assumption is that schools are describable by a body of knowledge that would be generic to all forms of human organization. That assumption, by the way, is still under debate in some academic circles. Most practitioners already make this assumption.

Question 4: *What has been the most serious drawback of the form of the audit you've utilized?*

Answer: Probably that it doesn't answer the <u>content</u> question. The standards don't assume that any set of objectives or content is necessarily any better than any other. I've never said to a board of education, "You've got the wrong objectives for math." I have said, "How do you know these objectives are right for you and your children?" Then I expect to see all of the processes used to validate the act of local choice.

But I'm fully aware that there is at work a set of values, often unstated, that are utilized to exclude some content from being considered. That's why I like Beauchamps' definition of this choice as "culture content." If the school is serving children from different classes and these have different cultures, there is a kind of "war" to determine primacy. That is what most of the theoretical debate is about in academia about curriculum and schools.

Because the audit doesn't assume or push any one culture over another, it ends up reinforcing the current one. If an individual is Marxist by persuasion, the dominant capitalistic ideology is repulsive, so the audit would be likewise objectionable. The audit process is not suited to supplanting the judgment of a duly elected board of education. As it pertains to value choices, the audit is reflective and probing at its best. At its worst it is mechanical. It is almost never radical, not because it rejects radicalism per se, but because it doesn't start with radicalism as a goal.

Question 5: *Why are some academics fearful of auditing and its impact on curriculum?*

Answer: There appear to be different reasons. Some are disturbed because they see auditing fostering a kind of control they may find repugnant. Some believe that the process is an insensitive application of another business technology in schools which is inappropriate.

I ought to remind my colleagues that academic peer review is a form of auditing and it could be conceptualized as both mechanical, routinized, and insensitive. There is the danger that it could be so, but the tradeoff is increased objectivity and rigor, or at least it is believed that these assets are attainable only through peer review. Of course, no human procedure is perfect. Errors in judgment can be made under any system.

Question 6: *Have you ever found some people less than candid in interviews? If so, what do you do?*

Answer: Remember the auditor usually has no legal authority to compel a response. The best recourse is a lot of interviews and data triangulation. Most people want to talk about their feelings and their jobs. They feel good and important being asked about them. Most of the time people provide more information than is really required.

I have come across some who withhold information. Normally, the body language gives them away. They may break eye contact or smile or shrug their shoulders. That means they probably know more but will not say, so I may try another question that is slightly different and in a different sequence. However, if I get the same response, I move on. There is always someone else to ask and other data sources to check. I've simply never found a level of distortion or collusion so widespread that the truth couldn't be ascertained with patience through triangulation.

Question 7: *Don't some of the questions involve more than one audit standard?*

Answer: Yes. This is because the standards are interrelated and are assessing how the functions are working together. A question about a long-range plan might incorporate a mission statement and indicate district organizational focus. It might also list objectives, test scores, or even financial priorities. There is no reason why some single documents can't be used to speak to several standards.

Question 8: *What about the issue of sampling? Financial accountants don't examine every transaction.*

Answer: I don't normally sample. For example, I read all of the curriculum guides, all of the board policies, and all test scores within a given time period. On interviews all board members are involved and all central office staff and principals. Teachers may be sampled along with parents, in which case it is up to the district to select a "representative" sample. Such a "slice" can be verified as accurate by asking people about the persons included. Statistically a table of random numbers could also be used. If the auditor has done a good job of triangulating the data, sampling does not normally become an issue.

/ III / *Writing the Audit*

THE DATA ARE in. The auditor often confronts pages of interview notes, stacks of internal memoranda, reports, minutes, curriculum guides and their analyses, test data and computer printouts, and boxes of texts and other materials. The writing task seems to be overwhelming.

From experience, the author–auditor has learned not to leave the writing to the end. The audit is written as the auditor goes, often in "sketches" or impressions and in partial stages of completion in file folders. For example, somewhere towards the end of the interviews, the auditor may attempt to pull together some impressions around a number of standards. Sometimes lists are made with short descriptive stages of findings. These are always considered very tentative and open to be examined with consistent triangulation.

In some audits where interviews are lengthy and many, interview notes should be reviewed and retyped to preserve accuracy, especially if direct quotes are going to be used within the text of the audit. The auditor should keep "working papers" in some orderly fashion so as to make the writing task easier, and to serve as a reference point if textual comments are challenged. Working papers should never be destroyed but kept for quite a while (ten years). Working papers are confidential, though in court cases the extent of confidentiality may be broached directly (problems in litigation will be discussed later).

The following points should be kept in mind in writing the final audit report:

- The writing style should be direct and in plain everyday English, as free from jargon as possible with little technical language.
- There should be no "surprises" in the audit, avoid playing "gotcha" with clients.
- The core of the audit is contained in the findings section.

- No attempt should be made to strike some sort of artificial balance between positive and negative findings or comments.
- The number of recommendations should be small, enabling the system to focus its energies on improvements.

THE WRITING STYLE OF THE CURRICULUM AUDIT

The primary audience of the curriculum audit is the lay board of education, the public, and the professional staff, in that order! For the audit to have the kind of power leverage it must attain to change things internally, it must be understood by the policy makers and their constitutents.

The auditor is not writing the audit for publication in a scholarly refereed journal, where the norm is to deal with complex thoughts and demonstrate a deep familiarity with the issues via intensive footnoting to a myriad of other writers and authorities. That kind of writing is too often dull, dry, and hard to follow. Furthermore, policy makers are not apt to be able to differentiate the really important issues from the trivial ones.

For these reasons audit prose is good expository writing that avoids jargon to a large extent (some is almost inevitable) and overly technical vocabulary. There are no footnotes to other authorities as a rule. The auditor and his standards are the only authority required. CPAs provide a reasonably good model here. The length of the audit should generally not exceed one hundred pages, double-spaced typing, if that long.

The temptation for professors who write audits is to view the document as a research effort. It is not. The auditor is a kind of consultant, doing a specific piece of work for a client. The job of the auditor is not to affirm or deny hypotheses, but to solve problems, specifically those relating to curriculum management.

THE DOCTRINE OF NO SURPRISES

The purpose of the audit is to provide the school system, its lay and administrative officials, with a clear, concise set of recommendations to improve the design and delivery of curriculum in the school district.

The data are produced by the system; the interviews reveal what people perceive, believe, or have observed about their own or others' actions in the system. The school buildings are part of the client system's daily ritual. A well-constructed and thorough audit comes as no surprise to most school system personnel, though occasionally a high level official or two may be surprised because he or she has cut himself/herself off from the data sources tapped by the auditor. Normally that person is the superintendent.

With few exceptions, the author–auditor always allows the superintendent or designee to read the draft audit. There are findings of error, findings of omission, or differences of opinion. For example, the auditor may state that there are fourteen courses in social studies when there are sixteen. Such errors are usually caught in the draft reading and are frequently caused by the fact that the system has failed to produce the correct documents.

Errors of omission occur because some documents were not presented to the auditor. For example, I once wrote that there had been no plan for budget reductions because of the failure of a tax levy in a school district. My interview data indicated that none of the board members could recall one. Even the superintendent was a bit foggy. However, upon checking he did find such a plan in the form of a memo to the board and it was in the board minutes. I subsequently changed the finding.

Errors of opinion occur because there is a difference of perception about the meaning of something. For example, a typical finding is that there is no long-range plan. I've often had district officials challenge me on this. They produce a document labeled "long-range plan." In some states, school districts are supposed to submit something called "a long-range plan" to the state department of education. Sometimes it is a single sheet of paper which has the budget totals for two years, enrollment projection for five years, and some other sketchy statistical data, perhaps test scores. In no way could such a document be construed as a bona fide long-range plan. Any review of a text on planning would provide ample evidence of what is missing.

I've had similar discussions about curriculum guides, alignment documents, budgets and budget formats, test analyses, scope and sequence charts, needs assessments, and board policies. One usually has to make clear why a document labeled a "plan" may not be a plan at all.

Audits are normally shared with the client prior to the time they are issued in final form. The only exception to that rule is when the school district may not be the client, but an agency outside of the school district, and the audit is part of a compliance review or legal proceeding. One of the audits in this book was conducted under the umbrella of long-standing litigation. It was not reviewed by the client prior to being issued in final form, but the school district did have an opportunity to challenge it—in a lengthy cross-examination of the auditor!

THE CORE OF THE AUDIT IS IN ITS FINDINGS

The heart of the audit document is contained in its findings. The most well-conceived "solutions" in the form of recommendations will fall on deaf ears unless a case has been made for them in the findings section of the audit.

So the auditor takes special pains to deal with what was found. In some of my earlier audits, I differentiated between findings and conclusions. This comes from the criteria used in assessing a dissertation. A finding might be that the auditor could not discover in the documents reviewed any reference to curriculum alignment (i.e., matching the test content to curriculum content). That could be affirmed or denied. The fact is that none of the documents reviewed contained any reference to the practice of curriculum alignment. However, a conclusion would deal with the meaning of an established fact. One conclusion might be "the system has made no efforts to deal with curriculum alignment." That would be a risky (and perhaps false) statement unless data triangulation from interviews and site visitations lead to the same conclusion. For the most part this distinction is academic (no pun intended). So it has been dropped. The outline of a typical audit is as follows:

Outline of the Contents of the Curriculum Audit

I. BACKGROUND, PURPOSE, SCOPE OF WORK
   - Background
   - Purpose
   - Scope of Work

II. METHODOLOGY
   - The Model for the Audit
   - Standards for the Auditor
   - Data Sources
   - Standards for the Curriculum Audit

III. FINDINGS
   - Reported by Standard

IV. RECOMMENDATIONS

V. SUMMARY

APPENDICES

In the writing process, the auditor groups the documents reviewed around the five standards discussed in Chapter 2. They serve as the "conceptual hooks" to cluster the data. Typically, the documents are grouped as follows:

Documents Usually Supporting Findings in Standard 1: The School District Demonstrates Control

- board policies
- long-/short-range plans
- job descriptions
- administrative regulations
- state law/federal statutes
- official memoranda from the superintendent or other high-ranking school officials
- compliance documents filed with intermediate, state, or federal agencies
- official reports, annual reports
- accreditation reviews
- other internal/external reviews of the control function(s)

Documents Usually Supporting Findings in Standard 2: School District's Objectives for Students

- curriculum guides
- course catalogs
- scope and sequence charts
- pacing charts
- curriculum planning documents
- grant applications
- compliance documents, state and federal
- long-/short-range plans
- budget documents (if programmed in nature)
- lesson plan guidebooks
- board policies (if specific)
- textbook/teacher guides
- needs assessment results
- variety of internal documents in memo form
- minutes from meetings of official groups which reflect consensus about goals/objectives
- state mandated course outlines or objectives

Documents Usually Supporting Findings in Standard 3: School District Program Documentation

- long-/short-range plans
- budget documents (if programmatic in nature)
- staff development surveys
- climate studies or results
- any system used for curriculum monitoring (pacing charts, lesson plans, etc.)
- state/federal projects
- formal reports on programs to board of education
- annual reports
- program evaluations
- accreditation reviews
- any relevant/current external review of a program

Documents Usually Supporting Findings in Standard 4: School District Utilization of Results

- test scores, data
- public reports on test scores and trends
- reviews (internal-external) of testing instruments or batteries
- internal memoranda linking test scores to curricular/instructional priorities
- graduate follow-up studies
- student evaluations of programs
- anecdotal data regarding dropouts
- data on college placement records
- statements about each graduating class (often in brochure form accompanying college applications and published by counseling department)

Documents Usually Supporting Findings in Standard 5: Improved District Productivity

- past budget documents and budget working papers
- public relations brochures
- budget election brochures or press releases
- official budget documents filed with intermediate agencies or the state
- school facility reviews
- long-range facility plans
- test scores/results and budget implications for programmatic changes (sometimes in memo form)
- enrollment projections and studies

The bulk of any audit's findings is supported through documents. Documents are considered very reliable sources of information because, particularly with the focus of the audit at the district level, it is through documents that systems exist and perform their functions. The absence of documents may mean independence, i.e., everybody is doing his or her own thing. Interviews reveal whether or not "informal" understandings have been used to fill in for documents.

While it may be possible for small schools to run well on informal understandings that incorporate "good practice," it is nearly impossible for larger school systems to do as well on the same basis. The reasons are not hard to discern. There are too many people, too many functions that have to be interrelated, too many clients that require individualization, in short, too much to remember.

When an auditor finds no documents that connect functions, and interviews reveal that there is no real coordination (triangulation), it is typical that there is no school *system*, but a *collection* of schools more or less operating independently. And that condition is acceptable as long as the system does not have to be responsive to improved test scores or other state mandates. Those requirements increase the necessity for centralization, i.e., for system-like responses. Any change or improvement that requires greater connectedness among the parts leads to the demand for documents as guides to attain it. They may be titled differently from place to place, but they must exist in some form to enable the school district to be responsive to the external environment.

The second working assumption about documents is that they are usually representative of the officials' best thinking on any given topic. The only detractor in this equation is the element of time. That can usually be ascertained by examining the dates on documents. For example, suppose the auditor is reviewing a long-range plan. The time period to develop the plan, as revealed in memos, is six months. The plan is not very good. It has many missing pieces. However, it is the best the officials could do in six months (given the fact that they also had other responsibilities). While the plan may not be thorough (i.e., contain all the elements), the level of planning reveals the sophistication of the officials with the planning process. When time is a factor, length may be sacrificed but not usually sophistication.

The lack of appropriate data in documents usually tells an auditor that the officials in the system didn't know what data were required; that is, they didn't know how to do it any better. It is a fairly reliable product (or outcome) of the best they know how to do. If documents are poorly put together, it is usually because the officials are equally poor in thinking about them. It is generally a safe assumption that any document one is reviewing is the best the system knows how to do under the circumstances in which it is functioning.

NO ARTIFICIAL BALANCE BETWEEN POSITIVE AND NEGATIVE COMMENTS

The auditor should never feel compelled to artificially strike a "balance" between positive and negative comments or findings in the audit. Accreditation reports are often examples of such phony practices where the visiting team feels obligated to say something positive. One of the results is that an often humorous juxtaposition is created such as the following:

(1) The department is to be *commended* for:

- paying attention to colorful hallways
- thinking positively about students in all circumstances
- believing in the power of stressing good attendance

(2) The department *should* spend some time:

- developing functional curriculum materials for all students
- examining test scores to use as a basis for creating workable student groups
- coordinating teaching so that students are not bored
- following the recommendations of the curriculum coordinator to achieve a better balance within areas of the curriculum dealing with basic skills

The "positives" are all "fluff" and are not even in the same ballpark as the areas requiring improvement. In this department, there is no or little functional curriculum, test scores are not used to create workable student groupings, teaching is uncoordinated resulting in pupil boredom, and the staff has ignored the recommendations of the curriculum coordinator about basic skills. On the other hand, the hallways are colorful, the staff thinks positively about students (they apparently don't do much about it, however), and good attendance is stressed.

One of the reasons accreditation reviews are not very useful and have little real impact is that they are filled with such drivel. Part of the problem is that an expectation has been created that there are always positives and negatives in every situation. An auditor who succumbs to this notion will soon find that his or her audits are debased and empty.

THE NUMBER OF RECOMMENDATIONS SHOULD BE FEW

School systems do not have unlimited time or resources to act on proposed changes. A certain amount of effort and energy has to go into keeping the system going, at the same time as those concerned engage in change activities called for in the recommendations of the audit.

For this reason, the number of recommendations should not normally exceed twenty, unless the system is quite large. Too many recommendations simply "flood" the system providing a good example of "input overload." Too many recommendations also confuse policy makers and may lead to the perception that the audit is, in the end, unworkable because it is unrealistic.

In this respect, the auditor must focus on those recommendations that will lead to improvements essential for the system to improve its operations. Keeping the number of recommendations manageable is also a requisite for a type of management in perpetual "crisis."

SOME SPECIFIC CONSIDERATIONS IN PREPARING THE AUDIT

The following points are presented so that the reader may consider them in preparing the final audit report.

On Confidentiality—The Use of Quotations

Generally, the auditor can guarantee confidentiality in interview situations. Field notes and other work document records are the property of the auditor. However, if the audit is going to be used in litigation, the auditor may not be able to guarantee anonymity if a quote is used.

In judicial proceedings the "evidence" is entitled to be known and subject to cross-examination. In such cases an auditor should not guarantee anonymity to those he or she interviews. It is a pledge that may not be able to be honored.

Quotations are a great source of power in an audit. Used sparingly and in the proper context, they can say succinctly what may take the auditor much longer to write. And there is no doubt that they add spice to the audit, improving its readability.

Yet of all the objections the author–auditor has received from superintendents and board members about the audit, it is most often about quotations that emotions run high. Partly, it is because quotations are very revealing about what kind of control really is operational. Take for example a quote from a superintendent that reads, "We've made every effort to improve our curriculum since I've been here," with one from a principal that states, "You won't find a complete set of curriculum guides at any school in this district."

One superintendent of a district was really upset with a remark from a principal to the effect that "these kids would learn on a desert island." That quotation negated all of the work of the district in providing for children with special needs, or at least the superintendent believed it did. Yet the quotation was accurate, and it was the perception of the principal. In fact, when the superintendent challenged the quotation in a board retreat, at least three board members said the principal's name out loud, though the principal's name was never used in the audit.

As a general rule I *never* use names when quoting. I write something like, "A veteran teacher remarked that" or "One high-ranking central office official said" or "A parent with children in this program remarked." Of course, an audit can be written without quotations. Interview data can be summarized with such phrases as, "Most principals interviewed indicated that the reading text was quite adequate" or "All board members believed that the policy on testing was fair."

An audit is not an ethnographic study, though there are sections of contextual ethnography which are part of many audits. The auditor is not compelled to use quotes or native language. It is a judgment call.

The Use of Boilerplate

Certain portions of all audits are the same. For example, a statement of the standards and their explanation is virtually identical in any audit. Repeated text of this sort is called *boilerplate*.

Sometimes recommendations become boilerplate when the auditor has the same findings from one site to another. For example, conventional budgets lack programmatic detail to be able to function in a productivity analysis. Almost all recommendations will indicate that the district officials must take steps to add budgetary detail in order to get into productivity assessment. That could be considered boilerplate.

There is nothing wrong with boilerplate. Without it, there wouldn't be much consistency from audit to audit. On the other hand, unique situations require unique responses, not boilerplate. The important criterion is knowing what is unique and what is not. Of course, the client normally considers everything unique and may resent boilerplate, particularly in framing some recommendations. In these circumstances the auditor must demonstrate that when the finding is the same from one place to another, so is the solution in terms of recommendations. No one objects to a medical doctor prescribing the same treatment, so long as the diagnosis reveals the same ailment for two or more patients. Functional boilerplate may be considered a form of a sound standard operating procedure (SOP).

Statistical Data

The primary audience for the audit is lay, i.e., nonprofessional. Particularly in presenting test data, there may be a tendency to get lost in statistical vocabularly and let the quantitative machinery "hang out." Lay audiences are unusually sensitive to this kind of technical one-upmanship. One of their reactions is simply to discount all statistics and let their own intuitions take over. Lots of statistics don't impress people; they confuse people and lead to mistrust and communications problems.

The author–auditor generally reviews test data in the same way district officials have chosen to review it in the past because there is at least a modicum of experience with it. However, if the district has consistently used grade equivalents in reporting scores, I have never hesitated to indicate that this form of reporting may present an inaccurate picture of pupil achievement and should be discontinued. Once, I took issue with a school district which was using an aptitude test and reporting it as though they were dealing with achievement test data. Yet even these are rare examples. In the main, the auditor should be more concerned about what the district does with its data to improve achievement and how clearly it communicates the meaning of the data to organizational stakeholders: teachers, parents, students, community, funding agencies.

The auditor is not generally trying to verify the actual data from testing as accurate, unless that becomes an issue. Rather, the auditor is looking for what the test results reveal in the way of patterns and what the district has done to change its operations to obtain better results over time. The auditor is therefore more concerned about what district officials know about tests and less about what he or she knows about tests.

There is also a tendency in the testing section to put in a lot qualifiers and disclaimers. The wording should be such so as to minimize the necessity to insert a lot of qualifiers and disclaimers. The author believes that one of the reasons the public puts too much faith in standardized tests is that professionals "protesteth too much." While they hear us say "tests aren't everything," our vociferousness says that if they were not important we wouldn't be concerned all that much.

The Inclusion of Photographs

Photographs can be a powerful way to illustrate the operational context of the school system. Yet they usually have to be accompanied by verbal accounts to take on meaning. Rarely can they stand alone. Take the two photographs shown on page 84.

What does the picture at the top show? A library? What does it mean? On my tour of a school, a district official said to me, "Take a picture of the books we don't have." See the empty shelves? Those are books the school can't afford to buy because of budget cuts. I doubt very much if any reader would have acquired that message by simply looking at the photograph.

The adjacent picture shows a school mission statement. What does it mean? Some school mission statements are examples of boilerplate. This one was special. It is situated in the main staircase in an old school in an inner-city system using the magnet concept. This is the magnet school for international studies. The statement was put together with a lot of faculty input and student involvement. It is not an empty piece of boilerplate. Rather, it is a reminder in the most strategic location within the school of the collective vision that drives the school's program.

Photographs that include students should not degrade them or be

The use of photographs can enhance a curriculum audit. However, they are highly interpretable and usually require grounding in the text of the audit to establish meaning.

considered demeaning. Handicapped children, some minorities, and adolescents experiencing acne or in compromising poses can be the grounds of lawsuits from unhappy parents. In district publications of a public nature, pictures of general school scenes and classrooms are somewhat exempt from the requirements to obtain parental permission to print. For any other use, however, as in this book, parental permission is necessary where a student in a photograph is distinctly identifiable. As a general rule of thumb, no picture should be included that could reflect unfavorably upon the subject, no matter who the person is, if the individual is identifiable.

ON DEVELOPING WRITING ABILITIES

Writing is a skill. The skill is improved with practice. The more one writes, generally the easier and better it becomes. Yet, there is an aspect of good writing that is simply clear thinking or thinking in a way that is conducive to writing in a linear, left to right manner. Parallelism has to be reduced to linear sequences. Open-ended thoughts or feelings have to be closed off and placed into linear patterns. That means that writing imposes constraints on thinking. Writing is a kind of coded thinking. The situation is not unlike being a good conversationalist and yet being unable to "capture" the conversation in a computer program.

In the process of getting a conversation into a computer, one has to "think like a computer."

Good audits are testimonials to clear, concise, uncomplicated prose that is not difficult to comprehend and is usually devoid of subtleties and other literary devices such as irony, surprise endings, or complicated plots (English and Steffy, 1984).

CHECKPOINTS

Common Questions Asked the Author–Auditor

Question 1: *How are questions of opinion finally resolved?*

Answer: My experience is that when the auditor finally determines that there are no errors of fact involved, stand firm. No audit is ever accepted totally anyway. The usual procedure is to have the superintendent affix his or her response to the audit. This maintains the accountability of the superintendent to implement the recommendations. It also enables the superintendent to disagree with anything the auditor finds or recommends and present contrary evidence. I've never had a superintendent reject a finding, once meanings are clarified. They will disagree with the recommendations sometimes. Every auditor should know that there will be some compromises made in terms of implementing all of the recommendations. That should be expected. That's why the auditor should not compromise at the outset because it will happen anyway, no matter what is recommended.

Question 2: *It seems that if a school district has produced enough paper trails, they would be in a better position to be audited than one which is simply doing the job, right?*

Answer: Paper is simply paper. It ultimately has to be connected to operations or it is useless. If a school system has only gone through the motions with paper, it is readily discernible through interviews. I wouldn't say it couldn't be faked, but it would take a deep level of collusion to do it. The likelihood of that happening is less probable, the larger the organization. The auditor is not only looking for documents, but how they are linked to the ongoing operation to direct it. Paper alone is not enough.

Question 3: *Do educational agencies, in contrast to individuals, perform audits?*

Answer: Yes. For example, Wisconsin Statute 121.02(2) requires that beginning in the 1988–89 school year, the state department of education will conduct a compliance audit of 20 percent of all school districts in the state. Every district is to be audited at least once every five years. Should a district fail to be in compliance after the findings are known and a period of time provided, the state can withhold up to 25 percent of the state aid to the school district. Some intermediate agencies in Pennsylvania have completed curriculum audits on a voluntary basis.

Question 4: *What changes in the audit process if the auditor knows it will be litigated?*

Answer: Based on experience I would not use any quotations. Also, I would include in an appendix every document that one examined. That prevents the opposing attorney from asking, perhaps months or even years after the audit has been completed: "Do you recall seeing this report, etc.?" If all the documents are listed in an appendix, that question can't be asked. It simply draws a tight circle around the data base upon which one's findings can be challenged. I've also found that attorneys often object to using data derived from newspaper clippings. Inasmuch as the press is not required to reveal their sources, some courts may consider newspaper data as a kind of hearsay evidence. The attorneys cannot cross-examine an article, particularly with confidential and anonymous sources. In social science, newspapers are considered legitimate, archival sources. Without them, historians would be left without original source material. However, courts view the matter differently.

Question 5: *What's the most challenging aspect of writing the audit?*

Answer: Not forgetting an important piece of information and placing it properly in the body of the audit. The audit requires the ability to synthesize large tracts of information and relate data to other important data. It's like putting a very difficult jigsaw puzzle together.

Question 6: *What's the most rewarding aspect of auditing?*

Answer: Helping a client organization focus energies, overcome problems, and attain a higher level of operational effectiveness and efficiency as a result of one's work. The auditor is a kind of very special change agent.

/ IV / *Auditing the Hidden Curriculum with the Camera*

THE *HIDDEN CURRICULUM* consists of the unstated values, implicit assumptions, rules, and meanings that lie behind and support the *formal curriculum* in schools. If the budget is the "mirror side" of the curriculum, the *hidden curriculum* is the often unrecognized face of social and political forces that look into the mirror.

THE HIDDEN CURRICULUM AND THE PROBLEMATIC

The *hidden curriculum* consists of what Giroux (1983) has called the *problematic*. The *problematic* is the questions asked in a curriculum and those not asked, and the relationship between them (p. 48). Eisner (1985) has called the curriculum left out of schools the "null curriculum." The "null curriculum" may consist of both curriculum content and intellectual processes.

In the past several years the U.S. curriculum has been criticized for both what is in the curriculum and what is left out. For example, a nineteen-member Study Commission on Global Education headed by a former university president released a report calling American students "globally illiterate" (Associated Press, 1987).

They recommended inclusion of what had been perceived as subject content left out of American curriculum such as study of two or more cultures including at least one non-European culture (p. B10).

Another battleground familiar to most front-line educators lies in the area of values and how they are taught. Christian fundamentalists want values based on their interpretation of the Bible included in the curriculum. Writes one, "The question in public education is what values will be taught. . . . This choice cannot be determined by a vote.

Where the majority stands on some issues makes no difference" (Ellis, April 7, 1987, p. 10A).

As a result of increased probing of the hidden curriculum, scholars have brought forth convincing arguments and data that curriculum content and the processes that accompany it are in no way neutral. A "value-free" curriculum is a contradiction in terms. It is a myth (Flinders, Noddings, and Thornton, 1986).

Schools and the curricula in them are increasingly seen as places of "sociocultural reproduction [and], also as sites involved in contestation and struggle" (Giroux, 1983, p. 115).

Much of the scholarship of the curriculum writers of the left has been sharply critical of the habit of thinking about curricular affairs purely as technical matters, as engineering (Apple, 1979). Schools are places where the values and ideas of the dominant classes in any society transfer them to each succeeding generation. Schools do this by taking the credenda, which are still contested beliefs, and making them over into sacranda, or sanctified dogma (Parenti, 1978, p. 85).

What both Christian fundamentalists and Marxists and neo-Marxists have done is attack the hidden curriculum and try to reopen the debate about what is really taught in the schools. Fundamentalists desire a more conservative curriculum where only their values are included, and leftists want a curriculum which is "emancipated" from class domination via "radical pedagogy" (Giroux, 1983, p. 115). The fundamentalists have chosen to fight in the legislatures via passage of laws forcing the inclusion of "creation science" in the schools, which have so far been struck down in judicial rulings, or by fighting in the courts to ban certain books labeled as examples of "secular humanism."

The leftists have chosen to espouse their cause in academic journals and scholarly books. Both attacks are indicative of the fact that indeed the overt and covert curricula in the schools are being contested and will continue to be matters of struggle in the years ahead.

The curriculum audit is one way of potentially opening this dialogue about the hidden curriculum. Rarely, however, is this the primary purpose of the audit. Most school systems want only the overt and formal curriculum examined. Yet the audit asks questions about how the school district officials know if such and such content is the "right" content. This is a search for a response of legitimacy, of asking what the mode of consensus was in determining content propriety.

In many instances, local schools are being responsive to state mandates. State curriculum guides are reflections of state law, and thus, the audit is thrust into the arena of policy development and politics.

SYMBOLS AS THE HIDDEN CURRICULUM

In the last half-dozen or so curriculum audits, the author–auditor has used a camera in attempting to record the *context of schooling* as it is being played out in classrooms and hallways. The camera was focused on the adequacy of school facilities to support a specified curriculum. However, the camera is an unsurpassed tool for dealing with many facets of school, including the hidden curriculum.

Take, for example, the photographs on page 92. Here are two examples of dealing with symbols. In the top picture, a teacher is giving direct instruction on "symbols of our country." The American flag is probably the most ubiquitous and omnipresent symbol in schools. The flag flies outside of the school and is in virtually every classroom.

The flag represents, in some scholars' opinions, a kind of civic religious symbol. Civil religion functions as "religiofication" of the nation as a concept (Bellah, 1970). The flag, the Pledge of Allegiance, the Constitution, the Alamo, and certain individuals are raised to a kind of transcendent level where they become sacranda. Indeed, the acquisition of the proper frame of mind regarding the nation can be defined as becoming "literate," as shown in a bulletin board in an Ohio elementary school in the bottom photo.

The purpose of the teaching of symbols is to raise them above the contestation level. In essence, the schools' hidden curriculum is to place the nation as a concept beyond struggle and certain beliefs beyond questioning.

The group of photos on page 93 shows other attempts to raise certain functions and concepts from credenda to sacranda. The top shot shows a teacher's desk plastered with buttons and bumper stickers. Signs such as "I'm supporting US" and "The Greatest American hero is a teacher!" represent an effort to move concepts and functions from an arena of discourse to one of dogma.

The second photo represents a way schools attempt to accomplish the same idea as an institution through creating a symbol of "school spirit." "Lion Country" is a tactic to reify a school, which is an abstraction, into something that is more concrete, i.e., a lion. A lion, in turn, has certain characteristics with which students can identify. Objects of reification for school spirit are rarely, if ever, passive creatures in nature. Most are aggressive. The hidden curriculum therefore includes lions, tigers, hawks, eagles, bearcats, bruins, badgers, owls, cougars, huskies, hornets, leopards, falcons, razorbacks, longhorns, or rams. Animals rarely selected are storks, cranes, sparrows, deer, mice, llamas, moths, butterflies, oxen, cows, or platypuses. School spirit symbols are overwhelmingly confined to predators or animals which are feared.

Two examples of the inclusion of symbols in the school curriculum as *sacranda*, unquestioned dogma. The symbols are to be observed and followed. The *hidden curriculum* is therefore how the symbols are presented. They are the tenets of *civil religion*.

The hidden curriculum at work in the schools. The top picture shows how a classroom teacher has reified both teaching and patriotism to one level. The second is an example of creating a symbol as an object of school spirit.

When humans are portrayed as objects of school reification they are also aggressive, such as "the Fighting Irish," "the fighting Illini," "the Trojans," or "the Crimson Tide." Rarely would school teams be called "the priests," "the musicians," "the hairdressers," "the philosophers," or "the artists." Characteristics of contemplation, thinking, beautification, and domesticity are not reified. Overt aggression, hostility, and war-related behaviors are held up as models for reification. There will never be any school cheers that echo in the stands such as "Go you ichthyologists!" But the message is clear. The hidden curriculum has selected some behaviors as virtuous. They often last a lifetime.

THE CONCEPT OF THE GOOD STUDENT

The schools work hard to cast the student into a largely passive role as students in their interactions with teachers. The "good" student is not rebellious in word, deed, or thought. Again, the camera aptly reveals the hidden curriculum at work.

Consider the two "portraits" of "good students" on page 95. The photo on the left was taken in a suburban junior high school. It is the painting of an "ideal" male student in the 1940s. It hangs in the school's cafeteria to this day. The second picture was taken in a large, urban high school comprised of mostly minority students. It shows a large drawing titled "Ordinary Guy" and is a product of the 1980s. It hangs on a door to the guidance counseling office suite.

The phrases written around the drawing say things like, "Learned not to wear hat indoors in first grade," "carries pen and pencil instead of brush," "carries books instead of candy," and "also learned not to wear coat indoors." These portraits are school-sanctioned. They are efforts to show students what the school thinks good students look like. They are undeniably passive and remarkably similar, from the sweater over the shirt to the facial expressions.

School officials know that forms of student dress can be symbols of student resistance to school authority. In urban high schools, school administrators and hall guards regularly discipline students who wear hats. A hat is considered a symbol of defiance. It therefore interferes with the mission of the school. The hidden curriculum teaches students how to "act like" students as the school believes they should act in order to partake of the official curriculum.

The hidden curriculum parallels the official curriculum all through school. It is most obvious in the early grades. Students must be taught to be "students" and how students behave. What do students do?

The set of photos on page 96 is an example of "learning to be students" in school.

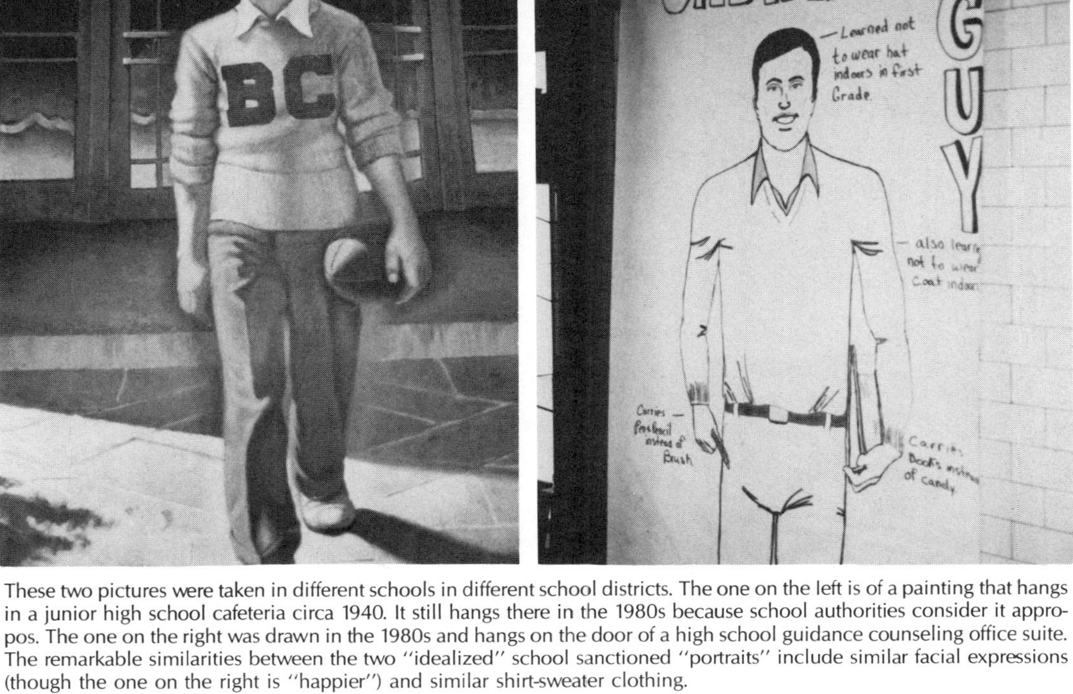

These two pictures were taken in different schools in different school districts. The one on the left is of a painting that hangs in a junior high school cafeteria circa 1940. It still hangs there in the 1980s because school authorities consider it apropos. The one on the right was drawn in the 1980s and hangs on the door of a high school guidance counseling office suite. The remarkable similarities between the two "idealized" school sanctioned "portraits" include similar facial expressions (though the one on the right is "happier") and similar shirt-sweater clothing.

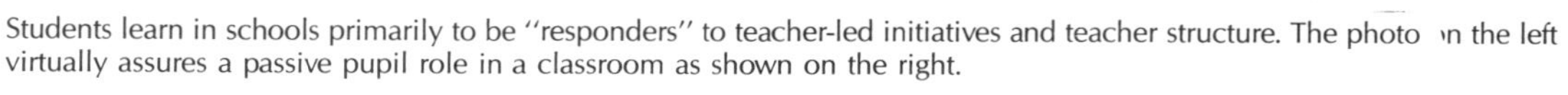
Students learn in schools primarily to be "responders" to teacher-led initiatives and teacher structure. The photo on the left virtually assures a passive pupil role in a classroom as shown on the right.

Everywhere in the primary grades in many elementary schools are visual "cues" as to what students do to "act appropriately." A good sample is shown in the left photo. Here in bold letters the teacher has spelled out the five "rules" students must observe. If they fail to follow the rules, there are consequences. They range in severity from a teacher warning, name on board, grounded in seat, lose recess, lose all privileges, to, lastly, meeting with the principal.

The photo on the right shows students doing the sanctioned behavior in a classroom learning circle.

The author–auditor has many such photographs of rules and "consequences." They are part of the techniques of "assertive discipline" which mark many school rooms today. Never once did any of these rules say anything like:

- "Question the teacher's opinions."
- "Ask why women and minorities are not considered heroes."
- "Notice when you are dealing with facts as opposed to interpreting statements made in your textbook."
- "Raise your hand when you think you have found a negative stereotype of a person based on race or sex."
- "Reject that which does not present the whole truth about anybody in history."
- "Think and question what you have read."
- "Who benefits from my believing this?"

In a classic study of classroom life conducted by Bellack, Kliebard, Hyman, and Smith (1966), fifteen high school social studies teachers were observed for four full class periods. Verbatim descriptions were transcribed of the verbal behavior of both students and teachers.

That analysis showed that students were overwhelmingly passive in classroom discourse, and that their responses were in the main empirical (fact-finding and stating) as opposed to analytical (interpreting and defining) (p. 239). Furthermore, the teacher did most of the talking.

CONTAINMENT AND CONTROL AS THE HIDDEN CURRICULUM

Schools are built and staffed with *containment* and *control* as paramount concerns. The placement of furniture in classrooms reveals that control of students is an overarching aim. The photos on page 98 are two examples of how classroom furniture is spaced so as to minimize pupil association by requiring each student to sit alone at a solitary desk. This enables the teacher to quickly isolate "deviant" behavior and focus "one on one" instead of having to confront a group. Clearly,

The placement of classroom furniture usually enhances teacher direction and control of students. Both of these pictures show how the location and spacing of furniture and equipment facilitate teacher control.

close supervision of pupils is vastly more efficient in this type of setting.

The camera has recorded visual data that shows the hidden curriculum at work. Every "place" has such a hidden curriculum. Rarely is it the subject of reports, but it is always there.

Much of the "effective schools" research reinforces a hidden curriculum that overwhelmingly favors a teacher-directed and system-defined curriculum. The measures for such a curriculum are standardized tests or state imposed criterion referenced tests. The effect is to "freeze" the existing modes of student initiative or to inhibit them.

Is this bad? The answer depends upon what one's ultimate goals are for schools. Clearly, schools as most people know them are places of conservatism. To preserve, one must reject or suppress change that threatens to undo what one desires to preserve. Preservation as a goal requires conformance as a method. The means are consistent with the ends.

Schools are therefore not places of liberation or emancipation from the rules of a society and those who are in power who define and enforce the rules. They are places to perpetuate a society in its existing form. Obedience, docility, passivity must become virtues. They are canonized. The rewards go to those who do it well.

The curriculm audit can deal with issues of the hidden curriculum. It can disclose and clarify them, even indirectly. Nonetheless, it is risky business since most school officials are not very interested in using it as a process to uncover the biases undergirding content selection and rejection. While audits can deal with the "givens," they cannot usually do it overtly.

Consider, for example, two photographs of activities in a fine arts curriculum that are more open-ended than academic areas and where student initiative is given a wider berth (see page 100). The top photograph involves the creation of a student mask, which is then painted. The student selects the facial expression he or she desires and then a fellow student actually does the work. In the bottom photo of the picture block, a female student works on her own design at a wood lathe. These curricular activities are of a much different nature than those previously pictured which tend to characterize the academic portion of the curriculum as very much less creative and analytical than these pictures would suggest. The learners depicted here are in an active, rather than passive, modality.

SOME CAUTIONS WHEN USING THE CAMERA

Despite it's mantle of "objectivity," the camera and the photograph it produces are not truly objective (Sontag, 1977). Since its earliest use on

The fine arts offer many students an active role as a learner in the school's curriculum. These two pictures show students pursuing projects which tap their initiative and creativity.

the American scene, the camera has been used as an agent of social change. This practice has raised questions about whether or not photographs are "truthful."

The best example of whether pictures tell the truth comes from the work of Jacob Riis in exposing the seamy side of tenement life in New York City in the late nineteenth century (Riis, 1890).

Riis did not go out and take pictures of "typical" urban scenes. He concentrated on New York City's Lower East Side where the population density reached 335,000 people to one square mile or as many as one person per square foot in storied tenements (Davidson and Lytle, 1986, p. 215). Within this environment he focused his rage on "The Mulberry Bend." Writes Riis in *The Battle with the Slum* (1902), "What was it like? . . . A crooked three-acre lot built over with rotten structures that harbored the very dregs of humanity . . . pierced by a maze of foul alleys. . . . Every foot of it reeked with incest and murder. . . . By night I have gone poking about their shuddering haunts with a policeman . . . and come away in a ferment or anger and disgust that would keep me awake far into the morning hours planning means of its destruction" (p. 40).

This passage amply reveals Riis' agenda. He wanted his photographs to condemn. In this sense he was not a scientist or a researcher, but a reformer. Riis was very sympathetic towards children. One of his most famous photographs was undoubtedly posed. It was entitled "street Arabs" and shows three boys sleeping on the sidewalk with a barred window clearly in the background. The message was clear: children left unattended will end up behind bars. The picture established a link between poverty and crime.

Riis's "street Arabs" utilized the camera technique of "ground on." What this means is that the photograph is shot "ground up" and usually close up. The photos on page 102 are examples of "ground on" shots. The top photograph was taken while following an elementary principal around a school. This was a principal who knew most of the students and took a personal interest in them.

The principal abruptly encountered a diminutive lad who was dressed up in a new suit for his birthday. As the principal stooped over to examine the boy's tie, I stooped to capture the moment. Had I remained standing, the angle and distance from the two would have put space between them and the camera. The sense of intimacy would have been lost as a result.

In the second photograph, an educator and a student are engaging in a conversation about the pupil's use of the computer. There is a sense that one is almost eavesdropping on a conversation. This photograph also has a sense of intimacy.

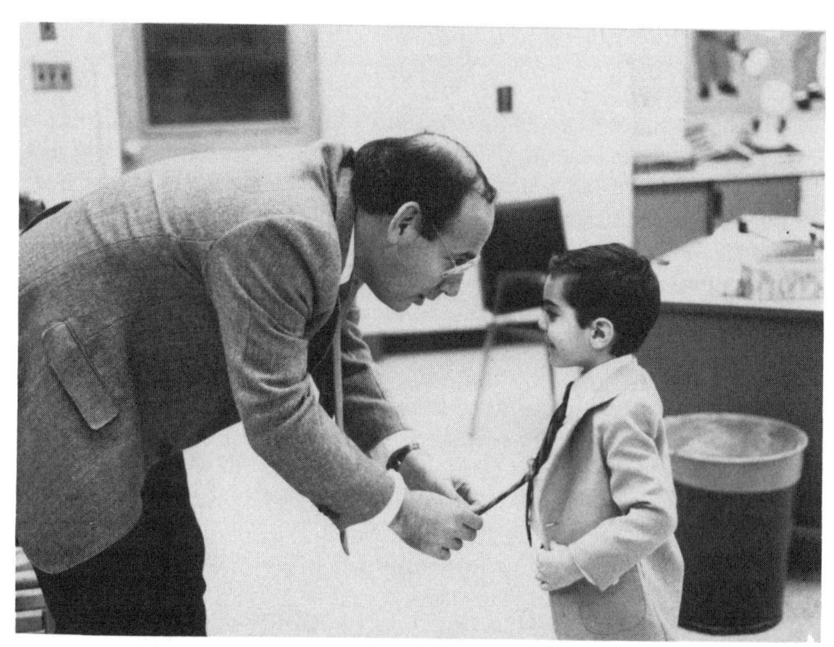

Two examples of "ground on" shots in the use of the camera in auditing. It would be impossible to know if either was "typical" without data triangulation or special randomized procedures being used, such as shooting scripts or multiple photographers.

These photographs represent choices made by the author–auditor. A different photographer may have decided to take a different picture or use a different angle. For this reason it is hard for any given photograph of any subject to be considered "typical" unless it was taken under special procedures spelled out by Wagner (1979). These procedures utilize shooting scripts, randomly assigned times, places, and angles to take pictures, and the use of multiple photographers (pp. 147–160).

If, however, photographs are not going to stand alone (they rarely do) and if they are considered one source of data triangulation, scripts, random shooting, and multiple photographers may be unnecessary.

Technical Problems

Other notes of caution in using the camera concern at least one technical problem. All of the pictures in this chapter, as well as in other audits in which the camera was utilized, were taken with natural (available) light. The use of "flash" photography is very distracting, particularly in schools with young children. To avoid disrupting the school, classrooms, and the setting, it is essential that the camera be as unobtrusive as possible.

The problem is that the auditor will require an exceptionally fast film, meaning one that is very sensitive to light. Most of the pictures in audits, as well as those in this chapter, were taken with Kodak Tri-X pan film with an ASA rating of 400. This simply refers to what the film is set at for normal film exposure. Instead of using a 400 rating, the meter in the camera is set at 3200, eight times its "normal" index. To compensate for the fact that less light will be permitted, the film is "overdeveloped," i.e., left in the developer eight times longer than normal.

A film has to be very hardy to do this. Some film becomes very "grainy" as a result of overdeveloping. Tri-X pan does not do so. That makes it an ideal film for such use. The disadvantage in following the aforementioned procedures is that the film must be taken to a photofinishing shop that can handle these special orders. Such photo processing is much more expensive than otherwise would be the case.

Photographs add a special feature to a curriculum audit. They are able to show contextual clues within and outside a school that exceed the descriptive capacity of words. When coupled with verbal descriptions, the audit is indeed a powerful and graphic document.

CHECKPOINTS

Common Questions Asked the Author–Auditor

Question 1: *Does one ever go into a school building looking for a special picture?*

Answer: No. I try to record on film what is happening to me in the way of visual impressions simultaneously. It's the equivalent of taking notes in an interview. For example, if a hallway looks dark and it creates a special kind of feeling, I take a picture of it. Later I go back and see what it might mean in the context of the full audit findings. In short, I have no "shooting script" predetermined to follow.

Question 2: *Have you ever been surprised after looking at a picture?*

Answer: Sometimes. What may happen is that as one sorts through pictures, one may pick up patterns, juxtapositions, contradictions, similarities missed because the pictures were taken in a long linear sequence. When one is sorting pictures, it is possible to reconstruct any number of sequences and combinations after the fact. That's what makes visual data so powerful. For example, I had "seen" the two photographs on page 95 at least a half dozen times prior to the time I combined them in an effort to portray student stereotypes put forth by the school. When that happened, the striking similarities just bowled me over because I was acutely aware of the two completely different school sites in which they were produced.

Question 3: *Have people ever objected to your taking pictures in schools?*

Answer: Not really, since I am usually in the company of the principal. His or her presence means that it is "OK" to take pictures. I try to work fast by presetting the meter reading and prefocusing where I can. That reduces the probability that kids will "mug" the camera, i.e., give me some very unnatural or "goofy" look which signals they knew a camera was around. If I'm in a classroom for any length of time, I will often "fake" taking pictures quickly so that the children get used to the idea. After the first initial "pictures," they usually go on about their business as usual. Then I begin taking the real pictures.

Question 4: *What's the worst "sin" one can make when taking pictures for an audit?*

Answer: Using "posed" pictures. Posing means that the auditor intervened in an otherwise "natural or ongoing" social setting to create (translate "fake") something that would not have occurred had the photographer not been there. It is the equivalent of fudging one's statistical data in order to get a high correlation or significant response. That's why "public relations" photos are useless in most audits.

Question 5: *For an auditor considering using a camera for the first time, what advice would you give him/her?*

Answer: Shoot, shoot, shoot. In a typical elementary school on an hour "walk," plan on using at least three rolls of film at 36 exposures to a roll. Shoot everything! Concentrate on pupil and teacher produced artifacts which are examples of "cultural residues." Try capturing the teacher–pupil(s) relationship in what is going on. Don't spare the film and don't be afraid to be repetitious. If you get three to four usable pictures per roll you will be doing very well.

Question 6: *Any other advice?*

Answer: Use black and white film, never color. Color is not fast enough and so it isn't very flexible. Furthermore, reproduction is very expensive and few school systems can afford color printing if they run multiple copies of the audit.

/ V / *Case Study 1: The Pergola Public Schools*

THE PERGOLA PUBLIC Schools is a pseudonym for a real school district in which the author–auditor completed a curriculum audit in 1987. All photographs have been removed to prevent identification of the district. Specific references which would reveal the name of the district or any person in the district have been deleted. Otherwise, the audit report is stated as it was filed with the Pergola Board of Education.

BACKGROUND, PURPOSE, AND SCOPE OF WORK

This document constitutes the final report of a curriculum audit of the Pergola Public Schools. The audit was conducted at the request of the superintendent and the board of education in accordance with a written agreement of September, 1986.

Background

The Pergola Public Schools consist of approximately 250 square miles of territory. The town of Pergola was created by a necessity of the railroad for a termination point, then called Frontier Town. A railroad station was constructed there which still stands to this day.

In 1885 the townspeople decided to move the town to a more convenient location. Land was acquired from the railroad, and Mr. Zachary T. Pergola, the chief engineer of the railroad, was sent to execute the move. Pergola was officially named a station on the route of the railroad on April 1, 1886.

The people of Pergola turned to agriculture as their future. Water was brought from the lake in 1880 and used to grow oranges and grain crops. Although this source eventually dried up, it was discovered that there was a plentiful supply of underground water.

With this invaluable source at hand, the Pergola area became known for its abundant alfalfa crop. Another major crop was potatoes. Later, sugarbeets became the mainstay of farming in the Pergola area. The Pergola schools were organized in August of 1897. From that time it enjoyed a somewhat "laidback" reputation until the opening of a large metroplex center seven miles south of the city in June of 1962. This was the catalyst which has propelled Pergola and the larger area into the current housing boom which is radically altering almost all features of the lives of the area's residents.

An automobile drive along most of the major arteries in the Pergola Public School District reveals a daily transformation taking place. Real estate signs show large plots of land for sale. New housing tracts are blossoming in packed clusters.

Building permits in Preston County are increasing at a 13–15 percent yearly rate with the highest growth (36 percent) in Pergola. The relatively affordable prices of homes in the Pergola area compared to those in Lakefront and Parkside counties are resulting in successive waves of in-migration. The in-migration is producing a strange bimodal distribution: a larger than typical population under fifteen years of age, and a skyrocketing senior citizen cohort of sixty-five years or older.

The population boom is expected to produce the need for at least three new high schools and five additional middle schools in the next ten to twenty years. By 1990 it is estimated by district officials that the total population of the area served by the school district will have increased by 26 percent.

However, the demographic data also reveal a high unemployment rate (9.8 percent) and a larger than typical number of overcrowded households (five or more people). The number of low economic households (under $12,830) is larger than typical (53.5 percent). The number of households headed by women is 11.7 percent. The minority population of the school district is approximately 43 percent.

The student enrollment of the Pergola Public Schools has shown a steady growth pattern which coincides with the overall growth of the Pergola area. The enrollment growth is shown in Exhibit 3.

In the 1985–86 school year, the Pergola Public Schools employed a total certificated staff of 156 persons and a total classified staff of 130 persons. The general fund budget was approximately $10,654,527 for four educational programs. They were Pergola High School, Pergola Valley Junior High School (now Pergola Valley Middle School), Pergola Lake High School, and the Pergola Adult School.

At the time of the audit, the district had completed a new adminis-

Exhibit 3
Pergola Public Schools
Student Enrollment 1977–86

Year	Enrollment
1977	2185
1978	2145
1979	2263
1980	2156
1981	2212
1982	2711
1983	2826
1984	3049
1985	3250
1986	3396

trative center by renovating two old portable classrooms and was nearing completion of a new middle school.

The Pergola Public Schools are governed by a five member board of trustees elected by the citizens of the school district. There are four major administrative officers in the district. They are a superintendent of schools, an assistant superintendent of business, an assistant to the superintendent, and a coordinator of instruction and projects.

Purpose

The purpose of the curriculum audit in the Pergola Public Schools was to determine the extent to which the officials and professional staff had developed and implemented a sound, valid, and operational system of curriculum management.

Such a system would enable the school district to make maximum utilization of its human and financial resources in the education of its secondary school students. If such a system were operational, it would also ensure the taxpayers and the state that their financial support had been optimized under the conditions in which the school system functioned.

Scope of Work

A curriculum audit is an independent examination of data pertaining to educational program practices that will indicate the extent to which a school district can meet its objectives (whether the latter are internally or externally developed or imposed). An audit examines management practice and system results. As such it is a type of quality assurance.

METHODOLOGY

The Model for the Audit

The model for a curriculum audit is shown in Exhibit 4. The model has been published extensively in the literature, most recently in the AASA publication *Skills for Successful School Leaders* (1985, p. 90).

Generic quality control assumes that at least three elements must be present in any situation for it to be functional. These are: (1) a standard, goal/objective, (2) work directed towards the standard or goal/objective, and (3) feedback about the level of attainment (performance).

Within the context of an educational system and its governance and operational structure, curricular quality control requires:

(1) *Documents*—These consist of board policies, memoranda, curriculum guides, checklists, test results, lesson plans, and any other source of information which would reveal elements of the written, taught, and tested curricula and the linkages between these elements.

(2) *Interviews*—Interviews were conducted to shed light on the same elements and their interrelationships. Interviews were held with the top-level administrative staff including the superintendent, all of the board of trustees, building principals and assistant principals, department chairs, mentor teachers, teachers, classified personnel, students, and parents.

(3) *Site Visitations*—Site visitations reveal the <u>context</u> in which curriculum is being implemented. Contextual references are important as they may indicate discrepancies in documents or unusual working conditions. The auditor visited all schools in Pergola, including the new middle school under construction.

Standards for the Curriculum Audit

The auditor utilized five standards against which to compare, verify, and comment upon the Pergola Public Schools' existing curricular management practices. These standards have been extrapolated from an extensive review of management principles and practices and were utilized in the previous sixteen audits in eight states conducted by the auditor.

As a result, the standards do not reflect a utopian or ideal management system, but rather working characteristics that any complex or-

Exhibit 4
A Schematic View of Curricular Quality Control

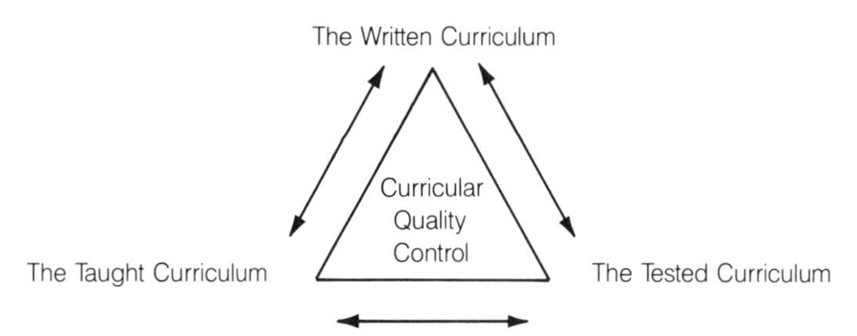

ganization should possess in being responsive and responsible to its clients.

A school district that is using its financial and human resources for the greatest benefit of its students is a district that is able to establish clear objectives, examine alternatives, select and implement alternatives, measure results as they develop against established objectives, and adjust its efforts so that it achieves a greater share of those objectives over time.

The five standards employed in the curriculum audit in the Pergola Public Schools were:

(1) The school system is able to demonstrate its control of resources, programs, and personnel.
(2) The school system has established clear and valid objectives for students.
(3) The school system has documentation explaining how its programs have been developed, implemented, and conducted.
(4) The school system uses the results from district designed or adopted assessments to adjust, improve, or terminate ineffective practices or programs.
(5) The school system has been able to improve its productivity.

FINDINGS

Standard 1: The School District Is Able to Demonstrate Its Control of Resources, Programs, and Personnel

Quality control is the fundamental element of a well-managed educational program. It is one of the major premises of local educational control within any state's educational system.

The critical premise involved is that via the will of the electorate, a local school board establishes local priorities within state law and regulations. A school district's accountability to its community rests with the school board.

Through the construction of policy a local school board provides the focus to direct the operations of a school system through its administrative staff. In this way the expression of popular will is assured and enables the district to be responsive to its clients and patrons. It also enables the system to assess and utilize meaningfully student learning as a critical factor in determining its success.

Although educational program control and accountability are often shared among different components of a school system, fundamental control of and responsibility for a district and its operations rest with the school board and top-level management staff.

What the Auditor Expected to Find in the Pergola Public Schools

A school system meeting Standard 1 would be able to demonstrate the existence of:

- a clear set of policies that reflect state requirements and program goals and the necessity to use achievement data to improve school system operations
- documentation of school board and central office planning for the attainment of such goals over time
- a direct, uninterrupted line of authority from school board/ superintendent and other central office officials to principals and classroom teachers
- teacher and administrator responsiveness to the school board policies, currently and over time

What the Auditor Found in the Pergola Public Schools

The auditor found generally ineffective board policies which were outdated and did not establish the framework for effective management of the curriculum. Furthermore, the new board policies were not much better.

The auditor found a workable management plan, newly developed curriculum, and renewed leadership stability in the school system. There was also a perceived workable relationship between the board of trustees and the superintendent, but long-standing tension between the board and the Pergola Educators Association was heightened by an impasse in negotiations at the time of the audit.

The auditor found severe understaffing present at the central level.

Existing personnel are stretched quite thin in attempting to provide for solid curricular leadership in the schools. Some leadership roles, most notably the supervising of teachers, are ambiguous as they pertain to curricular expectations.

The auditor also found a condition which presents a continuing problem for the school district. The condition pertains to the lack of control via curricular continuity among the five sending elementary districts that feed into the high school system.

Finding 1.1: Administrative Stability Has Been Restored to the Pergola Public Schools

The key to leadership continuity is administrative stability. The Pergola Public Schools have been wracked with administrative turnover, most notably at the high school, but in other areas as well. Given the rapid growth being experienced in the Pergola area, stability is a critical ingredient to firm, steady progress towards curricular improvement.

The current superintendent has succeeded in building a cohesive administrative team that works well together and shares common aspirations. This represents no mean accomplishment since it is the building block for designing, delivering, and maintaining a sound curriculum management system.

The relationships between the board and the superintendent are sound. The board is a dedicated body composed of strong and outspoken individuals. For the most part, they spend many hours in the study and review of items forwarded for action and are generally well prepared to vote on them.

Finding 1.2: There Is Evidence of Sound Planning in the Pergola Public Schools

The auditor reviewed a number of documents that were strong evidence of sound planning in the school district. Among these were *The Management Plan* or *Strategic Plan* of December 1986 and the *Long-Range Facility Plan Update* of June 1985.

The *Strategic Plan* contains a review of environmental trends including the financial conditions of the district and directions for the system through 1988. It deals with twenty-two program areas including curriculum development. It links at the mission level with a proposed board policy #0100 which will tie the *Strategic Plan* into a general policy statement (p. 2).

While the *Strategic Plan* is a most laudable effort, activities within programs were not always specifically linked to either goals for students or to achievement test scores included in the document. The document could be more tightly matrixed and cross-referenced to link programs and expenditures to goals, needs, and results.

However, the *Strategic Plan* does provide a workable and working framework for much of what the district is currently doing and the efforts it will be making in the future.

Finding 1.3: Existing Board Policies and Proposed Policies Are Not Effective Statements to Establish Sound Curriculum Management in the Pergola Public Schools

The auditor examined two sets of board policies. The first were generally approved in 1972, some fourteen years ago. They contain many vague phrases and unclear references.

For example, existing board policy #102 Intent to Provide Best Possible Educational Program states that ". . . the board pledges itself to constantly strive for improvement in instruction; to seek to obtain optimum development of the learner; and to provide and maintain an efficient school management. . . ."

When asked what data the board received to judge whether the optimum development of each learner had indeed occurred, no one could identify any specific information they had received which would bear on whether their intent had been realized in the school district.

In fact, board members cited their concerns about the curriculum as follows:

- "I don't know what the standards are."
- "We have to depend upon the principals to know what is going on."
- "Not enough of a comprehensive program for the remedial kids."
- "The minority kids are not helped."
- "Bilingual kids are not learning enough, fast enough."

These comments would suggest that the "optimum development of the learner" stated in policy #102 was not being met. Yet there was and has been no systematic data provided to the board that it could recall that would assist it in this matter. Board members had similar problems with existing policy #106 Individualization of Instruction which called for each individual to learn "to his maximum potential." What is maximum? What data have or would be used to determine "maximum potential"?

Board policy #402 indicates it is the board's intent to "make available to the youth and adults of the community the finest well-balanced program possible. . . ." No board member could define "balance," nor was it indicated in any policy examined by the auditor.

Board policy #406 Supervision of Instruction sets forth the dictum that "the major portion of the principal's time and energy should be concerned with the improvement of instruction." No board member interviewed indicated that he or she thought that the principals were devoting the major portion of their time to instruction, and for the most part the principals themselves concurred. Furthermore, the board indicated that it never received reports from the principals about what they did with their time or what their plans were for their buildings in the future.

Board policy #408 Course of Study was being followed. This policy required the board to approve courses of study and the superintendent to maintain them on file. All of the board agreed that this was being monitored and maintained.

The auditor examined the new proposed board policies. They contained many of the same flaws as the old policies. For example, proposed board policy #6000(a) Instruction states that "the district shall provide comparable educational opportunities for all students regardless of level of academic ability and to insure that each individual learns to his/her maximum potential."

What does "comparable educational opportunity" mean? Does it mean every student has the same program? If not, then on what basis will comparability be determined? Will it be cost? Test scores? Also, this policy has the same problem with defining "maximum potential." Does anyone know what the "maximum potential" of another human being really is?

Also, the policy makes it mandatory that the governing board "articulate the district's educational philosophy and goals." What does the board do to "articulate"? The policy indicates that the board approves district-wide instructional objectives. Does "articulate" mean simply "approval" or does the board do something else that "articulates"? If so, what?

The same policy indicates that the superintendent "decides the general methods of instruction to be used." On what criteria will the superintendent determine this? What methods may be discarded? How will the superintendent enforce this policy?

New board policy #6010 Instruction requires that the superintendent "annually review strategies to improve the quality of education provided to students." What will constitute this annual review? A report to the board? Will this be a summary of test scores, student ratings of the program or teachers, state compliance data, parental opinion, or a staff survey?

Newly proposed board policy #6140 Curriculum states that the curriculum of the Pergola Public Schools will be guided by "actual studies and information concerning the needs of the students, aspirations of the residents, and population mobility." The auditor could find no systematic needs assessment data of the student body in the school district nor any systematic sampling of the full community in past curriculum development efforts. Are these new conditions or extensions of old ones?

The same policy states that "the Governing Board desires the unnecessary duplication of work among the various school levels be eliminated." When asked how the board would determine "unnecessary duplication of work," no member could respond.

Proposed board policy #6141(a) appears to contradict policy #6140. In the latter policy the curriculum of the district was to be guided by "actual studies." However, in the former policy the board "shall adopt a district curriculum which to the extent possible reflects [underlining the auditor's emphasis] the desires of the community, the needs of society, and the requirements of law."

On the one hand, the board states it desires actual studies to guide curriculum development, but on the other it says it will determine what it believes reflects the desires of the community and the society. If the latter is to be the practice, why do the former?

The auditor could not find anywhere in either the old or the proposed board policies language that required curricular quality control, that ensured textbook and test adoption would be aligned with curriculum, or that stated these would be tracked systematically to approved goals and objectives.

The auditor could find no set of specific instructions by which curriculum would be developed nor how that process would be monitored or maintained. A large portion of existing and proposed board policies regarding curriculum are nonfunctional.

Finding 1.4: Long-standing Tensions Between the Pergola Public Schools Board of Trustees and Pergola Teachers Have Been Exacerbated

At the time of the audit, the board of trustees and the official representatives of the Pergola Secondary Education Association were deadlocked. The issue did not appear to be financial. Rather, it was the result of teacher perceptions of comments made by board members about teachers which had raised their ire.

The auditor found comments about the problem in all schools visited. Some teachers could recall negative comments made by board members extending back three to four years. The result was an atmosphere which made program and curricular change difficult, especially when teachers must trust the board and its sponsorship of curricular projects.

There were no negative comments about administrators encountered by the auditor from teachers interviewed. Many teachers had more than ten or fifteen years experience in Pergola and were only critical of board interference in the administrative affairs of the system and of the high levels of turnover at some administrative positions.

Finding 1.5: Severe Understaffing Exists at the Administrative Level in the Pergola Public Schools

An existing state regulation limits the number of administrators that can be hired by a school district. That regulation allows one school administrator for each 100 FTE (full time equivalent) certified staff.

Such a provision is absurd and makes sense only if one could assume that all districts had the same staff, the same students, and exactly the same working conditions, which clearly is not the case. Furthermore, it has to assume that curriculum is virtually in the same shape from one district to the next.

At the time of the audit Pergola employed a superintendent, an assistant to the superintendent, one coordinator of instruction and projects, and four principals. Given the need for curriculum improvement in Pergola, the expanding and changing pupil population, state requirements relating to curricular reviews in each of the content areas every three years, and other regulations, existing staff are severely overloaded.

Furthermore, supervising teachers do not and have not taken up the slack, and principals have little time to devote to curricular affairs in the district (see Finding 1.6 and 1.7).

Pergola appears to be at the maximum allowable limit with regard to the number of administrators permitted under state regulations. It is highly unlikely that the school system will be able to fulfill completely all of the demands upon it without attention to the lack of staffing in the curricular areas.

Finding 1.6: There Is Confusion Regarding the Curricular Responsibilities of Supervising Teachers

The audit revealed confusion regarding just what supervising teachers did to improve curriculum in the Pergola Public Schools. Some supervising teachers have worked diligently in curriculum, most notably in history and English. Great effort has gone into adhering to state standards and the development of curriculum around these indices. Other areas had not experienced the success of these two.

Supervising teachers with no formal job descriptions explained that they had encountered conflicts between administrators and, on occasion, had trouble knowing "who the boss was."

Supervising teachers reported that they had no secretarial support, limited access to test scores to utilize as feedback, and expressed ambivalence about monitoring the implementation of curriculum once it had been developed. Some supervising teachers reported doing some activities which could be construed as monitoring. Others expressed antipathy towards the idea in any form. They saw themselves more as "cheerleaders" for teachers or "helpers." At least one supervising teacher did not want any curricular responsibilities at all.

Finding 1.7: School Principals Report Little Time to Devote to Curricular Matters

Despite the presence of board policy #406 stating that "the major portion of the principal's time and energy should be concerned with the improvement of instruction," no school principal interviewed concurred that the major portion of his/her time was, in fact, spent on instruction.

Pergola principals reported they struggled to stay on top of day-to-day affairs, the paperwork, pupil problems caused by swift-moving demographic changes and mobility, discipline, and other demands to ensure a safe and orderly environment for learning in their schools. Said one principal, "You depend upon the teachers to work on curriculum."

The most obvious work on curriculum from an administrative standpoint was at the middle school level, both old and new. In some departments, the curriculum had been "mapped." This referred to a practice of developing highly scheduled daily or weekly content specifications.

This practice was not uniform, however, and did not enjoy universal staff support. Some teachers appeared to resent the tight structure, while others liked it.

Finding 1.8: There Is Little Actual Curriculum Monitoring Present in the Pergola Public Schools

The weakest aspect of sound curriculum management revealed in the audit in Pergola was the almost total lack of formal and regular curriculum monitoring.

There is no board policy which requires lesson plans, teachers do not develop such plans unless they are on probationary status, and principals do not formally review curricular content. Supervising teachers do not monitor what has actually been taught on a systematic basis. Indeed, there is no record of the taught curriculum anywhere in the district that could be reviewed. The data base for curricular improvement is therefore missing.

While great energy is going into developing a curriculum, there is no system to monitor it once it is in place. The superintendent is aware of the problem but has so few personnel available that most of the energy and focus have had to be devoted to development.

Finding 1.9: The District Lacks Control Over Lack of Pupil Mastery at the Elementary Level

The Pergola Public Schools are a receiving entity for five elementary school districts. There is considerable difference among these elementary districts as it pertains to curricular emphasis, despite their location in the same county and state. One high school board member commented, "Articulation between the feeder schools and the high school is about zero."

While some preliminary meetings have begun to be held between the elementary district personnel and the high school district administrators, there were no tangible data to indicate that the problem of articulation between these school districts was being systematically attacked.

It will be impossible for the high school district to improve pupil achievement without some continuity among all of the five sending districts. It will take more than talk and a few meetings to truly improve the K–12 curriculum.

High School administrators and teachers noted that there was a vast difference in achievement and ability among students coming from the respective five elementary districts. While some of the difference lies outside of the control of the school, some of it is within that sphere of influence. Improved coordination among and between all of the districts is a necessity for sustained long-range pupil achievement.

Standard 2: The School District Has Established Clear and Valid Objectives for Students

A school system meeting this audit standard has established a clear, valid, and measurable set of pupil standards for learning and has set them into a workable framework for their attainment.

Unless objectives are clear and measurable, there cannot be a cohesive effort to improve pupil achievement in any one dimension. The lack of clarity denies to a school district the capability of concentrating its resources through a focused approach to management. Instead, resources may be spread too thin and be ineffective in any direction. Objectives are, therefore, essential to attaining local quality control via the school board.

What the Auditor Expected to Find in the Pergola Public Schools

The auditor expected to find in the Pergola Public Schools a clearly established, district-wide set of goals and objectives adopted by the board of trustees. Such objectives would set the framework for the operation of the district, its sense of priorities, and explicit direction for the superintendent and the professional staff.

In addition, clarity of objectives must be matched by a record of consistent effort towards attainment and the creation of a working context in which the objectives are set into the structure of the school system.

What the Auditor Found in the Pergola Public Schools

The auditor found clear statements of objectives in both policy form and in other documents. These objectives were not always linked tightly towards curricular objectives.

The overwhelming thrust of the curricular activities in Pergola is to implement the state's document, *Curriculum Standards*. This forms, in essence, a state curriculum in all subject areas which require periodic assessment by local school districts.

The auditor found generally loose linkages between the respective buildings in the Pergola schools with a long history of teacher isolation and autonomy within departments, particularly at the high school.

The auditor found overall well-run school buildings being directed by caring and businesslike professionals at all levels. The schools in Pergola are places of genuine educational activities.

Finding 2.1: Objectives Exist at a Variety of Levels in Pergola

The auditor found goals and objectives in existing board policy #105 and in proposed board policies #0100, 0200, 0210, 0300. Within the *Strategic Plan, 1986–87* there was a linkage between the overall mission statement of the district and proposed board policies.

However, the tangible linkages between pupil objectives as set forth in proposed policy and the program plan in the *Strategic Plan* were not evident. For example, it was not possible to ascertain why certain elements of the program plan were stressed over others and what relationship these had to priority pupil objectives.

The result is that discussion at one level does not influence activities at another level. The only way policy impacts operations is that it must be visibly transposed from one level to the next. If such transpositions are not present, that often is indicative of the fact that there is a breakdown between policy directives and operational practices. This condition may also exist from one operational level to the next. For the most part, the auditor could not find clear transpositions among the documents reviewed in Pergola.

Finding 2.2: There Has Been a Strong Renewal in Pergola for Improved Curriculum

The auditor found, from interviews at all levels, renewed interest and commitment towards improving curriculum in Pergola. Board members commented that they were taking a more active interest in curricular matters and devoting more time to curricular issues in their meetings. Funds have been budgeted for curriculum development in the last several school budgets. A person has been designated at the district level to coordinate curricular affairs. New documents have been developed in the district that contain significantly more detail and information for teacher utilization in classrooms.

Finding 2.3: Curricular Efforts in Pergola Remain Partially Completed

The auditor did not find a complete set of curricular documents for all grade levels and all subjects currently within the Pergola educational program.

The reasons were not hard to ascertain for this gap. The district has planned to invest more in curriculum in the way of staff time but has been hampered by some revenue shortfall based on enrollment projections which did not fully materialize.

There has been a shortage of people who could lead curricular efforts on a district-wide basis. The current person is overwhelmed by the magnitude of the task, and curriculum development is only one of her myriad responsibilities.

Principals are busy maintaining a positive climate for learning and have little time to devote to curricular issues. Supervising teachers are not clear about their curricular responsibilities. Who is left to lead curricular improvement? Understaffing and underbudgeting have hampered the efforts of the school district to revamp its curriculum.

Finding 2.4: Curricular Documents in Pergola Have Not Been Completely Effective in Promoting Improved Program Consistency

The auditor examined curricular documents dated from the 1977–78 school year to the present. No document produced prior to the state's *Curriculum Standards* is relevant. Therefore, the auditor examined only those curricular documents that have been developed in compliance with the Standards volume.

The most recent and conspicuous of these documents is the English curriculum adopted in May of 1986. This document is two and a half inches thick in a three-ringed binder. It consists of course outlines, a scope and sequence chart, a curriculum guide, and appendices.

On the face of it, the document is imposing and bulky but contains some critical pieces of information. The course outlines contain statements regarding prerequisites, course length and amount of credit, specification of content together with suggested time allocations, specific course competencies, and a brief statement regarding a method for the teacher to evaluate student skill attainment. Where appropriate, the course outline indicates the textbooks and supplemental books relevant to the area.

The section marked as curriculum contains statements which could be classified as quasi-performance objectives and little else. The scope and sequence chart is keyed to the curriculum guide section and indicates if certain content is tested on one or more of three extant tests utilized in the district. At one of six grade levels, the designated English content is marked with one of three symbols that show a teacher whether the content is to be introduced, reviewed/reinforced, or extended.

In the appendices are indicated the core reading lists compiled from *Barron's How to Prepare for the Advanced Placement Examination in English Composition and Literature*, along with recommendations from the College Board, university reading lists, and other sources.

The appendices also contain a series of review worksheets which key the course content to the *State Curriculum Standards in English*. This format provides a quick and comprehensive method for determining whether or not the district is in compliance with these standards.

The English curriculum guide is exemplary in several respects and weak in others. First, the inclusion of time specifications is critical to effective curriculum monitoring. These are present, though not in sufficient detail. The cross-referencing to the *Curriculum Standards* is excellent in conception and design. The scope and sequence chart presents a short and effective method for illustrating how the curriculum comes together at all grade levels.

The weaknesses of the guide begin first with its sheer bulk. It is too large. Teachers interviewed indicated they found it non-utilitarian. The document did not offer explanations about how to use it effectively. For example, in what ways are the courses related to the curriculum? What is the difference between reviewing and reinforcing and extending? How are the worksheets in the back to be used? Who fills them out and who reviews them? How often?

A curriculum guide ought to be a stand-alone document, i.e., sufficiently clear and utilitarian to be understood by itself with no other information required to use it properly. The existing English curriculum guide fails on this criterion.

Finding 2.5: Curriculum Development and Implementation Have Been Hampered by Strong Traditions of Teacher Isolationism

A curriculum exists to provide and promote program continuity across school buildings and between classrooms. The classroom is the basic unit in which a curriculum is delivered. If classrooms have little correlation to one another in terms of content taught, the best designed program is nothing more or less than a patchwork quilt. Opportunities for maximizing student time and energy are lost by and through poor organization and utilization of limited resources.

A school must be more than a collection of classrooms. An educational program comes into existence when classrooms are integrated, one into the other, and coherence occurs by design. That coherence is contained in a curriculum.

The auditor found in Pergola a board of trustees and central administration acutely aware of the need for such program coherence. Site administrators and some teachers also exhibited and commented upon the necessity for improved program focus. These, however, have been offset by strong past traditions of teacher isolationism, most notably at Pergola High School.

However, the auditor found high school teachers extremely dedicated to providing quality education. Even veteran teachers were very positively oriented towards working with Pergola students. Teachers interviewed indicated they returned to work in Pergola because of strong morale, collegial working relationships, and a positive school climate.

Over the years high school teachers have withdrawn into their respective and isolated spheres because of the frequent shifts in site administrators. They have learned not to invest time in administrative priorities because that investment would be negated by the next administrator. High school teachers have learned to depend upon one another for survival and feedback. Thus, any kind of "normal" teacher–administrator relationship has been largely missing at Pergola High School. The current site administrator is now in her second year there. Many teachers commented upon this as a positive sign that stability had returned to the senior school campus in Pergola. Such a sign was welcomed.

The days when teachers could quietly go to their classrooms and "do their own thing" are over in Pergola and every other district in the state because of the creation and mandated review of the state curriculum contained in the state *Curriculum Standards*. A centrally imposed curriculum requires teachers working within schools to be more cohesive and directed in their energies than ever before. This condition exists in Pergola and all other districts. A tradition of teacher isolationism is a major barrier preventing the district and the school from becoming more effective as an entity. The district and the school cannot afford a permissive environment on this matter.

Finding 2.6: Site Visitations Revealed the Presence of Effective and Positive Learning Environments in All Schools in Pergola

The auditor visited every public school in Pergola. The auditor viewed classes and work areas, offices, and libraries and encountered the full range of teacher–pupil activities.

School administrators at all levels in Pergola were extremely sensitive to the fact that aesthetically pleasant facilities promote improved pupil discipline.

The auditor found a most unique and successful program at Pergola Lake High School. This program deals with troubled youth and students who have difficulty with a traditional secondary school program. The school has an exceptionally sensitive administrator and staff who have a "hard nose, warm heart" approach that works with their students.

The Pergola Public Schools have recently moved towards a middle school program. This movement has been led by an experienced and able middle school principal who was instrumental in the design of the newly constructed Plato Middle School.

Finding 2.7: There Is a Shortage of Counseling Support Staff in Pergola

An almost universal complaint from students interviewed in the audit was the lack of time with counselors. This was caused by the high pupil–counselor ratio. For a school of some 2000+ students, there are only three counselors.

This problem was highlighted in the *1983–84 Accreditation Report* filed with the district in May of 1984. It noted that at that time there were only two counselors for a 830/1 ratio. That report noted that ". . . this department is handicapped by the number of students to be served . . . students tend to be counseled and advised on a crisis basis rather than on an academic planning basis" (p. 53).

The importance of sound counseling to curricular effectiveness is integral. No matter how good the written curriculum may be, or no matter how sound classroom instruction may be, without proper guidance from the counseling staff, the delivery of a curriculum is compromised. To ensure the proper implementation of curriculum with any student population, a workable ratio of students to counselors is requisite. At the present time that ratio is not functional for anything but crisis intervention.

Standard 3: The School District Has Documentation Explaining How Its Programs Have Been Developed, Implemented, and Conducted

A school district meeting this curriculum audit standard is able to show how its programs have been created as the result of a systematic identification of deficiencies in the achievement and growth of its students compared to measurable standards of learning.

In addition, a system meeting this standard is able to demonstrate that, as a whole, it is more effective than the sum total of its parts, i.e., any arbitrary combination of programs or schools do not equate to the larger school district entity.

The purpose of having a school district is to obtain the educational and economic benefits of a coordinated program for students, both to enhance learning by maximizing pupil interest and by utilizing economies of scale where applicable.

What the Auditor Expected to Find in the Pergola Public Schools

The auditor expected to find a highly developed, articulated, and coordinated curriculum in the district that was effectively monitored by the administrative and teaching staffs. Such a curriculum would be:

- centrally defined and adopted by the board of education
- clearly explained to members of the instructional staff and building level administrators
- accompanied by specific training programs to enhance implementation
- monitored by central office staff and building principals

What the Auditor Found in the Pergola Public Schools

The auditor found in the Pergola Public Schools a school system in transition, moving from a somewhat informal set of operations to more formal operations.

The auditor found greater emphasis being placed on central planning, centralized curriculum development pushed by state mandates, and more sophisticated practices being utilized at all levels, from board policies to curricular documents.

The major weakness previously cited under curriculum audit Standard 1 (Finding 1.8) is the lack of any curriculum monitoring or any system or plan for monitoring at the time of the audit.

Finding 3.1: The District Is Moving Towards More Sophisticated Responses Governing Its Operations

The auditor found in the *Strategic Plan* document, the *English Curriculum Guide*, the documents pertaining to the design and construction of Plato Middle School, the *1985 Long-Range Facility Plan Update*, and the prepared *Accreditation Report 1983–84* a gamut of very sophisticated responses to a broad range of problems.

Such documents in most districts represent the "best thinking" that the combined professional personnel can produce under the conditions in which they work on a day-to-day basis. The documents reviewed by the auditor were examples of a high level of thought at work in Pergola. Morever, various personnel interviewed reflected the same thoughts as encountered in the documents, which indicates that they have made a difference in the thought processes of the people in the district.

The *Accreditation Report of 1983–84* and subsequent examination of Pergola High School by a visiting committee from the Regional Association of Schools and Colleges resulted in the first six-year accreditation of that school in eighteen years.

Finding 3.2: The Schools Are Better than the Curriculum in Pergola

The operations of the schools in Pergola are generally better than those described/prescribed in the curriculum reviewed. Instead of the curriculum leading operations, it has followed and still is absent in many cases for much of the full range of educational programs.

The absence of a generally accurate set of curricular documents prevents the school system from optimizing its resources across grade levels 7–12. Instead of behaving as a system, it is behaving as a confederation of smaller systems. For Pergola to function as a system, it must have a system-wide curriculum which pulls together all operations into one cohesive set of work actions.

Without such a cohesive set of operations, the school district consumes more resources than may be required because of unnecessary duplication of effort by students and labor by teachers, resulting in boredom and mismanagement of time.

For a school district to indicate to its citizens and taxpayers that every tax dollar is being used to maximum advantage, a school system must function as a system. Pergola has not attained that position yet. There is strong evidence derived from documents and interviews that it is moving in that direction.

The auditor encountered opinions from parents, students, teachers, and administrators that the school district had suffered from a poor image acquired in the 1960s because of a variety of factors. The resulting poor image was still shared by some of the larger populace and the press in the vicinity. Without exception, the same people indicated that the image and the actual educational program in Pergola were quite different. Virtually all parties could cite specific cases and programs that were exceptionally good and a school environment that was positive and improving.

The auditor has confirmed the generally positive and productive atmosphere of all schools in Pergola under curriculum audit Standard 2 and Finding 2.6. The only exception to these data was the ILP at Pergola High School. This program has not enjoyed the full success that some other areas have attained in Pergola.

This program is set aside in portable facilities and functions in small teacher/pupil ratios. Some student behavior observed by the auditor was not productive nor in keeping with the larger operations of Pergola High School.

Taken as a whole, the auditor could find no evidence that the schools in Pergola were not as good or perhaps even better than schools audited elsewhere which were serving a similar diverse pupil population and functioning in comparable settings. The poor image acquired by Pergola and reflected in comments by persons interviewed is no longer a reality, if it ever was a reality, for the school system.

Standard 4: The School District Uses the Results from District Designed and/or Adopted Assessments to Adjust, Improve, or Terminate Ineffective Practices or Programs

A school district meeting this audit standard of the process has designed a comprehensive system of testing and measurement tools that indicate how well students are learning designated priority objectives.

Such a system will provide:

- a timely and relevant base upon which to analyze important trends in the instructional program
- a vehicle to examine how well programs are actually producing desired learner results
- a way to provide feedback to the teaching staff regarding how classroom instruction can become more effective
- a data base to compare the strengths and weaknesses of various programs and program alternatives
- a data base to terminate ineffective educational programs

A school district meeting this audit standard has a full range of formal and informal assessment tools that provide relevant program information for decision making in the classroom, building (principals and/or grade/department chairpersons), district, and board levels.

The school system has taken steps to ensure that the full range of its programs are systematically and periodically assessed. Assessment data has been matched to program objectives and are utilized in decision making.

What the Auditor Expected to Find in the Pergola Public Schools

The auditor expected to find a comprehensive assessment program of all aspects of the curriculum, 7–12, which was:

- keyed to a set of goals/objectives adopted by the board of trustees
- utilized extensively at the building level to engage in program review and modification
- demonstrating consistent improvement over a longitudinal time period
- used to terminate ineffective educational programs
- used as a base to establish needed programs
- publicly reported to the board of trustees and the community on a regular basis

What the Auditor Found in the Pergola Public Schools

Finding 4.1: Test Scores in the Pergola Public Schools Indicate Modest Improvements

The auditor examined test scores contained in the *Strategic Plan* of the school district. Scores on the state achievement test were listed back to the 1981–82 school year through the 1984–85 school year, grades 7–12, and are presented in Exhibit 5.

Exhibit 5
Results of the Test Grades 7–12, (1981/82)–(1984/85)

		School Year				
Test Area	Grade	81–82	82–83	83–84	84–85	Trend Line
Reading	7	6.7	6.8	7.0	6.9	+
	8	7.9	8.1	8.0	8.0	+
	9	8.5	8.2	8.6	8.6	+
	10	9.1	8.7	9.1	10.0	+
	11	10.6	10.0	10.0	10.5	–
	12	11.1	10.6	10.6	11.1	0

The auditor examined whether or not the trend was towards improved performance (an increase no matter how small) or a decline (a decrease no matter how small) in this four-year period. Statistical significance was not determined. What was important was the emergence of a clear trend towards improvement which may become statistically significant if continued. The data are also reported in grade equivalents which are now passé. The district has also discontinued the practice of reporting the scores in this manner.

Data for language, mathematics, and total are shown in Exhibit 6.

The test data may indicate some important patterns. For example, in grades 7–8, pupil achievement is at grade level or extremely close (.1). However, achievement in all areas and total test is below grade level in the ninth grade and continues to widen in grades 10–12, so that by the twelfth grade Pergola students are .9 below grade level in math and one year and nine months below in language. On the total test battery they are one year three months behind grade level.

The SAT (Scholastic Aptitude Test) indicates that those Pergola twelfth grade students who took the battery were, on the average, twenty points below on the verbal section of the SAT and thirty-five points below the state mean in math. The scores were Pergola Verbal 401 compared to a state mean of 421. The math was Pergola 441 compared to a state average of 476.

The test data may mean that the curriculum is not well-aligned with the skills included on the test at the upper levels. It may mean that some factors of pupil mobility may be at play which impact the results and are not understood. It may mean that teachers are not teaching the proper skills even if the curriculum were aligned with the test. It may mean that all of these factors are at work simultaneously.

The district does recognize that these may be variables at work. There were numerous references in the *Strategic Plan* of the necessity to improve test performance (pp. 18, 22–23, 27, 31) and engage in curriculum alignment.

Exhibit 6
Results of the Test Grades 7–12, 1981/82–1984/85

Test Area	Grade	School Year				Trend Line*
		81–82	82–83	83–84	84–85	
Language	7	6.6	6.6	6.8	6.9	+
	8	7.8	8.1	8.3	8.3	+
	9	8.3	8.0	8.2	8.6	+
	10	9.3	8.3	8.7	9.5	+
	11	10.4	9.1	8.8	9.7	–
	12	10.1	9.6	10.1	10.1	0
Mathematics	7	7.3	7.3	7.5	7.4	+
	8	8.0	8.1	8.0	8.0	0
	9	8.2	8.1	8.6	8.6	+
	10	8.8	8.5	9.0	9.6	+
	11	9.9	9.6	9.2	10.0	+
	12	9.8	9.7	10.0	10.7	+
TOTAL CAT	7	7.3	7.3	7.5	7.4	+
	8	8.0	8.1	8.0	8.0	0
	9	8.2	8.1	8.6	8.6	+
	10	8.8	8.5	9.0	9.6	+
	11	9.9	9.6	9.2	10.0	+
	12	9.8	9.7	10.0	10.7	+

*NOTE: The designated trend pattern does not include a reference to the standard error of the mean, in which case differences reported by the district either positive or negative over the four-year-period may not be actual shifts but reflect relative stability in results. This may be an accomplishment given the factor of pupil mobility. The mobility factor was unknown.

The CAP (Critical Assessment Program) results are shown for the twelfth grade in four areas over a four-year period in Exhibit 7.

Once again, the same data caveats pertain to the CAP scores as for previous test scores. The 1985–86 CAP scores placed the district students in the eighty-fourth (84) percentile in written expression, the seventy-ninth (79) percentile in mathematics, and the forty-ninth (49) percentile in reading. Spelling data were not available. The greatest gains for Pergola students over the four-year period were in written expression and math, respectively. Reading showed a decline.

Several factors may be responsible for this improvement. The first is that the district's "Zap the Cap" efforts are bearing fruit. The second is that the pupil population has changed, i.e., those students least successful in the basic skill areas have dropped out, thus changing the population which is tested in the twelfth grade. The auditor did not find dropout data in the materials provided; however, the district's *Strategic Plan* did cite the statistic that expulsions were up 20 percent at Pergola High School (p. 25).

These data are cited in an effort to view the matter of test scores in perspective. Schools do not control all of the variables which impact pupil achievement as measured on standardized tests. They should neither be totally blamed nor lauded, no matter what the test scores might be. They should be held accountable for those variables over which they do have control and which influence learning. Such controls, however, are never absolute. They are always relative.

Finding 4.2: There Is Not a Comprehensive Assessment Program for All Curricular Areas in Pergola

State and standardized tests used in Pergola cover only a small fraction of the curriculum. There are few other district-wide assessments or tests which systematically examine other areas of the curriculum beyond the basic skills.

Teachers do their own testing in their own classrooms. Some areas and departments have developed a variety of means of assessing pupil progress. But there has been no systematic effort to engage in pupil assessment comparable to the testing in the basic skills. A large chunk of the curriculum in Pergola is therefore partially or totally unassessed in rigorous terms.

Finding 4.3: Use of Test Data Is Limited in Pergola as Positive and Relevant Feedback

Interview data with teachers revealed that test data is not utilized as a powerful avenue of feedback to improve pupil achievement. Test data were available, but never as accessible as teachers would like and require for it to have much impact on curricular improvement. Super-

Exhibit 7
Results of the Assessment Program—Twelfth Grade
(1982/83)–(1985/86) Total Percent Correct

	School Year				
Test Area	82–83 %	83–84 %	84–85 %	85–86 %	Trend Line
Reading	64.1	59.2	56.1	62.4	–
Written Expression	62.4	59.1	53.7	62.5	+
Spelling	64.2	62.7	62.7	Unavailable	–(3 years)
Mathematics	62.3	61.1	57.1	66.8	+

vising teachers reported they did not make much use of test scores as feedback nor monitor curriculum through test scores. They admitted to looking at test scores, but not in any systematic or thorough way.

Finding 4.4: The District Has Been Most Successful in Using Feedback and Goal-Directed Behavior at the Middle School Level (Grades 7–8)

The auditor found solid linkages between goals and action in the reshaping of the middle schools in Pergola. For example, in the district's *Strategic Plan*, one major district-wide goal for 1986–89 is "to improve student learning and student achievement as measured through standardized tests" (p. 18).

For the middle school level the auditor found these statements regarding the instructional program:

- "There will be increased emphasis on academic excellence and required academic courses" (p. 20).
- "The increased academic requirements will decrease the number of electives and exploratory programs" (p. 20).

Both of these statements can be tracked into the structuring of the curriculum at the middle school level (p. 21) and into brick and mortar at the newly constructed Plato Middle School.

The district has therefore modified the conventional view of a middle school to reflect both an increased emphasis by the state on academics and the nature of the students to be served in Pergola. The Pergola Lake High School also demonstrated similar linkages.

Feedback is more limited at Pergola High School for a variety of reasons previously cited (see Findings 1.5, 1.7, 1.8, 2.5, and 2.7). Of critical importance is administrative stability (Finding 1.1). Effective feedback is dependent upon stable linkages between operations to be utilized. Pergola High School has encountered a good deal of curricular fragmentation caused by administrative instability. The effective use of feedback at the key educational facility in the Pergola High School District is intimately linked to continued administrative stability to become operational.

Standard 5: The School System Has Improved Productivity

Productivity refers to the relationship between input and output. A school district meeting this standard of the audit is able to demonstrate consistent pupil outcomes, even in the face of declining resources. Improved productivity results when a school system is able to create a more consistent level of congruence between the major variables involved in achieving better results and in controlling costs.

What the Auditor Expected to Find in the Pergola Public School

While the achievement of improved productivity in a school system is a complex process, caused in part by the lack of a tight organizational structure, a school district meeting this audit standard demonstrates:

- planned and actual congruence between curriculum objectives, results, and financial costs
- specific means that have been selected or modified and implemented to attain better results in the schools over a specified time period
- a planned series of interventions that have raised pupil performance levels over time and maintained those levels within the same parameters as in the past

Any evaluation of productivity is a relative one and must include the fundamental recognition that neither the board of trustees, superintendent, principals, or professional staff completely control all of the important variables that will result in improved pupil performance. Nonetheless, there are substantial elements within their combined authority that do account for improved pupil learning. These can be subjected to productivity assessment.

What the Auditor Found in the Pergola Public Schools

The auditor found a generally stable financial condition in the school district. The 1983–84 school year saw a negative ending balance in the budget. The district's finances are overwhelmingly state controlled with less than 35 percent local support for the educational program.

The auditor found insufficient funds allocated for curriculum development and no visible linkages from curricular priorities to the process of budget development. Because of this condition, the auditor found no tangible way to trace dollars to programs nor any method used by the school system officials to do the same.

Finding 5.1: Budgeting in the Pergola Public Schools Follows a Traditional Format

The auditor reviewed past budgets in the Pergola Public Schools. In addition, the auditor reviewed several past financial audits from the accounting firm of Pride, Price, Jones, and Co. of Marberry.

These financial audits were generally complimentary to the district and did not reveal any major financial problems which would be unexpected with anyone familiar with the operation of a school district on an approximately $10 million dollar budget.

The Pergola Public School District's budget is a traditional one, called object item or line item with some programmatic definitions included.

However, the auditor was unable to find how curricular priorities were used to build the budget and how financial emphases were changed from curricular data.

When asked, board members were also unclear about the process. While conceding that they tried to get money as close to the kids as possible, said one, "I understand how it goes from fiscal to curriculum, but not the other way." This comment was revealing. The budgetary process directs curriculum unless the district takes steps to shake itself from this cycle. In most school systems the curriculum is budget-driven. In reality, the budget ought to be curriculum-driven. There should be visible and tangible linkages between curricular priorities and budgetary priorities. While they may be present in Pergola, they were not able to be demonstrated to the satisfaction of the auditor through the retrievable documents or interviews.

This is a critical problem for any remnant of local control of curriculum to remain in school districts. The breakdown of revenue for 1984–85 and 1985–86 indicates the following:

	Amount of Revenue in Pergola Budget	%	Source
1984–85	$ 385,804	5%	Federal
	$5,947,137	62%	State
	$3,290,029	34%	Total Local
	$9,632,806		
1985–86	$ 454,225	3%	Federal
	$ 7,243,604	63%	State
	$ 3,880,028	34%	Total Local
	$11,580,256		

NOTE: Figures derived from audited data in reports by Pride, Price, Jones, and Co., financial accountants to the school district.

The state has assumed the major portion of funding for the Pergola Public Schools. The state has also assumed an even larger role in determining the objectives and standards for all areas of the curriculum. Whatever remains for a local school district to determine is dependent upon adequate local support and sound curricular leadership.

Pergola faces a series of unique factors which make it hard to standardize any externally developed curriculum. Factors of historical demography, pupil mobility internally and externally, large blocks of senior citizens who have no children or grandchildren in the schools, and a varied mixture of racial, ethnic, and religious backgrounds of families from many socio-economic and cultural levels make a volatile and difficult body of clientele with which to provide effective and efficient education.

In order to maximize its capability to shape a curriculum that is effective for all students within the Pergola Public Schools, the board and professional staff must exercise their latitude in the determination and configuration of the local curriculum to the greatest extent possible within the law.

Finding 5.2: Local Funding for Curriculum Development Has Been Insufficient

The auditor examined budgetary data to determine how much money had been allocated for curriculum development. In the 1985–86 budget reviewed, $16,800 was allocated within a $10,134,527 school budget. In the same budget, the board allocated $15,000 for travel and conferences for itself. Both budget allocations represent less than 1 percent of the total budget.

A review of allocated funds within the 1986–87 budget showed curriculum development budgeted at $20,750.00. The amount is far too small to be meaningful in the school district. The amount ought to be increased and certainly not be less than one-half of one percent of the budget, particularly within the next three years when developmental costs will be high.

RECOMMENDATIONS

Based upon the auditor's findings, the following recommendations have been formulated to improve the curriculum management system of the Pergola Public Schools.

Recommendation 1: Maintain Administrative Stability

The superintendent has created a functional management team in the Pergola Public Schools. Administrators were very complimentary about the creativity they were afforded, the openness present, and at the same time the high level of expectations for improvement required.

The board of trustees have provided generally solid support to the superintendent and the administrative staff, even though their debates are hard fought and they are anything but a rubber stamp to the administration.

Of most critical importance is the continued administrative stability at Pergola High School.

Recommendation 2: Relieve Administrative Understaffing in Curriculum

The current administrative staffing for curriculum development, implementation, and monitoring and evaluation is inadequate. Existing staff have been overextended. Creative ways must be explored to provide for increased leadership, at the same time staying within state regulation. Such avenues as teacher leaders on assignment, external contracting for some curricular services, and other means should be explored to relieve an unhealthy and potentially debilitating problem from continuing.

Recommendation 3: Improve Internal Human Relations Between the Board of Trustees and the PSEA

The problems between the board of trustees and the PSEA are longstanding. Some board members have displayed individual insensitivity to the efforts of teachers working in the district, at least in many teachers' perceptions.

Also, the PSEA has worked to unseat some board members it has found who do not share its views about matters pertaining to contractual grievances and binding arbitration and other problems.

These political confrontations were exacerbated by an impasse between the board and the PSEA at the time of the audit. Even with the eventual resolution of the contractual differences, poor human relations, mistrust, and suspicions will continue to fester and provide an antagonistic environment. In this context meaningful curricular change and particularly an effective monitoring system cannot be developed. A good part of any such monitoring system is based on mutual trust.

Organizational trust is not based on personality preferences or placating opponents. It is based on mutual understanding of differences and respect. One can disagree and still maintain respect. These factors are necessary to restrain the destructive elements of the collective bargaining process from poisoning the climate in a school district.

The auditor recommends that an external human relations specialist be employed to conduct several sessions between the two parties in order to clear the air and reestablish a functional, working relationship between the board and the PSEA.

Recommendation 4: Develop Functional Board Policies to Ensure Sound Curriculum Management

Both the old and proposed board policies regarding curriculum are inadequate. The proposed board policies are vague, filled with high-sounding but non-functional references, and do not include the idea of creating functional local quality control of the curriculum.

Policies should be developed which contain statements regarding:

- the necessity of developing operational and measurable objectives for all curricular areas
- the requirement for curriculum alignment (both content and context) being a part of the curriculum development process to tests and textbooks
- the necessity for curriculum monitoring on an ongoing basis with a delineation of responsibility for such monitoring to appropriate professional personnel
- a specific procedure for annual curricular review which is directly linked to budget development
- the requirement to assess formally all areas of the curriculum on either a state, standardized, or locally developed and rigorous set of sound tests
- the requirement for sound curriculum planning expected of all staff at all levels, regardless of whether they are probationary or tenured

Recommendation 5: The Creation of a Policy Framework to Improve Curricular Articulation with the Feeder Elementary School Districts

The problem of articulation with the feeder elementary school districts has been approached as a technical one. The administrators have begun to establish professional linkages to work on a problem.

This is only part of the problem. The most important aspect of this problem is political, in the best sense of the word. Articulation is first a political problem, given the legal differences which separate the districts.

It is recommended that the Pergola board of trustees initiate policy invitations to jointly formulate and issue a policy directive to all five administrations of their desire to attain the maximum articulation possible, at the same time providing for the individual differences necessary to be responsive to their respective clientele.

A joint policy statement would then become policy for all feeder districts and the high school district to implement. That policy should call for common testing instruments, sharing of data to all parties regarding pupil performance in the high school system, and the creation and funding of a collegial curriculum advisory body which defines and monitors an operational relationship among and between the respective entities.

No real progress on the matter of articulation can be made without attacking the political context in which articulation as a technology is applied. As the board leads, so will the administration follow in each of the districts.

Recommendation 6: Improve the Linkages within the Strategic Plan of the District

There are not adequate linkages within the *Strategic Plan* of the district between goals, objectives, and activities. Furthermore, the evaluative data is not clearly related to priorities. The *Strategic Plan* is thus technically flawed in this respect. A cross-referencing system within the Plan would help in creating these linkages.

Recommendation 7: Clarify the Job Descriptions of the Supervising Teachers

The supervising teacher role is one of potentially enormous influence in the school district. Yet this influence is being squandered because of the lack of clarity and responsibilities that they are to perform.

Supervising teachers should be more than organizational "cheerleaders" or ombudspersons. They should exercise technical responsibilities for the improvement of curriculum and instruction and be held accountable for those improvements taking place.

The clarification should provide answers to organizational questions about who is the "boss."

Recommendation 8: Clarify Role Expectations of School Principals

School principals are devoting an enormous amount of time to maintaining order and stability in the district. It is unrealistic to believe that, given this paramount task, they can be expected to devote a majority of their time to observation or curricular affairs.

The auditor found Pergola principals to be dedicated and hard-working and vitally concerned about curriculum. Under existing conditions they will not be able to meet the existing board policy #406. One answer is to revamp the role of supervising teachers and department chairs in the curricular areas.

Recommendation 9: Design and Develop a Workable and Utilitarian Curriculum Monitoring System

Curriculum is not monitored in the school district. In some areas it does not exist to be monitored. After it is developed, it will have to be monitored.

Many monitoring systems create acres of paperwork. Attention must be paid to creating a system that is functional, not complex, and easy to use and apply.

Part of the monitoring system ought to be the development of lesson plans by all teachers, but not necessarily in the conventional format. The conventional "block plan" lesson format is largely non-functional in improving curriculum management in schools. It must be modified to include provisions for adjusting time and sequence in the application and delivery of the curriculum. Many districts are experimenting with a variety of designs that are easy to use and review by appropriate administrative or supervisory personnel.

Recommendation 10: Revise and Simplify the Design for Curricular Documents in Pergola

The existing three-ringed binder, two and a half inch thick curriculum guide is too bulky and complex to be effective. The guide should be revised and broken into smaller, more utilitarian documents easily used and transported by teachers. An emphasis on *curriculum alignment* should be the watchword. All redundancy should be eliminated, along with ambiguous words and phrases. Clear and concise directions should be present in all guides to facilitate their usage.

Recommendation 11: Lower the Counselor/Pupil Ratio in the Secondary Schools

The counselor/pupil ratio is unworkable for effective assignment of students to a curriculum in the secondary schools in Pergola. A ratio of 200–300 should become the standard for the schools over the next several years.

Recommendation 12: Develop a District-Wide Testing Program That Formally Assesses All Curricular Areas of the Educational Program

Only a small portion of the school district's curriculum is now formally and rigorously assessed by reliable instruments. That spectrum ought to be expanded to district designed and validated criterion referenced measures where appropriate.

The district must make better use of the test data it gathers. Comprehensive testing reports should be made available to all professional staff and be accompanied by analyses and specific suggestions as to what to change as the result of the feedback. This is a responsibility that can be subcontracted, if necessary, in order not to exceed state regulation regarding administrative personnel.

It should be noted that not all areas of the curriculum are appropriately assessed in the same way. Paper and pencil tests may not be appropriate measures for each and every objective. Observation, anecdotal data, and other approaches will have to be considered where necessary.

Recommendation 13: Improve the Budgeting Process to Reflect Hard Data and Curricular Priorities

The budget should contain appropriate data to justify changes in dollars and to substantiate desired changes in programs. Curricular priorities should be included in the budget and tangible linkages shown which indicate why and how dollars are to be spent based on such priorities.

SUMMARY

The Pergola Public Schools have no smug past to constrict its progress as one of the finest school districts in Preston County and the state.

Economics and demographics are fast pushing it to enter the next century and shed its mostly rural agrarian past. No sleepy little "burg" any longer, Pergola is on the first step of the space age.

Yet the legacy of problems which have historically plagued Pergola remains. Landed gentry, immigrants, middle-class migration, and senior citizen retirement centers provide an unusual and unique challenge to the professional leadership in the district.

A strong and vibrant secondary school system is at the heart of any consideration of the good life for Pergola children. This curriculum audit is filed with the board of trustees and the superintendent to fulfill that promise for each child.

That dream is captured superbly in a road sign when one enters Pergola by automobile. The sign promises the "good life" now. It can be done.

CHECKPOINTS

Questions to the Author–Auditor Regarding Curriculum Audit

Question 1: *In what ways was the Pergola audit typical and atypical of others you have completed?*

Answer: It was quite typical for districts of its same wealth. As I noted, I found understaffing present. This was not determined by arithmetic calculation, but by experience in knowing how much work it would take to accomplish the tasks given the level of personnel available and by interviewing key personnel. The use of test data was quite typical as well as the budgetary practices.

Pergola was atypical in that it had developed a pretty good strategic plan. Such an effort is relatively rare. Most districts have no plan whatsoever, let alone a strategic one. The atypical part of this audit was that I was scheduled to have lunch with the executive board of the PSEA. The district catered a lunch for about twenty people. Nobody showed but the president. I was told that the executive board considered it an affront to schedule the meeting with me on a Saturday. Remember the teachers association and the board were at impasse in a sticky labor situation. As it turned out, I got to interview most of the members of the executive board at site faculty meetings anyway.

Question 2: *The audit raised no questions about curricular content propriety? Why not?*

Answer: Pergola is located in a state where local curriculum development has been supplanted by the state education agency. To raise the issue in the district would have been addressing the wrong audience. The district had to comply by law. The compliance had to be demonstrated to the state's satisfaction. It was all the district could do to meet the state's regulations.

/ VI / *Case Study 2: The Junction City Public Schools*

THE JUNCTION CITY Public Schools is a pseudonym for a real school district in which the author–auditor completed a curriculum audit in 1986. All photographs have been removed to prevent identification of the district. Specific references which would reveal the name of the district or any person in the district have been deleted or changed. Otherwise, the audit is printed here as it was filed in final form.

BACKGROUND, PURPOSE, AND SCOPE OF WORK

This document constitutes the final report of a curriculum audit of the Junction City Public Schools.

Background

The Junction City Public Schools serve the municipality of Junction City. Junction City occupies approximately 10,000 acres of land or roughly 16 square miles.

Junction City was initially settled in the early 1600s, but remained sparsely populated until serious land investment began in 1804. Because of its strategic location, it became a major center of commerce. Its population peaked in the 1930s at 316,715 and thereafter began to decline. During the decade of the 1970s, there was a 14 percent loss in total population.

According to the 1984 U.S. Census, the population is now 220,248 and has undergone some significant changes. The percentage of

Asians in Junction City rose by 67.9 percent from the 1980 Census, from 9,793 to 16,444. The Hispanic population increased 10.8 percent, from 41,672 to 46,193. The Anglo population declined 11.5 percent, from 127,699 to 112,930. The Black population also declined 1.8 percent from 61,954 to 60,781.

At the present time Junction City is a community undergoing rapid change. Older buildings and historic property are being changed to condos. Land prices have soared. Former manufacturing plants are being converted to malls and boutiques.

Junction City is still plagued by a variety of urban problems, however. As of 1985, Junction City had the highest crime rate per 1,000 of any municipality in Hart County at 78.5 percent per 1,000 and the highest violent crime rate in the county at 15.2 percent.

The Junction City Public Schools have been steadily declining in enrollment in the past years. This has prompted the closing of several schools. The enrollment pattern is shown below:

Year	Total Enrollment Junction City
1975	36,758
1976	35,515
1977	35,057
1978	34,706
1979	33,524
1980	32,564
1981	31,737
1982	31,384
1983	31,380
1984	31,018
1985	30,418

The ethnic breakdown of the school population in Junction City is shown below for the past six years.

School Population Ethnic Breakdown

Year	Black	White	Hispanic	Native American	Asian
1980–81	47.7%	18.9%	29.5%	.1%	3.8%
1981–82	47.9%	18.8%	28.9%	.1%	4.3%
1982–83	45.8%	18.4%	31.0%	.2%	4.6%
1983–84	45.5%	17.7%	31.3%	NA	5.5%
1984–85	44.9%	16.2%	32.7%	.1%	6.1%
1985–86	44.2%	15.9%	32.4%	.1%	7.4%

The pupil mobility factor in Junction City was not available at the time of the audit.

The Junction City Public Schools are governed by a nine-person board of education which is appointed by the mayor of Junction City. The policies and politics of city hall strongly dominate the financial priorities and budgetary practices of the school system, as well as the selection, promotion, and demotion of central office staff and many non-instructional support staff as well. As of September 1985, the school system employed 128 administrators at both the building and central level and 2,288 instructional staff at thirty-seven schools/instructional/support centers. The 1985–86 school budget is approximately $140 million dollars.

At the time of the curriculum audit, the district was deep in the throes of many ongoing crises. These were caused by:

(1) A budget cut of $4 million in which the district reduced fourteen library media teachers, eight computer teachers, several classroom teachers, program coordinators, administrators, and pool substitutes. This was caused by failure to budget funds for forty special education teachers and twenty aides, state retirement costs, and out-of-district tuition.

(2) A federal fine of $1,200,000 for failures in the Federal Lunch Program in the 1984–85 school year. The government contended that it was charged for 327,000 school lunches that were never served.

(3) Notification from the county/state that they had failed to become certified. The district was rated "unacceptable" on thirty-two of fifty-one indicators.

(4) Public recognition that the school system was rated as the "worst" in Hart County and the state on state educational criteria (*Junction Journal*, 8/16/85).

(5) Inability of the board of education to evaluate its new superintendent. The board president initiated efforts, but lost a quorum during the meeting.

(6) Investigations and audits of various programs by a variety of agencies from the U.S. Environmental Protection Agency, Federal Lunch Program, or the state.

(7) The public resignation of one member of the board of education who cited "lack of curriculum revision" as a major frustration. He further claimed in a paid ad: "The board of education has now become a dumping ground for incompetents, liars, people who have been in trouble with the police, political hacks . . . people who are both morally and professionally unqualified

either to teach in or to administer the very schools they are sworn to serve" (*Junction Journal*, 5/30/86, p. 17).

(8) Being the only school district in the state (of 565 operative school districts) to miss the mandated deadline for striking a budget (*Junction Journal*, 4/3/86).

(9) Battles between the state and the city over school spending which was prompting consideration of how to cut $11 million from the proposed $162 million 1986–87 school budget (*Junction Journal*, 5/30/86, p. 135).

Purpose

The purpose of the curriculum audit was to determine the extent to which the Junction City Public Schools had implemented the principles and practices of sound curriculum management by which it then could be expected to:

(1) Fully comply with state directives and mandates regarding education in the future

(2) Implement sound and functional local curriculum control as required in statute 18A: 7A-7 and A.C. 6:83.5

(3) Make maximum use of its resources and revenues, local, state, and federal, in the process of improving pupil learning in the district

Scope of Work

A curriculum audit is an independent examination of data pertaining to educational program practices that will indicate the extent to which a school district can meet its objectives (whether the latter are internally or externally developed or imposed). An audit examines management practice and system results. As such, it is a type of quality assurance.

METHODOLOGY

The Model for the Audit

The model for a curriculum audit is shown in Exhibit 8. The model has been published extensively in the literature and incorporated into the regulations of at least one eastern state.

Exhibit 8
A Schematic View of Curricular Quality Control

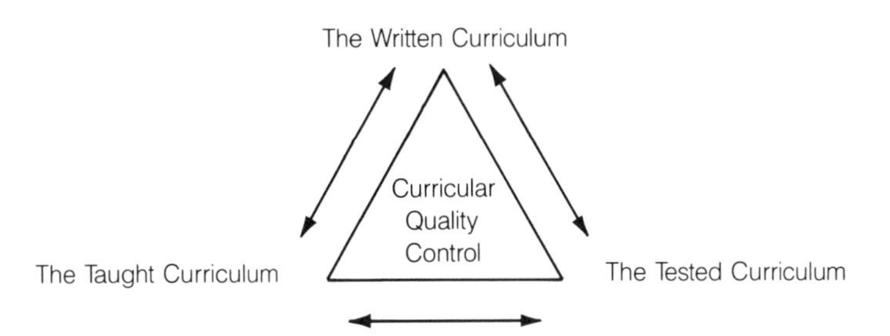

Generic quality control assumes that at least three elements must be present in any situation for it to be functional. These are: (1) a standard or goal/objective, (2) work directed towards standard or goal/objective attainment, and (3) feedback about performance. Performance in this context merely refers to any discrepancy between what the work accomplished and what it did not, relative to standard/goal actually desired.

Within the context of an educational system and its governance and operational structure, curriculum quality control requires: (1) a written curriculum capable of being translated into the work of teachers in classrooms, (2) a taught curriculum shaped by the written curriculum, and (3) a tested curriculum consisting of the utilized assessment tools of pupil learning which are linked to both the taught and written curricula.

A curriculum audit utilizes a variety of data sources to determine if each of the three elements are in place and connected one to the other.

The audit process also inquires as to whether pupil learning has improved as the result of effective utilization of curricular quality control.

Data Sources

The major data sources of the audit were:

(1) *Documents*—These consist of board policies, memoranda, curriculum guides, checklists, guidebooks, study guides, test results, lesson plans and any other source of information which would reveal elements of the written, taught, and tested curricula and the linkages between these elements.

(2) *Interviews*—Interviews are conducted to shed light on the same elements and interrelationships about available documents which explain their presence, form, meaning, or absence. Interviews in Junction City were held with the superintendent, top-level and middle-level management, board members, building administrators, and officials of the Junction City Education Association.

(3) *Site Visitations*—Site visitations reveal the context in which curriculum is being implemented. Contextual references are important as they may reveal discrepancies in documents or unusual working conditions as in the case of the adequacy or inadequacy of facilities.

Standards for the Curriculum Audit

The auditor utilized five standards against which to compare, verify, and comment upon Junction City's existing curricular management practices. These standards have been extrapolated from an extensive review of management principles and practices and were utilized in the previous twelve audits in seven states conducted by the auditor. As a result, the standards do not reflect a utopian or ideal management system, but rather working characteristics that any complex organization should possess in being responsive and responsible to its clients.

A school district that is using its financial and human resources for the greatest benefit of its students is a district that is able to establish clear objectives, examine alternatives, select and implement alternatives, measure the results as they develop against established objectives, and adjust its efforts so that it achieves a greater share of those objectives over time.

The five standards employed in the curriculum audit in Junction City were:

(1) The school system is able to demonstrate its control of resources, programs, and personnel.

(2) The school system has established clear and valid objectives for students.

(3) The school system has documentation explaining how its programs have been developed, implemented, and conducted.

(4) The school system uses the results from district designed or adopted assessments to adjust, improve, or terminate ineffective practices or programs.

(5) The school system has been able to improve its productivity.

FINDINGS

Standard 1: The School District Is Able to Demonstrate Its Control of Resources, Programs, and Personnel

Quality control is the fundamental element of a well-managed educational program. It is one of the major premises of local educational control within any state's educational system.

The critical premise involved is that via the will of the electorate, a local school board establishes local priorities within state law and regulations. A school district's accountability to its community rests with the school board.

Through the construction of policy, a local school board provides the focus to direct the operations of a school system through its administrative staff. In this way the expression of popular will is assured and enables the district to be responsive to its clients and patrons. It also enables the system to meaningfully assess and utilize student learning as a critical factor in determining its success.

Although educational program control and accountability are often shared among different components of a school system, fundamental control of and responsibility for a district and its operations rest with the school board and top-level management staff.

What the Auditor Expected to Find in the Junction City Public Schools

A school system meeting Standard 1 would be able to demonstrate the existence of:

- a clear set of policies that reflect state requirements and program goals and the necessity to use achievement data to improve school system operations
- documentation of school board and central office planning for the attainment of such goals over time
- a direct, uninterrupted line of authority from school board/ superintendent and other central office officials to principals and classroom teachers
- teacher and administrator responsiveness to the school board policies, currently and over time

What the Auditor Found in the Junction City Public Schools

The auditor found an outdated set of board policies concerning curricular quality control, lack of leadership stability, no long-range plans for curriculum, outdated curriculum, and much confusion regarding roles and authority within the school system.

Finding 1.1: There Has Been No Leadership Stability nor Curriculum Consistency in the Junction City Public Schools

The current superintendent in Junction City had served only nine months at the time of the curriculum audit. In the last two years there have been four superintendents in Junction City, one having served less than six weeks.

The major cause of the shuffle of chief executive officers in Junction City is the tight linkage between the school district and office of the mayor of Junction City. Mayoral politics have had a direct impact on board appointments and top-level school administrators in the school system.

With the election of Mayor Fred Cain, the board-appointed majority abolished in one "pocket resolution" sixteen top administrative positions, including seven assistant superintendents, its business manager, and the school board attorney in July of 1981 (*Junction Journal*, 7/22/81). This move left the then superintendent of schools with only two assistants for the coming school year.

This act was widely believed to have been done to rid the school administration of one assistant superintendent whose husband was a prominent figure in the previous mayor's regime. After extensive legal battles and costs to the district, this assistant superintendent was reinstated in her post some four years later. She is now serving in the same job after being in the classroom during this time period. In the ensuing months the following occurred:

(1) The district nearly lost $864,000 in ESL (English as a Second Language Program) from the state for various snafus in the program and an impending deadline date for filing a state grant:

> The snarls in the program were attributed to the recent action by the school board in abolishing a number of assistant superintendent and administrative positions, leaving very few people to actually run the programs that are required (*Junction Journal*, 9/16/81, p. 2).

(2) Charges of bribery to city officials and political figures and possible solicitations of bribes by them to save impending cuts of the supervisor of social studies position in the district were lodged. City and board figures had to testify before a Hart

County grand jury on the matter. The result was that one city official was convicted and sent to jail. The second official was coming to trial during the audit (*Junction Journal*, 9/24/81, p. 1; 6/12/86, p. 38S).

(3) In October the Hart County prosecutor's office investigated allegations that a dean of students at Franklin High School may have paid political figures or city officials to get his job.

> A highly-placed source in the school administration said the resolutions to hire the two deans and several others and to transfer the personnel who formerly occupied these positions were given to the board by its president Quinby Morse (*Junction Journal*, 10/12/81, p. 1).

(4) The Junction City council indicated it would launch its own investigation of school board hiring and firing practices based on the fact that the council had received numerous complaints from teachers who were not rehired (*Junction Journal*, 10/6/81, p. 1).

When the superintendent of schools, Moss, resigned in March of 1984, an interim superintendent was appointed, an elementary principal with no prior top-level central office experience, Dr. Rico.

When Mayor Cain was defeated by the now Mayor Rose, the outgoing board intended to give the interim superintendent a two to three year contract, give Mayor Cain's chief of staff a job as assistant school business manager, and provide a contract to the then assistant superintendent for personnel (now demoted to high school principal) (*Junction Journal*, 6/24/85).

The incoming Mayor Rose arranged to have five of the nine school board members taken to Lake Front so they couldn't vote on the proposed promotions. "Did I know about it?" said Rose in an interview. "Yes, I knew about it. I approved it" (*Junction Journal*, 2/18/86).

Then the third superintendent (Taylor) was appointed in Junction City but resigned within six weeks of taking the job. One of the reasons indicated in the press at the time was that Mr. Taylor would not appoint the grievance chairperson of the teachers' association to the assistant superintendency for personnel. The teachers' association president had backed Mayor Rose in the election. When the grievance chairperson of the teachers' association was appointed as assistant superintendent, one board member called it publicly, "A political deal. That's why Taylor is no longer the superintendent" (*Junction Journal*, 8/17/85).

The fourth superintendent (Hill) then reinstated nine assistant superintendents. Of these appointments, only two had any prior experience in the role. The shuffle of superintendents and other top-level management staff has had a disastrous and demoralizing impact on middle management, both central and at the building level.

In audit interviews, supervisors recounted that some had a new boss (often the same person reinstated after being gone for a time) once a year. One had two bosses in fourteen months, another eight to nine bosses in eight years.

Principals conceded curriculum had been given a back seat to the constant personnel movement within the district and that because of "so many changes of leadership, we are working on the same things we did ten years ago." Said another, "If you looked for consistency you won't find it. We work in spite of the system." Another said, "Basically, we are into survival." Confessed another principal, "I'm never sure which order to follow." Finally, another conceded, "The insidious part of this is it's very demoralizing."

The lack of leadership in the area of curriculum has been apparent. Many of the curriculum guides are outdated. Some have been simply re-adopted without substantial change and represent materials developed many years ago (see Finding 2.2 under Standard 2). Said one veteran principal, "I don't think that half the teachers in Junction City have a complete set of curriculum guides."

When the school district failed to pass the state criterion for curriculum because of lack of board approval of curriculum and the incomplete revisions in social studies, math, home economics, health and physical education, gifted and talented, and art, the state commented:

- Inconsistency and lack of supervision exist.
- Some of these programs have been put on hold pending assignment of personnel.
- Key positions relevant to the curriculum development process for the district remain unfilled.

Following this failure to pass the state's curriculum criterion, the then district director of curriculum said to the press, "We're in worse shape than even the state said." In that same article it was noted, "Peters is still looking at all the curricula, which he says nobody has done on a system-wide basis since they originally were approved" (*Junction Journal*, 10/3/84).

That director of curriculum is no longer in the central office.

Finding 1.2: Board Policies on Curriculum are Outdated and Generally Ineffective

The auditor reviewed existing board policies as follows:

Policy	Subject	Adopted
6140	Curriculum	1976
0200	Philosophy—Goals	1976
0200(a)	Goals	1981
0300(a)	General Objectives	1976
0400	State Goals	1982
6156(a)	Lesson Plans	no date specified
3100	Budget	no date specified
6162.5	Research/Testing	1976
6141	Curriculum Design	no date specified
6141.1	Experimental/Innovative Programs	no date specified
6142.1	High School Graduation	1981
6143	Curriculum	no date specified
6144(a)	Controversial Issues	no date specified
6150	Instructional Arrangements	1977
6151	Class size	no date specified
6152	Grouping	no date specified
6153	Field Trips	1976
6154	Homework	no date specified
6161	Equipment, books, materials	no date specified
6163(a)	Media Center	no date specified
6164.5	Child Study Team	1978

In a memo to the board of education of 2/25/86, the director of research, planning, and evaluation noted:

> I have recently completed a review of current District Policies, paying special attention to areas in which the Board has not developed clear policy statements. The policies, last updated in 1976, may not express the Board's current intent in various matters, do not give the Superintendent sufficient guidelines to prepare necessary administrative regulations, and do not acknowledge relevant and recent law.
>
> Our lack of a viable policy manual may have damaging consequences for the District. Such consequences may include:
>
> - failure to comply with statute and administrative code
> - likelihood of litigation
> - failure to pass the monitoring process
> - damage to the District and Board's public image
> - lost opportunities to improve programs and facilities district wide

The board authorized the allocation of funds to accept a proposal from the State School Boards Association to update their policy manual.

Nowhere could the auditor find reference to board policy as a guideline or motivating force to update curriculum, bring improvements in the curriculum management system, utilize test results as feedback, or to bring order to the district's current curricular practices.

Finding 1.3: Confusion, Inconsistency, and Ineffectiveness Are the Hallmarks of the Administrative System in Junction City

The constant shuffling of personnel within the administrative ranks in Junction City has created gaps and distortions in normal organizational relationships and has led to overstaffing and breakdowns within the total administrative system.

The major responsibility for the confusion stems from the politicization of the entire school system and the use of its payroll to place political figures and to pay off debts for friends and relatives to city hall.

Normal board/superintendent relationships were seriously disturbed when in 1980 the board appointed two assistant superintendents over the objections of the superintendent of schools (*Junction Journal*, 6/17/80).

The superintendent appealed the board's action and won before an administrative law judge in 1981. This opinion was upheld by the state superintendent in 1981 (*Junction Journal*, 10/8/81).

The board has acted similarly in the past, prompting the current mayor, Rose, to say:

> The board of education is like a runaway wild horse that needs to be lassoed, tamed, and domesticated. I will be involved as much as it's needed to get it going on the right track again (*Junction Journal*, 2/18/83).

Currently, the superintendent of schools is having difficulty in running the school district without active board interference. The mayor has conceded publicly that, "Fairchild (the current board president) has sometimes 'usurped' Hill's (the current superintendent) authority" (*Junction Journal*, 2/18/86).

In addition, the active involvement of the mayor in school board appointments has distorted the personnel function in the school system. This is indicated in the following news story:

> In the interview, Rose said he essentially made some appointments to board jobs, approved others, and was kept aware of many other board actions. . . .

> A case in point is the appointment of Leonard Tate—the former elementary school gym teacher and teachers' union grievance chairman to the position of assistant superintendent for personnel, a position that sometimes involves conflict with the union.
>
> Tate is an associate and protege of teachers' union President Roy Stits, and both supported Rose in the election. Rose said Tate requested the assistant superintendent's job from him, "and I approved it."
>
> Rose also said he personally put assistant superintendent for special education, Gene Somers, into his job. Somers, a friend and neighbor of Rose, had been a guidance counselor and administrator in Clear Lake (*Junction Journal*, 2/18/86).

In August of 1985, Mayor Rose's sister was appointed by the board of education to the newly created position of Audio-Visual Liaison/Graphic Arts Specialist at a salary of $23,000 per year. The mayor's stepdaughter was appointed (from the position of clerk typist) to the newly created position of Special Education Awareness Specialist. The brother of the board secretary was also appointed to the position of assistant superintendent (*Junction Journal*, 8/24/85). The board secretary then was quoted in the press as saying, "The board is being overburdened with personnel indiscriminately placed throughout the system" (*Junction Journal*, 8/24/85).

The loss of a clean chain of command within the Junction City Public Schools was noted in an internal audit conducted in 1982. This document, based on a survey of school principals which were "found to be consistent across schools," made the following observations:

- "There is no single channel of communication—the superintendent is lost in a welter of lesser officials."
- "Lack of effective central office staff results in confusion at the school level. Proper line/staff organization does not seem to exist."
- "Better coordination and direction needed. Presently a vacuum appears to exist with too many 'doing their own thing.' "
- "It seems that central office is more and more staffed by people who have not taught nor administered in any of the schools and who do not know what is really going on at the school level."
- "Central office seems to always be in a state of flux. For every step forward, there seems to be two steps backward. Crisis management is still prevalent."
- "It seems as if the ordering procedure is in a continuous state of change and central office staff very often cannot answer questions about the ordering procedure."

In 1984, school officials commissioned an external consulting firm, Rogers, Crane, and Dick (RCD), to do a management study of selected central office units of the Junction City Public Schools.

The RCD report found the business and personnel units of the Junction City Public Schools had these problems:

- unclear lines of authority
- duplication of responsibility
- unclear and cumbersome procedures
- duplication of records
- insufficiency of automation of procedures
- excessive paperwork
- lack of top-level control over operations

The lack of top-level control over operations was conceded to exist in Superintendent Hill's memo to the board regarding his evaluation when he stated:

> For the past four years, principals, assistant principals, and many other school administrators have had free reign to leave their buildings whenever they felt the desire, hold area meetings and even spend a great deal of time in the Central Office conferring with their peers (15 assigned to Central Office). This freedom prevailed while students' test scores continued to plummet, lunch program records ignored, asbestos records were being misplaced, and teachers were going unsupervised. Some principals had forgotten that they were supposed to be the educational and instructional leaders of their building. Some principals had forgotten that they were <u>in charge</u> of their schools (March 31, 1986).

The RCD study also commented upon the politics in the system:

> School board members often recommend candidates for teaching, custodial, food services, business, and other school district positions. No written records are kept of these recommendations. . . . The Central Office is staffed with many individuals who have little prior experience in the functions they are expected to perform.
>
> The board has initiated many staff termination actions for political reasons. In 1981, for example, several teachers about to achieve tenure were dismissed by the board; the teachers successfully proved to a grand jury that their dismissals were politically motivated. The board has also frequently abolished positions in order to terminate specific individuals.

In the area of personnel management, the frequent violations of contracts and agreements by the board have prompted a long list of lawsuits. At the time of the RCD report in 1984:

> School district employees filed more than 107 personnel-related grievances. RCD reviewed 31 cases and found that they related to failures to post jobs, improper assignment of teachers, failure to pay employees at their proper step. Approximately 60 percent of these grievances were

decided in favor of the grievants. During the 1982–83 school year, judgments against the school district totalled $1,921,618.

The current superintendent of schools has even had to sue the board for back pay along with some other administrators. These administrators won an out-of-court settlement of $130,000, inclusive of legal fees (*Junction Journal*, 5/31/86).

The RCD study also examined district purchasing and found that "the purchasing process of the Junction City Public Schools is characterized by poor managerial controls, overspending, and long delays in the acquisition of goods and services."

Rogers, Crane, and Dick commented on controls and accounting:

> Examples of poor or ineffective controls in the process are numerous. . . . The board does not have adequate central purchasing and storage and has not established an effective inventory accounting and control system.

The RCD study found overstaffing, lack of controls, duplication of services, poor management, and lack of records. It also recommended the elimination of 33.5 positions in the functions it examined, which would save the schools $694,000 in operating costs.

The RCD study was never issued in final form. Only draft copies remain at the board offices. The board president at the time, the campaign manager of the Junction City mayor, Cain, objected to the passage: "Political interference exists at the board of education" (*Junction Journal*, 7/9/84).

In interviews of top-level management leaders in Junction City, no one could remember any changes which were ever made in the schools as a result of this $80,000.00 study.

When in 1985, the superintendent was forced to cut staff to lower expenditures in the 1985–86 budget, only <u>one position</u> was abolished of the 33.5 recommended by Rogers, Crane, and Dick. This position, in the payroll department, was one of six recommended to be abolished by RCD.

The auditor reviewed the personnel action of December 18, 1985, prompted by the budget's $4 million deficit problem for 1985–86. Of fifty-three people impacted by this action, only four were in the central office, and three of the four were in the area of curriculum/instruction. The bulk of the cuts occurred in the library/media program, substitute teacher pool, or elementary guidance.

The school district officials chose to ignore an $80,000 external, objective study of noninstructional services that would have saved over a half-million dollars and improved effective operations. Instead, library and guidance services were reduced for thousands of students in the schools.

The current organizational chart reveals many line/staff problems. First, four current assistant superintendents split responsibilities for some twenty supervisors. Some supervisors report to the assistant superintendent for funded programs. Others report to the assistant superintendent for support programs. Others report to the assistant superintendent for curriculum and instruction.

Effective coordination is difficult because so many roles and functions are split among those who would direct or service principals and others in the schools.

There is a mixture of line and staff responsibilities among many offices. For example, the evaluation of principals is shared among three assistant superintendents (as a line function), but these are not separated on the organizational chart as line functions. They are mixed with staff functions such as personnel, curriculum, and testing.

Some functions which normally might be sub-functions to major functions have become separated. For example, funded programs should provide support to the line function instead of being a separate function. The same for testing and other support programs. This mixture of line/staff separate functions leads to fragmentation, duplication, and overstaffing, a definite trend noted in the RCD study of non-instructional central office functions in Junction City.

For one memo to be sent to school principals by a supervisor, four approvals may be necessary from: the assistant superintendent for funded programs, the two assistant superintendents for the schools involved, and the assistant superintendent for curriculum.

The current superintendent has conceded that, "The many changes in personnel in the central office and in the schools have created a serious morale problem among the staff within this district. Staff members were confused because they were not able to clearly discern who was in charge" (superintendent's memo to board of 3/31/86).

The new organizational chart does not clarify because it is not conceptually accurate about basic line/staff functions. It does nothing to take care of the problem that the district has but one elementary supervisor for some 900+ elementary teachers. Other supervisors have impossibly long spans of control, some in the hundreds of teachers. The current administration's solution is to ask for more (and more are necessary) but not to consolidate positions where consolidation would result in improved services (*Junction Journal*, 5/2/86).

The number of political appointees in the Junction City Public Schools would be impossible to trace accurately. The apparent reluctance of school officials to implement an objective study calling for the elimination of 33.5 "unnecessary" positions may provide some clue as to the extent of that patronage. The lack of written records on employees compounds the problem.

One other external study was reviewed by the auditor. This study was completed in 1984 by two professors from State College of the Bureau of Pupil Personnel Services. The study noted:

- "Lack of implemented curriculum existed in most classes. Curricula in certain areas missing."
- "Lines of authority were indistinct."
- "Too many directors and chief administrators. It is incessantly troubled by unpredictable change."
- "The management apparatus of the BPPS is plagued by confused, even contradictory, supervisory/administrative responsibilities. Some positions are characterized by divided authority."
- "There is a lack of definitional clarity between major functional units."
- "An unpredictable promotion process is in effect, allegedly based largely upon political, non-merit factors."

The auditor finds great confusion regarding supervision, divided authority in the area of curriculum, lack of clarity about who is doing what, unnecessary paperwork procedures, and inadequate staffing in the curricular areas of the Junction City Public Schools.

Finding 1.4: Curriculum Monitoring in the Junction City Public Schools Has Been Weak and Largely Rested on Principal Expertise and Initiative

The Central Office in Junction City has not published any specific guidelines for use by principals as to how to monitor the curriculum in the schools. The board does have a standing policy (#6156a) that indicates what should be in lesson plans, but no principal interviewed cited this as a source which they used to monitor plans.

When interviewing principals in groups and in schools, a variety of approaches about lesson plans are used. Almost all principals review them periodically, but what they look for varies quite a bit. In one elementary school, the principal carefully checks the pacing and even provides a curriculum timetable. In another, the principal only looks for basic coverage, objectives, statement of methods, and some type of evaluation. The question of alignment to the testing program was not addressed.

One principal did use a general required time indicator for various subject matter developed by the district in September, 1983. However, the use of this sheet was nowhere near universal.

One of the major impediments to monitoring the curriculum is a provision in the current contract with the Junction City Teachers Association. Under Article 20 (Section 20-4.4 it states that, "All teachers who are not under tenure shall be required to submit lesson-plan books" (p. 22). Another section of this article (20-4.6) states: "All teachers shall plan their work and have such plans ready for presentation to authorized personnel at the time of supervisory visitations."

These two clauses limit the ability of principals to monitor weekly the lesson plans of tenured teachers in the Junction City Public Schools. Given a shortage of qualified central office supervisors, the only remaining authoritative person in the schools to perform curriculum monitoring is the school principal.

Principals are constrained in Junction City by:

(1) The lack of proper procedures to engage in curriculum monitoring
(2) The lack of updated and aligned curriculum in the school district
(3) The lack of appropriate testing and feedback data
(4) The inability to require lesson plans to be turned in each week for review of content, objectives, inclusion of state proficiencies, results, pacing, and other critical data to make adjustments in the curriculum on an ongoing basis
(5) Lack of knowledge and sufficient training to monitor the curriculum

Whatever curriculum management system has developed in Junction City has been created in the 1985–86 school year since all memoranda regarding alignment with tests and texts were dated in this time period. The district was requested to provide such documents for a five-year period. It is significant and in keeping with other observations made by many people that Junction City could not provide any such information prior to the 1985–86 school year.

There has been no system for curriculum monitoring at work in the Junction City Public Schools which was system-wide and systematically employed nor was one in place at the time of the audit.

Site visitations in Junction City also indicated that where good learning situations were found, it was largely peculiar to individual schools and principals or even to some programs within some schools. These have been the result of individual initiative and not system planning.

Finding 1.5: There Is No Long-Range Plan for Curriculum Improvement in the Junction City Public Schools

The auditor could find no long-range plan for the development of curriculum in the Junction City Public Schools. Such a plan would specify the following:

(1) An assessment of where curriculum was outdated, weak, or non-existent
(2) Sources of data to be used in updating or creating curriculum
(3) A priority list of areas requiring changes
(4) A recommended overall approach which had been related to budget development, i.e., a list of procedures/committees which would work on specific curricular priorities
(5) A plan for curriculum field testing and evaluation
(6) Plans for textbook adoption to become part of curriculum alignment and part of the development of a curriculum in the district
(7) A publication schedule which would enable the district to publish curricular materials in a timely fashion

The auditor did find evidence of several internal audits of the school district completed in the past. The first was completed in October of 1981 by the director of research. It examined many facets of curricular quality control (*Junction Journal*, 10/7/81, p. 10S).

The second audit was completed in October of 1982 and was reported to the board. Since that time the auditor could find no further efforts by the district to examine its own procedures on a systematic basis.

At the time of the curriculum audit (May–June 1986), the district's newly appointed assistant superintendent for curriculum had developed approaches to curriculum development which included alignment of the textbook adoption process to extant tests the district utilized or were imposed by the state. This was the first effort of its kind validated by the auditor in document review or interviews. No earlier efforts along this line were available to the auditor.

Junction City has not had a reading curriculum per se, nor has it used a unitary approach or basal reading program which would bring some central focus to the reading program. In the past, each school chose its own approach; consequently, there were enormous qualitative and quantitative differences within the district as to teaching reading successfully. At the time period of the audit, district curricular officials were in the process of considering a unified adoption and bringing increased focus and consistency to the reading program. None of these efforts, however, were occurring within a concrete long-range plan for the development, implementation, or evaluation of the total curriculum of the school system.

Standard 2: The School District Has Established Clear and Valid Objectives for Students

A school system meeting this audit standard has established a clear, valid, and measurable set of pupil standards for learning and has set them into a workable framework for their attainment.

Unless objectives are clear and measurable, there cannot be a cohesive effort to improve pupil achievement in any one dimension. The lack of clarity denies to a school district the capability of concentrating its resources through a focused approach to management. Instead, resources may be spread too thin and be ineffective in any direction. Objectives are, therefore, essential to attaining local quality control via the school board.

What the Auditor Expected to Find in the Junction City Public Schools

The auditor expected to find in the Junction City Public Schools a clearly established, district-wide set of goals and objectives adopted by the Junction City School Board. Such objectives would set the framework for the operation of the district, its sense of priorities, and explicit direction for the superintendent and the professional staff.

What the Auditor Found in Junction City

The auditor found in Junction City an outdated set of board policies on curriculum that were not utilized by the professional staff in curriculum development nor referred to by field staff in its implementation. Although curriculum had begun to be adopted by the board in order to comply with state mandates within the past several years, this consisted of readopting old curriculum in many cases with new cover sheets and the name of the new superintendent. A reading of the curriculum documents produced the past names of superintendents. The curricular materials spanned a decade or more.

There is little order to curricular objectives in Junction City. This reflects many years of neglect with feeble efforts to improve it, constantly shifting personnel, and functioning under a variety of superintendents or other top-level officers. Since state review in 1984, in which Junction City failed the criterion relating to the development of a comprehensive curriculum and instructional program, there has been very little substantial improvement made. A systematic coherent attack on the deficits identified by the state have not been addressed until very recently and these are not comprehensive.

Finding 2.1: There Is No Set of Concrete and Measurable Objectives That Serve as a Focal Point for Curriculum Development in Junction City

The auditor could find no tangible evidence of a mission statement for the Junction City Public Schools which could be and must be translated into a set of organizational expectations. Existing board policies are inadequate in that they set no specific time horizons for specific work to be accomplished in the area of curriculum.

The superintendent or top-level management staff also have not established any substitute for such a mission statement. Such a statement would specify where the Junction City Public Schools as an entity should be at a specific point in the future. The mission statement would be capable of being translated into specific performance measures that would be observable.

At the present time there are no mission statements that would serve to explain to the public the tangible needs in the area of curriculum which would serve as the focus for:

(1) Summer curriculum development work
(2) Textbook adoption and curriculum alignment
(3) Test alignment
(4) Staff development

The auditor could not even find any specific references as to when the Junction City Public Schools would seek to attain state certification. There were no plans nor timetables. The district appears to be so caught up in management by crises and political hassles that there is little time to devote to setting the curriculum house in order.

Finding 2.2: Curriculum Guides in Junction City Are Not Effective Management Tools

The auditor examined sixty curriculum guides. Each was rated according to the rating sheet reproduced at the end of this chapter. The ratings of the guides appear in Exhibit 9. Most were mediocre and quite old. Many had new covers added, the name of the new superintendent, and some very minor revisions. They were simply readopted

Exhibit 9

Ranking of Curriculum Guides on Five Criteria of Sound Management Principles in the Junction City Public Schools

Guide Title	Date Published	Grade Levels	Rating on Each Criterion 1	2	3	4	5	Total Points
1. Industrial Arts Technology	1974—Readoption 1985	9	3	3	1	2	3	12
2. ESL	Unknown	Not Stated	2	1	1	3	3	10
3. Social Studies	1967	K–8	1	1	2	2	3	9
4. For. Language	Readoption 1985	7–12	2	1	1	2	3	9
5. Vocal Music	Readoption 1985	9–12	2	1	1	2	2	8
6. Keyboarding	1986	9–11	2	1	1	2	2	8
7. Instrumental Music	Readoption 1986	9–11	2	1	1	2	2	8
8. Vocal Music	1986	K–3	2	1	1	1	3	8
9. Life Science	1982	7	1	0	1	3	3	8
10. Math	1972	K–8	2	0	1	2	3	8
11. Home Economics	1980—Readoption 1985	5–8	2	0	1	2	3	8
12. Adv. English	Readoption 1985	11–12	2	2	0	2	2	8
13. Phys. Ed.	Readoption 1985	9–12	2	2	0	2	2	8
14. Ethnic Stds.	1977	9–12	2	1	0	2	2	7
15. New Studies	1979	9–12	2	1	0	2	2	7
16. Regional Stds.	1978	9–12	2	1	0	2	2	7
17. Anatomy/Physiology	Readoption 1985	11–12	2	1	1	3	0	7
18. Phys. Science	1983	8	1	0	0	3	3	7
19. Language Arts	1967—Readoption 1985	K–8	2	0	1	2	2	7
20. Family Life	1983	K–8	1	0	0	3	3	7
21. Data Processing	1982—Readoption 1985	12	2	2	1	2	0	7
22. Business Law	1981—Readoption 1985	11–12	2	1	0	2	2	7
23. Bookkeeping	1981—Readoption 1985	10–12	2	1	1	2	1	7
24. Latin I	Readoption 1985	9–12	2	1	0	2	2	7
25. Cabinet Making	1972—Readoption 1985	9–12	2	1	1	2	1	7
26. Science	Readoption 1985	9–12	1	1	1	2	1	6
27. Bio-Medical	1983—Readoption 1985	12	2	1	1	2	0	6
28. Honors Chem.	Readoption 1985	10–12	2	1	1	2	0	6
29. English #A-C	Readoption 1985	11	2	1	0	2	1	6

(continued)

intact as they were written over ten years ago, most in a board motion of January 16, 1985, to comply with state regulations. The data indicate there has not been substantial curriculum development in the Junction City Public Schools in over a decade. Only one curriculum guide of the sixty-one examined attained a rating over ten points. Guides were almost uniformly weak in the area of evaluation and congruence to the testing program. They were also silent on entry-level skills re-

Exhibit 9 (continued)

Guide Title	Date Published	Grade Levels	Rating on Each Criterion 1	2	3	4	5	Total Points
30. English 4A-C	Readoption 1985	12	2	1	0	2	1	6
31. English 1A	No date	9	2	1	0	2	1	6
32. Citizenship	1970	9–12	2	1	0	2	1	6
33. Honors Bio.	1985	9–12	2	1	0	3	0	6
34. A. P. Biology	Jan. 1986	11–12	2	0	1	2	1	6
35. Phys. Ed.	1983	1–8	1	1	1	0	2	6
36. Math	1982—Readoption 1985	9–12	2	1	1	2	0	6
37. Psychology	no date	11–12	2	1	0	2	1	6
38. Communication Arts	1983—Readoption 1985	11–12	2	1	0	2	1	6
39. Psych. Intro.	no date	9–10	2	1	0	2	0	5
40. French	Readoption 1985	9–12	2	1	0	0	2	5
41. Library Media	Readoption 1985	K–8	1	1	0	1	2	5
42. Art	Readoption 1985	K–8	1	0	1	0	3	5
43. Contemporary Law	1982	11–12	2	1	0	2	0	5
44. Afro-American History	no date	9–12	2	1	0	2	0	5
45. Economics	1981—Readoption 1985	9–12	2	1	0	2	0	5
46. Puerto Rican Culture	no date	9–12	2	1	0	2	0	5
47. Spanish I	1985	9–12	2	1	0	0	2	5
48. Italian	1985	9–12	2	1	0	0	2	5
49. Afro-American Literature	1982—Readoption 1985	10–12	2	1	0	1	1	5
50. App. Chemistry	1986	11–12	2	1	0	2	0	5
51. World Literature	1980—Readoption 1985	11–12	2	1	0	2	0	5
52. Business Math	1981—Readoption	9–12	2	1	0	0	1	4
53. Power Mechanics	1978—Readoption 1985	Not Stated	2	0	0	2	0	4
54. Poetry Guide	1960	K–8	1	0	0	2	1	4
55. U.S. History II	1974	10–12	2	1	0	1	0	4
56. U.S. History I	1974	10–12	2	1	0	1	0	4
57. Industrial Arts	1979	5–8	1	0	1	0	1	3
58. Futurism	1982	Not Stated	1	0	0	1	0	2
59. Sociology	1973	11–12	1	0	0	1	0	2
60. Science	1984	K–6	1	0	1	0	0	2

quired to complete successfully any curricular area. Most often all that was cited was the fact that a prior course at the secondary level was necessary to enroll in the one being examined.

At the time of the audit, the assistant superintendent for curriculum had developed a newer prototype curriculum guide which if implemented may prove to be more functional. It could not be rated because it is still in the developmental stages.

Taken as a body of work, the extant curriculum guides in Junction City are inadequate to direct unambiguously the work of instruction in the Junction City Public Schools and to use teacher and student time effectively to be able to meet the standards necessary to obtain state certification.

Standard 3: The School District Has Documentation Explaining How Its Programs Have Been Developed, Implemented, and Conducted

A school district meeting this audit standard is able to show how its programs have been created as the result of a systematic identification of deficiencies in the achievement and growth of its students compared to measurable standards of learning.

In addition, a system meeting this standard is able to demonstrate that, as a whole, it is more effective than the sum total of its parts, i.e., any arbitrary combination of programs or schools do not equate to the larger school district entity.

The purpose of having a school district is to obtain the educational and economic benefits of a coordinated program for students, both to enhance learning by maximizing pupil interest and by utilizing economies of scale where applicable.

What the Auditor Expected to Find in Junction City

The auditor expected to find a highly developed, articulated, and coordinated curriculum in the district that was effectively monitored by the administrative and teaching staffs. Such curriculum would be:

- centrally defined and adopted by the board of education
- clearly explained to members of the instructional staff and building level administrators
- accompanied by specific training programs to enhance implementation
- monitored by central office staff and building principals

What the Auditor Found in Junction City

The auditor found outdated and largely nonfunctional board policies and ineffective and outdated curriculum guides. While the latter had been adopted by the board in 1985, they were, as a whole, rehashed documents that had been given a superficial face-lift.

The auditor found little evidence of a centrally coordinated curricu lum or any meaningful central curriculum activity except in the most recent months of the 1985–86 school year.

Early in the 1980s the district had made some attempt to create a system of internal monitoring which resulted in the publication of two candid reports. This effort has largely been washed away in the subsequent shifts of personnel at the top level and in the general "management by crises" atmosphere which has prevailed in the Junction City Public Schools.

Finding 3.1: The District Has No Plan to Respond to the Findings of Previous State Reviews

In June of 1984, the superintendent and the board secretary were informed that the Junction City Public Schools had not passed state review. The school system did not meet thirty-two criteria. The auditor did review a progress report of 9/18/85 from the superintendent to the county superintendent. However, in June of 1986, some two years later almost to the month, no plan was in existence which could be reviewed by the auditor and which would direct the school system to become responsive to these documented shortcomings. The lack of responsiveness may be partially due to one or more of these conditions in the Junction City Public Schools:

- changes in the superintendency which resulted in four chief executive officers in the same two-year time frame. This meant that the current superintendent was in office only nine months at the time of the curriculum audit.
- sweeping changes in other top level administrative officers coming and going as a result of mayoral changes in city hall. These have been cited earlier in the audit. Some of these were directly responsible for curriculum in the schools.
- swiftly moving crises such as investigations of various programs, audits of accounts and finances, deficits, litigation and lawsuits over hiring or firing, fines for asbestos, etc.
- the lack of any system by which the school district could be responsive to these problems

The current superintendent stated in his evaluative report to the board in March of 1986:

> This evaluative report is a profile of the programs and activities the superintendent has had to organize, administrate, and implement. The impediments brought on from years of confusion, neglect, and lack of leadership have been identified and a great effort is being exerted toward ameliorating the district's weaknesses.

Finding 3.2: The Same Condition Identified in Previous Audits/ Studies Currently Exist in the Junction City Public Schools

The auditor found many of the same conditions in the Junction City Public Schools as identified from previous internal reviews, external consultant studies, and other external sources still prevalent in the school district. These were as follows:

Finding	Source Document	Curriculum Auditor Concurrence
1. Board policies outdated	Policy Development Memo to Board of 2/25/85	• Document review
2. Lack of effective line/staff relationships at central	• Internal audit 10/4/82 • Memo by superintendent to board of 6/3/83 • Consultant Study of 6/21/84 • Study of 12/10/84 • Superintendent Evaluation Memo 3/31/86	• Review of current table or organization • Interview data
3. Outdated curriculum	• State document 6/15/84 • *Junction Journal* coverage of Curriculum Director Smith 10/31/84 • Statement by former board trustee *Junction Journal* 5/30/86	• Interview data • Document review
4. Understaffing in curriculum	• Statement by superintendent *Junction Journal* 6/2/86 • Internal audit of 10/4/82 • Study of 10/4/82	• Interview data • Document review
5. Evidence of influence of city hall on personnel ap-	• *Junction Journal* articles: "Sixteen Top Heads Roll" 7/22/81; "Jury Prob-	• Interview data

Finding	Source Document	Curriculum Auditor Concurrence
pointments in school district	ing Bribery to Keep City School Job" 9/24/81; "Cain Allies Getting School Gravy Jobs" 6/24/85; "To the Victor Belong the Spoils" 8/24/85; "School and Politics Perfect Together" 10/24/85; "Hill Ousts School Trustee" 10/25/85; "Loser on Rose Ticket, Gets Board Job" 1/16/86	
6. Chronic lateness in meeting deadlines for budgeting and funding	• *Junction Journal* articles: "Second Language Program in Chaos 9/16/81; "Budget Not Ready, Cap Inaction Blames" 3/18/82 • RCD Report 6/21/84 • *Junction Journal* "School Board is Tardy in Presenting Budget" 4/1/86; "Junction City Only One to Miss School Deadline" 4/3/86; "School May Lose $1.2 Million in Federal Funds If They Fail to Complete Remedial Plan" 4/28/86	• Interview data

From a variety of sources both internal and external and over an extended period of time, the Junction City Public Schools have demonstrated a pattern of an inability to capitalize upon economies of scale and a chronic inability to implement effective, workable educational programs.

Standard 4: The School District Uses the Results from District Designed and/or Adopted Assessments to Adjust, Improve, or Terminate Ineffective Practices or Programs

A school district meeting this audit standard of the process has designed a comprehensive system of testing and measurement tools that indicate how well students are learning designated priority objectives. Such a system will provide:

- a timely and relevant base upon which to analyze important trends in the instructional program
- a vehicle to examine how well programs are actually producing desired learner results
- a way to provide feedback to the teaching staff regarding how classroom instruction can become more effective
- a data base to compare the strengths and weaknesses of various programs and program alternatives
- a data base to terminate ineffective educational programs

A school district meeting this assessment standard has a full range of formal and informal assessment tools that provide relevant program information to decision making in the classroom, building (principals and/or grade/department chairpersons), district, and board levels. The school system has taken steps to ensure that the full range of arts programs are systematically and periodically assessed. Assessment data have been matched to program objectives and are utilized in decision making.

What the Auditor Expected to Find in the Junction City Public Schools

The auditor expected to find a comprehensive assessment program of all aspects of the curriculum, K–12, which was:

- keyed to a set of goals/objectives adopted by the school board
- utilized extensively at the building level to engage in program review and modification
- demonstrating consistent improvement over a longitudinal time period
- used to terminate ineffective educational programs

- used as a base to establish needed programs
- publicly reported to the board of education and the community on a regular basis

What the Auditor Found in the Junction City Public Schools

The auditor found a school district which had not been able to attain the state standards in pupil achievement and which had not used test feedback to improve student achievement systematically at the school level. School principals exhibited a large variance in their ability to use such data intelligently. District level curriculum supervisors also showed a very large difference in how they perceived and used such data to engage in program interventions to upgrade pupil performance.

The auditor could not find any use of pupil data or programmatic state standards in pupil achievement and, thus, no test feedback to improve student achievement systematically at the school level.

The auditor could not find any use of pupil data or programmatic feedback that had been structured by the administrative staff to improve pupil achievement nor any such data used in the termination of ineffective programs.

Finding 4.1: Test Data in Junction City Shows Mixed Results

A review of the district's test performance on the SBS (State Basic Skill) tests did demonstrate a steady improvement in the secondary grades, according to a report developed by the district test coordinator in June of 1985. That report indicated the following:

Percentage of Junction City Ninth Grade Students Passing the SBS 1978–1985 Reading/Math

Area	Year	Number of Pupils Tested	Percentage Passing (75% required)
Reading	1985	1866	62.0%
	1984	1851	58.8%
	1983	1927	55.2%
	1982	2104	43.3%
	1981	2196	46.8%
	1980	2260	42.4%
	1979	2260	43.0%
	1978	2165	42.0%

Area	Year	Number of Pupils Tested	Percentage Passing (75% required)
Math	1985	1891	72.5%
	1984	1839	73.6%
	1983	1891	65.8%
	1982	2078	60.6%
	1981	2153	56.3%
	1980	2265	46.4%
	1979	2260	44.0%
	1978	2143	42.0%

The eleventh grade SBS test data were also gathered for the same time period. They present a slightly different picture. The data show that test performance declined in reading after peaking in the 1982 school year. In math the same trend showed as for the ninth grade, i.e., the percentage passing had declined since the 1984 school year.

Percentage of Junction City Eleventh Graders Passing the SBS 1978–1985 in Reading/Math

Area	Year	Number of Pupils Tested	Percentage Passing
Reading	1985	259	54.8%
	1984	449	63.9%
	1983	no data	no data
	1982	1370	72.3%
	1981	1458	70.4%
	1980	1434	62.9%
	1979	1387	57.0%
	1978	1436	55.0%
Math	1985	193	63.2%
	1984	325	69.5%
	1983	no data	no data
	1982	1342	65.1%
	1981	1456	62.5%
	1980	1430	62.5%
	1979	1979	48.0%
	1978	1412	55.0%

The auditor reviewed a memorandum of 8/21/84 from the director of testing and research and the district testing coordinator to the superintendent which pertained to state achievement test results for grades 2–12 for the time period 1978–1984. The results were reported in percentile scores. That study noted the following longitudinal trends:

> In math, grade levels 2–8 are performing above the national norm, while grade levels 9–12 are performing below the national norm.
>
> In reading, grades 7 and 8 are at or above the national norm, while grades 2–6 remain in the mid 40th percentile range. Grades 9–12 show lower performance levels, with scores in the mid 30th percentile range.
>
> For both reading and math, a significant drop-off occurs for our students after grade 8. In grade 8, grade level performance is noted in both reading and math. In grade 9, a significant decline occurs in both areas, and performance remains below grade level through grade 12.

The most recent results reviewed by the auditor were contained in a memo to Superintendent Taylor of 8/5/85 which showed that (as reported in normal curve equivalents):

- Second grade students were below the national norm (fifty) in both reading and math.
- Third grade students were below the national norm in reading but exceeded the national norm in math by five NCEs.
- Fourth grade students were below the national norm in reading but above the national norm in math by three NCEs.
- Fifth grade students were below the national norm in reading but above the national norm in math by five NCEs.
- Sixth grade students were below the national norm in reading but above the national norm in math by six NCEs.
- Seventh grade students were above the national norm in reading by one NCE and above the national norm in math by nine NCEs.
- Eighth grade students were above the national norm in reading and at the national norm in math.
- Tenth grade students were below the national norm in reading and at the national norm in math.
- Eleventh grade students were below the national norm in reading but at the national norm in math.
- Twelfth grade students were below the national norm in reading but at the national norm in math.

Finding 4.2: Use of Test Data as Program Feedback Is Limited in Junction City

All documents reviewed by the curriculum auditor in Junction City were reports of test results to the superintendent.

With only one exception, all of the memoranda are to the superintendent or assistant superintendent/director of research from the director of testing. The auditor reviewed no memoranda to school principals about testing or how to use or apply test results in formulating program interventions to improve pupil performance. A perusal of memoranda written to principals or teachers from supervisors indicated that only a few dealt with any use of test feedback to improve pupil performance. None were specific in outlining strategies for instructional change.

The only document that could be considered sensitive to feedback and which was reviewed by the auditor was a memorandum of 1/21/86 by the director of research, planning, and evaluation to the deputy superintendent, assistant superintendents, principals, and supervisors regarding district objectives.

This annual document of some six pages indicated twenty-three activities for the 1985–86 school year. They dealt with examples of feedback and curricular alterations/upgrading. One activity for the 1984–85 school year which was revised in October of 1985 dealt with reviewing results of the SBS through alternative high school programs. The staff accountable was designated as school principals and guidance staff. No other reference to this activity was reviewed by the auditor.

Standard 5: The School System Has Improved Productivity

Productivity refers to the relationship between input and output. A school district meeting this standard of the assessment is able to demonstrate consistent pupil outcomes, even in the face of declining resources. Improved productivity results when a school system is able to create a more consistent level of congruence between the major variables involved in achieving better results and in controlling costs.

What the Auditor Expected to Find in the Junction City Public Schools

While the achievement of improved productivity in a school system is a complex process, caused in part by the lack of a tight organizational structure, a school district meeting this standard demonstrates:

- planned and actual congruence between curriculum, objectives, results, and financial costs
- specific means that have been selected or modified and implemented to attain better results in the schools over a specified time period
- a planned series of interventions that have raised pupil performance levels over time and maintained those levels within the same parameters as in the past

Any evaluation of productivity is a relative one and must include the fundamental recognition that neither the board of education, superintendent, principal, or professional staff completely control all of the important variables that will result in improved pupil performance. Nonetheless, there are substantial elements within their combined command that do account for improved pupil learning. These can be subjected to productivity assessment.

What the Auditor Found in the Junction City Public Schools

The auditor found a school system reeling from one financial crisis to another, perennially late in its budget submissions, and with a history of financial mismanagement and questionable financial practices. Poor personnel practices have resulted in the loss of millions from the school system that might have otherwise been allocated to the improvement of curriculum and instruction.

The auditor found no tangible way to trace dollars to programs nor any method used by the school system officials to do the same.

Finding 5.1: Budgeting in Junction City Follows a Traditional Format

The auditor requested and was provided several Junction City budgets. These documents indicated the following:

Year	Total Current Expenses
1982–83	$116,836,956.75 (stated as actual)
1983–84	$123,804,457 (stated as actual)
1984–85	$125,993,590 (projected)
1985–86	$140,000.00 (proposed)
1986–87	$158,500,000 (a budget at about ceiling) discussed by the superintendent in memo of 3/31/86

The percentage of support for four years is as follows:

Year	Total Local Support	Total State Support	Total Federal Support
	24%	64%[2]	9%
1982–83	$28,336,155.18	$75,274,737.88	$10,802,854.96
	27%	64%	9%
1983–84[3]	$33,643,495	$80,963,790	$11,701,681
	23%	70%	7%
1984–85	$29,326,491 (projected)	$88,343,667 (projected)	$ 8,323,432 (projected)
	25%	67%	7%
1985–86	$35,316,783 (projected)	$94,280,125 (projected)	$10,403,092 (projected)

The figures indicate that the state share of funding in Junction City is considerably over 50 percent.

Finding 5.2: Budgeting Practices in Junction City Reflect Questionable Procedures

It seems clear from the data reviewed by the auditor that there was a budget surplus in Junction City in the 1983–84 school year. The surplus was used to keep local taxes low. This piece of information surfaced in the 1985 budget crises in an interchange at a board meeting reported in the *Junction Journal* of 10/30/85:

> When Jones wanted to know when the Board first became aware that there was a problem, Hill [currently superintendent—insert the auditor's] rose from his chair, tossed his glasses on the table, and snapped, "You were told two years ago when you took $5 million out of our surplus. . . . That's why we're in this fix."
>
> Under the former city administration of Mayor Cain, the Board of School Estimate chopped several million dollars from local school budgets. Jones served on the city council in the Cain era.

A review of revenue for the 1983–84 school year showed, in fact, that revenue exceeded total expenditures by $2,404,509.

[2]May not include state building aid in the amount of $2,917,363.

[3]Does not equal stated total budget expenditures. Exceeds amount by $2,404,509. Percentages calculated on total support (revenue) stated as actual.

Another practice which surfaced has been the use of the ceiling waiver. State law provides for a waiver to be granted by the state superintendent under two conditions:

(1) Increased enrollment
(2) A reallocation of resources or any other action taken within the permissible level of spending which would be insufficient to provide a thorough and efficient education

A local board of education must state the reasons why a waiver is necessary in resolution form and it must be presented to the county superintendent.

A charge by the current mayor, Rose, on past practices in this regard surfaced in the *Junction Journal* of 5/29/86:

> Rose also said the Board of Education under Cain repeatedly requested waivers and then adopted budgets below the ceiling.

A check with Junction City school business officials, indeed, indicated that this practice had been carried on in the past. A *Junction Journal* article of 8/24/85 indicated that the budget deficit was caused by former Mayor Cain's shifting money from the board's salary accounts to the surplus. While the salary funds were being depleted, there were still employees being added to the staff. The superintendent reported to the board in March of 1986 that one new school in the district was in operation without a planned budget, funded from one that was already deficit. In a letter to State Senator Pete Flan of Junction City, of December 20, 1985, Superintendent Hill admitted that part of the financial straits of the schools was caused by: (1) forty special education teachers not budgeted, (2) twenty special education teacher aides not budgeted, (3) out-of-district tuition not budgeted, and (4) state retirement cost increases not budgeted. This amount came to $2,115,000.

Finding 5.3: Poor Financial Management Practices Result in Loss of Productivity and School Funds

Shoddy management practices in the school's financial area have been noted for years as a problem in the Junction City Public Schools.

For example, in the school district's own internal audit conducted of school principals, these comments in 1982 were deemed typical and representative across the schools:

> While funding may or may not be adequate, the distribution and governing of funds assigned is almost to the point of disaster. Purchase orders may be lost routinely, funds taken from one school to another without

notification to original school getting to be common practice. Whole system needs complete overhaul.

Procedures have been established, but are not always followed. Many purchase orders are lost or misplaced by business office personnel, and the schools are penalized by loss of finances and lack of materials.

Late budget adoption hampers effective school administration. Meetings devoted to review fiscal policy and concerns are needed.

Two years later, the district authorized an $80,000 management study of its business operations. The RCD study noted:

The excessive delays and resultant overspending inherent in the Junction City Public Schools purchasing process reflect the labor-intensiveness and confusion characteristic of the process as it is now constituted. At least 23 different stations typically handle a purchase order from the time it is issued by a school or administrative department to the time that a check is finally generated and forwarded to the vendor.

Many purchase orders get lost in processing; consequently, the schools are not being adequately stocked.

The RCD study also noted the existence of poor reporting practices:

According to recent auditor's reports, as well as information gathered in the study, the Board performs certain mandatory accounting functions poorly, if at all. For example, the Board does not have a consistent internal audit system; it maintains neither a general ledger nor a formal accounting manual; it also does not reconcile its current fund bank accounts monthly.

In the payroll department, the RCD consultants noted that this area was overstaffed and that proper accounting and control of the payroll was lacking.

Not one school administrator, from the superintendent to principals, could recall any recommendation of the RCD study being implemented. Most indicated that this expensive study never saw the light of day.

Finding 5.4: Poor Personnel Management Practices Have Cost the District Millions

A review of *Junction Journal* articles reveals an extensive pattern of litigation and lawsuits in the time period 1980–1986. Because of the blatant disregard by the board and its officers for affirmative action, due process, and good personnel management practices, matters of loss of jobs and subsequent reinstatement, back pay, legal costs, and the like have had to be spent on what might have otherwise been materials, supplies, textbooks, and improved supervisorial services.

In 1984, the RCD study estimated that in the 1982–83 school year, judgments against the school district totalled $1,921,618. The auditor was not able to find any document that would have added up total costs. The current superintendent (Hill) conceded in his evaluation report to the board of March 31, 1986, that he had met with the board attorney and personnel administrator "to discuss the inordinate and escalating number of teacher and administrative grievances that have cost the board and this district many millions of dollars over the last five (5) years."

The superintendent himself was also a litigant in suing the board over a matter of back pay.

Finding 5.5: Overstaffing in Many Departments Costs the School District Efficiency

In the wake of understaffed supervisorial personnel in the district where one general elementary supervisor has a span of control over 900 teachers and many secondary supervisors are responsible for hundreds of teachers in the district's upper elementary grades and high schools, blatant overstaffing exists in the central office.

For example, the RCD study of 1984 noted:

> The noninstructional Central Office units are generally overstaffed, inefficient, and ineffective in providing support for the educational units of the Junction City Public Schools.
>
> . . . extensive Board involvement in personnel actions involving specific individuals has led to an excessive reliance on political influence in determining which candidate is hired or promoted. Instead of the superintendent hiring or promoting individuals on the basis of qualifications, some vacancies in Junction City Public Schools have been filled on the recommendation of Board members, with political acceptability, and not aptitude, the determining criterion. In short, the Board's involvement in selecting specific individuals for hiring or promotion may deprive the school system of the most qualified candidate.

That this condition still prevails in Junction City was the substance of an earlier reported "flap" between the superintendent and a now resigned board member, Raven. According to the *Junction Journal*:

> Raven, accompanied by a reporter and a photographer, went to the supply area to check on a new employee, Guy Train, hired Wednesday night as senior storekeeper at $17,735. Train told a visitor, "Rose put me in here." Asked who he meant, Train replied: "Rose. I grew up with him."

A review of *Junction Journal* articles indicates the following about the current persons functioning as assistant superintendents in the Junction City Public Schools:

Person	Title	Information from the *Junction Journal*
Gene Somers	Asst. Supt. Pupil Personnel Services	Friend and neighbor of Mayor Rose and appointed by him (*Junction Journal*, 2/18/86).
Leonard Tate	Asst. Supt. Personnel	Requested job from Rose. Rose approved. Former grievance chairperson of J.C.E.A.
Henry Stevens	Asst. Supt. Funded Programs	Appointed by board over objections of superintendent in 1980, lost job following Cain election. Recently reinstated by board as assistant superintendent (*Junction Journal*, 6/17/80 and 7/22/81).
Fred More	Asst. Supt. for Testing	Brother of board secretary. Promoted following Rose win for mayor (*Junction Journal*, 8/24/85).
Sharon Bliss	Asst. Supt. for Ele. Education	Lost job when Mayor Cain was elected. Her husband was sheriff and backer of Cain opponent. Reinstated after lengthy court battle (*Junction Journal*, 3/22/85).

Other officers in the Junction City Public Schools trace their positions to the influence of Mayor Rose. For example, Donald Hern, a defeated city council member who ran with Rose was made business administrator. Rose conceded, "He asked for assistant superintendent of languages" (*Junction Journal*, 2/18/86).

Robert Luke who was Mayor Rose's running mate but was defeated, was promoted. "Luke was promoted from a teaching job to teacher in charge of home instruction, an administrative job with a $7,000 raise and a board car" (*Junction Journal*, 2/18/86).

The current table of organization in which these administrative officers function was reviewed previously in the audit. Discrepancies in logical relationships abound.

Finding 5.6: Questionable Business Practices by the District and City Hall Impede Productivity and Lower District Performance

A review of external sources, most importantly the *Junction Journal* and *Globe*, reveal a long history of questionable business activities in the schools that involve the mayor and city hall. These are reviewed below for purposes of illustration.

Date	Newspaper	Article Contents
9/15/82	*Junction Journal*	Bus company sues the board
10/14/82	*Junction Journal*	Grand jury probed school bus contracts
10/26/82	*Junction Journal*	School board deal with successor to a bid rigger
10/28/82	*Junction Journal*	A judge throws out bus contracts
12/8/82	*Globe*	Prosecutor investigated board's insurance contract for prescriptions and dental care
12/27/82	*Junction Journal*	School board investigated its vendors
2/10/83	*Junction Journal*	Audit shows a mess in schools' business
2/25/83	*Globe*	A former board member backs accountant's charge that Mayor Cain tried to meddle in problem
3/29/83	*Junction Journal*	Mayor Cain's relatives have insurance contracts
9/2/83	*Junction Journal*	Mayor Cain's backers were awarded school bus contracts
10/14/83	*Junction Journal*	Superintendent Moss warns that the business staff was in chaos
1/1/85	*Junction Journal*	County superintendent probing hiring practices of the board
3/11/85	*Junction Journal*	Discussion of Mayor Cain's role in creating school budget
5/28/85	*Junction Journal*	Budget officer says that the school board will go broke over salaries
6/25/85	*Junction Journal*	Mayor Cain's allies getting school gravy jobs
8/17/85	*Junction Journal*	School board in uproar. Top personnel job to union activist
8/27/85	*Junction Journal*	Article about school board jobs for Mayor Rose's relatives
10/24/85	*Junction Journal*	Councilman Flise appointed as acting principal of Academic

Date	Newspaper	Article Contents
		High School (now standing trial for soliciting a bribe from social studies supervisor). Relatives of councilmen get jobs
2/12/86	*Junction Journal*	Mayor Rose feels the schools need a controller
2/18/86	*Junction Journal*	Who runs the schools? Article on mayoral influence on personnel promotions and jobs
2/27/86	*Junction Journal*	School employees and bus driver are objects of separate prosecutor's probe

The articles reveal a pattern of entanglement among the mayor, city hall, and the city public schools involving personnel decisions, promotions, demotions, and hiring and firing. They reveal business dealings with friends, associates, and political backers in which school contracts are involved.

On June 3, 1983, the then superintendent (Moss) wrote the board a memorandum in which he enclosed the results of the schools' failure to pass state monitoring:

> Deficiencies noted in fiscal, educational, and operational areas are examples of the absolute regression which has occurred as a result of a severely limited administrative organization and infractions of proper Board policy, regulation, and procedure.
>
> Since October of 1981, and consistently since then, I have called the Board's attention to the problems of administrative organization personnel. Again, I must notify the Board of the problems which we face and will continue to face unless action is taken; again, I must submit to you my recommendations for an effective school system. These recommendations are simple but fundamental.
>
> (1) Sufficient top administrative staff must be returned. The span of control assigned to the Superintendent, the Deputy, and the 1st Assistant is totally unmanageable for a district this size.
>
> (2) Board policy must be followed. Only then will personnel procedures, chain of command, staff accountability, and district operations become effective and responsive to the needs of our schools.

A review of the occurrences in the Junction City Public Schools since Dr. Moss' memos reveal that little has changed in three years since he wrote it. The district is still not certified. Lawsuits continue. Patronage persists.

Finding 5.7: Facility Needs Place a Large Burden on District Resources

Fifty percent of the school facilities in Junction City are fifty years old or older. The last bond issue approved by the Board of School Estimate was in 1985 for an amount of $6,122,800. The auditor visited some of the school sites. These ranged from classic high schools built at the turn of the century to more modern facilities.

CONCLUSIONS

The auditor has derived the following conclusions based on his findings in conducting the curriculum audit of the Junction City Public Schools.

The Junction City Public Schools Are Without a Focused Mission and Without a Sound Managerial Structure to Become Operationally Effective or Efficient

The curriculum auditor would independently concur with the conclusions reached by the county superintendent and which were sent in June of 1983 to the Junction City Public Schools:

> The district has not developed a comprehensive and coordinated plan of operation with the result that fiscal, educational, and operational support services are not integrated for effective and efficient control.
>
> The school district auditor's recommendations for the school year 1980–81 were acted upon by the Board of Education. The corrective action ordered by the Board was not accomplished, virtually every auditor's recommendation was repeated in 1981–82; and the auditors added many more procedural deficiencies for which the Board has taken no action. The impact of the current fiscal procedures has resulted in untimely and inaccurate reporting during the year.

The problems in Junction City are chronic. The school system is adrift. It is barely managing to survive. The managerial structure in the school system is a product of politics and patronage, lawsuits, and seniority. The structure has very little rationality to it, line/staff relationships are jumbled, and functions which are sub-functions of other functions become separate functions when they are attached to patronage promotions or demotions.

The school system has no concrete goals to attain, no long-range plan or mission by which to focus its resources, and no long-range plan for the development of curriculum. The system has at times sought external reviews, but the results of these reviews are then ignored because of political considerations. There has been no sustained or serious attempt to reorganize itself, streamline its operations, or improve its efficiency for at least a decade. There is continuing evidence of overstaffing in some of its departments and serious deficiencies in its financial operations, most notably in developing an accurate and timely budget.

The Junction City Public Schools' Leadership Is Characterized by Extreme Instability and Susceptibility to Political Influence

There have been four superintendents in Junction City in a two-year period. Dozens of other top and middle level leadership appointments have been made. There has been a steady shuffle of administrative officers up and down, to and from central to building level, each following the changes in mayoral fortunes at city hall.

The board of education has never sought to perform a national search for a superintendent, preferring short-term (usually one-year) appointments for the chief executive officer. This places the superintendent in a position of maximum vulnerability and deprives the system of a dispassionate view by the CEO on sensitive issues. The current superintendent was functioning on a one-year contract and was not sure it would be renewed at the time of the audit.

This extreme instability of top-level management for a $140 million dollar business has a chilling effect on the rest of the administrative cadre. No one is quite sure what tomorrow will bring. When bold leadership is required, boldness is discouraged. When commitment is demanded, only token responses are generated because no one knows who will be gone or in the driver's seat next.

The impact on the field is decidedly negative. Principals exhibited a great deal of negativism and cynicism about central office operations. They recounted at length the breakdowns, mismanagement, confusion, and frustrations caused by the politicization of the administrative ranks.

The Junction City Public Schools Remain Firmly in the Orbit of City Hall and the Mayor

Even a casual observer comes to the conclusion that little happens in the schools without the blessing of the mayor, no matter what party or person is in office. According to newspaper accounts, the mayor has personally appointed top-level administrative officers. These have been friends and political supporters. Relatives have been given promotions and raises in the schools.

There has been a positive linkage between those occupying seats on city council and professional appointments in the school system. The linkage between city hall and the Junction City Public Schools is not an accident. The ties are profound, deep, and long-standing.

The financial ills of the school system are directly linked to decisions made at city hall. By exercising veto power over the appointed board of education, the board of estimate can nix taxes, chop budgets, and stymie program development. It can and has postponed needed repairs and renovations to aging school facilities.

The Board of Education Has Not Exercised Required Responsibility for Curriculum Policy Development in Junction City

Board policy was outdated. The board is in a constant shift of personnel because of mayoral appointments. It is routine for board members to run ads in the press blasting officials and political appointments. There is a vacuum of leadership by the board in curricular affairs in Junction City.

There Is Not in Place in Junction City a Curriculum Management System to Improve Pupil Achievement on a Sustained Basis

There is no curriculum management system in place in the Junction City Public Schools that can utilize pupil test feedback to make intelligent interventions at the school level, refocus resources, and upgrade programs on a planned and systematic basis.

Curriculum affairs in Junction City have been subject to politicization in the form of personnel shifts. Supervisors have impossibly extended spans of control and little authority to bring about curriculum change. It is only within the last several months that the system has taken steps to perform curriculum alignment and improve its textbook adoption process accordingly. Current curriculum officials concede that almost nothing was done in the past in the curricular affairs of the schools.

While many of the existing curriculum guides were adopted in 1985, some simply represent a cosmetic face-lift of work done a decade or more ago. Curriculum in Junction City is in a serious state of disrepair.

Student Achievement in Junction City Is Below State Requirements and Barely at the National Average in Some Areas

Pupil achievement in Junction City is marginal. While showing some improvement over the years, it has recently begun to decline.

The auditor could find no evidence of any systematic work with school principals to use test data positively to formulate instructional interventions. Indeed, this facet of central leadership was almost totally absent in Junction City. There have been no regulations developed for test data utilization, lesson plan development, or monitoring to include test weaknesses. Tenured teachers do not even have to develop weekly lesson plans because of strictures within the existing teachers' association contract.

Given No Change in Existing Operations and Procedures, It Is Highly Unlikely Junction City Can Improve Pupil Achievement or Move Towards a More Effective or Efficient System of Operations

Money is not the answer for the Junction City Public Schools. What more money would do is accentuate the problems and trends now so apparent to the auditor.

Money will not solve the problems of overstaffing, the use of the school system's payroll for political friends and relatives, the serious deficiencies in budgetary calculations and oversights, the manipulation of surplus funds to keep local taxes down, the chronic inability of the system to meet basic deadlines that constantly jeopardizes its funds for programs, and egregious personnel mismanagement which has led to millions lost in litigation, fines, and back pay.

The simple fact is that the most basic type of required record keeping has not been performed in the Junction City Public Schools. It is this lack of sound procedures that led to charges by the Federal Lunch Program and, thus, a fine of over one million dollars against the school system and its officials.

The Junction City Public Schools had no system in place at the time of the audit to do anything but react from crisis to crisis, and the prospects of improvement are very dim. The short-term future of the district is not in the least assured. The long-term picture is even bleaker.

RECOMMENDATIONS

Based upon the findings and conclusions, the auditor has formulated the following recommendations to improve the curriculum management system and operations in the Junction City Public Schools.

Recommendation 1: De-Politicize the Junction City Public Schools

The politics of patronage dominate the Junction City Public Schools. The long arm of the mayor's office, no matter who the incumbent has been in recent years, has robbed the system of leadership stability; dissipated its energies and resources in lawsuits and conflicts, personnel demotions, and constantly changing priorities and crises; deprived it of cohesion and managerial focus; and drained its budgetary reserves to the point of deficit balances.

Qualified personnel see political cronies, friends, and relatives put on the payroll and given promotions although they have less experience or no experience in the positions in which they find themselves. It is hard to create a sense of urgency regarding finances or anything else when these flagrant abuses of privilege and influence are so patently obvious. As one current board member commented, "I don't know if this is a fiscal crisis or a political crisis" (*Junction Journal*, 8/24/85).

For any kind of professional stability to occur in Junction City, the system must be rid of mayoral patronage and interference with personnel appointments, budgetary schemes, and political ploys.

De-politicizing the Junction City Public Schools will require external intervention. This step is recommended because the problems run too deep, past excesses are still prevalent, patterns still persist, and the effects of patronage are too pervasive to expect significant internal change. What must occur are the following:

(1) Cleansing of the system of patronage appointments in the past six to seven years
(2) An intensive organizational study indicating where there is overstaffing and understaffing at <u>both</u> professional and nonprofessional levels
(3) Changes in the organizational offices which streamline existing overstaffed areas and add staff where required (the latter, particularly, being a need with instructional supervision) and which clarify line/staff responsibilities
(4) Extrication of all financial relationships from city hall and the establishment of independent financial authority for an independently elected board of education
(5) The immediate placing of the school district into <u>receivership</u>, suspending the current board of education from its responsibilities or creating an independently appointed oversight board which has veto power over all actions of the board and city hall—the panel to be appointed by the state superintendent of education
(6) The creation of independent "merit boards" which screen the credentials of all candidates for every position, professional or nonprofessional, and select only those that are qualified for

recommendations to appointment—all such positions to be fully advertised with open competition internally and externally

(7) The creation of automated business systems which more clearly pinpoint budgetary priorities, identify board actions, and indicate the responsibility for budgetary recommendations and expenditures

(8) The adoption of board policies which prohibit nepotism in any form and which make it impossible for relatives to be employed in the school system

(9) The requirement that all board members take an oath of ethics to refrain from administrative meddling or using their influence in personnel selections or any other financial matter after the district has been returned to the status of a fully functioning system, independent of receivership

Recommendation 2: Develop and Install a Comprehensive Curriculum Management System

Junction City must install a complete curriculum management system. Such a system is characterized by the following components:

- an effective framework of board policies that establish, maintain, and monitor the system once it is in place. Such policies include requirements for quality control and curriculum alignment which includes textbook adoption.
- the development of specific plans for curriculum development based on a comprehensive needs assessment and which set forth in a three- to five-year cycle of activities a plan for the upgrading of curriculum in the schools
- the development of new curriculum guides which are smaller and more functional, which show the required alignment to tests and textbooks and which are interfaced and part of weekly lesson plan development
- the establishment of a comprehensive monitoring system for the curriculum in a framework that principals and supervisors implement and use to improve pupil achievement
- the establishment of a data base of tests and other assessment tools which are directly aligned to state and local priorities and which are used by teachers and principals on a day-to-day basis to make decisions about the allocation of time, grouping of children, use of materials, and selection of curriculum
- the creation of a reporting system, internally and externally, by which curricular priorities are related to budgetary costs, and these in turn from the data for board decision making about

curriculum in the school district. This will move the system from a budget-driven curriculum to a curriculum-driven budget.

- the creation of an accurate and timely budget which is structured in such a way to identify program costs and serve as a functional guide to allocate the district's resources
- the linkage of a staff development to all of the above so that principals, supervisors, teachers, and other support personnel have the required skills to implement the upgraded curriculum

Recommendation 3: Increase Supervisorial Staffing in the Central Office

Current staffing in the Junction City Public Schools in the area of curriculum and instruction is inadequate. There should be at least one supervisor for every 75–100 teachers at the elementary level. The current superintendent (Hill) has asked for at least five elementary school supervisors (*Junction Journal*, 6/2/86). However, even this number is not adequate for the job that is faced in Junction City.

This adjustment ought to be made in keeping with reductions elsewhere in the central office, particularly in overstaffed noninstructional support services and departments highlighted in the RCD study. If all of the RCD staff reductions were made as recommended, the district should be able to afford approximately twenty supervisors at $30,000 per supervisor.

It is imperative to note that the current climate in the state with state-wide tests and accountability require a centralized response and not a decentralized response. School districts in the state are required to develop and maintain greater curriculum consistency than before across all schools. Since principals are only responsible for their schools, they cannot be the agents to insure system consistency outside of their respective buildings. The burden falls on the central office and central leadership.

Currently, there are too many assistant superintendents. A study should be undertaken to realign and streamline this level of operations of the school system to improve coordination and utilization of skilled people.

SUMMARY

Every day approximately 30,000 pupils in the Junction City Public Schools labor to climb the ladder of the "good life" to success. The schools represent a tangible form of a larger social promise.

Unfortunately, the Junction City Public Schools will not be able to deliver. Wracked by the politics of city hall that have robbed the schools of an ability to focus their human resources, stripped them of stability, bled away their finances in mismanagement, legal hassles, and outright patronage, the students will be denied a full chance to enter the American mainstream as functional and educated adults.

The tragedy of the Junction City Public Schools is not so much the corruption and mismanagement that has characterized its operation to date, but the fact that too many educators and politicians treat the situation as "business as usual." As one wise and long-time Junction City educator remarked, "You gotta understand the politics of Hart County. After you get past mid-state, everything else is Alabama."

There are good people laboring hard in Junction City on behalf of quality education for the children the public schools serve, but they are buried in the quicksand of politics and patronage, chronic mismanagement, and inefficiency. They will never be able to make a difference until the schools are accountable as a separate and functional enterprise, and free from mayoral meddling.

CHECKPOINTS

Questions about the Junction City Curriculum Audit

Question 1: *Why so many quotations and references to newspapers in this audit?*

Answer: Because of the turmoil at the central office, few people had a clear picture of what had happened. Those that did, evaded my questions or did not answer them. To fill in the "gaps," I spent a worthwhile day at the Junction City Public Library with some helpful library clerks.

Question 2: *How typical is Junction City? Isn't it an anachronism?*

Answer: There are plenty of school districts just like it in the U.S., some larger, some smaller. Most state education department officials know who they are.

Question 3: *How is it that the people allow such corruption to continue even in the wake of the newspaper articles?*

Answer: Machine politics have for so long dominated the life of Junction City, independents have no chance and no say.

Question 4: *On what criteria were the curriculum guides in Junction City ranked?*

Answer: On the criteria shown on the rating sheet which follows.

Curriculum Guide Rating Sheet

Criteria	3	2	1	0	Points
Clarity and Validity of Objectives 0. No goals/objectives present 1. Vague delineation of goals/objectives 2. States tasks to be performed or skills to be learned 3. What, when, how actual standard of performance and amount of time to be spent learning each objective	___	___	___	___	______
Congruity of the Curriculum to the Testing/ Evaluation Program 0. No evaluation approach stated 1. Some approach of evaluation stated 2. Skill, knowledge, concepts which will be assessed 3. Objective is keyed to performance evaluation and district tests in use	___	___	___	___	______
Delineation by Grade of the Essential Skills, Knowledges, and Attitudes 0. No mention of required skills 1. Prior general experience needed 2. Prior general experience needed in grade level 3. Specific documented prerequisite <u>or</u> description of discrete skills required	___	___	___	___	______
Delineation of the Major Instructional Tools 0. No mention of textbook in instructional tools 1. Must name the textbook used 2. Basic text and supplementary materials to be used 3. "Match" between the textbook and curriculum objective by objective	___	___	___	___	______
Clear Linkages for Classroom Utilization 0. No linkage cited for classroom utilization 1. Overall, vague statement on linkage for approaching subject 2. General suggestions on approach 3. Specific examples on how to approach key concepts/skills in the classroom	___	___	___	___	______
					______ Total

/ VII / *Case Study 3: The Locust Hill Schools*

THE LOCUST HILL Schools is a pseudonym for an actual school district in which the author–auditor completed a curriculum audit in 1987. All photographs have been removed to prevent identification of the district. Specific references which would reveal the name of the district or any person in the district have been changed or deleted. Otherwise, the curriculum audit which appears in this chapter was the same as reported to the superintendent and the board of education.

BACKGROUND, PURPOSE, AND SCOPE OF WORK

This document constitutes the final report of a curriculum audit in the Locust Hill Schools.

Background

The Locust Hill Schools are located in an historic area of the U.S. It is suburban. The district traces its roots to the late 1680s when the area was settled by early colonists.

The school district is approximately twenty-five square miles and includes two municipalities. The estimated combined population of the school district is 65,000 residents.

The public schools in Locust Hill have a long history of development. The Locust Hill Academy opened in 1813 to provide free education and instruction to the poor. That building still houses educational functions.

The pupil population of the school district has been declining. In 1968 the K–12 pupil population was 10,149. For the 1987–88 school year, it is projected to be approximately 5,449. Five schools have been closed, beginning in the 1978–79 school year. Discussions have been held about the possibility of closing Dinsworth High School in the future if enrollment decline continues.

At the time of the audit, the district continued to function with five elementary schools (K–5), two middle schools (6–8), and two high schools (9–12). Half the schools in the district have been recognized as models of educational excellence by the United States Department of Education in national competition. They proudly fly a flag of excellence.

The schools in the district are rich in support staff; the elementary sites have the services of guidance counselors, psychologists, speech therapists, and other specialized personnel. The director of personnel estimates that there will be approximately 420 full-time equivalent teachers in the system for the 1987–88 school year, a pupil–teacher ratio of thirteen to one.

The last school year in Locust Hill was marred by a teacher strike. While only brief in duration, it was followed by a "work to rule" action and several atrabilious exchanges in the local press between teachers, citizens, administrators, and students that carried over to the current school year. While the strike aftermath appeared to be subsiding, concern was expressed by all parties about the future of negotiations in 1988.

Purpose

The purpose of a curriculum audit was to determine the extent to which officials and professional staff had developed and implemented a sound, valid, and operational system of curriculum management.

Such a system would enable the school system to make maximum utilization of its human and financial resources to educate the children it was built to serve. If such a curriculum management system were operational, it would ensure patrons, citizens, and taxpayers that their financial support had been optimized under the conditions in which they functioned.

Scope of Work

A curriculum audit is an objective, independent examination of data pertaining to educational program practices that will indicate the extent to which a school system can meet its objectives (whether the latter are internally developed or externally imposed). An audit examines management practice and system results, however defined. As such it is a type of quality assurance.

Exhibit 10
A Schematic View of Curricular Quality Control

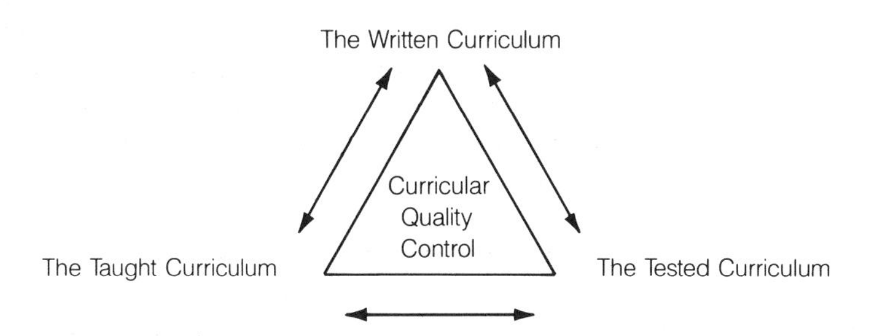

METHODOLOGY

The Model for the Audit

The model for a curriculum audit is shown in Exhibit 10. The model has been published extensively in the professional literature, most recently in the AASA book *Skills for Successful School Leaders* (1985, p. 90).

AASA has been using this publication in conjunction with the University of Texas at Austin to establish a national superintendent's assessment center.

Generic quality control assumes that at least three elements must be present in any situation for it to be functional. These are: (1) a standard, goal/objective (a work plan); (2) work directed by the participants towards attaining the standard or goal/objective (the work itself); and (3) feedback about the level of attainment (work measurement).

Within the context of an educational system and its governance and operational structure, curricular quality control requires: (1) a written curriculum capable of being translated accurately into the work of teachers in classrooms, (2) a taught curriculum guided by a written curriculum, and (3) a tested curriculum consisting of the utilized assessment tools of pupil learning (both system and teacher derived) which are linked to both the taught and written curricula.

Standards for the Auditor

While a curriculum audit is not a financial audit, it is governed by some of the same principles. These are as follows.

THE PRINCIPLE OF OBJECTIVITY

This standard means that curricular events are observable and verifiable, if not through observation, then by a review of the products of those events, i.e., documents. Such documents are considered representations of transactions. The standard also means that any two auditors using the same standards and data base would reach approximately the same conclusions.

THE PRINCIPLE OF INDEPENDENCE

This standard means that the auditor stands apart from the entity being audited and is not influenced in rendering an opinion about the curriculum by having any pecuniary relationship to anyone in the entity, nor will his/her judgments about the curriculum be influenced by having any preconsidered interest in those judgments.

THE PRINCIPLE OF CONSISTENCY

This standard means that the same procedures, techniques, and methods are followed with each audit so that the results are comparable over time.

THE PRINCIPLE OF MATERIALITY

This standard gives to the auditor broad authority to select that which is important from that which is not. It provides the auditor with discretionary authority to explore and investigate all aspects of the operation being examined.

THE PRINCIPLE OF FULL DISCLOSURE

This standard means that the auditor must reveal all information that is important to the users of the audit. The users of the audit are the board of school directors, the administration and teaching staffs, students, parents, and taxpayers.

Data Sources

A curriculum audit utilizes a variety of data sources to determine if each of the three elements are in place and connected one to the other.

The audit process also inquires as to whether pupil learning has improved as the result of effective utilization of curricular quality control.

The major sources of the data for the audit in Locust Hill were:

(1) *Documents*—These consisted of board policies, curriculum guides, plans, reports, test results, memoranda, contracts, informative bulletins developed for a variety of professional/lay audiences, and any other source of information which would reveal the elements of the written, taught, and tested curricula and the context in which the curriculum was defined, delivered, monitored, and utilized as a source of feedback to improve pupil learning.

(2) *Interviews*—Interviews were conducted to determine the relationships of the same elements within the quality control paradigm previously explicated in Exhibit 10, as well as to illustrate the context in which those elements did or did not function.

Interviews were held with school board directors, top-level central administrative officers, school principals, two groups of parents (Interschool Council representatives and Home and School presidents), students (Student Advisory Council), and officers of the Locust Hill Education Association.

(3) *School Site Visitations*—School site visitations reveal the physical context in which curriculum is being implemented. Such references are important as they may indicate document discrepancies or other unusual working conditions. The auditor visited Caliope, Delta, Pioneer, Fernwood, Seashore, River Bend, and Ajax elementary schools. Visitations were also made at Langdon and Irish Glen Middle Schools and Dinsworth and Locust Hill High Schools.

Standards for the Curriculum Audit

The auditor utilized five standards against which to compare, verify, and comment upon the existing curricular management practices in the Locust Hill School District. These standards have been extrapolated from an extensive review of management principles and practices and have been applied in previous audits by the auditor in eight states.

As a result, the standards do not reflect a utopian management ideal, but rather the working characteristics that any complex organization should possess in being responsive and responsible to its patrons.

A school district that is using its financial and human resources for the greatest benefit of its students is an entity that is able to establish clear objectives/priorities, examine alternatives, select and implement alternatives, measure results as they develop against established objectives, and adjust its efforts so that it achieves a greater share of those objectives over time.

The five standards employed in the curriculum audit were:

(1) The school system is able to demonstrate its control of resources, programs, and personnel.
(2) The school system has established clear and valid objectives for students.
(3) The school system has documentation explaining how its programs have been developed, implemented, and conducted.
(4) The school system uses the results from district designed or adopted assessments to adjust, improve, or terminate ineffective practices or programs.
(5) The school system has been able to improve its productivity.

FINDINGS

Standard 1: The School District Is Able to Demonstrate Its Control of Resources, Programs, and Personnel

Quality control is the fundamental concept behind a well-managed educational program. It is one of the major premises of local educational control within any state's educational system.

The critical premise involved is that via the will of the electorate, a local school board of directors establishes curricular priorities within state law, regulations, and good practice. A school district's final accountability to its community rests with the school board.

Through the construction of policy, a local school board provides the necessary focus to direct, via its administrative staff, the operations of a school system. In this way the expression of popular will is assured and enables the district to be responsive to its clients and patrons. It also enables the system to assess and utilize student learning meaningfully as a critical factor in determining its success.

Although educational program control (direction) and accountability are often shared among different components of a school system, fundamental control rests with the school board and top-level central administrative staff.

What the Auditor Expected to Find in the Locust Hill School District

A school system meeting Standard 1 would be able to demonstrate the existence of:

- a clear set of policies that reflect state requirements and program goals and the necessity to use achievement data to improve school system operations
- documentation regarding a clear division of authority and responsibility between the school board and the top-level management staff as it pertains to policy and operations
- documentation of sound planning by the board of school directors and top-level management staff
- a direct, uninterrupted line of authority from the school board/ superintendent to principals, teacher leadership roles, and teachers
- administrative and staff responsiveness to school board policies currently and over time

What the Auditor Found in the Locust Hill School District

The auditor found outdated and ineffective policies concerning curriculum design and delivery in the district. There were no explicit objectives for the district by which programs could be configured nor assessed specifically.

The auditor found evidence of a long-range plan, but this document did not establish any *strategic vision* for the district in the future.

The auditor found confusion regarding central level responsibilities for curriculum coordination and articulation within the district and no formal or consistent channel for teacher involvement in curriculum development, particularly in being responsive to teacher initiatives in curriculum.

The auditor found no formal system of curriculum monitoring in place in the schools and no clear understanding among principals as to how to monitor the curriculum.

The auditor found evidence of a lack of curriculum coordination within schools from students and parents and across schools from site visitations and interviews of principals.

The auditor found evidence of the lack of curriculum comparability to national standards from students and parents and evidence of inconsistency in evaluating pupil progress within the district.

Finding 1.1: Board Policies in Locust Hill Are Outdated and Ineffective in Establishing Curricular Quality Control

The auditor examined the following policies of the Locust Hill Board of Education.

Policy Number	Content	Date Adopted
101	Philosophy of Education	September, 1971
105	Curriculum Development	May, 1973
107	Adoption of Courses of Study	May, 1974
108	Adoption of Textbooks	July 15, 1985
131	Controversial and Value Issues	September, 1970
603	Annual Budget	No date

The policies fail to establish a framework for sound curriculum planning, configuration of courses, the problem of increasing time demands of new subjects, and the dilemma of "watering down" the curriculum. The policies did not indicate or mention any sense of curricular priorities as far as content was concerned, any procedure for evaluating the curriculum, or the establishment of any criteria by which curriculum was to be developed in the district.

Board policy #101, The "Philosophy," is a nonoperational statement. It was not cited once by anyone as a valuable reference in curriculum decision making.

Board policy #105 is mislabeled. It is not a policy about curriculum development at all. Rather, it is concerned with the adoption of program materials and publications.

Board policy #107 deals with the methods of adoption of courses of study. The criteria are student demand and budgetary support. The fact that many board members expressed doubt as to the prevailing wisdom of carrying some of the courses in the current curriculum should be ample evidence that their own criteria for course adoption are not adequate. Student interest is not the only focus to use in determining what should be included in a curriculum.

Board policy #108 indicates that the board must adopt all textbooks. It indicates that the superintendent should recommend all books but that the board can override the recommendation on a two-thirds vote. The policy indicates that the standards for adoption should be:

- suitability to pupil educational level
- relationship to curriculum
- freedom from bias
- cost
- appearance and durability

This policy does not contain any criteria by which suitability to educational level should be determined, fails to specify what relationship the proposed text should have to the curriculum (the issue of alignment), and does not mention any requirement for consistency of adoptions within specific curricular areas.

Some board members interviewed were critical of the plethora of textbooks used within common curricular areas. Yet the fact that the board's own policy is not specific means such practices will be continued until there is a change.

Board policy #131 is concerned with the matter of injecting into the curriculum controversial issues, "as long as carefully presented." What the latter means is undefined. No mention is made of "balance" in presenting such controversial topics. The way the current policy reads, a teacher could present a detailed lecture on Marxism, without feeling any compunction to present any critique or alternative to Marxist interpretation, and still be in compliance with the policy.

Board policy #603 regarding budget fails to connect the budgetary process to curricular or program priorities.

Board members interviewed by the auditor expressed concerns about the following:

- lack of control of the curriculum; too many doing their own thing
- lack of curricular continuity and consistency vertically and laterally in the curriculum
- lack of consistency in evaluating student progress
- lack of overall coherency in the curriculum
- lack of any definition of a core curriculum
- lack of emphasis on certain skills such as thinking and writing
- lack of a way to assess the adequacy of the curriculum or its comparability

Yet the board had not one policy which required curriculum to be developed in the district that was internally consistent or demonstrated coherency around a core, emphasized writing or thinking, or was comparable to like districts or to national indices or standards. By and large, the board gets what it demands via its policies. The board's failure to specify such demands within policy represents an error of omission. If the board has not required coherency in curriculum development, who is to blame if coherency is absent? These considerations have little to do with expertise within a curricular area. They have everything to do with the overall function of a curriculum within the school district. The board is responsible and accountable for much of the lack of existing coherency in curriculum across the district.

Locust Hill has had a long history of indigenous curriculum development. In the past thirty years, school buildings operated almost completely autonomously from one another. Curriculum development began and ended at the building level, with no thought as to the impact of changes in the career of the students when they left the school and went on to the next level.

While this practice has ended with the current administration, those efforts have not been totally successful. Disparities, inequities, and gaps still remain. Vestiges of courses popular in the 1970s still dot the curriculum. Whether they fit into a coherent curricular scope and sequence remains unknown. Action to create coherency begins with the board. If it desires coherency, it must require it within policy and insist that it be monitored.

Finding 1.2: The Long-Range Planning Development Fails to Establish a Strategic Vision for the School District

The auditor examined two long-range plans developed by the district. The first was an overall long-range plan approved by the board in June of 1984. It extended the district's activities into the 1988–89 school year. An update was filed with the county superintendent's office in September of 1986.

A second long-range plan for special education adopted by the board in 1979 and revised in 1987 was reviewed by the auditor.

The problem with the long-range plan for the district is that it fails to establish or define a *strategic vision* for the school district. A *strategic vision* refers to an organization's self-definition of its desired future. It is concerned with the creation of a framework which will guide current choices towards future desired ends based on a vision.

The creation of the vision and the framework and processes by which day-to-day choices will be made is an exercise in *metamanagement*. It is not concerned directly with the act of managing or administering. Rather, it is concerned with the processes by which such acts occur.

The act of routine administration is *micromanagement*. It is concerned with the technical details, the "how to's," and yearly objectives.

The so-called long-range plans are simply projections of annual plans. They are centered around issues of micromanagement. The chief problem of using micromanagement concepts is that one simply becomes a captive of current trends and conditions. The plans "verify" the status quo and lock the organization into a sterile and unproductive set of responses.

Take, for example, the matter of how to respond to declining enrollment. Here the district has closed schools and reconfigured curricula and programs. Some courses have been eliminated. In some respects courses eliminated simply followed apparent trends of student enrollment. That has left students without some offerings such as advanced physics or some upper-level offerings in a foreign language.

If the district had a vision of its curriculum within policy or a larger plan, those courses might have been retained and others eliminated instead.

Take another example. One scenario regarding declining enrollment has been to consider closing Dinsworth High School, that is, accepting the inevitability of current trends and past practices. In an effort to facilitate a smaller enrollment, the two high schools have developed schedule compatibility, with Dinsworth dropping its rotating scheduling practices. This would enable the two schools to become more tightly coupled. Course sequences have been made more consistent so as not to cause unnecessary gaps if all students had to transfer to one high school.

Suppose the district did not accept existing conditions. Suppose a strategic vision of the future boldly rejected this possibility and struck out in a very different direction. Suppose that Dinsworth High School were closed but reopened as a model of a selective prep school centered on a classical curriculum including Latin and Greek. Such a classical core curriculum housed in a superbly modern and beautiful plant, with small class sizes and rigorous academics, would be appealing to the 40 percent of the students who now live in the school district but attend a private or parochial school.

If the school district could attract back to Dinsworth half of the students who now attend private or parochial schools, the enrollment at Dinsworth would be in excess of 1,000 students. That would mean not laying off staff but perhaps even hiring staff. It would mean relieving some political pressure on the board to keep taxes down from those families who do not now attend a public school. Such "classical" schools now exist as magnet schools in many urban school systems, so the tradition is not new for public school districts.

This alternative scenario comes into being not as a result of simply extending current conditions and current modes of response into the future, but projecting current problems into the future as well. It is based on the idea of a strategic plan as opposed to a long-range plan. The public schools in Locust Hill are in a competitive situation for their clientele. This scenario would entail an aggressive departure from a largely reactionary and defensive posture to one set of conditions. Micromanagement techniques will not lead to bold thinking. The process must begin with metamanagement processes. These are strategic instead of tactical.

Finding 1.3: There Is Confusion Regarding Central Level Responsibilities in Curriculum Management

The auditor found ambiguity and some confusion among administrators about what central level responsibilities were needed in Locust Hill. In the past the district had supported an assistant superintendent who headed curriculum. When this person left the position to return to the classroom, he was not replaced. A director of curriculum was retained who had reported to the assistant superintendent. This person has had the full range of K–12 responsibilities. The position has functioned as a staff or support service role.

Currently, the district is advertising for an elementary curriculum person. The plan is that this role would be line as opposed to staff. This would reduce the span of control of the superintendent who now supervises all of the principals.

There is no doubt that this role is necessary. However, the role of a line officer in the area of curriculum is that of a generalist. There are generalist tasks required in Locust Hill. For example, a determination of the propriety of the total curriculum configuration is very much the province of a generalist.

However, another unmet need in Locust Hill exists for curriculum content specialists. This need was evidenced by numerous comments from principals who reported in interviews that they wanted help in making decisions about mathematics, reading, English, foreign languages, and the like.

The principal is also a curriculum generalist. Principals are also limited in that they have organizational authority and responsibility for only a building. Any role that would extend beyond the building requires a different base of expertise, particularly if the need is in relationship to questions of content selection or specialized methodological considerations.

The curriculum central level roles have been understaffed in Locust Hill. Improved content area coordination and articulation will not come from curriculum generalists. That can only come from curriculum specialists.

The problem is accentuated at the building level where there is a lack of department chairpersons. One high school utilizes chairpersons; the other does not. This responsibility is assumed by assistant principals. The assistant principals have multiple content area responsibilities. This practice presents a very uneven picture as far as resolving content specialization problems may be concerned. Curricular questions which involve advanced forms of specialized content knowledge cannot be resolved by curriculum generalists.

The existing solution to the problem of expertise has been, for some principals, to solicit external help. One elementary principal noticed that the upper elementary teachers were reporting that children had gaps in their mathematical backgrounds which were caused by the lack of a proper curricular focus at the lower grades.

Inasmuch as there was no district person to turn to, a consultant was secured from a local university in the area of mathematics to revamp the lower grades' curriculum. The staff determined a new scope and sequence. To what extent it meshes with other elementary schools and to what degree of impact it has at the middle school level are unknown. Said the principal, "This is our curriculum. If other schools want it, that's fine."

This process reinforces a long district practice of indigenous curriculum development that has led to curricular gaps and created problems of articulation among buildings and programs. Clearly the district cannot afford to (1) stifle initiative when the staff is ready to tackle an important problem or (2) allow the curriculum to be significantly altered without determining what the impact will be on the total curriculum, K–12. By not having on board a person who has responsibilities for mathematics, it has supported a principal and a staff at the risk of unbalancing the total curriculum in a curricular area that is heavily dependent upon sequenced content. The auditor heard numerous complaints from principals and parents about the mathematics curriculum in the district. Yet this has traditionally been one of the easiest curricular areas to sequence effectively. The fact that it has not been sequenced is indicative of the extent of the problem of both coordination and articulation of curriculum in the district. *Coordination* refers to the continuity of a curriculum in promoting consistency across grades within a single school. *Articulation* references the same problem across or between schools.

Finding 1.4: There Has Been a Lack of Formal Teacher Involvement in Curriculum Development as a Matter of Policy

Currently, there is no procedure or process that formally and consistently involves teachers in curriculum development on a district-wide basis in Locust Hill. Teacher complaints which have surfaced in the local press have referenced this lack of input and two-way communications (*Locust Hill Times* 3/20/86 and 3/27/86).

There is no district-wide curriculum advisory council comprised of teachers and administrators who ensure that curricular changes are considered across the board prior to implementation at a local school. Such a council of teacher specialists and administrator generalists would ensure that all aspects of a proposed curricular change would be fully anticipated. It would also deal with the problem of indigenous curricular change that continues to result in erratic curricular scope and sequence problems in Locust Hill.

There *has* been teacher input in curriculum in the district. Teachers have served on curriculum committees. Teachers have been able to initiate curricular changes within their schools. Yet there is strong evidence of a lack of coordination among these efforts and a lack of formalization with teachers of such efforts in the past, and this continues to the present day.

Finding 1.5: There Is No Formal System of Curriculum Monitoring in Place in the Locust Hill School District

With a few exceptions discerned by the auditor in interviews with principals and site visitations, there is no formal system of curriculum monitoring in place in the Locust Hill School District.

With some exceptions, principals do not review lesson plans regularly, even when they are developed. In some schools teachers are not required to submit lesson plans at all, substituting one-page quarterly reports of the curriculum they have included for that period. This practice denies to the district the opportunity of monitoring the ongoing curriculum and making adjustments within a time period instead of having to wait until after a time period has passed.

The issue of lesson plans is not a matter of trust. Rather, it is a matter of good practice. First, teaching is a complex process. Were it simple, perhaps verbal outlines of how it is organized would suffice. However, the process is complex and extends over many periods of time, involving many teachers, none of whom has the complete responsibility for the entire curriculum. This means that a coherent curriculum exists for a student when all of the individual pieces of the curriculum fit together. The purpose of curriculum monitoring is to ensure that the pieces fit together on a continuous basis and within a time frame in which adjustments can be made to obtain a closer congruence to the overall scope and sequence.

The purpose of lesson planbook monitoring is not only to ensure congruence to the overall curriculum plan within any one classroom, but to ensure that the individual work of one teacher reinforces and fits the total program in which all teachers are working. That responsibility rests first with the principal and secondly with curricular content specialists.

Complex and highly interdependent organizations depend upon a plan of work to ensure that the process remains an integrated whole. The first task is to design a sound work plan. The second task is to make sure that it is adhered to and that feedback about performance is used to improve individual and overall performance. An organization that does not use feedback within and across its many individual units cannot significantly improve its total performance.

Most teachers do use feedback from students within their classrooms. Feedback occurs in the form of responses to teacher-developed tests and teacher observation of pupil growth. However, the propriety of these responses has to be judged in comparison to the curricular role the teacher has within the total curriculum. That is a matter of comparison to the curriculum which is the overall work plan. Then that role must be compared to the work performed by all of the rest of the teachers. Without a record of ongoing teacher decisions in an individual classroom, no one can make judgments about whether or not the total collective efforts of a faculty result in a coherent curriculum for students that optimizes their talents within the time available.

Planbook supervision is an integral aspect of ensuring that the curriculum, on an ongoing basis, remains coherent for the student. It provides the basis for retracing what has occurred in a classroom and making immediate adjustments. Teaching is far too complex to trust one's memory on the details, no matter how long one has taught the same subject. Since each class and pupil are different, the adjustment of the curriculum is also situational and time specific. Without records regarding the ongoing curriculum, the daily and weekly adjustments necessary to modify the curriculum and still have all of the separate pieces remain coherent is left to chance.

The auditor encountered plenty of testimony regarding gaps in the ongoing curriculum in Locust Hill from students who noted that, whereas a curriculum should be continuous and interactive from one grade level to the next, it was in fact unrelated and disjointed. Parents recounted the same problem in their inability to secure a basic scope and sequence statement in any form from the district and in the necessity to hire tutors for their students to fill in the holes left by a lack of effective coordination.

Principals reported that in some cases they depended upon parental complaints to "right" a problem of curriculum balance or coordination within their schools. This means that the school lacks any formal mechanism to adjust its own curriculum internally before a parent might complain. What about coordination problems that go unnoticed by parents? How are they corrected?

If Locust Hill students were not of the caliber they are or if parents were unable or unwilling to secure outside help for their students, the problem might be of a different magnitude in the district. Said one veteran principal, "These kids would do well on a desert island."

Finding 1.6: There Is Evidence of a Lack of Curriculum Coordination and Articulation in the School District

The auditor encountered evidence from a variety of sources regarding the lack of curriculum coordination in the Locust Hill School District.

One example was a student comment about the English curriculum. Several students noted that while the courses were individually interesting and challenging, one did not prepare them for the next. They were unrelated. If the courses were electives, that might be a condition expected to be found; however, within the sequence of general English courses centered on language skills and knowledge of literary forms and expression, it represents testimony to the lack of "wholeness" of the overall English curriculum. A near universal criticism of the English curriculum encountered from students, parents, administrators, and board members was the lack of attention to the acquisition of writing skills. The students noted that writing skills were not really encountered in the English curriculum until the end of the sequence.

Students were very cognizant of ways teachers decided to vary from an expected course of study. They noted, for example, that within the same courses one teacher would spend approximately one-half a semester on Southeast Asia while another would spend about a week. The texts would also vary.

The student viewpoint was reinforced by a veteran secondary principal who observed, "Everybody did their own thing, but they did it well." One disadvantage is that Locust Hill students will be competing at the collegiate level with students who have perhaps encountered a curriculum with greater congruence and internal consistency than they have experienced. Such differences may not show up on more generic tests such as the SAT where Locust Hill students generally do very well. These differences are much more curriculum specific in nature.

The auditor requested information about follow-up studies of graduates from the school district. He was provided a computer printout of a random sample of the Class of 1983 of Locust Hill High School conducted by Action Research of San Francisco, California. The sample included 139 of the 339 members of the class, or 41 percent. The actual number of respondents was 117, or 35 percent, of whom 66 were males and 51 were females. Ninety percent had attended Locust Hill High School for four years and 82 percent were in the college preparatory program. Seventy-seven percent of the respondents had a GPA between 2.0 and 4.0. At the time of the survey, 58 percent of the respondents were in a four-year college or university. The students were then asked how many courses they had taken by curriculum area and whether or not they found them useful currently. The data from this survey is shown in Exhibit 11.

The follow-up data is difficult to interpret in light of student complaints about the lack of curricular cohesion. English is the second most "useful" curriculum in the "very useful" scores by Locust Hill High School graduates. It is quite possible that "utility" and "quality" may not be the same. It is possible that a student may find the "utility value" of a subject quite high and yet his or her own experience with the curricular area not as satisfactory as might be desired.

When asked what courses they wish they had taken more work in, the same graduates in the largest program area (college prep) indicated that it would be in the curricular area of "business" (see Exhibit 12). This was in turn followed by art/music (37 percent) and then English (35 percent). A review of the available test data base could not be related to specific curricular areas directly, nor would they necessarily be indicative of a strong or weak curricular sequence. The same would be true for the data gathered regarding graduates from the high schools. The best evidence is the testimony of students who have experienced directly a specific curricular sequence.

Exhibit 11
An Indication of the Utility of the Curriculum
Graduate Follow-up Study Class of 1983
Locust Hill High School (n = 139)

Curriculum Area	Percent Respondents Who Took One or More Courses	Utility Value to Respondents		
		Not Useful	Somewhat Useful	Very Useful
Art/Music	35%	44%	40%	15%
Drama/Speech	24%	18%	48%	33%
English	60%	5%	33%	60%
Foreign Language	54%	32%	3%	35%
Mathematics	60%	7%	35%	53%
Science	58%	19%	39%	38%
Social Studies	58%	20%	57%	14%
Business	25%	6%	37%	54%
Health	43%	27%	42%	30%
Home Education	29%	33%	45%	23%
Industrial/Tech	14%	37%	16%	42%
Work Experience	27%	5%	27%	62%
Physical Education	58%	42%	33%	22%

NOTE: Since respondents were in the main in college at the time of the survey, they may not be "using" some knowledge due to the collegiate curriculum focus. Utility was assessed by Action Research "in present activity." Data was not available from Dinsworth High School or for other years to the auditor.

Exhibit 12
Percentage of Students Who Wish They Had Taken More Courses in Some Curricular Areas by H.S. Program (n = 139)

	Percentage Who Wish They Had Taken More Courses by High School Program			
Curriculum Area	College Prep	General	Voc. Prep	Voc. & College
Art/Music	37%	50%	0	50%
Drama/Speech	32%	0	0	0
English	35%	29%	100%	0
Foreign Language	24%	40%	0	33%
Mathematics	31%	29%	100%	25%
Science	29%	17%	100%	0
Social Studies	14%	0	0	25%
Business	43%	100%	0	50%
Health	12%	40%	100%	25%
Home Education	6%	33%	0	25%
Industrial/Tech	19%	0	100%	0%
Work Experience	14%	0	100%	33%
Physical Education	9%	0	0	25%

NOTE: The numbers under vocational preparation and vocational and college are very small. Percentages may be misleading.

Finding 1.7: There Is an Indication of the Lack of Curriculum Comparability to Some Indices at the National Level

On national standardized tests Locust Hill students have done very well. The district is one of a dozen or so that has petitioned the Department of Education to cease giving the state's required testing program.

Certainly a review of a decade of SAT (Scholastic Aptitude Test) scores at both senior high schools in Locust Hill would reveal that, on the average, the students outscore the national average for every one of the years in the decade. Those data are shown in Exhibit 13.

However, the SAT is not a direct measure of any school's curriculum. It was created by Carl Brigham in the mid-1920s and was based heavily on Brigham's work with interpreting the widespread utilization in World War I of the Army Alpha intelligence test. Like many other tests of its type, the SAT is susceptible to the influence of ethnic and social class bias. These, in turn, are highly correlated with measures of wealth.

The indications of the true comparability of students in Locust Hill would be the Advanced Placement exams. The Advanced Placement Tests are specifically geared to assess the AP curriculum. While the auditor did not review any data supplied by the district regarding pupil success rates on the AP, he did receive information from some Locust Hill students about their success rate in taking the AP batteries. With a few exceptions, most did not do as well as they had hoped. In some specific instances, the students frankly admitted that their own honors courses were in no way effective preparation for an equivalent curriculum content AP exam.

Because the AP is a more direct measure of what is actually taught in a classroom than the SAT, it is a more accurate reflection of how well Locust Hill students are doing in comparison to other students at the national level. Based on student interviews, the data suggest that indigenous honors courses offered in both Locust Hill high schools are not strong comparable equivalents to the curriculum presented in the AP program.

Finding 1.8: There Is Evidence of Inconsistency in Evaluating Pupil Progress in Locust Hill

Both students and principals interviewed indicated that the curriculum across the district and within similar curricular areas differed substantially in some cases.

The problem is accentuated by test construction that does not assess common core elements within the same generic courses and by differing methods and criteria of assessing pupil progress. For example, one teacher in a common curricular area may count homework as one-fifth

Exhibit 13
A Ten-Year Comparison of SAT Scores of Students at Dinsworth and Locust Hill High Schools

School Year	Dinsworth High School			Locust Hill High School		
	Verbal	Math	Total	Verbal	Math	Total
1976–77	479(+50)	516(+46)	995(+96)	456(+27)	497(+27)	953(+54)
1977–78	477(+48)	507(+39)	984(+87)	475(+46)	506(+38)	981(+84)
1978–79	460(+33)	499(+32)	959(+65)	461(+34)	509(+42)	970(+76)
1979–80	467(+43)	498(+32)	965(+75)	472(+48)	510(+44)	982(+92)
1980–81	477(+53)	511(+45)	988(+98)	460(+36)	505(+39)	965(+75)
1981–82	473(+47)	506(+39)	979(+86)	468(+42)	511(+44)	979(+86)
1982–83	474(+49)	517(+49)	991(+98)	468(+43)	520(+52)	988(+95)
1983–84	475(+49)	514(+43)	989(+93)	485(+59)	535(+64)	1020(+124)
1984–85	490(+59)	538(+63)	1028(+122)	486(+55)	537(+62)	1023(+117)
1985–86	494(+63)	538(+63)	1032(+126)	495(+64)	558(+83)	1053(+147)

NOTE: The number in parentheses indicates how many points above the national average the average Locust Hill score was.

of the total grade. Another teacher may not count homework at all in a determination of the final grade. The inequities created by continuation of these practices for students are unfortunate and unfair to them. Furthermore, it presents a formidable obstacle to ensuring objectivity and equity in grading practices.

The current formula for determining the weight of the final exam is far too light for finals to be taken very seriously. At the present time the faculty handbook specifies that the final counts for one-fourth of the fourth-quarter grade. The only thing "final" about the final is that it is probably the last test administered. Other than that, it is a misnomer. In no way would it be comparable to a final at the collegiate level.

SUMMARY OF FINDINGS ON CURRICULUM AUDIT STANDARD 1

Perhaps the best way to summarize the findings regarding Standard 1 is to note that, individually, the schools in the Locust Hill School District are outstanding and effective on most conventional criteria. It would be difficult for the auditor to cite any he has seen that would be better. However, it would also be accurate to say that the school district is more a system of schools than a school system. At the system level there have been and continue to be many breakdowns and problems.

The superintendent has been working with his staff to create more continuity and coherency of the curriculum. Evidence was gathered that the curriculum possesses greater continuity than in the past. The superintendent has been working in the absence of an effective set of board policies which would require improved curricular consistency and focus in the district.

There has not been, nor was there at the time of the audit (April, 1987), an effective procedure for monitoring the curriculum in the Locust Hill School District. While student test scores indicate that, as a rule, they far exceed national averages, there is evidence of non-comparability as well, along with practices which are both unfair and inequitable to students still in operation.

Some of the findings in this section are not new. For example, the 1984 Report of the Regional States Accreditation of Dinsworth High School recommended (1) advanced placement courses be offered to the students in all subject areas in which they were available and (2) a written procedure be developed for the "systematic revision, evaluation, and development of curriculum." (Regional States, 1984). Such procedures were still not in place at the time of the audit some three years later.

At the district level, there is no clear picture by anyone as to where the district ought to be going in the future about curriculum. This lack of vision has impaired the ability of the board and administration in making closure on the matter of determining a curriculum core, dealing with the problem of curriculum balance and the number and type of electives and requirements, severing some curricular sequences and retaining others, and dealing effectively with the vestiges of indigenous curriculum development practices and attitudes of the 1970s. The times have indeed changed. A laissez-faire model of curriculum development is not functional any longer. Not everyone in Locust Hill has gotten the word yet. The ball is squarely in the board's court.

There has not been a systematic involvement of teachers in a district-wide set of administrative procedures that would draw upon their expertise and consistently solicit their advice and viewpoints about curricular changes. Locust Hill teachers have much to offer. The classroom environments observed by the auditor in site visitations were vivid testimony to their ingenuity, creativity, and dedication.

Standard 2: The School District Has Established Clear and Valid Objectives for Students

A school system meeting this audit standard has established a clear, valid, and measurable set of pupil standards for learning and has set them into a workable framework for their attainment.

Unless objectives are clear and measurable, there cannot be a cohesive effort to improve pupil achievement in any one direction. The lack of clarity denies to a school district the capability of concentrating its resources through a focused approach to management. Instead, resources may be spread too thin and be ineffective in any direction. Objectives are, therefore, essential to attaining local quality control via the elected school board.

What the Auditor Expected to Find in the Locust Hill School District

The auditor expected to find in the Locust Hill School District a clearly established, district-wide set of goals and objectives adopted by the board of education. Such objectives would set the framework for the operation of the district, its sense of priorities, and explicit direction for the superintendent and the larger professional staff.

In turn, an explicit framework is matched by the development of functional curriculum documents such as curriculum guides, pacing charts, and scope and sequence delineations. These tools connect purpose to work.

Courses of study identify explicit criteria by which the scope and depth of the curriculum has been derived, configured, and maintained. There are requirements and safeguards that insure coherency in any curricular path selected by students so that they do not miss requisite skills, knowledges, or attitudes while in school. In short, there is a system of curriculum.

What the Auditor Found in the Locust Hill School District

The auditor did not find any locally validated goals or objectives that were different for the state as a whole in Locust Hill. There were no local board-adopted educational objectives that drive local curriculum development in Locust Hill.

The auditor did not find a detailed scope and sequence for the curriculum in the school district. The curriculum guides that were reviewed did not embrace the entire curriculum and were of marginal quality.

The auditor could find no document or plan that would provide a central focus from which overall curricular coherency could be developed. School visitations and interviews of educational personnel did not produce any evidence that locally developed curriculum was useful or used in making day-to-day content, pacing, or sequential decisions in the classrooms of the school system. There is no system of curriculum in the Locust Hill School District.

Finding 2.1: There Is an Absence of a Central Focus for Curriculum in the Locust Hill School District

It has already been noted that the local board of education has not adopted any policy to provide an effective framework for curriculum development in the Locust Hill School District (see Finding 1.1).

What the Locust Hill Board of Education has done is simply adopt the goals of the state. These goals are not of an explicit nature. They are amorphous in nature. They cannot direct. They only absorb whatever an operational district might do. They are completely ineffective to establish a core curriculum.

In the district's long-range plan of 1984, individual courses are cross-referenced to the goals of the state. Inasmuch as the goals are nonspecific, any course in the district can be related one way or another. No course would be eliminated in such a procedure.

Therefore, such goals do not provide even the most basic and essential guideline for curriculum development, i.e., inclusion and exclusion in a school program via curriculum construction. It must be possible for a board, and especially the professional staff, to determine placement propriety (inclusion/exclusion) based on some criteria. Should this be included in the curriculum? If the answer cannot be derived from some criteria somewhere, whatever guideline does exist is ineffective.

Locust Hill principals complained about the expanding curriculum. Board members complained about the lack of a core in establishing some idea of essentials. The problem exists because existing policies and documents are not specific and do not provide the most minimum managerial responsibility required of any work organization, i.e., the definition of the essential tasks of the organization.

The major determinants of what stays or goes in the Locust Hill School District is not decided by policy or planned responses, but rather by funds availability, time, and pupil interest. This places the development of curriculum squarely on the passing fancies of the day. It produces a curriculum driven by fads and funds. Sound curriculum development should eliminate fads and drive budget development rather than be a product of it.

The current set of loosely related and nonspecific documents and policies fits rather well a confederation of schools that have been left to do "their own thing." It provides only the barest outline of structure for teachers in which to instruct pupils. While this type of framework might have been adequate for the 1970s, it is not appropriate nor adequate for the 1980s. The observations and complaints encountered from students, parents, board members, and administrators amply reveal the inadequacies of the current operational modality.

If the citizens and taxpayers of the Locust Hill School District desire an educational program that exceeds that of the state in terms of quality, the documents reviewed by the auditor would not indicate what or how it could be accomplished.

Finding 2.2: Curricular Documents Are of Marginal Quality in Locust Hill

The auditor examined the following curriculum documents:

- *Curriculum Guide K–12* (no date)
- *Special Education—Planned Courses* (no date)
- *Special Education—Speech and Language Goals* (no date)
- *Special Education—IEP Handbook* (no date)
- *Health Education Curriculum Guide* (April 1969), 385 pp.
- *Elementary Curriculum Guide for Instructional Swimming* (1983), 66 pp.
- Dinsworth High School *Planned Courses of Study*
- Locust Hill High School *Planned Course of Study*

These documents have been created in the absence of an explicit board policy framework for the district. As such they reflect little overall coherency or consistency when viewed as a totality. It would be impossible after reviewing all of the above documents to obtain any idea of what overarching purposes constituted the central focus of the Locust Hill School District. It would be impossible because the documents were created by a variety of people working on different agendas within different time periods and without much central direction. When summed, the documents do not reveal clarity, any grand design, or sense of mission. They do not establish purpose or direction.

When courses of study are summed, they do not equate to a curriculum. A curriculum is the grand design within which courses of study are developed to make it operational. Courses of study are designed to be operational documents guided by a curriculum. It is a curriculum that establishes direction. It is a curriculum centered on explicit purposes that should indicate what is essential and what is a fad. It is a curriculum that serves as the basis to determine sequence. It is a curriculum that defines coherency of all the separate parts.

The curriculum in Locust Hill is essentially a hodgepodge collection of disparate documents, courses, articles, textbook elements, objectives, goals, platitudes, skill or subject scope and sequences, content statements, and "philosophies." These have been developed in documents of widely differing sizes and formats, ranging from three-ringed binders to manila envelopes filled with planned courses of study. It is understandable why parents have complained that they have never received a coherent, concise statement of the district's curricular scope and sequence. The reason is that one does not exist. Furthermore, it would be impossible to construct one from these sources.

The auditor could find no set of specifications from which curriculum had been constructed. Such specifications would provide for commonality in design. Only at the level of planned courses of study was any semblance of consistency encountered in the document review. In this sense, the documents are revealing. They show that the level of understanding about the function of a curriculum does not extend much beyond the micro-management level. As such, the district runs the continuous risk of micro-managing the wrong things.

SUMMARY OF FINDINGS ON CURRICULUM AUDIT STANDARD 2

A school district is one kind of work organization in a society. The work of the schools is centered on education of the young, an essential social service. Schools are no longer simple uncomplicated places. They are staffed with hundreds of people engaged in activity directed at providing a continuous set of services within a specified time frame.

To insure that the efforts of hundreds of people are optimized, a work plan is required to provide purpose and direction. It is only within such a plan that the individual actions of a person can be properly assessed and the services of many people collectively evaluated.

It is a curriculum that is expected to establish the grand design of all of the individual people working in a school system. As such, it is not a product of whatever they decide to do. Were it only this, a curriculum could never guide an educational system to make intelligent choices about what it ought to be doing as a system. A plan is required for any human organization to improve its collective performance as a total organization.

Such a grand design does not now exist in the Locust Hill School District. For the district to move beyond its current set of operations into a more sophisticated realm, one will have to be created. In short, the school district will have to develop a curriculum.

Standard 3: The School District Has Documentation Explaining How Its Programs Have Been Developed, Implemented, and Conducted

A school district meeting this curriculum audit standard is able to show how its programs have been created as the result of a systematic identification of deficiencies in the achievement and growth of its students compared to measurable standards of learning.

In addition, a system meeting this standard is able to demonstrate that, as a whole, it is more effective than the sum total of its parts, i.e., any arbitrary combination of programs or schools does not equate to the larger school district entity.

The purpose of having a school district (as opposed to a collection of schools) is to obtain the educational and economic benefits of a coordinated program for students, both to enhance learning by maximizing pupil interest and by utilizing economies of scale where appropriate and applicable.

What the Auditor Expected to Find in the Locust Hill School District

The auditor expected to find a highly developed, articulated, and coordinated curriculum in the district that was effectively monitored by the professional staff. Such a curriculum would be:

- centrally defined and adopted by the board of education
- clearly explained to members of the instructional staff and building level administrators

- accompanied by specific training programs to enhance implementation
- monitored by department chairpersons, building level administrators, and appropriate central office staff

What the Auditor Found in the Locust Hill School District

The auditor found a very informal and loose set of operations concerning curriculum in the Locust Hill School District. The auditor found great sensitivity and awareness on the part of the school board, the superintendent, and other central level administrators to the need to promote greater system-wide consistency and continuity in the school district. However, the auditor found no plan to accomplish those ends in existence at the time of the audit.

The auditor found understaffing at the central level in Locust Hill, staff development efforts that were not always guided by a sound curriculum design, and spotty circular monitoring practices in individual school buildings that differed widely in scope, style, and intensity.

In addition, the auditor encountered widespread criticism about some curricular areas across the district from parents, students, and principals.

Finding 3.1: Awareness for Improved Curricular Consistency and Continuity in the School District Was Encountered at All Levels

The auditor encountered information in interviews that indicated great sensitivity to the lack of curricular consistency in the district. Some parents indicated that they didn't know what the curriculum was and that when they asked teachers about it, they were vague. "The whole thing is fragmented," said one parent. "There is no accountability."

Teachers interviewed doubted there was a curriculum as well. Comments like, "I do believe something exists in the principal's office" or "The principal probably has this document," were recorded.

Board members commented that the curriculum lacked rigor and focus. They appeared perplexed as to why some skills, like writing, were not taught across the curriculum in every area or why critical thinking was not emphasized more strongly. Members were struggling in their efforts to come to terms with measures of effectiveness of the educational program. On the one hand, all of the conventional measures showed the district was "outstanding." On the other, their instincts and raw data from patrons pointed to discrepancies in the school system that were unaccounted for in the information they did receive.

Said one board member, "I keep asking who's in control? I don't get any answers. No one is overseeing the curriculum." Another member observed, "Some people who did their own thing in the sixties are still doing it." One board member talked about "curriculum clutter" as a board concern and said, "I have no sense of a coherent curriculum."

Parents were critical of their lack of input into the curriculum. "We are complete observers," said one mother. Parents were also aware of the effect of "leveling" or "tracking" in the schools. Said one parent, "Choose a level, choose a curriculum at the high school."

The importance of parents in the process of education in Locust Hill was underscored in the previously reported stratified random sample of 1983 graduates of Locust Hill High School (see Finding 1.6).

When asked, "Who helped the most in planning for the future when you were in high school?" the respondents indicated the following (in descending order of importance):

1. parents and relatives	57%
2. teachers	17%
3. myself	11%
4. on-campus friends	10%
5. work experience advisor	8%
6. school counselors	7%

Various internal problems of curricular inconsistency were highlighted in the interviews with principals. One referred to the social studies area as "a loose confederation of states." Another principal noted, "We learn about the curriculum by the discovery method." One principal confessed there wasn't enough time to effectively deal with curricular consistency, "We do everything from toilets to textbooks."

Finding 3.2: The Curriculum Function in Locust Hill Has Been Understaffed

A review of the challenges and problems facing the district and the current state of curriculum documentation in Locust Hill leads rather easily to the fact that the curriculum function has been understaffed (see Finding 1.3).

While there are many ways to staff the function, none have been used in the school district except the "task force" approach which has yielded inconsistent results in the past. Curriculum staffing in the schools has also suffered from a lack of clarity.

SUMMARY OF FINDINGS ON CURRICULUM AUDIT STANDARD 3

Documentation on curriculum in Locust Hill is limited. The curriculum is not in one piece anywhere. A district-wide scope and sequence chart does not exist. The curriculum function has been understaffed centrally. There has been no clear and effective way to staff the function at the building level. There has not been a uniform method for taking on the curriculum function at the secondary level that appears to be particularly effective.

There has been great disparity in monitoring the curriculum in the schools. While some principals spend a great deal of time and closely review planbooks, others do not spend the time nor even require planbooks to be used by all staff (see Finding 1.5).

Central staff development which would be a validated means to implement a district-wide curriculum, has not occurred in Locust Hill. The closest the district has come was an attempt to implement the Madeline Hunter mastery teaching model. That effort became enmeshed in negotiations and was scuttled as one consequence of the negative fallout in the strike and "work to rule" action that followed. The Hunter model was misperceived as an attempt to superimpose a standardized procedure on all teachers. The positive benefits to the instructional program that could have accrued were therefore lost to the staff and the district.

Staff development that does not reinforce district goals will not lead to improved overall performance or desired pupil growth. To optimize time and finances, staff development must be coordinated on a district-wide basis. Purposive staff development is rooted in a strategic vision of the district. Staff development makes a difference to the district when there is a plan in place. In such circumstances it is possible to ascertain what difference staff development has made.

Standard 4: The School District Uses the Results from District Designed and/or Adopted Assessments to Adjust, Improve, or Terminate Ineffective Practices or Programs

A school district meeting this curriculum audit standard of the process has designed a comprehensive system of testing and measurement tools that indicate how well students are learning designated priority objectives.

Such a system will provide:

- a timely and relevant base upon which to analyze important trends in the instructional program
- a vehicle to examine how well programs are actually producing desired learner results

- a way to provide feedback to the teaching staff regarding how classroom instruction can become more effective
- a data base to compare the strengths and weaknesses of various programs and program alternatives
- a data base to terminate ineffective educational programs

A school district meeting this audit standard has a full range of formal and informal assessment tools that provide relevant program information to decision making in the classroom, building, district, and board levels.

The school system has taken steps to ensure that the full range of its programs are systematically and periodically assessed. Such data have been matched to program objectives and are utilized in decision making.

What the Auditor Expected to Find in the Locust Hill School District

The auditor expected to find a comprehensive assessment program of all aspects of the curriculum which was:

- keyed to sets of goals/objectives adopted by the board of education, these in turn being expressly linked to a strategic vision for the system
- utilized extensively at the building level to engage in program review and modification
- used to terminate ineffective educational programs
- used as a base to establish needed new programs or modify old ones
- publicly reported to the board of education and the community on a regular basis

What the Auditor Found in the Locust Hill School District

The auditor found that Locust Hill students score consistently above average on standardized tests utilized in the district. A very small fraction of students in the district fail the state mandated testing program.

The auditor found good reporting of the test data but a varied use of the data to evaluate programs or make adjustments in ongoing programs. The probable reason is largely rooted in the fact that none of the standardized measures is an accurate reflection of the district's curriculum.

The auditor found no district-developed, criterion-referenced tests to assess local curricular goals that would exceed those contained on standardized test batteries.

A review of documents regarding curriculum and instruction

showed an inconsistent use of test data as the basis to modify old programs or establish new ones.

Finding 4.1: Locust Hill Students Consistently Score Above Average on Standardized Test Batteries

The auditor reviewed a variety of test compilations and reports tabulated by the office of the director of curriculum. These were not only prepared for the immediate year, but included longitudinal data on the same instruments as well.

The data base included pupil scores on the following batteries:

- Metropolitan Achievement Test
- Otis-Lennon School Ability Test
- Stanford Test of Academic Skills
- Differential Aptitude Test
- Scholastic Aptitude Test
- State Test

The most recent report (11/10/86) prepared by the office of the director of curriculum on the Metropolitan Achievement Test (MAT) is shown in Exhibit 14.

Finding 4.2: Use of Test Data Is Marginal to Adjust/Terminate Educational Programs in Locust Hill

The district has conceded that the MAT was "not designed for our curriculum in particular" (memo from director of curriculum of 11/4/86 to middle school principals). Despite the unknown level of alignment from the test to the curriculum, principals have been urged to examine the data because "some test results are less impressive than others" (*Standard Test Report 1986–87*, 11/10/86, p. 8).

Despite a generally comprehensive reporting system on test results being published within the district, the auditor could not find any document that pinpointed specific local curricular weaknesses that had been identified at the same level nor any concrete suggestions for curricular change based on such analyses.

Principals interviewed reported a variety of uses of such data. Some engaged in individual item analysis; others did not. Thus, specific linkages from any of the test batteries to the ongoing educational program varied rather widely in Locust Hill.

The auditor did find the administration of tests and some items pertaining to test results on agendas of principals' meetings. However, he did not find documentation regarding specific linkages and sugges-

Exhibit 14
Results of the Metropolitan Achievement Tests for Grades 4–8 in Locust Hill (1986)

Test Area	Grade 4	Grade 5	Grade 6	Grade 7	Grade 8
Reading					
National Stanine	6	7	6	7	7
Median Gr. Equiv.	5.9	7.2	8.7	11.6	12.8
Mathematics					
National Stanine	7	6	7	6	7
Median Gr. Equiv.	5.1	6.2	8.2	9.2	10.9
Language					
National Stanine	6	6	6	6	6
Median Gr. Equiv.	5.7	7.0	8.4	10.0	10.9
Basic Battery					
National Stanine	7	7	7	7	7
Median Gr. Equiv.	5.5	6.9	8.6	10.1	11.6
Science					
National Stanine	7	6	7	6	6
Median Gr. Equiv.	5.5	6.7	9.2	9.6	11.0
Social Studies					
National Stanine	7	7	7	7	7
Median Gr. Equiv.	5.9	7.6	9.1	10.0	11.4
Complete Battery					
National Stanine	7	7	7	7	7
Median Gr. Equiv.	5.5	7.0	8.7	10.1	11.5

NOTE: A stanine is a normalized standard score based on dividing the normal curve into nine intervals. The mean is 5. The use of stanines is considered a gross and imprecise measure in reporting derived scores. Grade equivalent scores also rest on a number of questionable assumptions and are considered passe in reporting pupil achievement. Both measures are used by test companies.

tions which could be represented as action items for changes in school curricula as a result on any consistent basis.

Part of the problem is the lack of a coherent district-wide curriculum which is in place to relate feedback regarding pupil performance. A memo from one of the middle school principals to the director of curriculum on 3/4/85 (underlining the auditor's) is a good example of the problem:

> I have discussed with my sixth grade math teachers any gaps they see in the elementary math program which come to light in the sixth grade. The only area that they felt was a particular problem was addition, subtraction, and division of decimals.
>
> While they did see some problems with multiplication and division of fractions, number theory (primes, composites, factoring), and measurement other than metric they were not sure whether these areas are covered in the elementary program.

The fact that the middle school teachers did not know what was "covered" in the elementary math curriculum indicates that either: (1) a curriculum was in existence which specified what was taught and was not available to them or the middle school principal or (2) a curriculum did not exist or was unclear as to what was to be taught at the elementary levels.

Without clear curricular delineations both vertically (across grade levels) and laterally (within grade levels), feedback is impossible to use effectively to adjust/improve a curriculum. One doesn't know where to connect the feedback.

The fact that the above cited problem dealt with the lack of clarity regarding decimals was probably due to the problem of scope and sequence specificity. For example, the auditor reviewed a memorandum from the superintendent of schools to the board of education of 7/6/84 concerning the scope and sequence of the school district.

The memo was attached to a very broad document called "Curriculum Guide." Under the area of mathematics for the elementary grades the following statement appeared:

> Elementary schools develop concepts of numbers, measurement, geometry, graphing, ratio and proportion, problem solving, fractions and decimals, sets, and applications. Basic curriculum materials are either the Scott, Foresman, or the Holt mathematics program. Extensive supplementary materials are available.

The guide indicates that "concepts" are developed about decimals, among other things. But what concepts? This type of scope and sequence is not very useful for working on curriculum articulation problems. It is far too general to be helpful in resolving such problems or in relating test data to make changes in the curriculum itself.

The auditor reviewed a number of documents regarding changes in high school courses for 1987–88. None of these appeared to be prompted by any kind of feedback regarding pupil performance. Most changes appeared to be driven by enrollment rather than feedback. For example, a memo from the director of curriculum to the high school principals of 6/6/85 highlights this problem:

> How many different courses and course sequences do we need and how many can we support with our projected enrollments?
>
> We really have no choice. If the enrollment projections are accurate or even close, we will be faced with numbers that do not support as many different courses and/or levels as we might like to offer. Look at the numbers. . . .

The only course that appeared to be directly linked to a high school test was the one specifically geared to taking the SAT. That was addressed in a memorandum from the director of curriculum to the high school principals on 10/18/85. It was recommended that it be offered earlier than grades 11 or 12 since it had been criticized as "too little too late."

That same memorandum indicated (underlining the auditor's):

> We can delay change in the senior alternatives/electives by arguing that the course offerings will be evaluated and decisions made this year for inclusion in the 1987–88 program of studies, but the list of regular electives should probably be pruned.

Here is a directive or suggestion to change the number of courses. The directive does not emanate from (1) a district master plan or strategic plan or (2) feedback regarding pupil performance. There is no reference to the criteria upon which to engage in pruning. A review of related curricular documents by the auditor shows that the dominant impetus for course configuration changes relates to enrollment almost exclusively.

Other forces impinging at the high school level (as referenced in a review of department meetings agenda and minutes) were (1) a decision to bring "standardization" of courses among the two high schools and/or (2) the adoption of new textbooks which would impact course content and sequence or provoke changes in student grouping.

The auditor also found evidence that parent input was considered by the staff. For example, a memo of 4/24/86 in social studies concerned changing the local honors courses in social studies. The teacher's reaction is indicated below:

> In light of shrinking enrollment for subsequent years at Dinsworth, it would appear that another social studies course at the Honors level is not warranted. Students would be drawn from the Advanced Economics course.

Problems of sequencing and content selection appear with some regularity in in-house memoranda. For example, a memo of 12/1/82 about the math curriculum identifies as weaknesses "the sequence for those deficient in mathematics, a ninth grade program that is too diversified, and the limited numbers of students who pursue the honors track through four years of high school."

Problems in the English curriculum highlighted by high school students and previously reported in the audit (see Finding 1.6) were cited in a memo of 6/83:

> Each high school recommends adoption of its own sequence. Dinsworth prefers to place American literature in eleventh grade; Locust Hill has developed a course emphasizing American literature in the tenth grade. . . . Both high schools offer semester electives in twelfth grade, but the course offerings differ substantially between the schools.

The auditor reviewed agendas and minutes from the meetings of elementary principals and the same data base within the elementary schools regarding grade level meetings in the time period 1985–87.

These documents reveal a wide variety of concerns and actions taken at the elementary level. They pertain to everything from class trips to report cards, textbook adoptions, and homework time.

However, the auditor did not find any specific data which would show that precise test deficits were discussed at any level. Thus, pupil performance was not a strong motivating force for curricular change.

There are probably several reasons for this. The first is that the curricular scope and sequence continues to be too general to be used as the focus for specific behavioral changes in the district's classrooms. An updated (1/5/87) version of the *Curriculum Guide* (including scope and sequence) was not much more precise than the one reviewed in 1984.

The second reason for the lack of precision in linking feedback to curriculum is the manner in which test scores are reported. Grade equivalent scores have been subject to much criticism from testing authorities. It is often forgotten that a grade equivalent score is the median mark for performance, in which 50 percent of those tested will fall below the grade equivalent score. It is therefore an unreasonable expectation that all students at the sixth grade score at the sixth grade level.

Furthermore, a fourth grader scoring at the 6.0 grade equivalent does not know the same amount of information as a sixth grader, which is often the manner in which such a score is misinterpreted. Grade equivalent scores cannot therefore be utilized as sound curricular feedback.

The stanine is also not a precise way of linking test performance to curricular objectives. One of the reasons is that the same stanine score often contains (thereby concealing) very different raw scores.

The district's standardized tests are not direct measures of its curriculum. The actual alignment from the tests to the curriculum is unknown. It is impossible to use them to improve curriculum as a result.

The major problem with this approach is that the test then becomes the curriculum when it should be a reflection of the curriculum. If tests are properly aligned with a curriculum prior to adoption, this step minimizes the dangers of having the testing companies writing a school district's operational curriculum. Alignment prevents the misuse of tests and establishes a realistic framework for test interpretation. Any such data are currently not available in Locust Hill.

SUMMARY OF FINDINGS ON CURRICULUM AUDIT STANDARD 4

The use of specific data from the extant testing batteries has been limited in Locust Hill. The district has relied on available standardized tests which are not direct measures of its curriculum. This fact, and the imprecise manner in calibrating test scores, has not resulted in widespread use of such data to impact curriculum content, pacing, or sequencing or in other major adjustments in the instructional program, at least so far as documents and interviews revealed such practices.

The state testing program has shown that only a small fraction of the children tested in Locust Hill (around 1 percent) qualify for remedial instruction based on such competency tests.

The district has not moved towards developing its own criterion-referenced tests that would accurately reflect its expectations and be more useful in improving curriculum and instruction with more reliable feedback. In fact, final exams do not reflect, with any consistency, a district-wide focus. They are still largely idiosyncratic to peculiar courses, curricular areas, and schools.

One of the major problems in moving towards a more localized and accurate approach to testing is the lack of a validated, district-wide curriculum that is in place from which to derive and design such tests. For tests not to drive the curriculum, they must be developed after the curriculum has been developed.

The auditor could not find any evidence of a major curriculum decision that had been initiated as a result of examining pupil performance as an outcome of that curriculum being implemented in the district. For the most part, pupil achievement does not seem to be an important prime mover of curricular change in Locust Hill.

Standard 5: The School District Has Improved Productivity

Productivity refers to the relationship between input and output. A school district meeting this standard of the audit is able to demonstrate consistent pupil outcomes, even in the face of declining resources. Improved productivity results when a school system is able to create a more consistent level of congruence between the major variables involved in achieving better results and in controlling costs.

What the Auditor Expected to Find in the Locust Hill School District

While the attainment of improved productivity in a school system is a complex process, caused in part by the lack of a tight organizational structure (referred to as "loosely coupled"), a school district meeting this audit standard demonstrates:

- planned and actual congruence between curricular objectives, results, and financial costs

- specific means that have been selected or modified and implemented to attain better results in the schools over a specified time period
- a planned series of interventions that have raised pupil performance levels over time and maintained those levels within the same parameters as in the past

Any evaluation of productivity is a relative one and must include the fundamental recognition that neither the school board, the superintendent, principals, or teachers have complete control of all of the critical variables that will result in improved pupil performance. Nonetheless, there are substantial elements within their combined authority that do account for improved pupil learning. These can be subjected to productivity assessment.

What the Auditor Found in the Locust Hill School District

The auditor found a very professional and business-like set of operations in the Locust Hill School District. Over the past nine years, improvements in maintenance, buildings and grounds, cafeterias, transportation, and other support services have been systematically upgraded and improved. School facilities are impeccably kept and grounds manicured.

The budgeting process in Locust Hill would be characterized as "traditional." The auditor did not find financial data records that could be translated into programmatic thrusts or cost centers necessary to pursue productivity analysis. The auditor found no documents that formally linked curricular priorities and budgetary priorities.

The auditor found a stable financial environment and a fiscally conservative viewpoint regarding expenditures and finances in general.

Finding 5.1: School District Operations in Locust Hill Are Characterized as Business-Like

Administrators interviewed commented that the schools are run very much like a "corporate organization." These were not pejorative descriptors. The board of education is very stable. Five of the board members have served over a decade in that capacity. The least senior member has been a member for only three and one-half years.

The outlook of the board of education is conservative, educationally and fiscally. Members desire responsive and responsible education. Their comments indicated they desire excellence and believe that this ideal can be attained within reasonable cost parameters.

The teacher representatives interviewed also sensed the attitude of the board and administration. There were several comments about the fact that the school system was "run like a business." They expressed concern about morale and the climate in the school system. None of the concerns or feelings could be concretely identified, however. They appeared to be largely "perceptions."

Finding 5.2: Budgeting Practices in Locust Hill Assume a Traditional Format

The auditor reviewed three budgets from the Locust Hill School District. They were filed on form 1464 with the department of education comptroller's office.

They revealed that the budget for the school district was as follows for the last three years:

Total Budget	School Year
$32,377,077	1984–85
$33,381,076	1985–86
$35,992,245	1986–87

The budgeting process is a traditional, object item, line item fiscal document. As such, it is very difficult to move towards relating expenditures to results. Budgets have to assume a quasi-programmed form to do this.

The linkage from curricular priorities to budgetary priorities is strong, however, in Locust Hill. The fact is that whatever principals request, they receive. Said one secondary school principal, "I have everything I need."

Teachers reported some difficulty in ordering textbooks. However, these funds are controlled via formula and allocated differently than funds for program support and instructional materials.

Administrators were not opposed to developing more concrete linkages from programs to cost/benefit analyses. One of the major barriers to more effective fiscal management and allocation is the lack of precision in the overall curriculum in Locust Hill. At the present time there is no way dollars can be related to pupil outcomes because the latter have not been identified. In this sense improved financial management is highly dependent upon building a very different curriculum than that which is now in place in Locust Hill.

SUMMARY OF FINDINGS ON CURRICULUM AUDIT STANDARD 5

While the board of education and the school administration are not driven by the dollar sign in Locust Hill, they nonetheless expect a reasonable relation between costs and outcomes. Several board members were openly conscious of costs. "We hardly ever say no," said one member, "but are we getting what we should?"

In recent months the school board has pressed the administration for answers. First, some members wanted a review of SAT scores to examine trends. Others wanted to know how to measure final outcomes. At least one round with a measurement specialist was considered unsatisfactory.

Board members reflected varying degrees of frustration with getting answers and in trying to make connections between costs and quality in the schools. Said one, "It's very imprecise. The budgeting process that will support a curriculum is very loose." That same member expressed frustration in obtaining answers. "All we do is study, study. They (the administration) vacillate all over the place. We have a committee approach on everything."

At least one or two board members admitted that they did not feel that the board had created a very effective focus to study curriculum or deal with cost-quality relationships. It has been only recently that the board as a body has begun to focus squarely on the curriculum and curricular issues.

The auditor found the greatest dissatisfaction among board members over the relationship between costs (reflections of inputs) and pupil learning (outputs). The elusiveness of this equation was particularly galling to some members who had struggled in trying to answer it in their own minds over a prolonged time period.

The fact is that the curriculum in Locust Hill is in no shape to be responsive to such inquiries without substantial reworking.

RECOMMENDATIONS

Based upon the auditor's findings the following recommendations have been formulated to improve the curriculum management system in the Locust Hill School District.

Recommendation 1: The Board of School Directors Must Create a Functional Policy Framework to Require Good Practice in Local Curriculum Management

The board's policies are completely inadequate to create a sound curriculum management system in Locust Hill. New policies must be developed which:

- require the development of a strategic plan for the district
- require that a comprehensive curriculum be developed which

promotes continuity laterally and vertically within the school system
- require the publication of a district-wide scope and sequence chart for all parents
- require the development of pupil performance outcomes by which tests are adopted and reported to the public and which can be used to change curriculum to be more effective. Such outcomes will then be the basis to move towards programmed budgeting and the development of specific cost centers within the budget.
- require textbook alignment to the locally validated curriculum to insure that the curriculum drives the textbook adoption process and prevents the textbook from becoming the curriculum
- require the implementation of district-wide exams which assess common elements in the local curriculum and validated national exams (Advanced Placement) at the secondary level; local "honors" courses to be used only when an applicable national AP exam is not available
- require annual "state of the curriculum" report from the superintendent or designee which identifies progress and continuing strengths and weaknesses in the curriculum
- require formal parental input of an advisory nature to be a part of the curriculum management process

Recommendation 2: Develop a District Strategic Plan from Which to Configure Curriculum

The long-range plan of the district is not adequate for sound curriculum planning. It locks the district into a reactive, rather than proactive, posture in responding to local or state/national trends.

It is recommended that the district develop a strategic plan which will paint a broad-brush picture of the desired future for the school district at a specific time in the future. (Many school districts are using the year 2000 as an index.)

A strategic plan is not a detailed operational plan. It is not a "how to" plan. It is concentrated on the "what." A strategic plan would deal with the future of Dinsworth in alternative scenarios. The purpose of a strategic plan is to be cognizant of the existing trends impacting the district but not to be captured by them so as to be in a reactive posture.

A strategic plan begins by looking at the district's current mission and goals and identifying indicators of how well the district has been achieving its aims. This will mean that the school board will have to develop a mission statement, goals, and specific indicators of performance. Such indices are absent from board policies at the present time (see Findings 1.1 and 1.2).

After developing these statements, the board requires its professional staff to compile a data base of indicators as to how well the system is performing. These are called "results." They should be contained in a special and comprehensive report and organized under two headings.

The first should deal with how well Locust Hill students are doing at the end of their experiences at a particular school level, perhaps grades 5, 8, and 12. Probing questions should be raised about how well prepared students are for the next major level within the school district. Each subject area in the curriculum should be addressed.

The second area should deal with how well Locust Hill students do after leaving the school district in college, work, and life.

Data should be of all types, i.e., statistical, descriptive, anecdotal.

The report should end with specific *gaps* identified from the data, which are a result from the comparison of the data regarding performance to the mission, goals, and specific indicators.

The next step in developing the strategic plan is to determine what the future will be like. This is where demographic data is compiled about the world, nation, state, and local community. The question to be addressed is, "What sort of world will our students be entering?" Trends are identified. The impact of these trends are examined as they involve the school district.

From these trend impact areas, various scenarios are developed. The scenarios are labeled "optimistic" to "pessimistic" and "most likely scenario." All of the most likely scenarios are closely examined. From these, the strategic plan is developed. The strategic plan represents the desired future and contains elements which identify in broad terms what the district will do, given the most likely scenarios occurring. It is at this point that decisions are made about whether or not to conform to the trends or try to change them.

The strategic plan is finished when the critical decisions are listed as to what the district will do based upon what it should be like in the year 2000 (or whatever year is selected).

From the strategic plan, long-range plans are derived which contain detailed steps as to what the district will do in the areas of personnel, curriculum, budget, support service configurations, and school configurations. It is the strategic plan which is at the heart of establishing a more specific cost-quality relationship between inputs and outputs. At the present time many school districts, colleges, and universities are or have developed institutional strategic plans.

Until such steps are taken, the nagging questions raised by the school board regarding curriculum and programs in the audit interviews will not be answered.

Recommendation 3: Improve the Concentration of Staffing at the District Level in Curriculum

The central level staffing of curriculum has not been adequate in Locust Hill (see Finding 3.2).

Two types of curricular expertise are required to manage curriculum in a school district effectively. The first is a workable system of curricular generalists. These consist of line officers at the central level (assistant superintendents, directors, general coordinators) and building level (principals or assistant principals).

Curricular generalists are concerned with the overall focus of the curriculum and its internal balance and coherency. Generalists concentrate on the integrative functions of curriculum in the schools.

Curricular specialists, however, work on the same elements but within a specific content area. Their expertise does not extend beyond their content specialization.

The generalist function in Locust Hill has been concentrated in a staff position. Consequently, the district is moving towards replacing it with a line position. This will also reduce the span of control of the superintendent. That move appears to be necessary.

However, the district must consider the addition of content specialists. There are several ways to do this. The first is to create a role like a subject area supervisor that functions full- or part-time (the other time being in the classroom). These roles will be concentrated upon district-wide curricular continuity K–12 within each subject or content area.

Another way is to identify two or three curricular areas each year for review and move towards a task force approach where external university or educational lab consultants are utilized to create the required continuity. Once established, the necessary continuity (not standardization) is monitored by line officers already within the district. If three curricular areas were closely examined every year, over five years fifteen areas would be examined.

This latter approach avoids adding layers of supervisory staff to the table of organization. It would keep the administrative levels of personnel "lean and mean." It is, however, not without some problems, not the least of which is maintenance of continuity over an extended time period.

Finally, some resolution should be made towards resolving problems of general curricular supervision within the secondary schools.

At the present time, the use of department chairs is quite uneven at the secondary level in Locust Hill.

Some school districts have moved towards full-time chairs and require a supervisory certificate for this service. They then move towards removing the chairs from the bargaining unit. To have chairs in the bargaining unit puts the people occupying these roles in a "conflict of interest" position when it comes to evaluation of staff. If a grievance is filed regarding an evaluation, the union cannot grieve against itself. It cannot represent both parties fairly.

The evaluation of staff within subject content areas is one of the most important functions performed by department chairs. If they cannot perform this function, the value of maintaining the position is considerably diminished.

Recommendation 4: Move Towards Programmatic Budgeting

Once the board of education sets into place a specific framework by which concrete curricular objectives are validated and established, the process for programmatic budgeting can begin.

The major steps of installing programmatic budgeting are:

- Identify various educational activities or programs and group them into broad areas of need or purpose served.
- After grouping, a tentative program structure is derived.
- A goal statement is prepared for each basic program, expressing the purposes it serves.
- The goal statements are given to appropriate staff to gather data to describe service levels and program outputs.
- After data gathering, current and desired service objectives are defined.
- Guidelines are prepared and given to those who will develop the program budgets.
- Past cost information is assembled to guide budget estimates.
- Program work sheets and instructions are developed.
- Work sheets are completed and given to the respective budget directors.
- Work sheets are compiled and fed into master lists.
- Master lists are reconciled and established within a generic budget.
- The generic budget is passed and set into place.

Within such a budgeting system both finances and curriculum are monitored simultaneously. Thus, as the board of education receives quarterly reports regarding finances, it is also receiving information about curriculum. The process weds the budget and curriculum into one unified whole.

Such a system cannot be put into place overnight. At least a three- to five-year period is necessary for most school systems to engage in the transition. The most critical piece is the development of curriculum prior to loading it into any budgetary system.

Recommendation 5: Establish a Formal In-House Procedure for Teacher Involvement in District Curricular Discussions

At the present time there is no formal district-wide procedure for teacher involvement/input into curricular matters (see Finding 1.4). It is recommended that the superintendent establish a curriculum advisory council to be comprised of six classroom teachers (two from each level, i.e., elementary, middle school, high school) and six principals (likewise, two from each level). This group would be balanced among specialists and generalists. It would be a workable sized group. It would be chaired by the superintendent or designee who would not vote on matters.

The purpose of the curriculum advisory council is to serve as a central coordinating group and clearinghouse for curricular change in Locust Hill. All proposals for curricular change would be subject to review and discussion. This would ensure that the impact of initiative taken in one school was considered (not blocked) prior to implementation. It would insure that every level in the system was aware of changes at other levels.

It is not envisioned that this group would develop curriculum. That function would continue as before as a task force approach. The function of the group is to ensure continuity across the district and to be a receiving point for teacher-initiated changes and/or administrative initiated changes (or both) in curriculum. It would serve as a sounding board for the administration on new ideas to be explored in curriculum and/or instruction.

This group could also coordinate all staff development activities. It would ensure that such activities were consistent with and reinforced district priorities.

Recommendation 6: Develop Functional Curricular Documents in Locust Hill

Current curricular documents in Locust Hill are not functional (see Finding 2.2). They are nonexplicit, bulky and hard to use and monitor, and do not provide specific information to either teachers to coordinate the curriculum more successfully or to parents who want to know what the actual scope and sequence is (see Finding 1.3).

A complete set of curriculum guides should exist for all areas of the Locust Hill School District. These should be small, easy to use, readable, focused on the essentials of learner mastery, and ensure proper alignment to tests and texts in use. All guides should be referenced to an overall, valid scope and sequence document. There should be a workable system of cross-referencing objectives from scope and sequence to a grade level or course and from grade level to grade level and course to course.

Recommendation 7: Develop and Implement a System of Curriculum Monitoring in Locust Hill

Whatever curriculum is in place in the schools of Locust Hill is monitored very inconsistently at best. In most schools monitoring is largely perfunctory, with one or two exceptions and only at the elementary level.

A system of quarterly reports is largely a waste of time inasmuch as it is too late to modify the curriculum as it is being implemented. Rather, the quarterly system is merely a diary of composite decisions, however inconsistent they may be.

The purpose of reviewing planning documents prior to instruction and during instruction is to preserve the opportunity of engaging in modifications while instruction is being delivered. As such, it can prevent problems from occurring instead of documenting that they occurred.

Student and parent interview data provided abundant testimony of curricular breakdowns and lack of consistency and continuity still prevalent in the curriculum in Locust Hill (with the exception of mathematics, largely at the secondary level).

The best planbook supervision was observed in operation at the elementary schools in Locust Hill. Yet planbook supervision can be a waste of time in ensuring the delivery of the written curriculum (assuming one is present and valid) if it is not centered on the essential elements of sound curriculum management.

For a planbook to be useful in monitoring the written curriculum, the principal, chairperson, or supervisor must be able to ascertain the propriety of content selection (usually determined by a reference to the curriculum guide), the adequacy of time to be spent (by district guideline or curriculum guide reference), and the correctness of sequence (also determined by curriculum guide reference). Most planbooks typically include only a delineation of content and miss the remaining essential elements.

Most planbooks concentrate on objectives (with or without a reference to a curriculum), methods (the "how to"), and some sort of evaluation. These elements may be useful in evaluating an individual lesson apart from any other reference but are not useful in determining the meaning or value of any single lesson as it pertains to the flow of the total curriculum. Experienced teachers usually have no problem in determining methods or determining the propriety of specific outcomes. These may be somewhat repetitive.

Yet planbook supervision which is aimed at establishing adherence to the total curriculum is less concerned about methods and immediate evaluation than with matters of overall propriety and continuity. For planbooks to ensure curricular propriety and sequence effectively, they must be altered from the traditional format.

There are several simple and easy methods to do this. Paperwork should be kept to a minimum so as not to detract from the teaching process and, at the same time, to provide a means to adjust the curriculum should it be required. Flexibility should be preserved. However, flexibility does not connote no system at all or the lack of any adherence to the district's scope and sequence.

It is recommended that a system of curriculum monitoring be developed and implemented for all staff in the Locust Hill Schools. Such a system would provide a simple but effective means to ensure a high level of continuity to the overall curriculum and the ongoing data base for potential adjustments as instruction proceeds.

While any individual classroom teacher may be aware of this within his/her own environs, he/she may not be aware of the curriculum being delivered in other classrooms, at other grade levels, or in other schools. The data base should provide the means for adjustment from classroom to classroom, grade to grade, and school to school. It is the optimum of the flexible system in operation.

Recommendation 8: Replace All Local Honors Courses with Advanced Placement Courses if Available

Local honors courses do not appear to be solid equivalents to taking and successfully passing Advanced Placement. Local honors courses deny to Locust Hill students a means of successfully passing AP exams and in providing them, their parents, or the school district with any idea of comparability of the local curriculum to state and national norms. The Advanced Placement program was developed initially by some of the nation's most prestigious private schools and colleges. It is a rigorous and respected curriculum across the nation. All qualified Locust Hill students should have access to the Advanced Placement program.

Local honors may be continued in the curriculum but without the "honors" sobriquet. That should be reserved for only the AP courses. The only exception to the change may be those local courses in which students have consistently outperformed their counterparts who have taken the regular AP curriculum as determined by exam score.

The transition ought to take place within the next two years. Funds will have to be set aside for staff development as AP requires staff expertise in order to offer the AP curriculum.

Recommendation 9: Development of a Strong Local, Criterion-Referenced Assessment Program in Locust Hill

It seems highly unlikely that standardized tests will be of much use to the school district because of the manner in which data is reported and because Locust Hill students generally perform very well on them.

A more adequate and practical method for evaluating the growth of students in Locust Hill will be to develop exams that measure the more rigorous and demanding curriculum in the district.

The district can begin to move in this direction by requiring district-wide secondary school exams, a step being taken by many school districts in other states. Such exams will serve to focus on common curriculum content across the district and help identify the content to be taught and assessed by the respective faculties of the varying schools in the school system. It is a force for focusing the curriculum. Such exams ought to count for more than one-fourth of a fourth of the final grade for a course. They should count for at least one-fifth or one-fourth of the final grade.

It is recommended that the Locust Hill School District implement a system of district-wide exams at the secondary level within two years and a complete system of criterion-referenced measures in five years for mathematics, English-language arts, writing (using holistically scoring methods), science, social studies, and foreign language. Computer use and literacy may also be included in this arena.

Concomitantly, grading procedures should become uniform as well within the same time period. This inequity for students should be removed once and for all.

Recommendation 10: Redefine a Core Curriculum in Locust Hill That Includes Critical Thinking Skills

The curriculum is not managed per se in Locust Hill (see Finding 3.1). It exists in a more or less loose state, pushed and pulled by a variety of forces, many of which have no relationship to one another, and this results in a patchwork quilt of competing interests.

The absence of a sound board policy framework has served to hamper the capability of the district to make any closure on defining a common core to which all students would be served, prior to electing to move into a differentiated curriculum based upon future life choices.

It is recommended that a common core be defined for all (at least 90 percent) Locust Hill students in grades K–9 (which would contain some options within the core). Such a core would be characterized as having a strong basic skills focus which included the delineation of critical thinking skills. Such skills must be specifically identified by content area and taught in a multidisciplinary fashion across all curricular areas.

The core would also include the caveat that writing skills be taught in all subject areas within a district focused effort. This will necessitate a strong "writing in the content area" program.

The core curriculum should be accompanied by a detailed scope and sequence (as per Recommendations 1 and 6) and a reading list of books, plays, and artistic representatives/works that embody that core. Such a list should be published and be made available to students and parents within the school district.

SUMMARY

The Locust Hill School District enjoys a long tradition of excellence. By most conventional standards, it continues to uphold those traditions and expectations.

The board of education and the superintendent have not been content to rest on this comfortable tradition, however. Sensing that the district must move forward, they have commissioned this curriculum audit.

The audit imposes a set of standards that exceed many conventional criteria currently reflected in state and national standards. The district leaders desire to be assessed by the most rigorous criteria available. To this end, the audit is filed in the same spirit that is embodied in the phrase in stone above the old Adams Junior High School, "Enter to Learn, Go Forth to Serve."

CHECKPOINTS

Questions to the Author–Auditor about the Locust Hill Curriculum Audit

Question 1: *Since the Locust Hill students were doing so well on tests, how much better do you think they would do if the recommendations in the audit were followed?*

Answer: That would be difficult to establish from the data I reviewed. I think certain parts of the pupil population would do better on selected measures that were curricular focused. Without the focusing going on, I doubt the overall test scores would be improved significantly on standardized measures.

Question 2: *Since test scores were so high in Locust Hill, what were the real agendas in Locust Hill that propelled the audit?*

Answer: Curricular consistency among the schools, particularly the high schools. The pressures were quite strong from parents and these were reflected in many views of the board of education. The heart of this issue was control of the curriculum. The adversaries were, broadly, the teachers versus everyone else.

/ VIII / *Case Study 4: Cascade City Regional High School District*

THIS CASE STUDY is unique in that it is really three separate curriculum audits within one. The Cascade City Regional High School District is a separate and autonomous entity. It has its own superintendent and board of education. Two elementary districts send students to Cascade City, Eton Park, and Clumberville. The latter are small K–8 districts, which also have their own superintendents and respective boards of education.

All three districts are pseudonyms for three actual school systems audited by the author in 1987.

BACKGROUND, PURPOSE, AND SCOPE OF WORK

This document constitutes the final report of a curriculum audit commissioned by the Cascade City Regional High School District Board of Education.

Background

The Cascade City Regional High School (RHS) District was established in September of 1971. Formerly, high school students attended the Clumberville High School. A new arrangement was partially prompted by a fire in the old high school complex.

At the present time Cascade City RHS is struggling with a declining enrollment. Enrollment peaked in the 1976 school year when the plant accommodated some 885 students. At the time of the curriculum audit, the student population had shrunk to approximately 450 students.

The two feeder elementary school districts have also been faced with declining enrollment and aging facilities. At the time of the audit, both K–8 districts were discussing the possibilities of school closings and realignment of enrollment patterns. Such considerations have proven to be highly emotional topics in both communities.

The pupil enrollment in the Clumberville Public Schools was approximately 568 and in Eton Park, 419.

Purpose

The purpose of a curriculum audit in the three school districts was to determine the extent to which officials and professional staff had developed and implemented a sound, valid, and operational system of curriculum management.

Such a system would enable the respective school systems to make maximum utilization of their human and financial resources to educate the children they must serve. If such a curriculum management system were operational, it would also ensure the taxpayers and the state that their financial support had been optimized under the conditions in which they functioned.

Scope of Work

A curriculum audit is an objective, independent examination of data pertaining to educational program practices that will indicate the extent to which a school system can meet its objectives (whether the latter are internally or externally developed or imposed). An audit examines management practice and system results however defined. As such, it is a type of quality assurance.

METHODOLOGY

The Model for the Audit

The model for a curriculum audit is shown in Exhibit 15. The model has been published extensively in the professional literature, most recently in the AASA publication *Skills for Successful School Leaders* (1985, p. 90).

Generic quality control assumes that at least three elements must be present in any situation for it to be functional. These are: (1) a standard, goal/objective, (2) work directed towards the standard or goal/objective, and (3) feedback about the level of attainment (performance).

Within the context of an educational system and its governance and operational structure, curricular quality control requires: (1) a written

Exhibit 15
A Schematic View of Curricular Quality Control

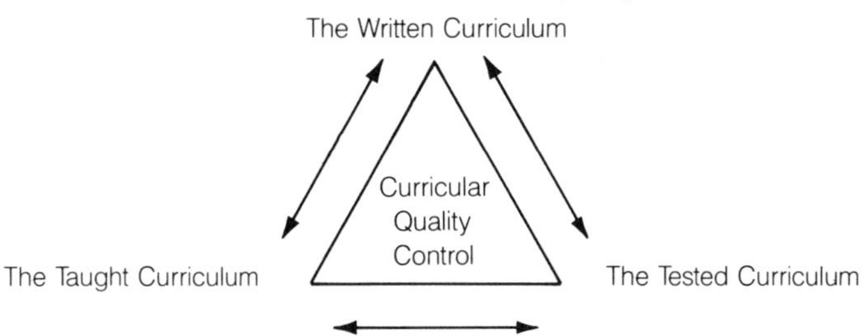

curriculum capable of being translated into the work of teachers in classrooms, (2) a taught curriculum shaped by the written curriculum, and (3) a tested curriculum consisting of the utilized assessment tools of pupil learning which are linked to both the taught and written curricula.

Standards for the Auditor

While a curricular audit is not a financial audit, it is governed by some of the same principles. These are as follows.

THE PRINCIPLE OF OBJECTIVITY

This standard means that curricular events are observable and verifiable, if not through observation then by a review of the products of those events, i.e., documents. Such documents are considered representations of transactions. The standard also means that any two auditors using the same standards and data base would reach approximately the same conclusions.

THE PRINCIPLE OF INDEPENDENCE

This standard means that the auditor stands apart from the entity being audited and is not influenced in rendering an opinion about the curriculum by having any pecuniary relationship to anyone in the entity, nor will his/her judgments about the curriculum be influenced by having any preconsidered interest related to those judgments.

THE PRINCIPLE OF CONSISTENCY

This standard means that the same procedures, techniques, and methods are followed with each audit so that the results are comparable over time.

THE PRINCIPLE OF MATERIALITY

This standard gives to the auditor broad authority to select that which is important from that which is not. It provides the auditor with discretionary power to explore and investigate all aspects of the operation being examined.

THE PRINCIPLE OF FULL DISCLOSURE

This standard means that the auditor must reveal all information that is important to the users of the audit. The users of a curriculum audit are the board of education, the administration and teaching staffs, students, parents, and taxpayers.

Data Sources

A curriculum audit utilizes a variety of data sources to determine if each of the three elements are in place and connected one to the other.

The audit process also inquires as to whether pupil learning has improved as the result of effective utilization of curricular quality control.

The major sources of the data for the audit in Cascade City, Eton Park, and Clumberville were:

(1) *Documents*—These consisted of board policies, curriculum guides, plans, previous reviews by state agencies, accreditation reports, board reports, test results, other external reports, memoranda regarding curriculum and instruction, and any other source of information which would reveal the elements of the written, taught, and tested curricula and the context in which the curriculum was defined, delivered, monitored, and utilized as a source of feedback to improve pupil learning.

(2) *Interviews*—Interviews were conducted to determine the relationships of the same elements within the quality control paradigm previously explicated in Exhibit 15.

Interviews were held in the three school districts with board members, top-level administrators, building principals, counselors, department chairpersons, teacher association officials, classroom teachers, and auxiliary personnel.

(3) *Site Visitations*—Site visitations reveal the physical context in which curriculum is being implemented. Such references are important as they may indicate document discrepancies or other unusual work conditions. The auditor visited all schools in all three districts. They ranged from turn of the century facilities to those constructed in the 1970s.

Standards for the Curriculum Audit

The auditor utilized five standards against which to compare, verify, and comment upon the existing curricular management practices in the three school systems. These standards have been extrapolated from an extensive review of management principles and practices, as well as having been utilized in the previous audits conducted by the auditor in eight states.

As a result, the standards do not reflect a utopian management concept, but rather the working characteristics that any complex organization should possess in being responsive and responsible to its patrons.

A school district that is using its financial and human resources for the greatest benefit of its students is an entity that is able to establish clear objectives, examine alternatives, select and implement alternatives, measure results as they develop against established objectives, and adjust its efforts so that it achieves a greater share of those objectives over time.

The five standards employed in the curriculum audit of the three school districts were:

(1) The school system is able to demonstrate its control of resources, programs, and personnel.
(2) The school system has established clear and valid objectives for students.
(3) The school system has documentation explaining how its programs have been developed, implemented, and conducted.
(4) The school system uses the results from district designed or adopted assessments to adjust, improve, or terminate ineffective practices or programs.
(5) The school system has been able to improve its productivity.

FINDINGS

Standard 1: The School District Is Able to Demonstrate Its Control of Resources, Programs, and Personnel

Quality control is the fundamental concept behind a well-managed educational program. It is one of the major premises of local educational control within any state's educational system.

The critical premise involved is that via the will of the electorate, a local school board establishes local priorities within state law, regulations, and good practice. A school district's final accountability to its community rests with the school board.

Through the construction of policy, a local school board provides the necessary focus to direct, via its administrative staff, the operations of a school system. In this way the expression of popular will is assured and enables the district to be responsive to its clients and patrons. It also enables the system to assess and utilize student learning meaningfully as a critical factor in determining its success.

Although educational program control (direction) and accountability are often shared among different components of a school system, fundamental control rests with the school board and top-level management staff.

What the Auditor Expected to Find in the Three School Districts

A school system meeting Standard 1 would be able to demonstrate the existence of:

- a clear set of policies that reflect state requirements and program goals and the necessity to use achievement data to improve school system operations
- documentation regarding a clear division of authority and responsibility between the school board and the top-level management staff as it pertains to policy and operations
- documentation of sound planning by the board and the top-level management staff
- a direct, uninterrupted line of authority from the school board/superintendent to principals, teacher leadership roles, and teachers
- administrative and teacher responsiveness to school board policies currently and over time

What the Auditor Found in the Three School Districts

CASCADE CITY REGIONAL HIGH SCHOOL

The auditor found ineffective board policies which were outdated and did not establish the framework for effective management of the curriculum. The auditor found a current record of frequent board violations of interference in and assumption of direct management of the school system in violation of good practice and the code of ethics of the State School Boards Association.

The auditor found no long-range planning capability of the district, poor central office and building leadership and coordination to lower levels of the high school, and inconsistent and ambiguous division of labor among the top-level administrative staff.

The auditor found an extremely negative, confrontational, and polarized situation between the Cascade City teaching staff and the Cascade City Regional High School Board of Education.

The auditor found a generally reactive approach to curricular improvement and innovation by the administrative staff, a conflict of interest among department chairpersons and their expected curricular/instructional leadership duties, no formal system for curriculum development, inequalities among persons with the same curricular responsibilities, and little formal use of feedback with the singular exception of the math and English departments.

The auditor found no formal mechanism in place of curricular articulation to the elementary school districts, with the exception of teacher-led efforts of the math and English departments at the high school.

The auditor found evidence of some board coordination among the three school districts which had recently been abandoned and, with the arrival of a new superintendent at Cascade City, renewed efforts of improved coordination with the elementary districts at a variety of levels on a number of common areas.

The auditor did find documents produced by teachers of the three districts which were considered by the developers as good and which were reported by teachers as useful and important products of curricular articulation.

ETON PARK

The auditor found some excellent policies pertaining to curriculum and instruction but no comprehensive policy which would require quality control of the curriculum as a totality.

The auditor did not find a comprehensive long-range plan for curriculum but did find evidence of aspects of long-range planning guiding the district.

The auditor found the Eton Park Board of Education generally in compliance with the State School Board Association's Code of Ethics, with only two occasions reported where it violated the Code on personnel appointments.

The auditor found evidence of provision for improved curricular coordination via the appointment of a part-time coordinator, though this position is understaffed, as is the guidance function. The auditor found excellent use of curricular feedback to classroom teachers, an operational monitoring system in place which assured that the curriculum was being delivered.

The auditor found a generally effective division of labor among the administrative staff, though some ambiguity was still present in the job descriptions reviewed.

The auditor found a generally positive climate in Eton Park, despite recently concluded negotiations with the teaching staff. The auditor found teachers extremely sensitive to perceived board transgressions into operations, particularly as it pertained to classroom grouping procedures and textbook adoptions. The auditor shares these concerns as well.

CLUMBERVILLE

The Clumberville board policies were mixed as far as continuity and comprehensiveness were concerned. The goals were vintage 1977, though the curriculum development policy was 1985. In the main, the policies did not provide the framework for a sound curriculum management system.

The auditor found evidence of board violation of the State School Boards Association Code of Ethics in the switching of the school principals—absent a recommendation from the superintendent to do so. The superintendent has also been excluded from a role in negotiations.

The auditor found a somewhat negative climate in Clumberville because of recently concluded negotiations where the amount of preparation time was a critical issue.

The auditor found a severely understaffed guidance function and a nonexistent, central curricular coordination function. Use of feedback data to improve pupil performance was informal and not systematic.

Job descriptions were somewhat detailed and provided some clarity regarding duties; however, they were unclear regarding curricular responsibilities. The auditor could find no long-range plan for curriculum development in Clumberville.

Specific Findings by District

CASCADE CITY REGIONAL HIGH SCHOOL

Finding 1.1: The Climate at the Regional High School District Has Been Volatile, Disruptive, Negative, and Confrontational

The climate at Cascade City Regional High School (CCRHS) has been subject to upheaval and disruption. Beginning with the adoption by the board of a controversial drug testing program for all students that brought national media attention to Cascade City, legal confrontations by the ACLU, and a public reprimand of the former superintendent for disobeying a board directive and ultimately his resignation, the turmoil became politicized in the community, resulting in a change in board membership, a change in board disposition, and a new superintendent.

Throughout this time there have been a continuing series of board/CCEA (Cascade City Education Association) skirmishes and clashes, both public and private, in which the board called for an assembly with students only, excluded teachers to discuss program and staff cuts, and attempted to exercise greater control of the student newspaper.

The confrontation between the board and the CCEA continued through the audit in which the board charged the staff with unprofessional behavior by engaging in a job action and gave every faculty member a written reprimand to that effect. The reaction of the teaching staff was bitter, emotional, and further resulted in their radicalization.

The basis of the confrontation between the CCRHS Board and the CCEA is heavily mixed with issues of job security, control, mistrust, outright personal antagonisms, and political club-wielding and provocations. Some members of the board are convinced the CCEA is engaged in deliberate acts of sabotage to their legal authority to govern the district. The CCEA and many teachers are convinced the board, and in particular some members of the board, are on a "power ego trip" of personal revenge and retribution for largely political reasons.

The resulting polarization has created an extremely negative and atrabilious school climate in which to function. Teacher energies are increasingly directed towards reactionary actions and outright hostility and alienation from the school and the system. Some faculty members have withdrawn and are in the process of severing their emotional ties to the ongoing educational process. The situation is unproductive and unhealthy. It is destroying the fabric of trust necessary for any human organization to remain a positive force in its environment.

When asked in interviews, neither board members nor teachers could indicate where such a destructive cycle of action and reaction would or could end in the future. While board members and teachers believed the climate to be injurious to good human relations and to any kind of productive work, with some expressing real regret at the circumstances, no one knew how to end the conflict and de-polarize the situation.

Finding 1.2: Board Policies in Cascade City Are Ineffective in Establishing Curricular Quality Control

The auditor reviewed the following policies:

Policy Number	Content	Date Adopted
3100	Budget Schedule	1978
3160	Line Item Transfer Authority	1979
3170	Budget Implementation	1979
5121	Examinations	1986
6010	Instructional Priority Objectives	1978
6010.1	Prioritized Goals	1977
6141.3	Curriculum Development	1978
6146	Graduation Requirements	1978
6147	Academic Achievement	1978
6160	Instructional Resources	1978
6161.2	Complaints/Instructional Materials	1984
6171	Remedial Instruction	1978
6171.1	Non-Discriminatory Programming	1984
9200	Commitment to Accomplishment	1978
9311	Curriculum Policies	1978

The above policies did not result in the development of specific curricular outcome statements, relate testing or test data to such outcomes, develop necessary textbook alignment with textbook adoption, or lead to the creation of any plan reviewed by the auditor that could be called comprehensive, despite the fact that Cascade City board policy #9200 required one along with "specifications of how their [students'] successful achievement will be determined." This policy has been in effect since November 1978.

The auditor did find examples of quality control in the curriculum. These were largely present in the English and math departments but only as a result of department chairperson initiative and not as a result of board policy or administrative leadership. Other curricular areas did not exhibit the same commitment or level of sophistication as these two curricular areas.

That fact was readily apparent in a recent "flap" over the use or misuse of audio-visual (AV) aids in the regional high school program. Despite the fact that Cascade City board policy #6160 states that the board, "shall provide a diversity of instructional resources including textbooks, and other printed materials, audio-visual aids and devices . . . to implement the district educational goals and objectives and meet pupil needs," the board vetoed continuing participation in the county film library because it was felt some teachers abused the privilege.

The new superintendent of one-half month had to require that the linkages between classroom objectives, course proficiencies, and AV applications be stated in planbooks. Such linkages should have been required in policy form prior to such an incident. The fact that they were not also indicates shortcomings in extant board policies.

The incident has also served to exacerbate tensions between the board and teachers. Some teachers have simply given up the use of AV and moved to a straight textbook oriented program, while others bring equipment from home to avoid having to fill out another form for equipment utilization. Teachers reported to the auditor the feeling that the AV imbroglio is another example of board mistrust of their professional judgments and, at best, an overreaction to one or two teachers.

Finding 1.3: There Is No Long-Range Plan for Curriculum Development/Quality Control at the Regional High School

The auditor could find no long-range plan for curriculum development in the regional high school. A review of the state's accreditation report of January, 1985, indicated that the state believed the district had established annual planning capabilities and complied with a requirement for multi-year program planning. However, neither of these represents a long-range plan for curriculum per se. Interviews and document review both indicate such a plan did not exist at the time of the audit.

Finding 1.4: The Lack of a Long-Range Plan Has Resulted in Budget Confusion and Misdirected Emphasis on Program/Staff Reduction at the Regional High School

Since the regional high school district does not have a long-range plan, establishing fiscally based program priorities has been difficult. The situation is worse at budget time when the teachers turn in their "wish lists," and the board has found examples of poor planning and duplication among fiduciary requests.

In addition, the lack of a long-range curriculum plan which would establish some sort of strategic vision for the district has resulted in a misemphasis on budgetary reductions and staff cutbacks.

The most serious problem facing the regional high school is declining enrollment. The extent of that enrollment decline is shown in Exhibit 16, from 1974 to 1984.

The Cascade City Board has responded with a variety of staff reduc-

Exhibit 16
Enrollment Decline at Cascade City Regional High School

School Year	Grade by Grade Comparison				Total Enrollment*
	Ninth	Tenth	Eleventh	Twelfth	
1974–75	217	210	209	197	833
1975–76	232	220	211	199	862
1976–77	212	217	205	199	833
1977–78	210	194	198	194	796
1978–79	201	187	182	186	756
1979–80	172	181	179	171	703
1980–81	164	169	165	168	666
1981–82	151	165	161	156	633
1982–83	129	149	157	149	584
1983–84	135	130	148	140	553
1984–85	136	132	125	133	526

*Figures extrapolated from Figure 8 (p. 19) Long Range Facility Plan.

tions, some through attrition and others more directly, though not on a one to one basis with enrollment decline.

The Cascade City Regional High School District will soon face the prospect of reducing a basic high school program that is not now comprehensive in nature as enrollment continues to decline. Board members in Cascade City, staff, and administrators all realize that the school must "reach out" to more students in other areas beyond Eton Park and Clumberville to compensate for this decline. Yet what would entice such students to come to Cascade City in lieu of giving up the high school where they now attend? One factor would be the prospect of encountering a richer curriculum than the school of current attendance. If this were not the case what incentive would there be to attend Cascade City rather than somewhere else?

In this respect, staff cutbacks which result in curricular reductions pertaining to quality and quantity become self-defeating to the long-range problem of institutional survival. The board should be building, expanding, and enriching the curriculum at Cascade City to provide the basis of expanding the enrollment beyond those students from Eton Park and Clumberville.

A review of students from the sending districts who do not attend Cascade City reveals that, with the exception of those pupils who attend the satellite vocational program, it is the more academically able student who opts out of the Cascade City program. Academically able students require program depth and diversity. To this extent the board recently moved to fill a music position on a full-time basis. Other programs, however, may not offer a full slate of rigorous curricula. This is true in foreign language, art, and social studies, to cite a few. While Cascade City offers some honors courses, it offers no Advanced Placement (AP) courses. The latter are considered the national barometer for academic excellence and provide a much more reliable guide as to the capability of enabling the "best" Cascade City students to compete with the "best" anywhere.

The Cascade City Board has taken actions in the short-term which on the surface appear prudent, i.e., reductions of expenditures to correspond to a declining requirement in the scope of the educational services provided to a diminishing student body.

Yet a longer view of the matter will indicate that this is a strategy for the demise of the school as a viable secondary educational institution. It is also crippling the institution in meeting its greatest challenge to its continuation. In short, there is no future in any further curricular reductions, and only a future with curricular expansion.

The problem is intensified with the recent drug test controversy which has established the school as a kind of "druggie heaven" in Clark County. How can such an image be dealt with? Certainly it is not by reducing the quality or quantity of the curriculum/programs at Cascade City. It is moving in the opposite direction.

The lack of a long-range plan has meant that there has been no guidance from the board of administration about the total configuration of the curriculum in the high school. At the same time no one is accountable either.

Finding 1.5: There Has Been a Lack of Leadership in Curriculum at the Regional High School

The auditor found no evidence of strong, proactive, central curriculum leadership at the regional high school. The auditor reviewed the job descriptions of the key administrative personnel. The following duties were listed for the superintendent in the area of curriculum.

Superintendent's Curricular Duties

#2. Devote the major portion of time to instructional leadership and curriculum work.

#3. Work with the chief administrators of the constituent elementary districts in developing coordinated programs and vertical curriculum disciplines.

A review of the principal's job description revealed no curricular duties listed. The same situation prevailed for the vice-principal and guidance chairperson.

The job description for the department chairperson revealed these curricular duties:

Department Chairperson's Curricular Duties

#5. Review and make recommendations concerning curricular revisions.

#11. Take the initiative in implementing and revising the approved course of study.

Interview data yielded a consistent pattern of curricular change at Cascade City. Department chairs would submit course change requests through the principal. These would be submitted to the board. Budgetary requests were given to the former superintendent. Teachers interviewed indicated that the pattern was clear in this regard.

This division of labor is in direct contradiction to duties as outlined in the job descriptions reviewed by the auditor. Central curriculum coordination was neglected. Teachers reported having to wait months for curricular decisions. The role of the administration in curriculum leadership has been reactive to whatever teacher initiative has been taken.

The lack of leadership was also evident in the 1983 Regional States Association Report. A team of seventeen teachers and administrators spent three days at Cascade City. They filed a unanimous report which made the following comments about leadership, curriculum, coordination, and communication at the school:

- It is recommended that leadership roles be carried out and evaluated in reference to Board Policy, job descriptions, and the school's philosophy and objectives. In doing such the potential of all concerned can be better realized and the quality of the educational program enhanced (p. 11).
- With developing good communications between administration and staff it is felt that shortcomings can be resolved or there can be an easing in the severity of the problems (p. 12).
- A curriculum leader be clearly identified as the individual responsible for the articulation of curriculum throughout the school and to structure a continuous, ongoing process for curriculum evaluation and development in concern with department chairpersons and librarian (p. 15).
- The position of building principal carry with it the responsibility for educational leadership. A more assertive role by him in the daily administration of the school would make this leadership more evident among the staff and students (p. 33).
- A program of cooperation to achieve curriculum compatibility with sending districts be implemented (p. 33).
- The separation of administrative authority, duties, and roles of the principal and vice-principal in the daily operation of the school should be more clearly defined to all staff and students to improve the decision-making process (p. 33).

The auditor concurs with the Regional States evaluation. Most, if not all, of the same conditions cited in 1983 still persist at Cascade City. It was precisely this vacuum that prompted some board members to become more aggressive than in the past.

Board members reported to the auditor their frustrations with the lack of information about curriculum, the lack of a comprehensive plan by which to relate budgetary requests, the "status quo" orientation of the administration, and its inability to admit to problems that were all too apparent to the board.

Board members cited the following additional concerns that directly relate to leadership in the school.

- obsolescence in some courses of a technical nature and with some equipment
- the duplication of budgetary requests which indicate a lack of internal coordination and review
- lack of coordination with the elementary districts
- the lack of a comprehensive set of offerings in some departments
- the lack of rigor in every course that the school offers
- lack of alternatives for unsuccessful children
- lack of attention to continuous skill building in the curriculum (sequence)
- inability to make sense of a multitudinal barrage of requests from the staff, each demanding their area be given priority with no way to establish priorities

Seasoned board members reported these conditions existed long before the incident with the drug testing brought matters to a head.

The auditor did review an external consulting report filed with the board in 1984 by Kermit Jones Rice, Inc. (KJR). This report dealt exclusively with seven areas: budgeting, purchasing, employee relations, tax collection methods, food services, warehousing, and building and grounds. It did not examine curriculum.

On the one hand, this external review corroborated this auditor's findings regarding curriculum. The superintendent had no curricular responsibilities. The report does indicate that the principal "participates fully in the development of the budgets, curriculum, and administrative procedures" (p. 2).

The KJR report is flatly at odds with the Regional States Association's seventeen member review. KJR interviewed only administrators and department chairs. No board members were interviewed, nor classroom teachers, association representatives, or auxiliary personnel.

The KJR report was not focusing on the educational programs or curriculum. It was solely focused on the business functions. Therefore, the two reports had a different scope and utilized a different functional base from which to gather data. It is quite possible that good communication may exist in the areas of budgeting, purchasing, food services, and building and grounds, but not in the curriculum or the educational program. Therefore, the KJR report cannot be used to invalidate the observations and recommendations of the Regional States, or this auditor, as has apparently been done in the First Progress Report of May 1, 1986, filed by the high school principal who cited this report in response to the Regional States recommendation that he take a more "assertive role" in the school.

The auditor asked to review the monthly reports filed by department chairpersons to the principal. These revealed that what was reported to the principal were departmental activities, some test scores, field trips, conference attendance reports, class projects, report on audio-visual utilization, and one incident of comments regarding the evaluation of staff. The auditor did not find in the time period review (Sept.–Dec. 1986–87) one example of a report regarding long-range curriculum needs or suggestions for specific curricular revisions.

A review of the job descriptions reveals many ambiguities. For example, the principal's job description states: "Coordinate the entire testing program with the guidance department." What does this mean? Coordinate what? The principal indicated that this meant that he determined that the test dates did not interfere with the SAT dates.

In relationship to "Be responsible for the student handbook," the principal publishes the handbook. Regional States found problems with the job descriptions between the principal and vice-principal. One problem is imbalance. In short, the vice-principal handles scheduling, attendance, discipline, lunch program, transportation, student activities, in-school suspension, parking permits, locker assignments, the scheduling of testing (also a part of the principal's job description), and responsibilities for athletic events and scheduling.

In comparison the principal's job description does not formally deal with any day-to-day specific duties despite the statement, "Supervise the daily operation of Cascade City Regional High School and the instructional staff."

Interviews and documents reveal that the day-to-day operations of the school are run by the vice-principal, with the principal selecting what other duties he may wish to pursue or subbing for the vice-principal in case of conflicts.

There is no formalized channel for curriculum review which would coordinate the efforts of the respective departments together in the school, such as a curriculum advisory council. The auditor found no sustained example of systematic, proactive curricular leadership at the regional high school by the school administration. The lack of that leadership extends back at least until so recognized by the Regional States Accreditation Report of 1983, a period of four years, and even before that in order to be identified in the Report.

Finding 1.6: There Are Inequalities Among Department Chairperson Duties as Well as a Conflict of Interest in Carrying Them Out

Some department chairs at the regional high school district teach four periods, others five periods. The basis for this difference was never made clear to the auditor nor was it understood by the chairpersons except to indicate to them that their areas were not as important as those with only four teaching periods. Those chairpersons with five teaching periods were those for physical education and special areas.

A conflict of interest arises as the chairpersons go about formally evaluating teachers in their respective areas. If such observations/evaluations are grieved, the chairpersons belong to the same union/association as the teachers they are evaluating. A union cannot grieve against itself. One result is a tendency on the part of chairpersons to be careful in such situations. At least one recounted an unpleasant incident in which an unfavorable teacher evaluation became confrontational.

Finding 1.7: Curriculum Articulation Between the Three Districts Has Been Limited to Technical Levels

There have been occasions where the staffs of the respective three school districts have worked together to write curriculum. According to teachers and administrators interviewed, some of these efforts have been quite successful in promoting improved articulation. These would be examples of technical articulation.

Another level of articulation is the political policy level. That has not been functional. At least one effort was made in the past, but it collapsed when some members perceived it as a "finger pointing session" instead of a joint policy development effort.

Curriculum articulation should be contained as a provision in the policies of all three boards. The policies provide an unbrella for the technical work of the professional staff. With those policies comes funding support and a systematic and coordinated technical effort by the respective three superintendents to work together on a variety of mutual problems.

ETON PARK PUBLIC SCHOOLS

Finding 1.1: Curricular Leadership in Eton Park Has Been Proactive and Effective

The auditor found in the Eton Park Public Schools a superintendent strongly interested in curriculum and program. The auditor found numerous documents pertaining to program and staffing and testing analyses that sketched out alternatives and options for the board in time for due deliberation.

In addition, the Eton Park Public Schools have funded a one-half time curriculum coordinator who is establishing operational linkages between the written, taught, and tested curricula.

The Eton Park Public Schools have seen fit to add a full-time science teacher at the elementary (K–6) levels, enabling the schools to partake of increased subject matter specialization in a field which has been traditionally weak at the elementary level.

Finding 1.2: Board Policies in Eton Park Are Marginally Effective and the Board Sometimes Strays into Operations

The auditor examined the following board policies in Eton Park:

Policy Number	Content	Date Adopted
5121	Grading System and Related Areas	1986
5123	Promotion and Retention	1986
5124	Reporting Pupil Progress to Parents	1986
6140	Curriculum Adoption	1983
6141	Curriculum Development	1983
6142	Basic Curriculum	1984
6142.1	Family Life	1983
6142.6	Testing Program	1983
6142.7	Alcohol and Drugs	1983
6147	Standards of Proficiency	1986
6156	Instructional Scheduling/Classroom Procedures	1985
6161	Textbook Selection and Adoption	1983
6171.1	Remedial Instruction	1983
6171.2	Academically Talented Students Programs	1983
6171.3	Compensatory Education Program	1984

Most of the policies reviewed were accompanied with detailed administrative procedures and one with exhibits. The accompanying administrative procedures enabled the auditor to determine if they were congruent with the intent of the policy. The same would be true of the board or public. This was one of the strong points of the policies reviewed.

The policies also made clear that it was the board that must approve all curricula (#6140); curricular priorities were explicit (#6142) and it was this policy that demonstrated how the curriculum was to be apportioned in minutes per week. Through this method the district was confronting the issue of instructional time availability in view of an ever-expanding curriculum. Basic adoptions for textbooks were also part of this policy.

Board policy #6147 made clear the standards for promotion at each grade level as well as accompanying administrative procedures which established the responsibilities of students and parents to engage the school's formal educational program.

The policies were weak because they failed to tie together elements of the written, taught, and tested curricula. For example, in the curriculum development policy (#6141) nothing is mentioned about the necessity for the curriculum to be aligned with extant tests or textbooks. Likewise, the testing and textbook policies (#6142.6 and #6161) make no reference to the requirement for alignment to the locally adopted curriculum or proficiencies.

Through the work of the newly funded curriculum coordinator's role, the district is, in fact, making a substantial effort to strengthen these linkages. If they had been required on the front end within policy, they would not now be having to spend time on establishing them.

Data derived from interviews of Eton Park board members, administrators, and teachers revealed that the board has expressed concern and made decisions regarding grouping practices. The auditor examined the policies of the board and found no reference to grouping practices directly. Indirectly, the board has required some grouping practices in its policies #6147, 6171.1, 6171.2 and 6171.3. These policies carve out provisions within the educational program for grouping.

Some board members expressed concern about the grouping practices, fearing that grouping leads to social stigmatization. Yet there is practically no way to avoid the necessity to group children on the basis of their achievement to enable instruction to be maximally efficient within the current structure of schools.

Without explicit policies which would clearly establish the board's intent or set forth criteria for grouping to guide operations, dealing with grouping on an ad hoc basis is clearly straying from policy and dabbling in operations, i.e., the actual administration of the school district. The board is out of line.

In addition, the board has expressed some interest in changing the primary textbook in reading (*Open Court*) despite the fact that the teaching staff feels strongly that it is an effective approach to teach reading.

Boards should rarely dictate methods/means of operations. That is the major responsibility of the professional staff via the superintendent. When methods/means become ends, then they are the proper subject of a policy. One example would be school integration. Racial integration is both a means and an end in itself. Therefore, it is the proper subject of policy development. Grouping may fall into this category if properly approached.

Policy development for a board of education is primarily the statement of intent. It establishes the "what" and the "why" for operations to follow. Operations are concerned with "how to" and "when." Boards should clearly delineate the purpose and rationale for operations but stay clear of dictating the methods/means to realize those purposes. If purposes are not realized over time with the existing methods/means, it is not unreasonable to require the professional staff to consider changes in operations which more closely conform to the board's stated intent.

To perform the above in a logical and rational manner, both the board and administration must engage in long-range planning. It is within the constraints and specifications of a long-range plan that the board sets forth the timeline by which it will determine if present methods/means are working and/or if they require changes. The data produced by the professional staff is thus logically linked to a systematic (and not emotional/political) review process. To do otherwise sets forth a confrontational climate between the board and the professional staff in which the board is perceived as meddling in professional affairs, and the staff feels compelled to enter the political arena to change board membership.

Finding 1.3: There Is No Long-Range Plan for Curriculum Development in the Eton Park Public Schools

The auditor did not find any comprehensive plan for curriculum development in the Eton Park Public Schools. The auditor did review a document which pertained to a long-range schedule for program evaluation which extended to the year 1989–90. Yet this would only be a piece of a long-range plan for curriculum development. The other pieces would include systematic and periodic needs assessments, validation of content selected, review of objectives and proficiencies, cost projections, and benefit analyses which would systematically link budget development to curriculum development.

Finding 1.4: There Is a Formal Procedure in Place for Curriculum Development in Eton Park

The auditor found both a formal system in place for curriculum development, a curriculum development policy by the Eton Park Board, and administrative staffing to operationalize this procedure.

Finding 1.5: The Central Curriculum Function Is Understaffed in Eton Park

The district has established a one-half time position for curriculum development. This person does more than merely supervise the curriculum developmental functions. The person also monitors the curriculum and becomes involved in the daily delivery of curriculum and the use of feedback data to classroom teachers. The position has been in operation less than a year.

It is not only critical that these functions be continued, but expanded for at least the next two to three years to a full-time position. One of the major responsibilities of this role as stated in the job description is the development of a long-range curriculum plan. The developmental process can be accelerated with increased staffing. Some of the delivery functions ought to be assigned to the two school principals as well. Their role at the present is largely perfunctory.

Finding 1.6: Some Job Ambiguities Remain in Eton Park

The auditor examined the board of education approved job descriptions in the Eton Park Public Schools. The language in the job descriptions is generally clear with some exceptions.

However, curriculum per se is not mentioned in either the job description of the superintendent or the principal. It is cited in the job description for the curriculum coordinator.

What is not clear is whether the curriculum coordinator is a line or staff officer. While it seems apparent that the development of curriculum is the responsibility of the coordinator, it is not clear who monitors the curriculum once it is in place.

Data from interviews indicated that both the coordinator and the principal did some monitoring of the curriculum, yet this responsibility is not cited in any job description. If both the principal and the coordinator monitor, this is mixing a line and staff function and results in the teachers perceiving that there are two bosses in curricular affairs, a violation of the unity of command concept.

It is not clear if the superintendent reviews the curriculum developed by the coordinator since this is not mentioned in any job description. There are citations regarding program evaluation and instructional materials in the job description of the curriculum coordinator but not the principal. Program evaluation is not the same as curriculum evaluation.

These ambiguities do not ensure clear accountability of the top-level administrative staff for all curricular functions.

CLUMBERVILLE

Finding 1.1: Curricular Policies of Clumberville Contain Similar Flaws to Those of Eton Park

The auditor examined the following policies of the board of education in Clumberville:

Policy Number	Content	Date Adopted
6000	Philosophy of the Schools	1977
6010	Goals of the Schools	1977
6111	School Calendar	1985
6114.1	Bomb Threat Procedure	1985
6115	Flag Displays	1985
6121	Affirmative Action	1985
6140[4]	Curriculum Adoption	1985
6141[4]	Curriculum Development	1985
6141.3	English as a Second Language	1985
6142.1[4]	Family Life	1985
6142.4	Physical Education Policy	1985
6142.6[4]	Testing Program	1985
6142.7[4]	Alcohol and Drugs	1985
6145	Academic Standards and Athletic Eligibility	1985
6147	Standards of Proficiency	1985
6151	Class Size	1985
6152	Grouping for Instruction	1985
6153	Field Trips	1986
6156[4]	Scheduling for Instruction	1985
6161	Textbook Selection and Adoption	1985

[4]Policy the same as in the Eton Park Board Policies.

Policy Number	Content	Date Adopted
6162.4	Community Resources	1985
6163.1	School Library	1985
6164.2	Guidance Services	1985
6164.4	Student Special Services	1985
6171.1[4]	Remedial Instruction	1985
6171.2[4]	Programs for Academically Talented Students	1985
6171.3[4]	Compensatory Education Program	1985
6171.31	Comparability of Personnel	1986
6171.32	Comparability of Materials and Supplies	1986
6171.4	Education of Handicapped Children	1985
6171.6	Evaluation of Special Education Programs	1985
6171.7	Services for Non-Public School Pupils	1985
6173	Home Instruction	1985

The auditor found that seven policies were nearly the same or exactly the same as those utilized in the Eton Park Public Schools, adopted for the most part some two years earlier. However, where the Eton Park policies were accompanied in some cases with significantly more detail, the Clumberville policies lacked that detail. The one exception was that Clumberville had adopted a policy regarding grouping which was not present in the policies of the Eton Park Board reviewed by the auditor.

The result is that the Clumberville policies suffer from the same deficiencies as the Eton Park policies, and, with the exception of the very precise policy about students with handicapping conditions present in Clumberville but not Eton Park, the same lack of solid policy framework for sound curriculum management was lacking in Clumberville as in Eton Park.

Specifically, no policy mandated that the curriculum be aligned with extant tests or textbooks or that regular monitoring of the relationships among all three elements of quality control (written, taught, and tested curricula) be systematically established and maintained over time and annually reported to the respective boards of education.

A positive finding is that, as the policies are the same for both elementary districts, the problem of organizational variance at the Cascade City Regional High School District is lessened in this respect. To the extent that both sending districts to the regional high school employ similar educational practices, texts, tests, and materials, the utilization of resources ought to become more focused and efficient. This would not be the case if the students of both districts were substantially dissimilar, which appears not to be the case at this time, or if the respective boards had vastly dissimilar aspirations for the clientele they represent.

Finding 1.2: The Clumberville Board of Education Has Acted on a Personnel Matter in Violation of the State School Board Association's Code of Ethics

The State School Board Association's Code of Ethics stipulates that personnel recommendations will be acted upon with "proper recommendation by the appropriate administrative officer."

A majority of the Clumberville Board, without a recommendation of the superintendent, voted to transfer two seasoned administrators in the district after many years of satisfactory service at those levels to opposite positions. The move caused a community uproar and a parental petition to the highest levels of the State Department of Education.

The parental suit was vitiated by the fact that the parents "lacked standing" and was subsequently dismissed by the Department.

The move by the Clumberville Board of Education represented an administrative decision to run the district directly in personnel matters, also a violation of the State Association's Code of Ethics. The board clearly entered the arena of administrative decision making instead of maintaining its position in the areas of policy making, planning, and appraisal. The board apparently acted on a whim of the moment, inasmuch as the auditor did not review any policy of that body which required or stipulated that professional personnel would be transferred under the contextual referents present in the district at the time of the board directive to do so in Clumberville.

When a board of education acts preemptively in administrative matters, it removes the accountability of the professional administration for the operations of the district, thus impairing the board from objectively evaluating administrative performance. If the board at a subsequent date determines such performance is not satisfactory, it cannot fire itself. Thus, poor administrative performance cannot be reasonably and fairly assessed, and if the board should act pejoratively, it seriously injures its own case to do so by eroding its own legal standing in case of appeal by the administrative officer in question. In short, a board of education administers a school district at its own peril, legal and otherwise.

The action has not only polarized some segments of the Clumberville community against the incumbent board, but established a cloud of doubt within the minds of the administrators as to the real reasons for the board's actions. If the board was not pleased with past administrative performance, why were not the customary legal and professional personnel procedures followed? Adherence to ethical practices would have protected the professional reputations of the administrators involved.

Finding 1.3: Centralized Curricular Staffing Is Nearly Absent in Clumberville

At the time of the audit, there was no central role devoted to curricular affairs in Clumberville. The job description of the superintendent does not include any curricular responsibilities of a specific nature, and only one is present in the job description of the principalship. Indeed, there is a conspicuous gap in this regard in Clumberville. There is no curriculum coordinator in the system.

Finding 1.4: Guidance Staffing in Clumberville Is Marginal

For approximately 230 children in grades 5–8, there is less than a 30 percent guidance counselor in the Clumberville Public Schools. Interview information with the guidance counselor yielded data that showed he had many administrative chores along with regular teaching responsibilities in the Faubus Intermediate School.

The paucity of time spent on guidance by this less than half-time counselor appeared to contradict directly board policy #6164.2 which mandates that a guidance program be comprehensive in nature and go beyond crisis counseling. This is simply not possible in the circumstances now regnant at the Faubus Intermediate School.

The importance of sound counseling to curricular effectiveness is integral. No matter how good the written curriculum may be or no matter how sound classroom instruction may be, without proper guidance from the counseling staff, the delivery of a curriculum is compromised. To ensure the proper implementation of curriculum with any student population, a workable ratio of students to counselors is requisite. At the present time that ratio in Clumberville is not functional for anything but the barest of crisis interventions. Both the children and the curriculum are being shortchanged as a result.

Finding 1.5: Job Descriptions in Clumberville Do Not Include Critical Curricular Management Functions

The word "curriculum" was not found in the job description of the Clumberville superintendent of schools and only once in the job description of the elementary principal (#20). However, the curricular responsibilities contained within the principalship were only for the purposes of ensuring visitations occurred in more than one area of the curriculum. There were no citations regarding curriculum development or validation, alignment, monitoring, or evaluation. While some of these functions were described by respondents interviewed by the auditor, they were nowhere as formally developed or systematic as those found in Eton Park.

The auditor did find evidence that a central coordinator role had been discussed and got to the point of being advertised but at the last minute was not funded by the Clumberville Board of Education.

Finding 1.6: There Is No Long-Range Plan for Curriculum Development in the Clumberville Public Schools

The auditor found no evidence of long-range planning for curriculum development in the Clumberville Public Schools. There was some evidence of short-range planning, normally not more than one year in length. These data were usually illustrated in annual reports to the county superintendent or contained within annual reports to the Clumberville Board of Education by the superintendent of schools.

The lack of an effective long-range plan denies to the district the benefit of a sound curricular focus for a longer period of time and prevents the district from relating curricular priorities to financial planning. It also means that short-term curricular priorities may take on a significance of disproportionate emphasis, and some overlooked needs will continue to be ignored until the system is caught up in a crisis. Management is crippled by a lack of sound multi-year planning.

Finding 1.7: The Climate in Clumberville Remains Rocky as the Result of Recent Negotiations with the Teachers' Association

The working climate within the Clumberville Public Schools was not positive at the time of the curriculum audit. The recently concluded negotiated agreement saw the board and the association at loggerheads over the issue of prep time for teachers.

That issue saw the principals drafting several simulated schedules based on many unknowns and the consideration of the board of a reprimand for the principals. Once again, the board was directly issuing orders to the professional staff in areas pertaining to the daily operations of the district. The superintendent was not a direct participant in this process.

While the board apparently felt that too many teachers had too much "free time," the auditor found evidence that many functions, such as curriculum planning and guidance, which took place during these preparation periods, have been lost or severely reduced as a result of the reduction in prep time. Whereas in the past the board may have paid for such services indirectly, they will now have to pay for them directly, in addition to the regular salaries paid to current persons on the payroll.

SUMMARY OF COGENT FINDINGS ON CURRICULUM AUDIT STANDARD 1

Viewed as three entities, the three school districts have similar problems with creating effective policy and managerial control over curriculum. Two of the three boards of education have strayed significantly into the operational affairs of the actual administration of the respective school districts, though the apparent motivation for doing so was different.

The most effective control of curriculum was being implemented in the Eton Park Public Schools where the most positive climate was also noted in operation by the auditor. It was also in Eton Park that the most consistent and formal operations regarding curriculum management were observed in action. The reason is that in Eton Park the board of education has funded the necessary administrative positions to some extent, whereas this support is absent in the Clumberville Public Schools and at the Cascade City Regional High School.

All three school districts have not created workable and functional long-range plans for curriculum development, nor have they developed a full set of functional curriculum policies necessary to gain curricular quality control.

While the job description of the Cascade City superintendent made curricular articulation an imperative with the two sending elementary districts, there has been a lack of initiative in this regard over the past several years. The new Cascade City superintendent has already begun to take some initiative to fully comply with the content of his job description.

Whatever articulation has occurred among the three districts, the linkages have been almost exclusively limited to technical matters. While the policies of the two sending elementary districts were virtually the same on many issues, the respective boards of education have remained largely isolated from one another. This has accentuated the problem of political insulation and program fragmentation, K–12.

The tendency of at least two of the boards of education has been to engage in staff cutbacks or increased work loads for remaining staff. If enrollment and curricular/legislative variables also remained constant, there might be some economies of scale realized with these measures.

However, there is a good deal of evidence to indicate at both Cascade City and Clumberville that the economies of scale are illusory. At the former district such reductions may lead to matters of institutional survival and, at the latter site, issues pertaining to diseconomies caused by having to pay more and not less for services already received. A pronounced lack of multi-year planning by the administration and boards cripples the districts from grappling with true economic and educational measures of efficiency and effectiveness. In spite of these obstacles and problems, sound teaching remains the cornerstone of all three school systems' daily operations.

Standard 2: The School District Has Established Clear and Valid Objectives for Students

A school system meeting this audit standard has established a clear, valid, and measurable set of pupil standards for learning and has set them into a workable framework for their attainment.

Unless objectives are clear and measurable, there cannot be a cohesive effort to improve pupil achievement in any one direction. The lack of clarity denies to a school district the capability of concentrating its resources through a focused approach to management. Instead, resources may be spread too thin and be ineffective in any direction. Objectives are, therefore, essential to attaining local quality control via the elected school board.

What the Auditor Expected to Find in the Three School Districts

The auditor expected to find in the three school districts a clearly established, district-wide set of goals and objectives adopted by the respective boards of education. Such objectives would set the framework for the operation of the district, its sense of priorities, and explicit direction for the superintendent and the professional staff.

In addition, clarity of objectives must be matched by a record of consistent effort towards attainment and the creation of a working context in which the objectives are set into the structure of the school system.

What the Auditor Found in the Three School Districts

CASCADE CITY REGIONAL HIGH SCHOOL DISTRICT

While a variety of goals and objectives do exist for courses and programs at Cascade City Regional High School, the board-adopted prioritized goals were not influential in their derivation. The auditor found no planning body or document that integrated such curricula together, no formal procedure for such integration, and largely isolated curricular development efforts. The most conspicuous gap at the Cascade City Regional High School District was the lack of any central leadership for curriculum development, integration, or articulation within the school or from the district to the elementary districts. The initiative which had occurred was decentralized and up to the department chairpersons.

Cascade City curricular documents varied in quality from those which would be considered generally high in content and structure to those which were marginal or ineffective.

ETON PARK

The auditor found no board-adopted goals and objectives in policy form for the Eton Park Public Schools though proficiencies had been developed and adopted. The auditor found very limited curriculum per se in Eton Park; what did exist had been prompted by the Cascade City department chairpersons in English and math. One additional guide existed for science.

CLUMBERVILLE

The auditor found almost exclusively courses of study in the Clumberville Public Schools, which were created or revised in 1985. They were very marginal as effective curricular documents and not linked to board policy. The auditor found no central thrust for curriculum development in the Clumberville Public Schools and no staff assigned to that responsibility.

Specific Findings by District

CASCADE CITY REGIONAL HIGH SCHOOL

Finding 2.1: Most Curricular Documents in the Cascade City Regional High School District Are of Marginal Quality

The auditor reviewed courses of study in the following areas:

- home economics (1983)
- industrial arts (1983)
- music (1983)
- special education (1973)

- art (no date)
- social studies (no date)
- science (1983)
- physical education (1983)
- math (no date)
- foreign language (1983)
- business (no date)

In general, the courses of study were simple outlines of the content to be taught in each course in a department. The content was stated in quasi-behaviorial objective form. The courses of study did not indicate the sources used to derive the content, the means of their evaluation, or the approximate amount of time to be spent on them within the course. They were the minimal required statement to comply with the High School Graduation Standards Act (18A:7c1) and the parallel Administrative Code section (AC 6:8-4.2). There was nothing exemplary about them.

The auditor reviewed curriculum guides in the following areas:

- mathematics K–8 (1986)
- English language arts, 5–8 (1985)
- mathematics (1986)
- business (1986)
- social studies (1983)

The Social Studies Curriculum Guide listed objectives for various units but not validation sources for the objectives. Validation simply means that the objectives have been suggested as appropriate by the state, the textbook companies, the College Board, the National Council of Teachers of Social Studies, or other sources/agencies.

It is not hard to write objectives. It is difficult to know that the district has stated the "right" ones as opposed to those of lesser importance. The curriculum guide lists topics and concepts. Some are related to chapters in the books corresponding to topical delineation. In some cases textbooks and other sources are identified. In other cases this has not been done.

The social studies area at Cascade City includes the following courses:

(1) U.S. History I
(2) U.S. History II
(3) Contemporary World Affairs
(4) Anthropology
(5) Sociology
(6) Psychology

(7) Economics
(8) Patterns of Civilization (World History)
(9) Mass Media
(10) Ecology and the Environment

The Social Studies Curriculum Guide is little more than a collection of courses of studies. It presents no suggested time for important topics; major objectives are not keyed to texts or audio-visual materials; and extant evaluation instruments are not referenced.

The *1983 Regional States Study* made eight recommendations regarding this area of the curriculum. Very few of these recommendations have been accomplished. Map skills have been emphasized to a greater degree than before, but the area suffers from a lack of truly rigorous offerings. There are no Advanced Placement courses. Courses such as mass media, anthropology, and sociology are of dubious value, given the small size of the school. In short, the social studies area suffers from a lack of depth. It has also been in this department where criticism has been leveled about too much "seat work," as opposed to real teaching, and an overuse of films. The latter prompted the Cascade City Board to question publicly the use of AV in the entire high school.

The curriculum guide in social studies is deemed very weak as an effective management tool for sound program operations.

The Business Curriculum Guide is also a collection of courses of study, the most recent being a course in keyboarding for information processing added in 1986.

The business area at Cascade City offers the following courses:

(1) Keyboarding
(2) Business Arithmetic
(3) Accounting I
(4) Accounting II
(5) Stenography I
(6) Stenography II
(7) Typewriting I
(8) Typewriting II
(9) Consumer Problems
(10) Office Practice

Many of the Regional States Study's recommendations were being implemented in the business education area. However, personal typing was not offered as an elective as recommended. Some computers had been added. The auditor encountered some criticism of the lack of modernization of the business education curriculum at Cascade City. Enrollment has recently declined in this area. Much more emphasis on computers and word processing should characterize the business area than is the case at the present time. The curriculum guide suffered from the same weaknesses as those cited for social studies. As a document for sound curriculum management, it is inadequate.

The Mathematics Curriculum Guide revealed a stronger and more diverse curriculum with a variety of groupings and tracking present. Most of the courses of study were revised in 1986. They included goals, delineation of the basic text, objectives, and methods of evaluation, including some oral recitations.

However, even the math curriculum guide suffered from the shortcomings of no alignment data present, from objectives to texts in use or mandated tests. Recommended time delineations were also not present. Evaluative methods were far too general to be effective curricular management tools.

The mathematics area offers the following courses at Cascade City:

(1) Algebra I and II
(2) Geometry I and II
(3) Trigonometry
(4) Pre-calculus
(5) Computer science I and II
(6) Practical math
(7) Advanced mathematics
(8) Basic skills math

There are a variety of available derivations of math at Cascade City, and the department does a good job in working with students who must pass the state proficiency test.

However, there are no Advanced Placement courses in the math department. The curriculum guide for the high school was not a strong management document.

The English Curriculum Guide reviewed was constructed during the 1982–1984 time period. It included fifteen courses. A recent revised course of study indicated that it did include the competencies from the state test. These were delineated as an addendum to the English I course of study. The state writing competencies were also indicated for the course remedial composition. However, other courses did not indicate the state competencies.

The English area offers the following courses at Cascade City:

(1) English I
(2) Ninth grade remedial composition
(3) English II
(4) English IIA
(5) English III
(6) English IIIA
(7) Business English IIA
(8) English IV
(9) English IVA
(10) Speech
(11) Dramatics
(12) Journalism
(13) Creative writing
(14) SCE remedial reading
(15) Developmental reading

The English Curriculum Guide, like others reviewed, was merely a compilation of courses of study. The guide was not a strong management document per se. The English department also did not offer Advanced Placement courses.

Finding 2.2: Some Curricular Areas at the Cascade City Regional High School Lack Sufficient Scope

Unlike the previous finding where curricular areas appeared to be reasonably strong as far as scope (number of offerings), some curricular areas at the Cascade City Regional High School lacked such scope.

Among the most noticeable in this regard was the curricular area of foreign language. Only two languages are offered at the high school, Spanish and Italian. If only two languages are offered in the future, one of them should be French.

However, for the foreign language program to be viable as a strong academic area, there should be at least four languages, one of which should be Latin.

The art program also suffers from a lack of sufficient scope. The course outlines reveal a strong proclivity towards crafts and practical projects such as bulletin board displays, advertising, and paper techniques. There was only one course in which the artistic achievements of various civilizations were the centerpiece.

The music program at Cascade City also lacks scope inasmuch as it only includes music appreciation, instrumental music, and band. There is no choral music program at the high school. It was only recently that a full-time band instructor has been added to this program in order to build a functional band program.

The science program at Cascade City includes earth science, general biology, C.P. biology, physical science, chemistry, physics, and advanced science. There are no Advanced Placement science courses in the science program.

The physical education program area at Cascade City had been considered by some a model program. However, staff cutbacks in this area have reduced the program somewhat. The area includes family living, driver education, and first aid.

The emphasis in physical education appears to be physical fitness and lifetime sports. Some of the activities within the curriculum, such as archery, fencing, juggling, pillow polo, and scooter activities, have been questioned as a bit esoteric.

Other sports activities appear to be more practical, such as aerobics, badminton, golf, jogging, self-defense, square dancing, tennis, and weight training. The physical education curriculum appears to be both broad and deep.

The industrial arts (I.A.) and home economics programs appear to be traditional in nature. The I.A. program includes the usual woodworking and mechanical drawing. The home economics program offers clothing and foods. These programs appear to be unusually truncated in scope.

Finding 2.3: There Have Been Collaborative Curricular Efforts Between Cascade City and the Two Sending Elementary Districts

There have been two successful collaborative curricular efforts involving Cascade City staff members and teachers from Eton Park and Clumberville. These efforts have been centered around mathematics and language arts.

Administrators and teachers interviewed considered these efforts successful, in that a great deal of cooperation among staff in these curricular areas had ensued from such work, and the curriculum was improved via expanded coordination (across grade levels) and articulation (across buildings).

The efforts also are testimony to the revered and respected work of the two Cascade City high school teachers in math and English who have spearheaded the developmental work and tended to its monitoring once the curriculum was in place.

Finding 2.4: Inter-District Curricular Documents Are More Comprehensive and Rigorous Than Those Produced within the Three Districts Separately

The auditor found the two curricula in math (K–8) and language arts (5–8) more effective management tools than those developed in any of the three districts separately.

The Language Arts Curriculum Guide produced in 1985 included a statement of goals that referenced the state competencies and utilized other external experts in the field in the state department and other school districts. Thus, curricular validation was enhanced with these efforts.

The guide also included some generic suggestions for program evaluation and proffered suggested instructional activities that would be helpful in the implementation process.

The guide was not strong on creating specific linkages between the sequential content and textbook alignment, nor was it clear about when and where specific types of evaluative activities could be utilized. It also did not include a curriculum timetable (i.e., pacing chart) to ensure staff that such content could be taught in the time available. In short, the greatest weakness of the curriculum guide was its silence regarding monitoring and the use of appropriate feedback to subsequently improve pupil performance over time.

Perhaps most instructive about this product of joint collaboration was the list of recommendations included in the document. Many of these related to needed policies and practices among the three districts to implement the tripartite curriculum successfully. The auditor considered these suggestions seminal:

- joint inservice meetings among teachers in the three districts
- establishment of a common policy for manuscript form among the three districts
- coordination of the standardized tests used in the three districts
- improved monitoring of the curriculum to ensure that reading and writing skills were being taught and reinforced in all disciplines
- suggestions as to what all teachers in the three districts could do to promote improved language arts proficiencies, such as insisting on the use of correct spelling, proper mechanics, standard English usage, good sentence structure, and unified para-

graphs in all written work. At least one essay question should be included on all tests.

These suggestions make it clear that a closer level of collaborative work must occur among and between the three districts. However, not one policy of any of the boards of education would appear to require such effort except as contained in the approved job descriptions of various professional roles. To date, such prescriptions have not proven to be effective measures to promote improved coordination and articulation among the three respective educational entities.

The Mathematics Curriculum K–8 developed in the summer of 1986 does demonstrate the sources utilized in validation. This guide references local and state sources in developing a general framework for each grade level. The document utilizes a two-column format which includes a statement of the objective in general terms and a specific example of what the students will be able to do once the objective is learned.

A graphic method is used to trace the strands that run vertically through the K–8 sequence. Then the guide shows a format which illustrates the objectives to be taught; those with an asterisk mean that they will be included on the state test, and a boxed lowercase letter means that the concept is introduced for the first time at the grade level. An unboxed letter means that the strand is to be extended or continued from a previous grade. In another column, a specific example of what the student should be able to do is shown once the objective has been taught.

The document also includes checklists which are used by teachers in utilizing the guide. There is one for each grade level. Three columns indicate the reference (or text) used, the date started, and the date completed.

A section on methodology was included which reflected suggestions for teaching division of fractions, simplification of complex fractions, and percentage.

The auditor found the Mathematics Curriculum K–8 the single most outstanding curricular document reviewed. It contained almost all of the elements of curricular quality control required including monitoring.

There were several small shortcomings. First, recommended time ranges were not included. Second, linkages to available texts in use in both districts were not indicated nor connections to extant AV materials. The latter would resolve the question of the propriety of AV with specific math curricula recently raised in another subject area at the Cascade City Regional High School. Lastly, the document is too large and cumbersome.

ETON PARK

Finding 2.1: The Curriculum Reviewed by the Auditor in Eton Park Is Limited

The auditor only found curriculum in three areas in Eton Park: language arts and math and science. This does not mean there were no programs in Eton Park in all of the curricular areas. What it means is that there was curriculum for only three programs.

Most programs were largely shaped by the textbook adoptions contained in board policy #6142. That board policy appeared to mandate curriculum in all areas of the district; however, it speaks largely to reading and the mastery of fundamentals and to desired characteristics of an instructional program in general.

Perhaps one of the reasons textbooks appear to be the center of some controversy in Eton Park is that there is no curriculum guiding their selection. The textbook is the curriculum instead of reflecting the curriculum. Eton Park has only enjoyed the services of a part-time curriculum coordinator for less than one year at the time of the audit. That lack of appropriate staffing may explain some of the reasons for the lack of curriculum extant in the district.

CLUMBERVILLE

Finding 2.1: Locally Developed Curriculum in Clumberville Has Been Limited to Courses of Study

The auditor reviewed the following courses of study in Clumberville:

	Date	
Course of Study	Revised	Updated
Kindergarten Course of Study	1980	1985
Grade One Course of Study	1980	1985
Grade Two Course of Study	1980	1985
Grade Three Course of Study	1980	1985
Grade Four Course of Study	1980	1985
Grade Five Course of Study	1985	N.A.
Grade Five Family Life	1985	N.A.
Grade Six Course of Study	1985	N.A.
Grade Six Family Life	1985	N.A.
Grade Seven Course of Study	1985	N.A.
Grade Seven Social Studies	1985	N.A.

Course of Study	Date Revised	Date Updated
Grade Seven Family Life	1985	N.A.
Grades Seven–Eight Mathematics	1985	N.A.
Grade Eight English-Reading-Spelling	1985	N.A.
Special Education Course of Study	1980	1985
Grades One–Eight Remedial Reading	1980	1980
Grade Eight Typing Course of Study	1980	1985
Grade Eight Family Life	1985	N.A.
Grades One–Eight Compensatory Math	1985	N.A.
Grade Eight Social Studies	1985	N.A.
Grade Eight Science Course of Study	1985	N.A.
Grades Five–Eight Computer Literacy	1985	N.A.
Grades Five–Eight Career Awareness	1985	N.A.
Grades Five–Eight Drugs, Alcohol, Tobacco	1981	1985
Resource Room Course of Study	1985	N.A.
Speech/Language Therapy Course of Study	1980	1985
Spanish Course of Study	1985	N.A.
English as a Second Language	1985	N.A.
Physical Education Course of Study	1980	1985
Art Course of Study	1980	1985
Vocal Music Course of Study	1985	N.A.
Grades Four–Eight Instrumental Music	1980	1985
Grades Five–Eight Industrial Arts	1980	1985
Grades Five–Eight Home Economics	1980	1985
Gifted and Talented Course of Study	1985	N.A.

The courses of study were curricular documents only in the most rudimentary fashion. Most were simple listings of content to be taught. Some included textbook references but none were specifically aligned to designated content. Content was not validated. Some appeared to be extrapolated directly from the textbook in use at the time.

The courses of study did not indicate which content would be tested nor prescribe time to be spent on the designated content. In short, these documents are not effective management tools. The lack of quality curricular documents can be traced to the lack of central attention to their development and implementation in Clumberville.

SUMMARY OF COGENT FINDINGS ON CURRICULUM AUDIT STANDARD 2

The curriculum developed within the three school districts has been of a generally poor quality, with the exception of the two K–8 documents most recently created in language arts and mathematics in 1985 and 1986, respectively.

The lack of high quality curricular documents has been due to a lack of leadership of a central nature at Cascade City and, in all three districts, the lack of sufficiently trained central personnel in the curriculum area. Only Eton Park has seen fit to fill this critical gap with a part-time appointment in the area of curriculum.

In all of the districts, there is lack of tangible and documented linkages from board policy and goal statements to curriculum content selected to be taught. In some cases board policy is simply inadequate as a platform to anchor this process realistically. This means that the board is simply not in control of its curriculum, having surrendered that responsibility to textbook adoption rather blindly and/or test adoption or utilization specifically.

The statement of objectives in all three school systems is either nonexistent and/or nonfunctional. This precludes tracing of control via direction from policy to operations within each of the three school districts. In short, there is no audit trail to trace. There are isolated documents which exist at a variety of levels and in some areas and not others. The curriculum management system for the total curriculum is weak or not operational at all intra-system and functional only in language arts and mathematics inter-system. In the latter case, this has only been the product of two very energetic high school teachers and cooperative superintendents at the two elementary districts.

The absence of high-quality curricular documents cannot only be traced to inadequate board policies and the lack of trained central curricular personnel, but also to the total lack of sound curricular specifications developed by the administrative staffs to which teachers have been expected to be responsive. If one finds a poorly designed house, one does not blame the contractor, but the architect who created the plans.

Standard 3: The School District Has Documentation Explaining How Its Programs Have Been Developed, Implemented, and Conducted

A school district meeting this curriculum audit standard is able to show how its programs have been created as the result of a systematic identification of deficiencies in the achievement and growth of its students compared to measurable standards of learning.

In addition, a system meeting this standard is able to demonstrate that, as a whole, it is more effective than the sum total of its parts, i.e., any arbitrary combination of programs or schools do not equate to the larger school district entity.

The purpose of having a school system is to obtain the educational and economic benefits of a coordinated program for students, both to enhance learning by maximizing pupil interest and by utilizing economies of scale where applicable.

What the Auditor Expected to Find in the Three School Districts

The auditor expected to find a highly developed, articulated, and coordinated curriculum in the three districts that was effectively monitored by the administrative and teaching staffs. Such a curriculum would be:

- centrally defined and adopted by the boards of education
- clearly explained to members of the instructional staff
- accompanied by specific training programs to enhance implementation
- monitored by central office staff and building principals

What the Auditor Found in the Three School Districts

CASCADE CITY REGIONAL HIGH SCHOOL DISTRICT

Perhaps the most obvious hiatus at Cascade City Regional High School in the curriculum area is the total absence of a systematic and formal mechanism for curriculum development. Curriculum development at Cascade City has been a "hit or miss" affair, uncoordinated and decentralized in nature, sporadic, and unplanned. This is above the departmental level. At the departmental level some curricular areas have developed mechanisms for using feedback and systematically reviewing program needs. The success of such efforts has largely been because of the energy and expertise of the department chairpersons. There has not been a high level of consistency across departments, however. The uneven nature of curriculum development has been reinforced by a generally reactive administrative posture that was not directed by sound central planning. Curriculum development has been very much an idiosyncratic phenomenon.

The monitoring of the curriculum has been mostly of a perfunctory nature by the principal and varies within departments depending upon the requirements of the respective chairpersons.

In short, Cascade City Regional High School is a collection of departments and not a school in any operational sense of the word. Despite these shortcomings, the data indicate there are many positive programs in effect at the high school. They are simply uncoordinated and unfocused by leadership or past practice.

ETON PARK PUBLIC SCHOOLS

While the Eton Park Public Schools have lacked formal curricular documents, there has been a generally "tighter" coordination of the curriculum because of the presence of policies which specified proficiencies (#6147), the level of time allotted (#6142), grading standards (#5121), promotion and retention (#5123), and regulations/past practices regarding planbooks and the utilization of testing data in developing/redesigning programs. Eton Park has developed tighter procedures which govern operations and by so doing created more functional linkages between the elements of quality control.

The new coordinator of curriculum has also succeeded in creating a workable system of monitoring and the utilization of feedback, and the school principals reinforce these procedures with teachers. The system has been formalized to a large extent.

CLUMBERVILLE PUBLIC SCHOOLS

The Clumberville Public Schools have no formal system in place to develop a strong central focus for total curriculum development. There is no coordinator of curriculum and no formal professional body that convenes regularly and systematically to examine curriculum or use feedback on a district-wide basis. The use of test data is informal. The monitoring of curriculum is also informal and not rigorous or systematic throughout the district.

Specific Findings by District

CASCADE CITY REGIONAL HIGH SCHOOL

Finding 3.1: There Is No Systematic and Operative Monitoring System of the Total Curriculum at the Regional High School

The curriculum at Cascade City Regional High School is only marginally monitored as a totality. The auditor found a primitive sort of lesson plan format which has been in use over many years. This format asks the teacher to indicate the objective to be taught, the content to be taught, the assignment to be employed, and the references, resources, and aids required. Many teachers found the form inadequate. Some chairpersons have modified the form. The new superintendent has indicated that the objectives should be tied to approved course proficiencies because of the recent flap over the alleged misuse of audio-visual materials in the social studies department. However, even with this linkage, there is doubt about the validity of the course proficiencies themselves being the correct ones to pursue. Many are simply not validated at all because of past practices of poor curriculum design procedures being followed.

In general, only the department chairs review the lesson plans of staff. The principal does not review the plans. What this practice does is reinforce the isolation of the departments within the school. It prevents the curriculum from having an overall school-wide focus. It works against any interdisciplinary practices being fostered, and it works against any possible economies of scale being utilized to support the total educational program. It also reinforces whatever weaknesses are inherent within the programs of the respective departments and isolates the strengths. It becomes impossible to develop total school synergy. The curriculum remains fragmented and uncoordinated. No one is minding the total curriculum "store" at Cascade City Regional High School. The principal does receive monthly department chair reports, but these are not tools of curriculum monitoring, and they rarely touch upon the daily evolving educational program within the respective departments therein.

Finding 3.2: Some Departments at the Regional High School Make Excellent Use of Feedback Data to Improve Educational Programs

The auditor found documents that indicate that the most consistent use of feedback to improve the curriculum and program at the regional high school has occurred within the English and math departments. These two departments have systematically tracked data (principally from the state test) regarding pupil attainment and emphasized programmatic adjustments in content to be taught, with procedures and methodologies to be altered as a result.

The English Department presented to the high school administration six new courses of study utilizing the Regional States Evaluative Criteria for English, a report of the Joint State-wide Task Force on Pre-College Preparation from the State Department of Education, and the State University president's statement on pre-college preparation dated 9/29/86. The auditor found a programmatic statement regarding course termination in math dated 9/22/86 for one program based on the changing needs of students at the high school.

One additional memorandum was reviewed of 11/5/86 regarding course title changes in the business department which would reflect the changing technology of the times.

Finding 3.3: While Follow-Up Studies Have Been Conducted at the High School, No Programmatic Changes Were Observed to Have Been Made with the Data

The guidance department does gather certain types of follow-up data about the graduating classes. For example, the data shown below were gathered about the classes of 1985 and 1986 at the regional high school.

Percentage of Students Who Will	1985	1986
• matriculate to four-year institutions	48.2%	37.5%
• matriculate to two-year institutions	6.8%	16.1%
• matriculate to trade/technical schools	12.2%	9.8%
• enter the military	1.5%	.9%
• directly enter the work force	31.3%	34.8%

The auditor reviewed the results of a graduate follow-up study of the 1984 students. Only forty-seven students responded on the post-cards reviewed. It is not known what percentage of a response this number represents of the total class. Approximately 42.5 percent of the responses indicated that they were engaged in full-time employment. Approximately 40 percent were attending a four-year college.

The postcard survey did not ask the students any curricular questions that would be helpful to revise the curriculum. The auditor did not review any document supplied by the guidance department or from any other source that would indicate in what ways any follow-up data had been used in redesigning the programs or curriculum at the Cascade City Regional High School in any planned, formal manner on a consistent basis in the past.

Finding 3.4: The Climate at the Regional High School Was Positive and Students Were Well-Behaved

Unfortunately, the reputation of the Cascade City Regional High School student body has been besmirched by the media attention drawn by the abortive board policy regarding mandatory drug testing. As mentioned earlier, that effort made it appear that Cascade City was some sort of "druggie paradise."

Actually, the *Lantern*, the award-winning student newspaper at

Cascade City Regional High, conducted a student poll in February 1986 on drug and alcohol use of Cascade City students. The results were considered valid for 76.7 percent of the total student body. The data showed that while 51 percent of the students admitted that they had experimented with drugs, 80 percent had done so before they had entered high school. Seventy-nine percent of the students indicated that they had never come to school under the influence of drugs or alcohol. These data do not indicate that the drug or alcohol problem at Cascade City is any more severe than anywhere else—rich or poor, urban, suburban, or rural settings notwithstanding.

The climate is the tone of a school. The tone at Cascade City was positive, relaxed, disciplined, and open.

A universal comment from teachers interviewed at Cascade City was that they enjoyed working with their students. They found them to be unpretentious, questioning, hard-working, ambitious, and teachable. While some complained about the actions of the board and were critical of some administrative practices, most found working with their students the single most rewarding and positive plus about their jobs. It kept them coming back in spite of the negative reinforcement of bad publicity, a perceived hostility towards them by the Cascade City Board, and past weak or ineffective administrators.

ETON PARK PUBLIC SCHOOLS

Finding 3.1: A Functional Monitoring System Is in Place for Some of the Curriculum in the Eton Park Public Schools

The newly appointed coordinator of curriculum in the Eton Park Public Schools was able to demonstrate to the auditor how he systematically used feedback data from the CTBS to develop specific suggestions for changes in the taught curriculum.

Furthermore, principals were able to show how the development of lesson plans showed connections to the written curriculum in math and language arts, particularly, and how they monitored such connections on a weekly basis via the use of grade-by-grade checklists.

The auditor also examined several reports of the Eton Park superintendent and the curriculum coordinator to the board of education indicating performance on the CTBS. Specific data had been summarized for children scoring below grade level.

For these areas of the curriculum, a functional monitoring system was in place. The system was creating the necessary linkages between the written, taught, and tested curricula.

Finding 3.2: The Superintendent in Eton Park Had Taken a Proactive Role in the Improvement of the Curriculum Monitoring System

The reason for the functional relationship in quality control in the basic skill areas in Eton Park was due to the leadership of the superintendent and the responsiveness of the board to that leadership. The board has seen fit to fund the increase required in staffing and not to make reductions in staff vitally necessary to make curriculum management truly operational.

The only area where the board has not been responsive has been on the issue of grouping. The board's position on this matter is not realistic, given the constraints faced by the district and its personnel in the existing educational environment.

Finding 3.3: The Eton Park Public Schools Have Increased Curricular Specialization at Some Levels

Most recently, the Eton Park Public Schools have seen fit to increase specialization in the area of science, K–6, by adding a teacher specialist at those grade levels.

The science teacher works with classroom teachers and introduces elementary school children to "hands-on" science experiences which go far beyond the usual textbook approaches normally found there, if any are found at all.

Finding 3.4: Staff Development in Eton Park Has Reinforced Curricular Priorities

The auditor reviewed a log provided by the Eton Park superintendent which indicated the major topics of staff development between the time periods April 1982 and February 1987. During this time period the district provided some fifty experiences for the faculty or selected faculty members in Eton Park.

Speakers were brought before the staff in classroom management, computer use, learning styles, mainstreaming, science, reading, general instruction, and critical thinking. Other areas included drugs and alcohol, family life, the use of specific diagnostic tools, special education laws and procedures, and mathematics.

Finding 3.5: The School Climate in Eton Park Was Positive

The auditor toured all schools in Eton Park. He found the climates positive and productive.

CLUMBERVILLE PUBLIC SCHOOLS

Finding 3.1: There Is No Formal System of Monitoring Curriculum in Place in the Clumberville Public Schools

The Clumberville Public Schools have no formal system in place to monitor curriculum. The auditor found no evidence of central monitoring of test data nor use of it at the central level. While teachers developed lesson plans, a review of those plans showed them to be informal compared to the procedures at work in Eton Park.

The Clumberville superintendent had worked unsuccessfully to secure funding for a curriculum coordinator position, only to see the position lost in budget reductions.

The auditor examined the Clumberville superintendent's annual reports for six years. While test scores were usually reported to the board, they were often not accompanied with any specific recommendations to improve pupil achievement.

A full-time guidance counselor was recommended for the Faubus Intermediate School beginning in the 1982–1983 annual report and repeated in the annual reports for the years 1984–85 and 1985–86 to no avail. This is still a critical and largely unfilled need at that site.

With no central staffing for curriculum or curricular support services, the burden for quality control has fallen on the shoulders of the two principals in Clumberville. Even a cursory review of their functions and time spent in touring the facilities indicates they have little time to spend on curricular affairs. Most is spent on the maintenance of order and stability in the buildings, on issues involving students and parents, and on daily matters pertaining to staffing and teaching as well. The recent board-initiated "shuffling" of the principals has further exacerbated the problem by bringing about a need for restored administrative harmony. In short, there is less time spent on curricular affairs because more time must be spent on achieving administrative stability than before.

Finding 3.2: The Schools Are Better than the Curriculum in Clumberville

The building operations of the schools in Clumberville are generally better than the curriculum reviewed. However, instead of the curriculum leading operations, it has followed and still is absent in many cases for much of the full range of educational programs. Extant courses of study are not effective surrogates for real curriculum.

The absence of a generally accurate set of curricular documents (with the exception of the two K–8 guides in math and language, see

Finding 2.4) prevents the school system from optimizing its resources across grade levels. Instead of behaving as a school system, Clumberville behaves as a confederation of smaller systems, i.e., buildings. For Clumberville to function as a system, it must have a system-wide curriculum which pulls together all operations into one cohesive set of work actions. Real economies which are not destructive of the educational program will not be possible without a system-wide curriculum in place.

Finding 3.3: Individual Schools in Clumberville Are Positive Places for Learning

The auditor toured all of the school buildings in Clumberville. He found them to be places of genuine learning and very positive. Veteran teachers related how much they liked their work, despite having to teach in antiquated facilities.

SUMMARY OF COGENT FINDINGS ON CURRICULUM AUDIT STANDARD 3

The very best use of data for feedback to improve pupil performance has been largely confined to two departments at Cascade City Regional High School and to the basic skill areas in the Eton Park Public Schools. The most functional total curriculum management system was observed in Eton Park. The weakest in Clumberville.

The general caliber of teaching in all three districts was very strong overall with the expected exceptions here and there. But, as a rule, the teaching going on within the three districts is stable, solid, focused, and effective, given the conditions in which teachers must function, including all of the physical, emotional, and psychological factors which impact the work they do. Teaching is exhausting work, and this fact is understood only by those who have to do it year in and year out and retain enthusiasm and vitality.

Teachers observed in all three districts displayed a disciplined enthusiasm for their work somewhat atypical of such a veteran teaching staff observed in other places in the state and nationally. Only at Cascade City was this enthusiasm dampened by the combative climate prevalent at that facility.

Standard 4: The School District Uses the Results from District Designed and/or Adopted Assessments to Adjust, Improve, or Terminate Ineffective Practices or Programs

A school district meeting this curriculum audit standard of the process has designed a comprehensive system of testing and measurement tools that indicate how well students are learning designated priority objectives.

Such a system will provide:

- a timely and relevant base upon which to analyze important trends in the instructional program
- a vehicle to examine how well programs are actually producing desired learner results
- a way to provide feedback to the teaching staff regarding how classroom instruction can become more effective
- a data base to compare the strengths and weaknesses of various programs and program alternatives
- a data base to terminate ineffective educational programs

A school district meeting this audit standard has a full range of formal and informal assessment tools that provide relevant program information to decision making in the classroom, building, district, and board levels.

The school system has taken steps to ensure that the full range of its programs are systematically and periodically assessed. Such data have been matched to program objectives and are utilized in decision making.

What the Auditor Expected to Find in the Three School Districts

The auditor expected to find a comprehensive assessment program of all aspects of the curriculum, which was:

- keyed to a set of goals/objectives adopted by the boards of education
- utilized extensively at the building level to engage in program review and modification
- used to terminate ineffective educational programs
- used as a base to establish needed programs
- publicly reported to the board of education and the community on a regular basis

What the Auditor Found in the Three School Districts

CASCADE CITY REGIONAL HIGH SCHOOL DISTRICT

The most consistent use of test data as feedback has been in the math and English departments and has involved the results from the State Competency Test.

Other use of test data has been sporadic or nonexistent except as teachers might make adjustments within their own courses based on exam data. After a long hiatus, the regional high school has reinstated mid-year and final exams, something long advocated by the faculty but resisted by past administrations.

The district administration has refused to examine its policy on early dismissal for seniors, despite being urged to do so by the 1983 Regional States Association Study. Members of the faculty interviewed and members of the Cascade City Board were also critical of this practice.

The auditor found no comprehensive Cascade City board policy regarding testing or its purpose in the district. The auditor found no evidence of any administrative recommendation to abolish programs or curricula based on test data and which was reflective of the existing program. The auditor did find evidence of teacher leadership on this question.

ETON PARK PUBLIC SCHOOLS

The auditor found board policies on testing and its functions, a comprehensive policy accompanied by administrative regulations on final examinations for grades seven and eight, and explicit rules for teacher-made tests contained in materials distributed to all faculty in Eton Park. The auditor found analyses of test results from the curriculum coordinator to the superintendent and from the CEO to the board.

CLUMBERVILLE PUBLIC SCHOOLS

The auditor found one board policy on testing and test data formally reported to the board in the superintendent's annual report to the board, but little use of such data at the building level in a formal systematic manner to modify or terminate programs.

Specific Findings by District

CASCADE CITY REGIONAL HIGH SCHOOL DISTRICT

Finding 4.1: The Existing Board Testing Policy Is Inadequate in Cascade City

The current Cascade City Board of Education policy on testing is inadequate. First, there is no explicit policy at all. Secondly, under the policy Academic Achievement #6147 it states:

> The assessment of student needs and measurement of academic achievement shall be based on well-defined and board approved educational

> goals and objectives developed in conjunction with the minimum proficiency levels identified for each student.

The auditor did not find well-defined board objectives, though course proficiencies did exist as required under state statute. However, these proficiencies have in the main, never been adequately validated.

The same board policy (#6147) required that the CEO annually report to the board and community the evaluation of student achievement toward meeting district and school goals and objectives. The auditor was not provided any such annual reports developed by the CEO in this regard and, therefore, must assume there were none.

Despite the fact that the last paragraph of policy #6147 states: "Low student achievement shall be regarded by the board as an indication that revisions are needed in educational programming, general strategy, staff resource utilization, and/or other aspects of the learning program," the auditor could find no documented evidence of any administrative recommendation which referenced this paragraph at all. Yet test data did indicate some low student performance in the past.

Finding 4.2: Despite Recommendations to Abandon an Outdated Practice, the District Continues to Use It

The 1983 Regional States Accreditation Report recommended the high school reconsider the practice of early dismissal of seniors. The rationale stated by the principal in support of this practice in his first progress report to Regional States of 5/1/86 states:

> With the policy now in operation there are too many advantages to the program to rescind it. Some seniors have home responsibilities, those involved with sports or activities have an opportunity to accomplish some library work or homework, and many have jobs.

This rationale is certainly not an educational one. The taxpayers of the district are providing an educational program at some expense, for which seniors may never again have an opportunity to utilize if sacrificed for a short-term, small economic gain or because of sports or other extracurricular activities. The educational resources of the high school are squandered for the very students who will need it the most later in life. The practice is outdated.

Finding 4.3: Standard and National Academic Barometers Are Missing at the Regional High School

The standard academic barometer of a sound high school curriculum is the Advanced Placement (AP) program. Most of the nationally prominent academic high schools utilize the AP program as their most advanced curriculum.

The Advanced Placement program includes the presence of a national AP exam, and it is against this measure that the quality of instruction at a school can be judged against other schools and students competing in the same curricular area.

Currently, Cascade City Regional High School offers its own honors programs. However, these programs are not reliable benchmarks upon which to assess the academic curriculum at the high school for the most able student.

Finding 4.4: Cascade City Seniors Taking the SAT Do Moderately Well

The auditor was provided SAT (Scholastic Aptitude Test) data for the years 1985 and 1986. SAT data should be used with caution. First, not all students take the SAT at Cascade City or nationally. Secondly, the SAT does not assess any specific curriculum, nor all of any curriculum anywhere at the secondary level. The two-year analysis showed the following:

1985 SAT MEAN SCORES

Cascade City (n = 78)		State		The Nation	
Verbal	Math	Verbal	Math	Verbal	Math
423	488	425	464	431	475

1986 SAT MEAN SCORES

Cascade City (n = 68)		State		The Nation	
Verbal	Math	Verbal	Math	Verbal	Math
383	449	424	465	431	475

Data provided by the College Board for 1986 also indicate how well students do by self-reported class rank. This barometer provides some clue as to how well the best Cascade City students do compared to the best students nationally on a common testing instrument. In 1986, the students at Cascade City who were in the top tenth of the class obtained a total SAT verbal mean score of 420 compared to a national top tenth of 514. In the SAT math, the top tenth at Cascade City obtained a mean score of 583 compared to 579 nationally. The state top tenth was 525 and 586, respectively.

In the second decile of the 1986 class, Cascade City students obtained an SAT verbal mean score of 397 compared to a national mean score of 454. The math mean score for second decile students was 457 compared to 507 nationally. The state second decile was 460 and 511 respectively.

What the data appear to reflect is that Cascade City students do better on the SAT math as opposed to the SAT verbal (also a state and national trend). The best Cascade City students (top tenth) scored below the nation and the state on the SAT verbal. The best Cascade City students scored above the national mean on the SAT math but slightly below the mean state SAT math for comparable students statewide.

The second tenth of the 1986 graduating class who took the SAT scored below the state and the nation in both verbal and math. Achievement results are always an intimate combination of factors of schooling and home/community variables. Conclusive findings are difficult to sustain.

The auditor could find no specific use of the above reported data anywhere in curriculum planning or program utilization at the regional high school. This finding alone appears to contradict the intent of Cascade City board policy #6147 previously cited under Finding 4.1.

Finding 4.5: Cascade City Scores Show Improvement on the State Competency Test

The state competency test is a more accurate and isomorphic measure of the curriculum and the results than the SAT in Cascade City.

The department chairpersons in English and mathematics have used the state data to: (1) make suggestions to teachers in the two sending elementary districts as to what to stress via workshops and (2) make curricular adjustments at Cascade City in terms of sequencing and remediation activities. The results of the state test demonstrate a steady increase in scores as shown in Exhibit 17.

The review of the three-year state data shows a steady improvement in every area tested from 1984 to 1986. Math scores exceeded every comparable score of other like districts, communities, county, and state except in one category, number concepts.

Cascade City scores were not as superior in reading. They were better in English in which sentence structure and actual writing attained a mark of E4.

The auditor's review of documents and data obtained from teacher interviews revealed a consistent use of feedback data over the three-

Exhibit 17
An Analysis of State Test Results 1984–1986 Cascade City Regional High School

Test Area	Mean Equated Cluster Scores			Legend
	1984	1985	1986	
1. Literal Comprehension/Vocabulary	80	85	89	E3(CO)
2. Inferential Comprehension/Vocabulary	76	81	89	E2(CO,CT)
3. Study Skills	78	79	88	E2(CO,CT)
4. Sentence Structure	78	80	86	E4
5. Organization of Ideas—writing	82	81	86	E3(CO)
6. Editing	73	82	86	E3(CO)
7. Writing Sample	7.9	7.8	8.4	E4
8. Computation of fractions	80	78	81	E4
9. Computation of decimals	76	75	81	E4
10. Computation of percents	56	68	88	E4
11. Number Concepts	55	68	77	E3(CO)
12. Measurement and Geometry	52	73	82	E4
13. Pre-Algebra	71	70	82	E4
14. Problem Solving	60	68	80	E4

Legend Explanation: state scores are reported for comparative purposes with four other scores. A district's mean equated cluster score is reported with a score derived from like school districts called DFG = district factor group, similar communities called CT = community type, the county called CO = County, and the state called ST = State. E4 as reported in the legend means that Cascade City exceeded all other four reported scores, i.e., its results were better than the mean equated cluster score for similar districts, community types, county, and state. E3 would mean that it exceeded three of the four mean equated cluster scores except the one which appears in the parentheses.

year period. For example, the math teachers have determined to do the following to improve pupil performance in the lowest state test area of number concepts:

- extension of local objective on proportion to include more than two ratios
- emphasis on vocabulary in identifying place value in decimal numerals
- more instructional emphasis on order and conversion on the correct ordering of a set of rational numbers
- working toward student mastery of the concept of prime number
- working towards having students demonstrate an understanding of scientific notation
- stress on the mathematical vocabulary in rounding decimal numbers
- improved instruction so that students demonstrate equivalent forms by reduction within fraction/decimal/percent equivalency
- increased stress on estimating answers as it pertains to sums, differences, products, quotients, and square roots

Clearly the instructional staff at Cascade City has been using the concept of curricular quality control and it has been working in regard to the state test.

ETON PARK PUBLIC SCHOOLS

Finding 4.1: The Eton Park Public Schools Make Systematic Use of Test Scores to Improve Pupil Performance

Eton Park has developed a fairly "tight" coupling within its administrative staff structure to analyze and use test data as programmatic feedback. The presence of a curriculum coordinator part-time greatly assists in the matter. The division of labor between this person and the principals has created an initially effective monitoring capacity.

The auditor reviewed several compilations and analyses of data from the performance of Eton Park students on the state test to the CTBS. In 1985 the Eton Park superintendent gave a report to the board of education on how ninth grade Eton Park students performed on the state test. That data indicated that Eton Park ninth graders equalled or surpassed Cascade City students in all writing clusters of the state tests. The same was true for reading. The math section was not reported in the same manner. However, a comparison was made to county scores in which Eton Park students were equal to or surpassed that index with the exception of pre-algebra and problem solving. The report concluded that 10 percent of the Eton Park students failed the state test.

Finding 4.2: Eton Park Students Perform Well on Standardized Test

Eton Park utilizes the CTBS Basic Battery in grades K–3. From grade 4–8, the Basic Battery also is supplemented with sections pertaining to science and social studies. A report by the superntendent and the curriculum coordinator on the April 1986 CTBS administration are shown in Exhibit 18.

With only one exception (seventh grade reading), Eton Park students scored in the 70–80th percentile in the basic skills of reading, spelling, language, and math for grades K–8. Similar results were shown in grades 4–8 in the acquisition of tested reference skills, once again with the exception of the seventh grade. Science scores were not as strong, though still above the national mean. Social studies scores were generally better with the same seventh grade exception.

What is important is that educational personnel in Eton Park have developed specific thrusts to improve pupil test performance and this was evident in a variety of documents reviewed by the auditor.

Exhibit 18
Results of the 1986 CTBS Test Administration
Eton Park Public Schools (reported in mean percentile ranks)

Grade (total district)	CTBS Subtests						
	Reading	Spelling	Language	Mathematics	Reference Skills	Science	Social Studies
K	85.5	NA	NA	87.8	NA	NA	NA
1	70.9	NA	81.8	73.1	NA	NA	NA
2	82.1	80.6	82.8	83.7	NA	NA	NA
3	71.4	79.6	81.3	85.4	NA	NA	NA
4	72.8	71.2	72.5	72.1	72.4	67.5	76.1
5	71.9	71.9	80.6	84.8	78.5	64.1	71.2
6	71.1	74.5	79.7	85.3	85.4	66.7	75.2
7	68	70	75	72	64	58	65
8	74	80	83	81	79	62	78

CLUMBERVILLE PUBLIC SCHOOLS

Finding 4.1: The Clumberville Schools Make Marginal Use of Test Data

In comparison to the Eton Park Public Schools, there is no operational system of the formal utilization of any test data back through the curriculum in the Clumberville Public Schools.

Test data is given to the principals. The use they make of the data to go about the systematic improvement of pupil performance is marginal and very informal. There are no central personnel available to assist in this process. There is no system of monitoring results and using them as feedback to teachers in Clumberville.

Test data have been annually reported to the board for at least six years in documents reviewed by the auditor. The formal connections from reported data to modifications in program/curricular emphasis so evident at the regional high school and in Eton Park were not specifically demonstrated in either the annual reports or in practice in Clumberville. Clumberville reports the data. It does not do much else with it. Unlike Cascade City or Eton Park, there were no audit trails to follow in Clumberville.

Finding 4.2: A Six-Year Review of Aptitude Data Shows Little Change in Results and Little Use of the Information in Clumberville

The auditor reviewed the scores of Clumberville eighth graders on the Differential Aptitude Test (DAT) for six years as reported in the superintendent's annual report to the board of education. The results are shown in Exhibit 19.

The DAT was developed in 1947 as an instrument for use as a guidance battery in counseling for application in determining vocational abilities. It is not an achievement test, yet it appears as though it has been viewed incorrectly as such in Clumberville. In virtually all of the six annual superintendents' reports the DAT results are accompanied by a column which states, "% above or below median." This is precisely the way an achievement test score would be reported. In the 1986 report (p. 7) it states: "In all of the nine tests administered, the class average exceeded the 50th percentile."

The DAT is highly susceptible to cultural differences because scores are reported by sex. In the past, females did not do as well as males in mechanical applications. Therefore the DAT score is not a measure of so-called "innate" ability or even of the curriculum but, rather, a measure of the cultural taboos or expectations prevalent at the time. To report the data as an achievement test is a serious misuse of the purpose of the test as designed.

Furthermore, the cutback in guidance services in the Clumberville Public Schools (see Finding 1.4) makes the use of the data for high school preparation ludicrous at the Faubus Intermediate School. Not only has the DAT data been reported incorrectly, its proper application has been denied by the absence of an effective counseling program to apply it, despite repeated recommendations by the administration to develop a functional guidance program there (see Finding 3.1).

Finding 4.3: Standardized Test Scores Indicate Good Achievement Over Time in the Basic Skills

The superintendent's annual report also included test data regarding achievement on the basic skills derived from the Metropolitan Achievement Test (MAT). Historically, the data have been reported in grade equivalents, now a passé form in reporting achievement data. In has been replaced by a generally more accurate interpretation in normal curve equivalents (NCE). However, this reporting was used only in the 1986 MAT report and not in the earlier reports, thus preventing some longitudinal examination of achievement results using normal curve equivalents.

The auditor examined longitudinal data in the basic skills to determine patterns over the years using grade equivalents. This is shown in Exhibit 20.

The data show that in reading Clumberville students test at grade level in the first grade, slightly above in second and third, and then

Exhibit 19
Results of a Six-Year Analysis of the Differential Aptitude Test in the Clumberville Public Schools (Eighth Grade Average Scores)

Test Section	1981 (n = 84)	1982 (n = 83)	1983 (n = 70)	1984 (n = 70)	1985 (n = 64)	1986 (n = 53)
Verbal	43.23	52.75	57.5	54.2	51.5	56.0
Numerical	58.24	51.93	50.5	51.4	59.5	53.0
Verbal & Numerical	50.56	49.63	57.5	52.8	55.0	53.0
Abstract Reasoning	57.21	51.9	55.5	54.2	57.0	56.0
Clerical	68.12	51.65	51.0	54.2	54.0	54.0
Mechanical	49.7	53.66	48.0	55.7	53.0	54.0
Space	50.02	52.1	59.0	54.2	51.5	56.5
Spelling	51.23	52.1	55.0	52.8	53.0	55.5
Language	56.23	53.05	53.0	52.8	53.0	55.0

begin to move towards significantly greater achievement from the fourth grade on.

By examining the scores of Clumberville students in grades 1–4 using NCE's, a clearer picture emerges as to what the net effect of instruction really is in Clumberville on the MAT for the 1985–1986 year tested in reading.

Reading	Clumberville First Grade Mean NCE	Clumberville Fourth Grade Mean NCE	Clumberville Difference
	51.6	59.4	+7.8

The national expectation for growth in the same period would be ±0.

Exhibit 20
A Review of Reading Scores in Grades One–Eight on the Metropolitan Achievement Test Clumberville Public Schools

Grade	1980–81	1981–82	1982–83	1983–84	1984–85	1985–86
First	1.8	1.7	1.8	1.8	1.8	1.7
Second	2.5	3.0	2.9	3.0	3.1	2.9
Third	4.1	3.9	4.0	3.9	4.8	4.6
Fourth	5.8	5.8	6.1	5.7	6.2	5.6
Fifth	7.0	6.7	6.9	6.6	7.3	NA
Sixth	8.5	9.2	9.6	8.9	8.9	NA
Seventh	9.4	9.2	10.1	10.2	9.3	NA
Eighth	10.2	11.2	11.0	12.0	12.6	NA

The math scores are reviewed in Exhibit 21, first in grade equivalents.

The grade equivalent data indicate that in the first and second grades in Clumberville the students were generally above grade level and moved significantly ahead from the third grade onward. Some regression appears to have occurred between sixth and seventh in three of the years shown.

Once again, using NCE data from the 1985–86 MAT, the net effect of instruction in Clumberville is shown below in mathematics.

Math	First Grade Mean NCE	Eighth Grade Mean NCE	Clumberville Difference
	51.6	60.0	+8.4

SUMMARY OF COGENT FINDINGS ON CURRICULUM AUDIT STANDARD 4

A review of test data from all three school districts indicates, generally, that pupil achievement is solid and stable. None of the three districts examined had very explicit test policies, the most specific being in Eton Park.

Solid gains have been made on the state test through very diligent analytical work and the use of feedback to staff of all three school districts by the Cascade City chairpersons in math and English.

The SAT data reviewed for two years indicated that the top Cascade City students were competitive with other top students only in math.

Exhibit 21
A Review of Mathematics Scores in Grades One–Eight
on the Metropolitan Achievement Test
Clumberville Public Schools

Grade	1980–81	1981–82	1982–83	1983–84	1984–85	1985–86
First	2.2	2.1	2.3	2.3	4.0	1.7
Second	3.2	3.4	3.3	3.3	3.3	2.9
Third	5.9	5.6	4.9	4.8	5.8	4.6
Fourth	6.3	6.4	6.3	5.8	6.0	5.6
Fifth	7.9	6.9	7.6	7.7	7.8	7.0
Sixth	10.4	10.7	10.0	10.0	9.6	9.3
Seventh	9.8	10.4	11.0	10.3	9.6	8.8
Eighth	10.6	11.9	12.6	NA	NA	10.5

NOTE: Most of the annual reports indicate the test was administered in the seventh month of the school year so the grade equivalent should be 1.7 for the first grade to be "on grade level," etc.

One possible reason is the lack of upper level rigorous academic courses commonly the hallmark in academically oriented high schools with the Advanced Placement (AP) courses.

Eton Park provided the best overall framework for the systematic use of test data. Clumberville had only a marginal framework at best. One instrument in Clumberville was apparently either misused and/or misreported to the public.

Standard 5: The School District Has Improved Productivity

Productivity refers to the relationship between input and output. A school district meeting this standard of the audit is able to demonstrate consistent pupil outcomes, even in the face of declining resources. Improved productivity results when a school system is able to create a more consistent level of congruence between the major variables involved in achieving better results and in controlling costs.

What the Auditor Expected to Find in the Three School Districts

While the achievement of improved productivity in a school system is a complex process, caused in part by the lack of a tight organizational structure, a school district meeting this audit standard demonstrates:

- planned and actual congruence between curricular objectives, results, and financial costs
- specific means that have been selected or modified and implemented to attain better results in the schools over a specified time period
- a planned series of interventions that have raised pupil performance levels over time and maintained those levels within the same parameters as in the past

Any evaluation of productivity is a relative one and must include the fundamental recognition that neither the board of education, superintendent, principals, or teaching staff completely control all of the important variables that will result in improved pupil performance. Nonetheless, there are substantial elements within their combined authority that do account for improved pupil learning. These can be subjected to productivity assessment.

What the Auditor Found in the Three School Districts

CASCADE CITY REGIONAL HIGH SCHOOL DISTRICT

The auditor did not find financial data capable of being translated into programmatic thrusts or cost centers necessary to pursue productivity analysis. The auditor found no documents which formally linked curricular priorities and budgetary priorities. Cascade City had no such system in operation at the time of the audit.

ETON PARK PUBLIC SCHOOLS

The same situation regarding linkages between curriculum and budget was applicable in Eton Park. However, some documents reviewed by the auditor related to general organizational plans and the various types of consolidations possible to reduce costs and strengthen the educational program in specific curricular areas. Some of the schools in Eton Park are old and under-utilized.

CLUMBERVILLE PUBLIC SCHOOLS

The Clumberville Public Schools budgeting process was not any more tangible in terms of linking programs to dollars than the others reviewed by the auditor. The school system is also struggling with old and under-utilized school facilities. Sinking money into such structures is not prudent management.

Specific Findings by District

CASCADE CITY REGIONAL HIGH SCHOOL DISTRICT

From the board's viewpoint, the process of budget development is almost a non-system. The auditor concurs.

Finding 5.1: The Budgeting Process in the Cascade City Regional High School District Has Been More Political than Educational

Politics is simply the "art of influence." As the board has tried to confront budgetary problems, they have been strenuously lobbied by the staff to spend funds or not engage in program reductions based largely on noise and muscle.

The lack of a sound long-range planning system by which priorities are set ahead of time and to which the budget is shaped would obviate much confusion. Since all cuts are fought, some board members have become cynical about listening to the staff at all since they appear to be opposed to any reductions. In turn, some staff see the board as only interested in reducing dollars and not interested in program scope or quality.

As some board members have taken to review budgetary requests, they have found duplication and unnecessary repetition. The budgetary process does not revert to "ground zero" each year. Rather, staff start with last year's budget as a base and continually add to the same categories. This practice irritates some board members who know that some expenditures do not have to be repeated at the same level from year to year.

Finding 5.2: School Facilities at Cascade City Are in Generally Excellent Condition

A long-range facility plan for the Cascade City Board was revised by Jones, Wagner, and Associates, Inc. in September of 1985.

According to Jones, Wagner, and Associates, the academic classrooms exceed minimum standards. The main gymnasium exceeds the minimum recommended area for a two-station. The auditorium seats 1,008 persons. It contains a large well equipped stage. The library contains the minimum recommended area based on maximum anticipated enrollment. It has a collection of approximately 12,500 volumes.

ETON PARK PUBLIC SCHOOLS

Finding 5.1: Budgeting Follows a Traditional Format in Eton Park

The budget in Eton Park is adequately prepared in a traditional line item format. It is not programmatically shaped. While the auditor did not find a programmed budget, he did find two documents developed by the superintendent that included a consideration of possible program and staffing changes from which the budget was cast into its format.

Finding 5.2: Consolidation of Buildings Would Improve Program Offerings and Productivity in Eton Park

A perusal of the superintendent's proposed plans for program and staffing for 1987–88 reveals several possible ways both program and building utilization can be improved. There are two old buildings in Eton Park: the Hamilton Elementary School constructed in the 1930s and the Dewey Elementary School built in 1910. Both of these sites are under-utilized. One school could easily be closed without injury to the curriculum or the program in Eton Park. The most modern facility is the Grant Avenue School built in the 1970s.

Continuation of two old and under-utilized buildings is neither educationally nor economically sound. Increased program/curriculum specialization is possible with more children present. There is also less duplication of services, not to mention a permanent cost reduction to the district in regards to the maintenance of under-utilized buildings.

CLUMBERVILLE PUBLIC SCHOOLS

Finding 5.1: Budgeting Follows a Traditional Format in Clumberville

The Clumberville Public Schools budgeting format also does not permit modern cost analysis techniques to be applied for the same reasons cited in Cascade City and Eton Park. Without linkages between programs and costs, budgets take on a rationale of their own and instead of reflecting the curriculum, they drive the curriculum.

Finding 5.2: Several Older Elementary Schools in Clumberville Are Under-Utilized

Clumberville also is suffering from the under-utilization of three old elementary schools. They are the Carson School, the Fremont School, and the Sierra School.

The Faubus Intermediate School is still well-utilized and offers facilities unavailable to many similar schools because it once served as a high school.

The continued maintenance of these old facilities is neither educationally nor economically sound. At least two of these buildings could be closed in the future.

Funds spent on expensive maintenance could be diverted to the purchase of additional computers sorely needed elsewhere and the addition of critical staff such as a full-time guidance counselor and a curriculum coordinator. These additions would substantially improve academic achievement.

SUMMARY OF COGENT FINDINGS ON CURRICULUM AUDIT STANDARD 5

None of the three school districts have very sophisticated budgeting systems. The budgets of the three systems do not permit the kind of programmatic comparisons by which costs and results can be aligned. It means that there are no operational measures of productivity available for the staff, the respective boards, or the taxpayers to determine if increased costs lead to improved learning.

In addition, the boards and their constituents are denied the basis for judging whether better decisions about programs would result in greater benefits to pupils. The respective budgets are, therefore, neither educational nor analytical tools that would provide the means for effective cost containment or evaluation of marginal educational programs.

The problem is accentuated in Eton Park and Clumberville by the perpetuation of very old elementary schools which are costly to operate and not as viable educationally as revised and consolidated programs.

The Eton Park community already had rejected one plan for consolidation several years ago. The issue is also a volatile one in the Clumberville community.

RECOMMENDATIONS

Based upon the auditor's findings, the following recommendations have been formulated to improve the curriculum management systems within and across the three school districts.

The first set of recommendations pertain to what the three school districts should do collectively. Then recommendations follow for each school system separately.

RECOMMENDATIONS FOR ALL THREE SCHOOL SYSTEMS

Recommendation 1: Creation of a Master Policy Committee (MPC)

It is recommended that the three school boards elect two representatives each to serve on a tripartite joint policy group called the Master Policy Committee.

The purpose of this MPC will be to:

- formulate umbrella policies to require the districts to work together to improve curriculum and program articulation
- act as a clearinghouse to share data regarding textbook and test adoption, grading procedures, and standards and integrate support programs that require special funding such as computers
- monitor the efforts of the respective superintendents to create operational and technical linkages within the respective school systems

- to supervise the creation of a common budgeting system that is automated and programmatically sensitive to reduce the costs of implementation and operation
- to create a framework for the sharing of staff expertise through joint scheduling of personnel to act in leadership and supervisory roles.

All three superintendents would be participants of the MPC but as non-voting members.

Recommendation 2: Creation of a Collaborative Task Force to Equalize Funding Support for the Regional High School

It is to the benefit and interest of all three districts that the problem of uneven assessments and support of the Cascade City Regional High School District be resolved. That issue stands in the way of the enlistment of additional elementary districts selecting Cascade City as their regional high school.

The task force should have on its agenda a legislative thrust to enlist political support to change the state's current funding formula for regional high schools via a planned program of publicity within the State School Boards Association and other professional/political avenues to improve Cascade City's long-term survival.

Recommendation 3: The Establishment of a Strategic Planning Task Force for Cascade City Regional High School

All three school districts are part of each other; each depends upon the other to maintain a viable K–12 educational system.

The purpose of this task force would be to develop a *strategic plan* for the Cascade City Regional High School that includes <u>both</u> elementary school districts. The creation of a strategic plan is to indicate <u>what</u> the Cascade City Regional High School District should be like in the future to prepare students in both Eton Park and Clumberville to function effectively in the future.

A strategic plan is not a detailed operational plan. Its purpose is to paint a broad-brush picture of what the Cascade City Regional High School District should be like to serve the graduating class of the year 2000, the classes which will enter kindergarten in both Eton Park and Clumberville in the fall of 1987.

A strategic plan has several major parts. It begins by looking at the district's current mission and goals and identifying indicators of how well the district currently achieves its aims. As discrepancies are identified, these are called "needs."

Then the strategic planning process projects into the future. What skills, knowledges, and attitudes will Cascade City graduates require in the year 2000 to function economically, politically, socially, and personally? What resources and programs will be required and available to meet these future goals?

As the projected requirements become detailed, these are specified in a broad and general plan. Once the plan is approved, then more time-specific events are spelled out in short- and long-range plans. Finally, these plans are cast into likely budget requirements which will be necessary to arrive at the collective vision which has been described in the process.

It is recommended that the three superintendents form the nucleus of the strategic planning task force with the addition of the principals and key subject area supervisors. The task force may require some training and the use of consultants as well. A time line of one year with adequate funding should be enough to create a preliminary plan for presentation to all three boards of education by September of 1988.

Recommendation 4: Creation of a Common, Programmatic Budgeting System

Once approved by the MPC,a common, programmatically focused budgeting system should be put into place in all three school districts. The current budgeting system is very primitive. All three must become more program oriented so that costs can be identified and realistically controlled. The current traditional line item budgeting format is hopelessly inadequate to be related to curricular priorities or to efforts to use funds more effectively in the school systems.

It is recommended that the three school districts move progressively into a program-based budget. It should take anywhere from two to four years to fully implement this budgeting system. The major steps are:

- Identify various educational activities or programs and group them into broad areas of need or purpose served.
- After grouping, a tentative program structure is derived.
- A goal statement is prepared for each basic program, expressing the purpose it serves to the communities.
- The goal statements are given to appropriate staff to gather data to best describe service levels and program outputs.
- After data gathering, current and desired service objectives are defined.
- Guidelines are prepared and given to those who will develop the program budgets.
- Past cost information is assembled to guide budget estimates.

- Program work sheets and instructions are developed.
- Work sheets are completed and given to the respective budget directors.

It should be noted that the budgetary system developed must be backed up with a congruent accounting system that tracks transactions and financial decisions within the three school districts. Such "trails" are only available in the most cursory sense now. It should no longer be necessary for any individual board member to track purchase orders or budgetary requests to isolate duplications. All of the data should be available on computer and in as much detail as required.

The respective boards are in charge of multimillion dollar businesses. They cannot be effectively managed with the primitive procedures now in place. Effective cost controls are only possible with a vastly upgraded budgeting system. To fail to put into place such a system runs the risk of cutting out substantive parts of the educational program, something that at least two of the three boards have already done.

A common system among the three school districts will reduce the developmental costs and the costs of hardware acquisition and operations. Each board should share in the planning and developmental costs. The task force should be comprised of the three superintendents and respective business managers/secretaries. They will require some consultative support as well.

RECOMMENDATIONS FOR CASCADE CITY REGIONAL HIGH SCHOOL DISTRICT

Recommendation 1: Declare a Moratorium on Confrontations with the Cascade City Educational Association (CCEA)

The Cascade City Board has dissipated the energies and focus of the district in continual clashes with the Cascade City Educational Association. The continuation of the "tit for tat" one-upmanship confrontations, both public and private, is deleterious to morale and to the energy of the professional staff being channeled towards the real issues facing the survival of the high school as an institution.

Of course, it takes both parties to engage in a kind of "positive disengagement" to abort any further negative and destructive battles from marring a collaborative effort to work towards a better Cascade City Regional High School. Too much is at stake to avoid such disengagement.

It is recommended that some members of the board meet privately with CCEA officials to agree formally or informally to a cessation of all such activities in the future, without either party feeling it has capitulated on some important issue. The session should be used to clear the air and to establish an "action agenda" towards better working relationships.

Recommendation 2: Freeze All Staff and Program Cuts Until the Development of the Strategic Plan

The auditor believes that short-term cuts of both staff and program are unwise and possibly debilitative until the board, the administration, and the teaching staff fully understand what Cascade City must do and be in the future.

For Cascade City to survive, it must expand its appeal to students not now in either Eton Park or Clumberville. It will not offer anything very attractive or different if it has reduced itself to a "bare bones" secondary school program that is neither broad nor deep. It is now at a very critical crossroad. Further cuts may spell out its demise as a comprehensive high school. That would surely seal its lack of appeal to anyone but a captive audience in the two captive elementary school districts. That would mean an unhappy ending to a once proud high school.

Recommendation 3: Clarify Leadership Responsibilities and Roles

The leadership at the high school has been reactive and idiosyncratic. There has been a lack of formal staff involvement in program and curricular design. Long delays have often meant teachers have had to wait to know if their ideas would bear fruit at all in the future. The principal should review lesson plans.

A major effort must go into creating a positive, proactive, and planned approach to curriculum development at Cascade City Regional High School. Leadership roles must be clarified. A better balance must be struck for operational responsibilities between the principal and assistant principal.

Recommendation 4: Add a General Curriculum Coordinator

The auditor must agree with the 1983 Regional States Association Study which recommended improved curriculum leadership. It is doubtful that existing staff have the necessary expertise to do such a job. The new superintendent will not have time for at least two years because his attention must be directed to activities that relate to the long-term survival of the high school. Someone with the necessary expertise must work internally to create a cohesive curriculum and plan for many of the improvements sketched out in the curriculum audit.

Recommendation 5: Develop and Implement a Marketing Plan for Cascade City Regional High School

The major thrust of the new superintendent should be directed towards: (1) spearheading the development of the district's strategic plan and (2) marketing Cascade City Regional High School to a larger constituency. However, to be successful, he must have something to sell. That will mean developing something special at Cascade City that cannot be found anywhere else. What that something "special" is should emanate from the strategic planning process.

The superintendent's marketing plan must include a large component of public relations since the district succeeded in giving itself a very large public relations "black eye" over the drug testing fiasco.

It is recommended that the superintendent work with an established school public relations expert to turn this image around within a short time period not to exceed eighteen months.

Recommendation 6: Reduce the Number of Department Chairs, Expand Their Supervisory Responsibilities, and Remove Them from the Teacher Bargaining Unit

Most department chairpersons are effective. Some are very effective in the curricular area. Some additional consolidation could even up their supervisory duties and qualify them as teaching supervisors. All now have supervisory certificates.

It is recommended that the district change their responsibilities and remove them from the teacher bargaining unit. This will remove any possible conflict of interest from hampering their evaluative duties.

It is also recommended that plans be explored systematically to share their expertise in a planned, formal fashion with the two elementary school districts on a regular basis, with some funds from these two districts offsetting the necessary release time required to perform such curricular articulative duties. Such sharing could be accomplished on an annually rotating basis.

Recommendation 7: Revise Board Policies So That They Are Effective in Defining and Making Operational Curricular Quality Control

The Cascade City Board must update, revise, and create a more workable and sound framework for curricular quality control. Policies should be developed which deal with testing and test selection, textbook adoption and alignment, the necessity to have an annual curriculum report on the entire curriculum prior to initiation of the budget development cycle, the use of lesson plans and curriculum monitoring, the structure and timing of public reports, and the necessary interrelationship between the budget and the curriculum.

The Cascade City Board has renewed its efforts to remove itself from operations with a new superintendent. It should develop an effective set of bylaws and procedures that relate to its staying away from operations except in a monitoring capacity. It should also establish a set of procedures to govern itself, having none now by policy.

The lack of effective and agreed upon internal procedural rules means that a good deal of time is wasted by the board in sloppy board operations. It means that the board lacks the internal discipline to deal with itself. *Robert's Rules of Order* is recommended. It has been the standard reference work for Congress, state legislatures, political parties, and business, communitive, and civic groups for over 100 years. The board may wish to avail itself of a service of the State School Boards Association in this regard. The board cannot expect (or demand) professional behavior of the staff when it fails to apply the same standard to its own behavior as a primary legislative body in the district.

Recommendation 8: Systematically Institute Advanced Placement Courses in the Curriculum at Cascade City Regional High School

There are no Advanced Placement courses presently in the Cascade City curriculum. It is recommended that the department chairpersons investigate the addition of AP courses within their respective departments so that at least three such courses are operational by the 1988–89 school year and six by the 1989–90 school year. Funds will have to be set aside for training and development.

Recommendation 9: Delete Certain Courses in Social Studies and Add French to the Foreign Language Curriculum

Certain courses in social studies are not rigorous and are leftovers from the old "mini-course days." Such courses as mass media, sociology, anthropology, and even psychology or ecology are not rigorous enough for a sound academic program in this area. The social studies department must expand its depth.

Foreign language is limited to two languages. French is considered a basic international language. It ought to be added to the curriculum within a year, beginning in the 1988–89 school year. Ideally, Latin should also be offered.

Recommendation 10: Diversify Music and Art

There should be a vocal music program at Cascade City along with a more diversified program in art. The band instructor must be given increased administrative support to make connections to the two feeder elementary districts.

Recommendation 11: Revise and Modernize the Lesson Plan Form

The current lesson plan form is obsolete. It should be replaced by one that is more functional and easier to monitor.

Recommendation 12: Eliminate Early Dismissal for Seniors Except for Cases of Extreme Hardship

The practice of early dismissal for seniors should be eliminated beginning in the 1987–88 school year. The only exception should be grounded in cases of extreme financial hardship upon the senior or his/her family circumstances. Early dismissal for sports or other extracurricular activities should be abandoned.

Recommendation 13: Fund Future Summer Curriculum Work That Follows a Uniform Format

The best format for curriculum development was the one developed for K–8 mathematics. It ought to be followed in the future with modifications as suggestion in Finding 2.4.

Recommendation 14: Regular and Systematic Follow-Up Studies of Graduates Should Ask Curricular Questions

The two follow-up studies reviewed by the auditor were much too limited to be of use in revising the curriculum at Cascade City Regional High School. No curricular questions were asked. It is recommended that in the future, curricular, programmatic, or educational questions be asked that will be useful in the process of revising curriculum.

Recommendation 15: The Guidance Department Is Charged with Formulating a Plan of Curricular Feedback Using SAT Data in a Similar Fashion as the State Test Data

The same procedures and principles apply to improving the SAT score results as the state test. It is recommended that the Cascade City guidance department take the lead in developing an annual detailed and systematic analysis of the SAT data as the auditor has seen developed at Cascade City with the state data. Copies should be widely circulated among the respective curricular areas at Cascade City and be incorporated into lesson plans and instruction.

RECOMMENDATIONS FOR THE ETON PARK PUBLIC SCHOOLS

Recommendation 1: Revise and Update Board Policies Regarding Curricular Quality Control

Eton Park has developed a fairly good set of policies. However, the testing policy requires provisions for curriculum alignment as does the textbook policy. A policy should be developed which clarifies the board's role to setting goals and objectives jointly, planning supervision, and the monitoring of results of the curriculum. This will prevent the board from directly entering operations. Specific textbook adoptions and grouping practices should not be a matter of direct board interference unless agreed upon results with the superintendent are not forthcoming after a reasonable period of time.

Recommendation 2: Develop and Implement a Long-Range Plan for Curriculum Development

A long-range plan is required in Eton Park for curriculum development to be maximally effective. At least a five-year planning horizon should be part of such a plan. It should identify the major areas of the curriculum to be developed and relate to all aspects of curriculum development: needs assessment, development of alternatives, cost-effective analysis, criteria development, and selection of alternatives. The alternatives are then cast into a planning period with accompanying responsibilities by appropriate personnel.

Recommendation 3: A Full-Time Curriculum Coordinator is Required for at Least Two Years

Eton Park does not have a locally developed curriculum for every area which could be called an appropriate management tool. The current position is staffed only part-time. For at least two years it should be a full-time responsibility with the aim of developing a complete curriculum K–8 with accompanying monitoring provisions now being put into place with the CTBS feedback.

Recommendation 4: Clarify All Curricular Functions in Extant Job Descriptions

A better delineation of specific curricular responsibilities is required in Eton Park. This will clearly specify who develops, refines, monitors, and modifies curriculum as an ongoing process in the district.

Recommendation 5: The Board of Education Should Adopt a List of Validated Goals and Objectives Which Anchor the Curriculum Development Process

The board of education should cause to be developed a validated (cross-referenced by consensus) set of goals and objectives which will anchor the curriculum development process in the district well into the future. These should be periodically examined and modified based on feedback provided by the administration.

Recommendation 6: The Superintendent Should Submit an Annual State of the District Report on Curriculum

The superintendent of schools already submits testing and other data to the board. However, there should be an annual report in which all of these data are submitted collectively so that the board can see the overall process of the written, taught, and tested curricula. This report should be provided to the board each year prior to the budget development process.

Recommendation 7: Close at Least One School in Eton Park and Consolidate the Educational Program in the Remaining Sites

Eton Park has not optimized the resources provided by the taxpayers of the district. Some of the schools in Eton Park are under-utilized. The resources expended for the under-utilization of the sites could be better spent on staff and support to expand and enrich the curriculum and program in Eton Park.

Consolidation is never popular because most communities want their "cake" and eat it too, i.e., the convenience of neighborhood schools and low taxes. There comes a time when enrollment decline will no longer justify the current building configuration. That point has been reached in Eton Park.

The superintendent has developed a variety of options and ideas regarding program consolidation. The one selected should be the one that is educationally the soundest and maximizes the opportunities for the children of the district.

RECOMMENDATIONS FOR THE CLUMBERVILLE PUBLIC SCHOOLS

Recommendation 1: Refine and Expand Board Policies Regarding Curriculum Quality Control

Board policies are inadequate in Clumberville. New policies should be developed and adopted that insure that quality control will occur in the schools. That means that test, textbook, and curriculum adoption must be congruent with one another and these to a sound and explicit set of validated board goals and objectives. The current list is in need of revision.

Recommendation 2: Refrain from Activities That Encroach on the Actual Administration of the School District

The intrusion of the board into personnel matters regarding the principals should not be repeated. All personnel actions should be acted upon with a recommendation by the superintendent. Not only has this action served to stir up a section of the community, it has undermined the confidence of many people in the principals transferred. Their professional reputations have been publicly tarnished by this ill-conceived decision.

Recommendation 3: Develop a Long-Range Plan for Curriculum Development

There is very little curriculum per se in Clumberville. The district requires its own locally validated curriculum in areas that are not directly part of the Cascade City program. A long-range plan should be developed similar in content and scope to that recommended for Eton Park (see Eton Park Recommendation 2).

Recommendation 4: Fund a Curriculum Coordinator Role for at Least Three Years

Clumberville is considerably behind Eton Park in the creation of a working, effective, and monitored curriculum. The coordinator should be charged with creating a formal system of curriculum development similar to that emerging in Eton Park with very similar responsibilities.

Recommendation 5: Fund a Full-Time Guidance Position at Faubus Intermediate School

The guidance situation at Faubus is deplorable. Both the critical nature of the program and the volatility of the age of the students requires a full-time guidance position.

Recommendation 6: Revise the Testing Program

The testing program should be revised. The DAT has not been used or reported correctly. It should either be changed or employed correctly.

Recommendation 7: The Board Should Receive an Annual In-Depth Curriculum Report Each Year

The current annual report by the Clumberville superintendent should be modified and focused more clearly on yearly and long-range curricular and educational goals/objectives. The report should indicate how curricular priorities have been realized and trace their linkages to budget priorities. The annual report should be a more coherent document than what it has been in the past.

Recommendation 8: At Least One School Should Be Closed in Clumberville

None of the elementary schools in Clumberville are very modern. All are under-utilized. Clearly, one school could be permanently closed, perhaps two depending upon program decisions.

The current board is in the process of considering options regarding facilities in Clumberville. Funds saved from school closings could fund the two recommended positions in the curriculum audit, purchase additional computers and extend that program more formally into the elementary level, and add needed specialization in science similar to that option selected in Eton Park.

SUMMARY

Eton Park and Clumberville are two established and solid communities that have conspired to create a regional high school. That school is supported by two K–8 school systems in the respective two communities. All three have a common purpose in providing for a K–12 educational system.

Such a system has probably never worked K–12 in the past except at isolated moments and in very specific curricular areas such as the state tests, which demanded inter-district cooperation.

All three school systems face stiff challenges in the future. Declining enrollment, aging facilities in the two elementary districts, rising costs, new state mandates in curriculum, and the necessity to keep pace with educational changes will require constant attention.

The easy remedies have all been tried. None of the districts can take more staff cuts or program reductions. In fact, contemporary challenges require program expansion and staff additions.

The hard solutions are school closings. The savings here are both necessary and prudent. They are the most politically sensitive of almost any that can be made at the local level. But they will make a difference and they will last. That payoff ought to be worth the risks involved.

As for the Cascade City Regional High School there is precious little time remaining before it slides substantially more from the kind of rigorous and comprehensive school it must be to survive. The board, administration, and teaching staff must work collectively to turn the corner and enter the twenty-first century with confidence. For the latter scenario to become reality, a lot of people at Cascade City among the board, administration, and teaching staff will have to swallow hard and learn to work with former adversaries to ensure any future at all. That payoff also ought to be worth the required humility and humanity to guarantee the best possible future for the students now at Cascade City and those yet to come.

CHECKPOINTS

Questions to the Author–Auditor About the Cascade City Audits

Question 1: *What were the politics behind the audit? Were there three clients or one?*

Answer: While all three boards and superintendents were cooperative, the "client" board was Cascade City. The Cascade City Board had influence on the other two. However, the Cascade City Board actually paid for the audit.

Question 2: *What was the most sensitive part of the audit?*

Answer: There were several aspects that were sensitive. First, some of the elementary district superintendents were suspicious of the motives of the Cascade City Board. Secondly, the recommendations dealing with school closings were acutely sensitive. Board members in the respective elementary districts were critical of this aspect of the audit, not all, but several.

Question 3: *Were you able to discern any short-term impact of the audit?*

Answer: There were several. First, there was an immediate "thaw" in the relationships between the Cascade City Board and the CCEA. Secondly, the new Cascade City superintendent got some important reinforcement for what had to be done to improve things in Cascade City.

Another short-term impact was a negative newspaper article in the local press about the audit. The article concentrated only upon the negative findings and did not cite any "positive" findings. Since several Cascade City board members were up for reelection, they were upset with the local press.

/ IX / *Pre- and Post-Audit Activities*

AFTER THE DECISION has been made to undertake a curriculum audit, there is a scenario of activities that leads to the successful completion of the process. Also, after the audit has been completed, there are a number of events that will facilitate the changes recommended in the audit. This chapter explicates those which have been used with success in a dozen or more sites in several different states and school systems in the U.S.

KNOWING WHAT TO EXPECT

Knowing what to expect in the audit process can be ascertained by reading about it, reviewing copies of previous audits completed in other school districts, and talking personally with those who have already been audited.

The emotional "set" is important to understand. What does it "feel like" to be asked questions about some of the most difficult aspects of school and curriculum management? Does one "feel stupid" or "embarrassed"? If so, why?

One of the crucial questions that might be asked to those that have already been audited is: "What were the unanticipated consequences of the audit?" In almost all activities there are results that one simply didn't expect. What were they?

For example, one superintendent who wanted to delve deeply into the adequacy of the management of curriculum at individual schools was surprised to discover that, by implication, his own lack of leadership was partly responsible for the deficiencies uncovered. He hadn't considered this outcome, believing that "they" (the principals) "out there" (in the buildings) were the culprits, not "us" (central leadership). He simply had never connected the two. But the audit clearly showed the connection. He felt "stuck."

One of the ways the author–auditor attempts to deal with this problem is to give the school district officials a copy of a completed audit from another district. Some superintendents have wisely circulated the audit to board and staff prior to the audit being finally considered. At least two have opted to withdraw from the process, claiming that they had decided that they "did not need" an audit after all.

What that normally means is that the district officials and the board cannot withstand the criticism they would inevitably encounter if the audit similarly revealed gaps in their district. The auditor should endeavor to avoid any surprises with a possible client. I've insisted as much as possible that the superintendent talk with another superitendent candidly and privately prior to any decision to go ahead in the first place. Even with examining previous audits and talking with other superintendents, some chief school officers express "surprise" at the findings of an audit in their system. Most of the time, it is the result of their own lack of experience with the real problems of curriculum management and their isolation in their own school systems from them. For some, it is a rude awakening.

After the decision has been made to proceed, the superintendent should do as follows.

1. Inform the Staff

The staff ought to be informed, preferably face to face if possible, or by memo in larger systems. The information should proceed something like this.

> At the Monday night meeting of the board of education, it was determined to undertake a curriculum audit. This is a process to examine how well the district is managing its curriculum. The audit is not an evaluation of any person's teaching or activities. It is a collective examination of the way we, as a system, deliver our own curriculum.
>
> The board appointed Dr. Joe Doakes, an experienced curriculum auditor to do the audit. Dr. Doakes has performed similar audits in Newtown, New Jersey; Franklin, Ohio; Coopersburg, Pennsylvania; and San Xaviar, California.
>
> The board believes we have an excellent school system. They expect to use the results to improve an already good set of operations. We know we can be even better.
>
> For those teachers interested in reading a prior audit completed by Dr. Doakes, a copy of the one performed in Newtown, New Jersey, is in the superintendent's office.
>
> Dr. Doakes is expected to begin the audit the third week of March and

> conclude his review the first week of May. He will be interviewing teacher association leaders and building representatives, principals, other administrators, board members, and some parents and students. Any teacher desiring to conference with Dr. Doakes separately and privately may request an interview through Dr. Sally Reins' office. Dr. Reins will function as the audit coordinator.
>
> Dr. Doakes will also visit each school in the district to get a firsthand "feel" for each building's "learning environment." Please join us in welcoming Dr. Doakes to our school district. We look forward to his visit and to his report. If there is a better way to do things, we want to know how.
>
> Questions about the audit or Dr. Doakes may be directed to Dr. Reins or the superintendent. Thank you.

The message that should be communicated is not only what the audit is, but more importantly what it isn't. Teachers must definitely get the message that the audit is: (1) not a witch hunt to "get" anybody or any program or school and (2) not an evaluation of them or any other teacher.

The opportunity to allow any teacher to confer with the auditor is controversial. Some superintendents are frankly scared to do this. I insist on meeting with the full teacher association or union officers. That is a must meeting. And I know full well that some of the teachers will use the meeting to grind their own axes or to proffer the union line. The auditor must know the difference between the "union line" and legitimate concerns and problems. That is why experience is crucial in such instances. Novice auditors without much real firsthand experience can be misled. Even if one encounters the "union line," the agenda is usually attached to real events. It is the real events, as the union perceives them, that must be examined by the auditor.

Real events are things like the union's perceptions of administrative actions and intent. The "union line" is usually the solution to the problem created by the event. For example, one union official said, "The administration looks at us as troublemakers with no brains. It's like we only work here and wouldn't have the foggiest idea of how to improve the district."

When questioned as to "how" the official knew this, he said, "Because principals never ask us, never involve us, never take the time to initiate any inquiry prior to actions they may take." This perception may be accurate. If it is confirmed by other teachers outside the union's inner circle rather consistently, it may be true. The finding is that teachers perceive that their opinions are not valued by the administration. The union has simply articulated the feeling held by the teaching staff.

The union agenda to solve the problem, however, is another matter.

Suppose that when asked "How could this perception be changed?" the union responds, "The answer is to have teacher advisory councils to each principal that can veto any action or decision with which they may disagree." Here, a possible bona fide feeling and perception has been translated into a union strategy to take control of the schools at the building level. The auditor may cite the perception without embracing the union solution.

Opening the audit interviews to volunteers runs the risk of inviting in the kooks and chronic complainers to use up the auditor's normally precious and costly on-site time. However, the advantage is that no one can later complain they were "shut out" of talking with the auditor so they couldn't tell him or her what was really going on.

In one district where the superintendent decided to open the interviews, the author–auditor got a string of hard-core union supporters. It became clear that their agenda was to create an image of an ogre-like board trying to "crush them" i.e., engage in "union busting."

Despite the obvious agenda the auditor did encounter some new information unrevealed up to this point. It included:

- On two occasions the board president had ripped up the state's code of ethics for school boards in front of witnesses.
- On one occasion the board had called a meeting for all students in the auditorium and then dismissed all of the teachers and barred them from listening to what the board said to the students.
- The board president had received a near failing grade as a student in the high school from a union teacher, who later felt the president was trying to "get back" at him in his actions as president.
- The board tried to "censor" the student newspaper as a result of receiving what they perceived to be less than complimentary support for their actions from the students.

When this information was triangulated, almost all of the information was confirmed by the administration and the board. The differences were:

- The code of ethics was torn up only in one meeting.
- The board president denied trying to "get" his former teacher. He did acknowledge he was not a "superior student" in school.

Furthermore, the board president added a piece of information on the code of ethics imbroglio. He said another board member was reading from it in an effort to chastise him for some of his views and actions. However, that board member was only citing areas which contradicted him. When he pointed out that the critical board member had also violated the code of ethics but had failed to cite those, he said that either we live by all of the points in the code or none, whereupon he said he ripped up the code of ethics to make his point.

The teacher union officers left out this piece of the episode, pointing only to the substantiated fact that the board president had indeed publicly torn up the state's code of ethics for school boards. However, none of this affair would have been known had it not been for the fact that unsolicited interviews were accepted in the audit.

The information revealed the depth of the animosities between the board and the teachers' union. It was during the audit interviews that the auditor observed the traumatic effect of that hostility when the board ordered every single teacher to be officially reprimanded for engaging in a "job action."

The reprimand was triggered by an incident in which a teacher was attacked by a student while supervising a restroom. The teacher, in turn, struck back. The pupil's parents complained. The teacher was suspended from duty.

The remainder of the faculty demanded a meeting with the principal (a recluse) to know why their colleague had been suspended under the circumstances. When the principal refused to divulge his reasons and ordered them to their classes, they refused to budge until they were told.

The standoff was resolved when the union president suggested the teachers go to their classrooms. Because the teachers were all late (not more than five to ten minutes), the board decided to place a written reprimand in every teacher's file.

I interviewed teachers as they went in to receive their reprimand and after they got it. Many were shaking. All were angry. The actions of the board had "radicalized" even the most timid into crusty protagonists. While the board clearly demonstrated its "power," the effect was not to discourage the staff but to strengthen and unite them. Their differences congealed into a toughened cadre.

That experience further resulted in recommendations concerning dealing with the "climate" problem. The fact that I had interviewed a good number of teachers led to some candid interviews, where their real feelings about the events occurring were revealed.

2. Inform the Media

Another party that does not take kindly to "surprises" is the media. If the audit comes to be reported publicly and the media never knew one was undertaken, the impression will have been created that the district or the board was up to something "sneaky." The press is already suspicious of public officials. Don't hand them an issue.

Inform the press that an audit has been undertaken. Explain what it is and who will be doing it. Provide the cost of the audit. Indicate what benefits the school district expects to gain from having it done. If necessary, give the press the same references of previous audits undertaken by the auditor so they can do their own checking.

3. Publish the Schedule of the Auditor

Once the schedule has been established for the audit, publish it widely. Staff, parents, and community should be aware of whom, when, and where the auditor is meeting. Make arrangements for a contact person if someone becomes ill and has to rebook an appointment.

4. Establish a Document Storage and Work Room

A central place should be designated for storage of all documents to be reviewed by the auditor. Preferably, all of the documents should be boxed and catalogued for easy reference. Other items in the room should be a telephone and a typewriter and easy access to a copy machine.

5. Establish a Contact Person for the Auditor

To avoid contacting too many people and disrupting the schedules of many administrative officers, the school district should establish one person as the liaison administrator for the audit. This person works out schedules, rearranges conferences if necessary, and works out all the required details to perform the audit.

6. Prep Those to Be Interviewed

There will be some natural uneasiness for people to be interviewed by an auditor. Board members, particularly, may be nervous because they don't know what to expect.

I've found it necessary to have the district contact person provide some explanation of what I'm looking for. For example, parents can be told, "He wants to ask you about the curriculum, your perceptions of its strengths and weaknesses." Board members have to be reassured that they are not expected to possess detailed technical knowledge of curricular processes. They will be asked about board policy development and board decision making about curriculum.

Interviewees should be reassured that their responses will be kept confidential (assuming litigation is not involved).

7. Insist on Business as Usual

The last thing the auditor wants is a show. The auditor wants to encounter the system as it runs each day. The auditor wants to be as unobtrusive as possible. The longer the auditor is there, the more this becomes a reality.

POST-AUDIT ACTIVITIES

After the audit, district officials will want to do the following.

1. Issue a Press Release at a Press Conference

It is important to get the results of the audit out as soon as possible. This quells any rumors and insures an open climate to address the audit's recommendations. It should be made clear just what next steps

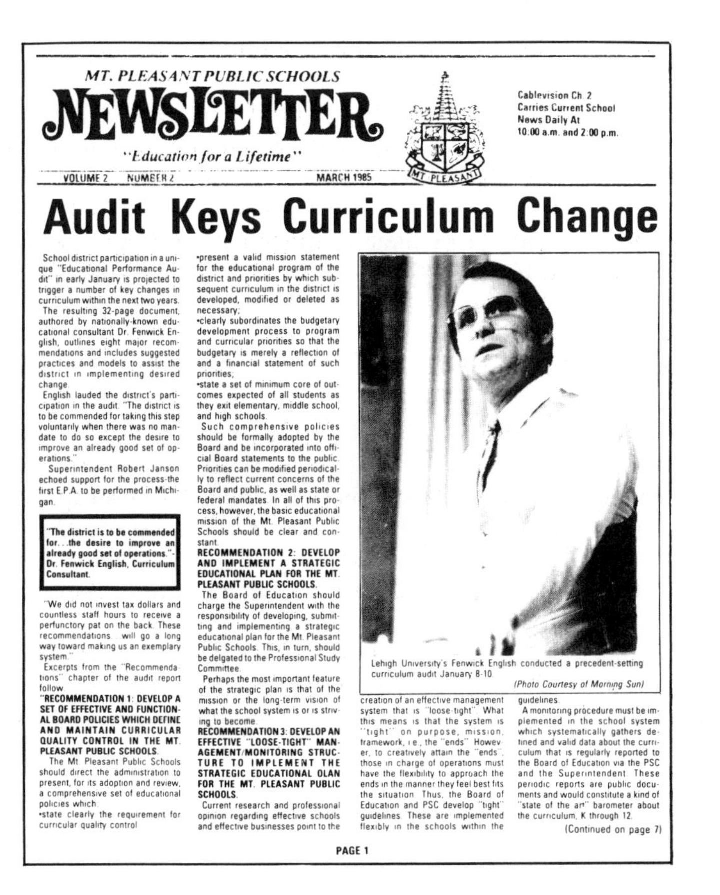

MT. PLEASANT PUBLIC SCHOOLS

NEWSLETTER

"Education for a Lifetime"

MT PLEASANT

Cablevision Ch. 2
Carries Current School
News Daily At
10:00 a.m. and 2:00 p.m.

VOLUME 2 NUMBER 2 MARCH 1985

Audit Keys Curriculum Change

School district participation in a unique "Educational Performance Audit" in early January is projected to trigger a number of key changes in curriculum within the next two years.

The resulting 32-page document, authored by nationally-known educational consultant Dr. Fenwick English, outlines eight major recommendations and includes suggested practices and models to assist the district in implementing desired change.

English lauded the district's participation in the audit. "The district is to be commended for taking this step voluntarily when there was no mandate to do so except the desire to improve an already good set of operations."

Superintendent Robert Janson echoed support for the process-the first E.P.A. to be performed in Michigan.

"The district is to be commended for. . .the desire to improve an already good set of operations."-Dr. Fenwick English, Curriculum Consultant.

"We did not invest tax dollars and countless staff hours to receive a perfunctory pat on the back. These recommendations . . will go a long way toward making us an exemplary system."

Excerpts from the "Recommendations" chapter of the audit report follow.

"RECOMMENDATION 1: DEVELOP A SET OF EFFECTIVE AND FUNCTIONAL BOARD POLICIES WHICH DEFINE AND MAINTAIN CURRICULAR QUALITY CONTROL IN THE MT. PLEASANT PUBLIC SCHOOLS.

The Mt. Pleasant Public Schools should direct the administration to present, for its adoption and review, a comprehensive set of educational policies which:

•state clearly the requirement for curricular quality control

•present a valid mission statement for the educational program of the district and priorities by which subsequent curriculum in the district is developed, modified or deleted as necessary;

•clearly subordinates the budgetary development process to program and curricular priorities so that the budgetary is merely a reflection of and a financial statement of such priorities;

•state a set of minimum core of outcomes expected of all students as they exit elementary, middle school, and high schools.

Such comprehensive policies should be formally adopted by the Board and be incorporated into official Board statements to the public. Priorities can be modified periodically to reflect current concerns of the Board and public, as well as state or federal mandates. In all of this process, however, the basic educational mission of the Mt. Pleasant Public Schools should be clear and constant.

RECOMMENDATION 2: DEVELOP AND IMPLEMENT A STRATEGIC EDUCATIONAL PLAN FOR THE MT. PLEASANT PUBLIC SCHOOLS.

The Board of Education should charge the Superintendent with the responsibility of developing, submitting and implementing a strategic educational plan for the Mt. Pleasant Public Schools. This, in turn, should be delgated to the Professional Study Committee.

Perhaps the most important feature of the strategic plan is that of the mission or the long-term vision of what the school system is or is striving to become.

RECOMMENDATION 3: DEVELOP AN EFFECTIVE "LOOSE-TIGHT" MANAGEMENT/MONITORING STRUCTURE TO IMPLEMENT THE STRATEGIC EDUCATIONAL OLAN FOR THE MT. PLEASANT PUBLIC SCHOOLS.

Current research and professional opinion regarding effective schools and effective businesses point to the creation of an effective management system that is "loose-tight". What this means is that the system is "tight" on purpose, mission, framework, i.e., the "ends". However, to creatively attain the "ends", those in charge of operations must have the flexibility to approach the ends in the manner they feel best fits the situation. Thus, the Board of Education and PSC develop "tight" guidelines. These are implemented flexibly in the schools within the guidelines.

A monitoring procedure must be implemented in the school system which systematically gathers defined and valid data about the curriculum that is regularly reported to the Board of Education via the PSC and the Superintendent. These periodic reports are public documents and would constitute a kind of "state of the art" barometer about the curriculum, K through 12.

(Continued on page 7)

Lehigh University's Fenwick English conducted a precedent-setting curriculum audit January 8-10.

(Photo Courtesy of Morning Sun)

PAGE 1

the superintendent will take. The customary procedure is for the board to receive the audit. The board does not accept the audit. Instead, it waits for the superintendent's recommendations. It then decides what to do based upon actions suggested by the superintendent within the context of the audit's recommendations. That should be made clear at the press conference.

2. Issue a Newsletter about the Audit to the Community

Many school districts publish their own newsletter. After an audit, the results are often included in the newsletter. An example is shown here (previous page) from Mt. Pleasant, Michigan, after an audit was performed in that district in 1985. This newsletter was mailed to the entire community. All of the recommendations of the auditor were included.

3. Devote One Public Board Meeting to a Full Discussion of the Audit

At least one public board meeting should be devoted to a discussion of the audit. The meeting is explanatory and is aimed at developing awareness of the audit's recommendations and the implications if they were followed as framed. Sometimes the auditor is present to explain his/her reasons. This is preferable, though not always possible, because of time and distance.

4. Hold a Staff Briefing

In some districts, I've conducted a full staff briefing. At this time, teachers and administrators are free to challenge or criticize the audit. This provides a healthy give and take and often clarifies expectations.

5. Assist the Superintendent in Developing an Action Plan

I've often helped the superintendent frame out an "action plan" in response to an audit. Normally, a matrix is constructed in which the audit recommendation is followed by a response by the superintendent, a scenario of events, time line, and a column for budget implications.

Sometimes the action plan has been presented at the same time as the audit is made public.

6. Arrange for a Follow-up Visitation or Second Audit

In most cases, an audit is a "single shot" affair. What happens after the audit is dependent upon the tenure of the superintendent, board support, budget allocations, and staff response. However, districts are becoming more aware of the necessity for continuity in engaging in large-scale, deep change. This requires more than a single audit, but a continuing series of audits over time.

Activities before and after the audit are critical to its success. Careful attention must be paid to scheduling, maintaining an atmosphere of openness about what the auditor is doing, and what the results are expected to be.

After the audit, how the district officials handle themselves and what they say to staff and the community will be important bellweathers for shaping the response to the audit's findings.

District officials must look at both the pre- and post-audit activities as bridges which connect the audit process to the district's operations and the major players that shape and support the district's functions. In this respect, while there is no substitute for substance, perceptions by stakeholders of the audit will often overshadow the actual changes included in it. These perceptions have their roots in the pre-audit activities and blossom in the post-audit activities.

CHECKPOINTS

Questions Commonly Asked the Author–Auditor

Question 1: *You didn't say anything about an exit interview? Are they done?*

Answer: It depends upon the client. Sometimes the superintendent schedules one. In that case I have one. I make sure the persons in attendance understand that they are simply impressions at that point. The danger in an exit interview is that one requires time to ponder an enormous amount of data. The interview may foster premature closure on both findings and recommendations.

Question 2: *How does one know what recommendations are most acceptable and will be acted upon?*

Answer: The auditor is actually building a consensus throughout the audit towards acceptability of the recommendations. The interviewing process is more than just fact finding. It is a dynamic process of give and take. I use it to try out ideas, secure reactions, provoke thinking, and obtain reactions to possible solutions. Interviewing is thus a proactive process and not merely sitting passively waiting to be told.

I can't think of any recommendations I've made that came as a surprise to a client. That doesn't mean they agree with all of them or necessarily implement all of them. But they do know what they probably will be.

Question 3: *Doesn't this strategy compromise the integrity of the audit?*

Answer: Only if the auditor is searching for what will make the client "happy" as opposed to doing what is right by the client. There are usually many ways to act upon a problem. Recommending a course of action beyond the capability of the client organization, or one which is absolutely not acceptable, is a waste of time to everyone involved.

The audit is not a search for "eternal" truth. It is, rather, a search for a better course of action that will lead to improved results as the school system defines results. It is a thoroughly pragmatic endeavor.

Once again, we are problem solving and not doing research. A researcher would be concerned about "contamination." The auditor is an active player. The auditor is problem solving, preferably with a client and not trying to "sentence" a client.

Question 4: *What have been the most common problems you've encountered in the pre-audit stage?*

Answer: The most common fault is that school system officials don't really understand the assumptions and limitations of the auditing process. Some believe it will be a "PR" exercise and validate their preformed opinions about "educational excellence." Others want a "quick fix" and are not willing to consider deep change.

Question 5: *And post-audit problems? What are the most common problems there?*

Answer: I think making the audit fully public quickly. I've known some systems to wait many months for the "right" time to release the results. The real leverage of the audit is its public visibility. Time quickly erodes this valuable asset.

Question 6: *Have school district officials ever tried to influence the shaping of an audit through bribery or intimidation?*

Answer: Never overtly. Of course, everyone is trying to influence the auditor by stressing their view of reality. But outright bribery I've never experienced in any form, and I've worked in systems where bribery was a practice at certain levels of the school district.

The most subtle form of intimidation is when a person intimates that "follow-on" work may be available if some people are "happy" with the audit. The auditor must never be tempted. One simply calls it the way it is and the chips fall where they may as far as the "happiness factor" is concerned.

Question 7: *Can you predict the kind of criticism an auditor can expect to encounter after the audit has been concluded?*

Answer: If the audits are litigated, the oppositional parties will search for errors and inconsistencies in the factual presentations within the audit. Unless the auditor has been sloppy, this will not be a problem.

Question 8: *Where is the audit most vulnerable?*

Answer: On its axioms or critical assumptions. For a good review which will be presented as a contrast, read the next chapter on auditing non-rational systems.

/ X / *Auditing Curriculum in the Non-Rational System*

RATIONALITY REFERS TO the extent to which an organization is goal-directed (Silver, 1983, p. 77). Even if a school system doesn't have goals, it may believe it should. Goals mean that a school system is trying to direct itself towards certain ends. In so doing, it appears to act thoughtfully, to marshall its resources accordingly, and to obtain desired results which have been sanctioned or mandated.

Almost all school systems function using this assumption. There is considerable effort to install planning approaches that strive to delineate a consensus, sketch out what the organization ought to be like in a specified planning horizon, and attempt to make budget projections based on the aforementioned activities. The case studies cited in this book reinforce that view of organizational life.

THE RATIONAL ORGANIZATION

Briefly stated a rational organization develops goals, translates them into activities which are congruent with the goals, portions its resources based on goal priorities, and translates both into tangible jobs to be performed and subsequently evaluated. Based upon feedback obtained from evaluation, the cycle is repeated until the desired results are obtained at the lowest possible cost.

There is plenty of evidence to indicate that the cycle doesn't occur as it has been described. The discrepancies are primarily viewed as breakdowns to what otherwise should occur. Recently, however, some organizational writers have challenged this model.

Weick (1985) avers that "organizations use rationality as a facade when they talk about goals, planning, intentions, and analysis, not because these practices necessarily work, but because people who supply resources believe that such practices work" (p. 110).

Organizations use the guise of pretending to be "rational" to bolster themselves within their environment, defend themselves against attack, and guarantee a flow of resources to support their activities (Weick, 1985, p. 110).

School systems are therefore, according to this view, much more likely to act first and then invent reasons for their actions. This is a kind of post-hoc approach to organizational rationality.

SCHOOL SYSTEMS AS NON-RATIONAL ORGANIZATIONS

Any school superintendent knows that decisions are often required prior to a full discussion or disclosure of a data base. Then school systems have to be responsive to stakeholders with contradictory claims and desires. The result is that such an organization resorts to ambiguous goals (Hasenfeld, 1983, p. 92). Only ambiguity shields the organization from having to deal with such contradictions. Goals then absorb the contradictions and enable the organization to appear rational in the eyes of its constituents.

If there are no goals in reality for organizations, the whole concept of planning as it has been practiced is thrown into question. If organizations simply are in the process of responding to the exigencies of the moment, plans cannot help because they are usually always anchored to larger statements of purpose as encased in the idea of organizational goals.

Curriculum is believed to be a means to attain organizational goals as they are finally stated in terms of learner achievement. If goals are simply political agreements about resource allocation (White, 1974, p. 369) and nothing else, the effort used to create system-wide curriculum which drives budget allocations is a waste of time.

And finally, if an organization is nothing more than its contextual actions, current notions about "reform" and change are also severely negated.

Exhibit 22 illustrates the "polarized" differences between rational and non-rational systems. The polarization represents a pulling apart of the variables which may be considered falling on a continuum. In reality, no organization would be totally one or the other, and some rational systems may act non-rational at times, and vice versa.

However, for purposes of discussion, the polarization enables the auditor to consider a different scenario and set of challenges and constraints than heretofore encountered.

As shown in the exhibit the differences are identified with the key words that differentiate between how each system views the problem or confronts reality.

Exhibit 22

A Comparison between Rational and Non-Rational Systems on Selected Variables

The Rational System	The Non-Rational System
Goals	
• focused, formal, sanctioned, or mandated	• ambiguous or non-existent • process anchored
Planning	
• formal, based on goals • macro in design	• no long-range planning • process statements • micro in design
Involvement of Stakeholders	
• formal, pre-determined • minimal • participants but not shapers	• organic, major players • informal and formal • spontaneous
Change Strategy	
• macro movement • holistic	• incremental • appears uncoordinated
Outcomes	
• predefined • predetermined prior to implementation • grandiose, comprehensive in nature	• specificity unknown • broad ranges may be anticipated • the unexpected is expected
Leadership Conception	
• search for generic "best" models or actions • anchored in formal roles	• situationally defined • contextually determined • spontaneously generated
Guide to Action	
• shaped by role pre-determinants in sanctioned structures • action limited to small, "authority" figures	• role free • situationally defined • task specific • action focus flexible and unlimited by formalized role constraints

Goals

Rational systems spend a lot of time on goals. Goals are considered pivotal for the mustering of organizational energy and resources. All organizational behavior is believed to be directed towards goal attainment. It is therefore important that goals be legitimized by having them approved by various internal groups and sanctioned by external groups or agencies.

The non-rational system spends little time on defining goals prior to the occasion when activities begin. Non-rational systems believe that actions define goals. They are therefore prone to act first and consider what the actions meant second. Goals are contextually defined as "right action" for a specific situation.

If the non-rational system does define goals, they are apt to be "process"-based as opposed to "product"-based. this means that the goals are shaped by the means to be used to carry on the essential work of the system as contrasted with what finally happens after the work of the system is done.

Planning

Rational systems seem to be always planning. They appear "possessed" by the necessity to pre-establish actions and legitimize them. The reason is not hard to ascertain. For any work situation, the possible "actions" which may be taken are almost limitless, especially for policy makers. This is because at the upper levels of an organization, management is not directly involved in the actual work of the system but is, instead, attempting to shape the processes utilized to do the work (Weick, 1985, p. 114). In order to avoid some of the political risks involved, administrators resort to obtaining organizational sanctions for their work. Plans are one way of sanctifying work design.

The scope of most plans for rational system is broad, often multi-year in approach. Strategic plans may reference time in decades with very wide brush strokes. This is an attempt to extricate the system from the iron grasp of the annual budgeting cycle.

The planning activities for non-rational systems are considerably less formal and complex, simply because the actors in this organization are more action oriented. They also believe that most consequences of plans are largely unanticipated and they want to be able to examine them firsthand without having to deal with whether or not they were "legitimate" outcomes.

In this sense traditional planning may be part of the reason failure appears to be "built in" from one cycle to the next. Suppose that the planners failed to account for some significant outcomes in their plans. But because these consequences were not anticipated, they are considered unimportant and they go unexamined. Suppose these variables "control" much of the outcome itself. The situation is one where the planners are concentrating only upon the expected outcomes as encased in their plans and ignoring the outcomes they could not explain. With each successive cycle they simply refine the plans more clearly, but still fail. One has only to think of the successive five-year plans in Soviet agriculture as examples of faulty plans or the many attempts to "wage war" on poverty in the U.S.

Because administrators in the non-rational system are not bound by their predetermined ideas, they are more free to examine the unanticipated outcomes of their actions. They may have a larger and more accurate data base upon which to construct future actions as a result.

Why don't more systems try this approach? Think of presenting a board of education, state or federal government, or even a foundation with a "plan" that says, "We don't know what we may accomplish, but give us money to muck around until we find something that works." Such requests would be laughed out of existence and dismissed out of hand.

Instead, funds are allocated to specific, "well-thought out" projects, replete with PERT charts and diagrams about predetermined actions on selected variables. These, in turn, are anchored to "roles" of investigators arranged by area of expertise and authority. The result is project management.

Public agencies have to justify "experimental" thrusts. They are awarded on a competitive basis. There is precious little room for very risky "experiments" and for the unanticipated. The cloak of rationality must cover such "experiments" by legitimizing them in psuedo-scientific terms, which means largely extending the tenets of logical positivism (see Lincoln and Guba, 1985) requiring cause and effect relationships which, because of limited knowledge, may exist only for trivial variables.

Involvement of Stakeholders

Rational systems may either exclude stakeholders or minimally involve them in very structured ways. This is because rational systems believe that their "expertise" precludes active stakeholder structuring of activities, even when the stakeholders are the recipients of the system's efforts.

Stakeholder ignorance or political proclivities cast them into an arena of suspicion by rational systems. Rational systems shield themselves from stakeholder influence by parading their authority in objective guise or structuring involvement so as to co-opt stakeholder anger and mask the manipulative behavior of the system itself.

Asking constituents what they "think" about a certain predetermined action, forcing that response into the format of a "semantic differential" attitude inventory, may distort stakeholder involvement, despite the fact that reliability is assured in the response.

Stakeholders are viewed as "objects" rather than human beings who have power and can take their own destiny in their own hands. That's the last thing any rational system desires for it erodes the base of social support for the system itself.

Non-rational systems view stakeholders as major players. They invent ways the stakeholders can participate, even with the absence of technical training. The work of Christopher Alexander and associates at the Center for Environmental Structure, Berkeley, California (1979) has developed such an approach in architecture. Their strategy has been to put into the hands of the users an organic, non-technical language by which they participate as active shapers of buildings.

Change Strategy

Rational systems desire macro or large change. Sweeping change as encapsulated in "The Great Society" of Lyndon Johnson or "The Nation at Risk" of the Reagan era aims at nothing less than grandiose alterations in large panoramic strokes.

What actually happens is considerably less dramatic, perhaps even pedestrian. Rational systems are forever tinkering with cosmic change and ending up with cosmetic change.

One reason is that, because they ignore the major variables, minimally involve stakeholders, and view incremental change as too small, their efforts are squandered on rhetoric and political verbiage at the expense of less dramatic but solid movement rooted in committed participants.

Non-rational systems are much less apt to engage in sweeping indictments or clarion calls for revolution. They appear to be user-oriented and satisfied with organic, incremental movement that is not "coordinated" top down.

When users are actively involved in changing their own situations, they may temporarily be working at cross purposes. Actions may be contradictory. Such a situation is not viewed as "bad," but natural as new avenues of synthesis are formulated with old data. Since unanticipated outcomes have been legitimized, contradictions (and powerful variables) are not eliminated at the outset because they don't match predetermined and anticipated ones.

Outcomes

Rational systems pride themselves on being results-oriented. The "bottom line" is always aimed at answering the question, "Did we get what we expected to get?" While the organization may have changed immeasurably and resolved long-standing internal problems or external conflicts, the measure of the worth of the change itself is rooted in outcome congruence with predetermined finality. From this perspective many of the world's great medical and mechanical discoveries were outright failures. Sir Arthur Fleming wasn't looking for penicillin when he "discovered" it.

Take the case of inventor Elisha Otis, father of the modern-day elevator, a creation that made skyscrapers possible. Otis also "invented" the wood-turning lathe, railroad brake, steam plow, lift bridge, and rotary bread oven. According to his son Charles, he "never used a drawing board, a blueprint, or a prototype model. He designed his inventions freehand, without working them out on paper first" (Drain, 1987, p. 44).

Otis also never asked anyone for advice or assistance, and he never used even a pen or pencil in design. His sketches were only minimally drawn to apply for patents. Rational system people would have had a terrible time with this solitary inventor. They would have been pressing him for "work plans," "outcome statements," "outlines of activities" "problem definitions," and Gantt charts. Had he been forced to comply, the world may have never known the "products" of a creative mind.

Non-rational systems are less concerned about knowing what the precise outcomes may be for any activity prior to engaging in the activity. This doesn't mean non-rational systems are unconcerned with outcomes; it means that they accept the fact that many of the real outcomes are unknown and it is not productive to try and define all of them. It is a waste of time.

Actors in non-rational systems think in broad ranges of possible outcomes, and they fully expect the unexpected and, therefore, are less apt to ignore important outcomes because they weren't specified ahead of time than actors in rational systems.

The Conception of Leadership

Rational system officials think in static terms of leadership. Leaders are those people in largely official roles who are responsible for thinking about the future. They are the administrators and planners with technical expertise. Their official roles are firmly attached to their plans. Vested interest solutions are perpetuated in such plans. Those in power are enhanced by the nature of the planning events.

Leadership becomes a search for the "one best way" to solve sanctioned problems that do not disturb existing power relationships, i.e., the status quo. Rational systems which are largely bureaucratic in design and function define leadership as synonymous with a bureaucratic role. Leaders are those people in the "top" positions who make decisions for the rest of us.

Non-rational systems have a more fluid definition of leadership.

Leadership in the non-rational system is what Alinsky (1969) called "native leadership" or "indigenous leadership." Notes Alinsky in his typical trenchant style, "The understanding of what constitutes a genuine native, indigenous leader is rarely found among conventional social do-gooders" (p. 67).

Alinsky notes that leaders vary with the situation: "Just as people have a variety of interests, so, too, they have a variety of leaders (p. 72) . . . one rarely stumbles across what might be defined as a complete leader—a person who has a following of forty or fifty people in every sphere of activity" (p. 73).

The non-rational system takes advantage of indigenous leadership that is site and issue specific. Leaders come and go and are not good for all times and challenges. Leadership is therefore not static and not role anchored. Such "informal" leadership is, however, capable of making significant changes, if supported. Such changes tend to be incremental but lasting.

Guide to Action

Rational system action is guided by logical, goal-directed policies and plans. Such actions are not necessarily a guarantee that what is desired really happens. A tragic national example occurred in the Vietnam War in which American forces won every battle in which they were engaged but lost the war because, "this generation of Americans had failed to study the history books well enough to discover that it was not possible to impose a people's government on a people" (Hoyt, 1987, p. 472). Saul Alinsky said the same thing in 1946 when he wrote "but only the people and their own leaders can build a people's organization" (1969, p. 74).

Rational systems circumscribe power to a few roles at the apex of the bureaucratic pyramid. Everyone else must "follow the rules." Compulsive rule following has long been the hallmark of the bureaucrat.

Non-rational systems are role free, situationally defined, and roles are linked to specific tasks. The range of possible actions is less circumscribed by both the nature of the analysis permitted and by the fact that role hierarchies do not stand as barriers to forcefully attacking a problem at any level.

The question may be asked, "Why aren't school systems moving towards a so-called non-rational model?" The answer comes from a variety of sources. The non-rational system is not very conducive to accountability, as is illustrated in the case of the E. F. Hutton scandal of 1985.

Hutton was one of the "darlings" of Wall Street. It was a "go-go" outfit, marked by an absence of corporate hierarchy and bureaucratic trappings.

When, however, the firm got entangled in an elaborate check-kiting scheme that may have bilked banks out of $250 million a day in free loans (Koepp and Constable, 1985, p. 54), the lack of clear lines of "control" for cash management produced a disaster. When ex-U.S. Attorney General Griffin Bell examined the situation after he and fourteen lawyers interviewed more than 370 persons, characteristics of the non-rational system were abolished as ambiguity regarding decisions was clarified. No longer could certain individuals in Hutton exist as "orphans." Roles had to be connected. People had to be supervised.

A freewheeling organization can be abused, especially when it comes to money. The accounting function is paramount, particularly in tax-supported institutions. For this reason, it will probably be impossible to create a fully non-rational organization in public education. The agencies regulating the schools demand, via laws and regulations, goals and goal-directed actions. Such agencies provide mandates for all of the trappings of rationality. They demand curricular-driven means led by explicit goals and objectives for learners, despite the fact that it is extremely difficult to anticipate every reaction in any situation by human beings, much less over an extended period of time.

Why then spend time talking about auditing curriculum in such a system? The answer is two-fold: first, to show that auditing as a function does not require a rational system in order to be performed and, secondly, to demonstrate how certain programs within rational systems which are non-rational can be audited.

Critics of auditing may want to point out that auditing literally demands a kind of system response that is inimical to "creativity," however defined. Such definitions of creativity, in an organizational sense, take on aspects of the non-rational system elaborated thus far. Auditing doesn't require them, however.

Secondly, it may be imagined that non-rational systems can't be audited because they function on contrary notions of the auditing process itself. That, too, is not true.

CURRICULUM IN THE NON-RATIONAL SYSTEM

Curriculum in the non-rational system has a very different function than in the rational system. First, it is not conceived as a tool to facilitate a centralized, top-down decision to carry out preconceived goals sanctioned by legislative-fiduciary bodies or agencies.

Curriculum in the non-rational system is much more open-ended, user-shaped, and site specific. Rather than being designed a priori, it it would be designed in situ. It is conceivable that it would be far more dialectical and spontaneously generated than the usual notions inherent in forming the tried and true curriculum committees which published curriculum guides the size of city telephone books.

Such a curriculum would and could contain inherent contradictions within itself. The "scope and sequence" would be a jumble, perhaps even chaotic by contemporary rational standards.

Suppose, however, that the designers were willing to tolerate such logical-positivistic dilemmas because they believed that contradictions are really inherent in reality. The trick is to get students to see them. That would be encapsulating the idea of dialectic as a "thread" for curriculum development. This internal organizing idea provides the locus for organized teaching instead of an externally imposed scope and sequence embedded in subject content characteristics or chronology.

By using such a principle, curriculum development shifts from a kind of inert state document imposed on teachers to an organic, user-based, and situationally shaped model. In this model, curriculum sheds a kind of superficial logical modality to become one which accepts contradiction as a way of life. Such contradictions are built into curriculum development on purpose.

AUDITING IN THE NON-RATIONAL SYSTEM

This situation would not be difficult to audit. The auditor would not ask what outcomes you were trying to obtain if the decisions were not outcome based. The auditor would ask, "What decisions did you make about curriculum? How do you know they were made as you believed? Did the results indicate to you your decisions were properly carried out? How do you know if you should continue to make the same decisions?"

Audits do not necessarily require goals. They require them if the entity being audited requires them. The audit process merely "tracks" the actions, ideas, beliefs, and decisions made by officials and participants in the entity being examined. What is required is an audit trail. That consists of documents primarily and, in the case of the audit methodology discussed so far, data derived from interviews and site visitations.

An audit is an organized probe and review of decisions, events, and processes employed by a group of people doing most any kind of activity. In the case of curriculum development, if spontaneity were the only guiding principle of the creation of curricula, the auditor would want to know if the users/designers of that curriculum were satisfied that spontaneity was working and that it enabled them to continue doing it. It would flesh out the criteria by which spontaneity was selected as the paramount criterion and others eliminated or considered less important. It would hold these data back to the client as a kind of mirror and ask, "What do you see? Is this right? Are there ways you can do it better? Are there things you should additionally consider?" Broadly conceived, auditing is simply an activity of evaluation.

And in this context as in the rational system view, auditing verifies the "truthfulness" of the records kept by the people in the organization. Are they true and credible representations of what they say is going on, whatever that may be? Auditing thus investigates the "believability" of any system, however it is defined, on whatever value base that may be employed. If it is important for any entity to be considered credible and an external verification is deemed proper, an audit and auditing become a logical derivative and process. Audits do not require any particular form of organization or belief to serve a useful purpose.

Two polarized models of system behavior are shown in Exhibit 23. Both are capable of being audited.

The two scenarios present the extreme view. In the rational system column/scenario of curriculum development, teachers are literally "left out" of the curriculum development process. They are relegated to the role of passive recipients and implementers. There is no room for involvement or any localized shaping of the curriculum.

Exhibit 23

Curriculum Development in Two Types of Organizational Systems

The Rational System Scenario (nonorganic)	The Non-Rational System Scenario (organic)
State Law	State Accepts the Curriculum
Essential Elements	
State Curriculum Framework	Board Accepts Curriculum
District Curriculum Guides (objectives correlated to essential elements)	Teachers Publish Curriculum (contradictions and all)
Teacher's Lesson Plans	Teachers Create Curriculum which Matches Organizing Principles
Teacher's Grade Book	Teachers Decide on Organizing Principles

In the non-rational system view, the "system" is "left out." In this scenario administrators, the board, and the state passively "accept" decisions made by teachers, no matter how contradictory or poor they may be. The scenario does not show that teachers may collectively decide to alter curriculum on mutually agreed criteria. Some of the contradictions could therefore be resolved. Furthermore, it does not show a board of education with any guidelines that have to be met or a state with any mandates about what ought to be included in a curriculum.

Both approaches to conceptualizing curriculum are amenable to using an audit, despite the fact that the values embraced may be quite different and the outcomes desired oppositional to one another.

Audit "logic" is shaped and determined by the nature of the enterprise being examined and the requirements and rules to which a system must be responsive, whether self-imposed or externally imposed, or combinations of both conditions.

Audits per se do not require centralization any more than they would require decentralization. They do not demand nonorganic approaches any more or less than organic ones. They can be as flexible as the situation permits. However, they all use data in its three basic forms (documents, interview, observation), and they all are indicators of organizational system credibility.

In rational systems audits tend to reinforce the values of that system because the system itself provides the judgmental criteria upon which the audit proceeds. The same is true for the non-rational system.

The critical decision is not whether to audit but what is to be audited because audits can be constructed which incorporate contrary or oppositional values to that which is being audited. For example, if a non-rational system selected a rational system audit approach, it would be blasted from all the assumptions of the rational system. The non-rational system's "strengths" would be labeled "weaknesses" in the rational system's value structure.

Once the decision has been made to conduct an audit, then it is incumbent upon the auditees to select an audit model that is congruent with the system's value structure. In that decision lies the utility of the audit's findings and recommendations.

CHECKPOINTS

Questions Commonly Asked the Author–Auditor

Question 1: *A review of the case studies of the audits you've conducted amply reveals that the districts' shortcomings were all embedded in the rational system model. Doesn't this contradict your point in this chapter?*

Answer: No, not at all. All of the school systems shown in the case studies desired to be considered rational system exemplars. Furthermore, they all functioned in states with legal mandates requiring rational system responses. Their shortcomings were congruent with the model they had adopted.

Question 2: *You said that accountability was a driving force for rational system responses—doesn't this depend upon who is defining accountability?*

Answer: Very much so. If teachers controlled their own profession in absolute terms, audits would probably follow the non-rational model and reinforce teacher control of the curriculum. Accountability under the present set of circumstances means that the state controls the schools.

Question 3: *Do you know of any school systems trying to be non-rational as you described them?*

Answer: No, not completely. I know some systems who thought they were implementing that model, only to have a board election provide a rude shock that such a non-rational system would not be tolerated, particularly where the people were shut out of the process and totally captured by the teachers.

Question 4: *What were the situations that stimulated the board reversals?*

Answer: It was either prolonged negotiations or a strike or a sharp drop in test scores. These two situations can dramatically illustrate to parents how "powerless" they really are when they perceive damage to their children's education. They normally result in movement to prevent teachers from obtaining absolute control of the curriculum or anything else in schools. In this sense teacher strikes provide a constant reminder to parents that teachers cannot be allowed to totally control the schools. They are counter productive to expanded teacher control of their own professionalization.

Question 5: *Do you really believe that time spent on goal formulation is wasted?*

Answer: Not usually. The creation of goals is usually purposeful even if nothing more than a symbolic exercise, which it is for many school systems. Symbols are important organizing points for social actions. My own work simply reveals that, as statements to impact work, they are not functional. However, as statements of social legitimization, they may be quite functional. In this sense they are serving a political, rather than operational, purpose.

Question 6: *Are most school system planning documents you've examined useful in impacting curriculum development?*

Answer: About half the time they impact curriculum development. The primary way they impact curriculum development is to designate which content areas are "developed" first. It's a rare document that does much else.

Question 7: *Why aren't plans more influential?*

Answer: Because of the fact that budgeting is conducted on an annual basis and is the dominant force for all district movement and because of the lack of stability in both board and administrative leadership in most school systems. Plans don't control anything. People control things through plans. When the people are constantly shuffling about the organization, the plans become empty reminders of previous administrators' thoughts. As stand-alone documents, they are rarely influential when the authors of them pass on.

Question 8: *What's the most appealing characteristic of the non-rational system?*

Answer: Organic change that is based on indigenous leadership. Change is much slower but does it last! However, such efforts ought to function within certain guidelines. In that way, the efforts of indigenous leadership can be supported in the larger political system, rather than be at odds with it. The only folks who would question that tactic would be those who desire fundamental changes in the existing political structure.

/ APPENDIX A / *The Essential Curriculum Audit Reader*

THERE ARE AS yet no university courses that specifically prepare curriculum auditors. In order to help the reader know what background reading the author–auditor has discovered to be most valuable, the following sources are compiled and annotated for reference purposes. They appear in alphabetical order.

(1) Apple, Michael, W. *Ideology and Curriculum.* London and Boston:Routledge and Kegan Paul. 195 pp. (1981).

Michael Apple is a professor of curriculum and instruction at the University of Wisconsin. His writing is highly influenced by neo-Marxist ideas. He deals with the concept of "de-skilling" teachers which relates to pre-packaged curriculum. He advances and clarifies the concept of the "hidden curriculum." His viewpoint of curriculum is political in nature. A reading of Apple should convince curriculum auditors that they are not doing a "neutral activity" in the auditing process. It should also make the would-be auditor much more sensitive about who will do what to whom as a result of an audit.

(2) Aronowitz, Stanley and Henry A. Giroux. *Education Under Seige.* South Hadley, Massachusetts:Bergin and Garvey Publishers, Inc. 225 pp. (1985).

The product of two professors of sociology and education at CUNY and Miami of Ohio, this book is a radical critique of business applications to education, as well as of many Marxist ideas pertaining to schooling and curriculum. Aronowitz and Giroux are intellectually rigorous and will frame for the reader stimulating and forceful attacks on conventional thinking about schools and curriculum. Especially helpful are thoughts about the problematical nature of school knowledge, how schools reinforce the dominant society with its ideas about social relations and class, and "structured silences" that teach values and social relations informally in schools and classrooms.

(3) Beauchamp, George A. *Curriculum Theory*. Wilmette, Illinois:The Kagg Press. 210 pp. (1975).

Beauchamp is a retired professor of curriculum at Northwestern University. His book is the last of a line of thought that attempts to codify curricular concepts and terminology in use in the field. I have found myself returning many times to clarify concepts and terms, at least from an historic, in-house view of them. Many contemporary curriculum writers, especially the leftists and radicals, pooh-pooh Beauchamp, but I've found him to be helpful on more than one occasion.

(4) Drucker, Peter F. *Management*. New York:Harper and Row. 803 pp. (1973).

Anybody dealing with human organizations and contemporary issues will encounter Peter F. Drucker. His popularity makes him suspicious to academics at the outset because professors assume that rigor and fashion are not complementary. They are wrong. Drucker is wide and deep. Furthermore, he is readable. My edition of *Management* is riddled with notes and the pages are dog-eared. I have used his concept of the "fallacy of creativity" many times to counter neo-romantic views of life in school systems. Consider Drucker to be "core" reading.

(5) English, Fenwick W. and Betty E. Steffy. *Educational Consulting*. Englewood Cliffs, New Jersey:Educational Technology Publications. 209 pp. (1984).

I'm recommending this book because it deals with all of the practical side of consulting–auditing. It's based on many years of experience. I'm told by many professional consultants that the chapters on profitability and marketing are the best thing around. For the would-be auditor to know how to "price" an audit, this source provides the best explanation.

(6) English, Fenwick W. *Curriculum Management for Schools, Colleges, Business*. Springfield, Illinois:Charles C. Thomas Publisher. 297 pp. (1987).

This is a comprehensive source for detailed background reading of the audit concepts. It also deals with curriculum alignment and mapping, two related technologies to auditing. There is a chapter in the book on auditing itself.

(7) Hasenfeld, Yeheskel. *Human Service Organizations*. Englewood Cliffs, New Jersey:Prentice-Hall, Inc. 265 pp. (1983).

Schools are one form of human service organizations. This text includes an up-to-date reference for many current ideas about human organizations. I thought Hasenfeld's review of Karl Weick's concept of "loose coupling" was one of the best I've seen. The book will provide the reader with a good grounding in organizational theory.

(8) Hill, John C. *Curriculum Evaluation for School Improvement.* Springfield, Illinois:Charles C. Thomas Publisher. 219 pp. (1986).

My colleague at Cincinnati, John Hill, has written a readable review of the many ways of evaluating curriculum. I consider Hill's book a basic primer for the curriculum auditor to begin any activity of an evaluative nature.

(9) Glatthorn, Allan A. *Curriculum Leadership.* Glenview, Illinois:Scott-Foresman and Company. 360 pp. (1987).

This is perhaps the very best contemporary view of the curriculum field by one of the most able and practical writers on the subject. Glatthorn is an experienced school administrator of many years, having been principal of Abington High School in Pennsylvania during its heyday as an innovative secondary school. The book deals with the foundations of curriculum which include history, theory, and politics. It also includes chapters about developments in the subject fields, planning, and alignment.

(10) Hartley, Harry J. *Educational Planning-Programming-Budgeting: Systems Approach.* Englewood Cliffs, New Jersey:Prentice-Hall, Inc. 277 pp. (1968).

Because the tie between budget and curriculum assumes a programmatic format, this book explains the "classical" PPBS solution. While some of the ideas are outdated, the text still provides a basic conceptual grounding of PPBS. For examination of school budgets, Hartley's book is still important.

(11) Kaufman, Roger A. *Planning Educational Systems.* Lancaster, Pennsylvania:Technomic Publishing Company, Inc. (1988).

I consider Kaufman's book the most holistic of all planning books ever written. The reason is that his "system approach" prevents fragmentation and jumping on the bandwagon with solutions before adequate problem definition. For the auditor to grasp what essential educational planning is all about, this book is basic.

(12) Kliebard, Herbert M. *The Struggle for the American Curriculum 1893–1958.* Boston:Routledge and Kegan Paul. 270 pp. (1986).

This is an excellent source book to understand both the figures and ideas that have moved American curriculum thought since the turn of the century. Kliebard has put together valuable historical data and does an able job in fleshing out the contextual sources of many contemporary curricular and schooling ideas. Too many educational administrators are ahistorical in outlook. Their naivete is embarrassing. This book would go a long way in bringing the auditor "up to speed" in the curriculum discipline itself.

(13) Lincoln, Yvonna S. *Organizational Theory and Inquiry: The Paradigm Revolution.* Beverly Hills:SAGE Publications, Inc. 228 pp. (1985).

To fully understand the dramatic shift occurring in how school systems are being viewed, this book is a "must." School systems are a lot more "irrational" than we formerly believed. Two chapters in this text by Karl Weick and David Clark lay it all out. Some familiarity with organizational theory is required to fully confront the ideas Weick and Clark present.

(14) Majchrzak, Ann. *Methods for Policy Research.* Beverly Hills:SAGE Publications, Inc. 109 pp. (1984).

A curriculum audit is a kind of policy analysis tool. This small but very helpful book will explain concisely the parallel approaches to policy analysis and curriculum auditing, though the latter is not cited by name in the text.

(15) Murnane, Richard J. *The Impact of School Resources on the Learning of Inner City Children.* Cambridge, Massachusetts:Ballinger Publishing Co. 118 pp. (1975).

Consider this little book a "classic" study using time-honored economic concepts of the examination of inputs and outputs in schools. The connections reviewed by Murnane are the basic assumptions of the curriculum audit. The fact that they are positive and interrelated is documented in this text, as well as some of the shortcomings, too.

(16) O'Neill, William F. *Educational Ideologies: Contemporary Expressions of Educational Philosophy.* Santa Monica, California:Goodyear Publishing Company, Inc. 403 pp. (1981).

What's a book on educational philosophy doing on this list? This isn't just any book on philosophy. It's a readable and very current categorization of figures and writers espousing a variety of solutions to education's problems. O'Neill has rejected the traditional view of educational philosophy of Theodore Brameld as too confusing. His ideas and constructs are much more akin to what school administrators bump into managing schools. An excellent source book to view some of the current political battles over education at the state and federal levels.

(17) Sayle, Allan J. *Management Audits.* New York:McGraw-Hill. 181 pp. (1981).

A curriculum audit is a special kind of management audit. This book deals with applications in the private sector. It is an excellent overall source book, concise and practical. Chapters in the book include the use of checklists, interviewing, questioning techniques, and auditor tactics. A simply superb reference for the auditor.

(18) Wagner, Jon. *Images of Information.* Beverly Hills:SAGE Publications. 308 pp. (1979).

If the auditor is considering the utilization of photographs in a curriculum audit, this is the book to read. Both technical and research oriented, the rules of visual data will be made more comprehensible. This source is one of a kind.

/ APPENDIX B / *Survey Instrument on Good Curriculum Management Practices*

THIS IS A kind of self-survey to look at a school district's curriculum management practices. The "cut off" scores have been established on the basis of experience in auditing and not by empirical/statistical studies.

AREA	YES	NO	DON'T KNOW
Policies			
1. The local school board has developed and adopted a policy which requires quality control of the curriculum.	____	____	________
2. Policies are followed by the administration and regularly reported to the board at public meetings.	____	____	________
3. Policies adhere to state laws and regulations.	____	____	________
4. Policies are regularly reviewed to incorporate suggestions as per national studies.	____	____	________
Curriculum			
1. Locally produced curriculum guides exist for all areas of the curriculum.	____	____	________
2. Local curriculum guides have been subject to external review and critique to demonstrate validity.	____	____	________
3. Local curriculum guides indicate clear objectives for teachers and recommended time ranges to be spent by objective.	____	____	________
4. Curriculum guides have been keyed to all utilized tests by grade level and objective and to teaching methods.	____	____	________

5. Curriculum guides have been officially adopted by the board of education. _____ _____ __________

Textbooks

6. Textbooks are adopted on the basis that their content matches locally adopted objectives (the key to local control). _____ _____ __________
7. Curricular objectives are keyed to each adopted textbook by page reference and listed in curriculum guides. _____ _____ __________
8. Textbooks are adopted with tests and curriculum and not separately. _____ _____ __________

Tests and Testing

9. Tests are adopted because of their "match" to local curricular objectives. _____ _____ __________
10. Test data are regularly and publicly reported in an understandable manner. _____ _____ __________
11. Test data are regularly used in program and classroom evaluation and planning. _____ _____ __________
12. Areas of the curriculum not regularly tested are assessed by some other appropriate and reliable method and are publicly reported. _____ _____ __________

Teaching

13. Teacher adherence to the locally adopted curriculum is monitored by school principals on an ongoing basis. _____ _____ __________
14. Teachers are test data as feedback for planning their educational programs. _____ _____ __________
15. Pupil achievement is considered an important aspect of teacher evaluation, but teachers are not rated or paid on the basis of standardized test results. _____ _____ __________
16. In-service training of teachers is aimed at improving their capability to deliver the adopted local curriculum. _____ _____ __________

Planning

17. The planning process shows evidence of the necessity to establish, maintain, and improve management control by the board and superintendent. _____ _____ __________
18. The plans developed by the administration are clear, regularly reviewed, and monitored by the board of educa-

tion, and they are used to assess administrative performance. _____ _____ __________

19. Plans cover at least three to five years as a "horizon" and include a consideration of how "problems" will be overcome in implementation. _____ _____ __________
20. The planning process for curriculum is integrated with the budgeting cycle. _____ _____ __________

Budgeting and Finances

21. The budgeting process indicates a linkage to instructional priorities based on test and other evaluative data. _____ _____ __________
22. The budgeting process is able to use as a rationale for increased costs expected benefits in terms of results. _____ _____ __________
23. Priorities of the educational program can be found in past budgets and future cost projections. _____ _____ __________
24. Costs are calculated in terms of not doing anything about priorities (ignoring the problem). _____ _____ __________
25. Costs can be shown to be related to benefits that are visible and explainable. _____ _____ __________

TOTALS _____ _____ __________

Gauging Your Results

Score Range	Comment
22–25 points	Excellent control of the curriculum. Congratulations!
18–21 points	Fairly sound control. Could stand some tuning.
15–20 points	Marginal control. Will require attention.
14 or below	Little or no control. When are you going to start?

/ APPENDIX C / *Sample Board Policy to Establish Curricular Quality Control*

AFTER BEING ASKED by more than one board of education to provide them with a policy about quality control because they didn't have one, this sample was finally developed.

In order to maximize local control of the curriculum and to be responsive to the community, the board sets forth these tenets to be followed by the superintendent and professional staff in the development of curriculum in the district.

(1) There shall be locally developed written curriculum guides for all grade levels and subjects in the school district. These guides shall be revised and re-adopted by the board every five years or sooner and:
   (a) identify the specific content, skills, attitudes, and processes to be taught.
   (b) state the means for the evaluation or assessment of each of the content areas, skills, and attitudes to be taught.
   (c) be integrated with and consistent with the adoption of textbooks.

(2) Curriculum developed for the district's elementary schools shall concentrate upon the basic skills and provide for consistency and clarity of instructional focus among the elementary schools of the district. Common textbook adoptions and curricular materials shall be aimed at promoting consistency and clarity of instructional focus.

(3) Curriculum shall be developed in harmony with state guidelines and relevant federal mandates where applicable. It shall be congruent with those subject areas and skills tested by the state and locally adopted criterion referenced or standardized tests.

Accordingly, the superintendent shall take steps to conduct a major review of three curriculum areas per year and organize a report/presentation to the board of education which demonstrates how this policy has been implemented and to present such recommendations as may be necessary for the improvement of pupil growth as may be required, except in the first year of implementation of this policy in which only one curricular area is required to be reviewed.

The areas to be reviewed are mathematics, physical education, reading language arts (elementary), English (secondary), writing (creative and expository), foreign language, science, social studies (including geography, patriotism, civics, history), art, music, industrial arts/home economics, computers, special education, vocational education, health, and safety.

The review process shall include a statement of instructional goals by grade level, assessment or testing trend data as may be relevant, important new trends that are to be incorporated into the curriculum, recommended textbooks in the curriculum, and input from the teaching staff. The superintendent shall employ one or more externally identified content area curriculum experts to critique the proposed or existing curriculum in light of available knowledge regarding appropriate curricula in the areas being reviewed, and those reports/critiques shall be appended to the board support.

Copies of the curriculum guides in complete sets shall be available for all teachers and the public in each principal's office and in the public libraries of the community for parental review and reference.

The superintendent shall develop a set of administrative regulations that will effectively carry out this policy in its entirety and ensure its consistent implementation at all schools of the district.

Definition of Terms

Curriculum—The content (process, attitudes, skills, knowledges) that is to be taught and/or learned at the appropriate level/area/course.

Basis Skills—Defined as mathematics, reading, penmanship, writing (all forms), related writing skills (grammar, spelling, etc.), science, geography, history, music, and art.

Adopted:

Re-Adopted:

/ BIBLIOGRAPHY

ALEXANDER, C. *The Timeless Way of Building*. Oxford University Press (1979).

ALINSKY, S. *Reveille for Radicals*. New York:Vintage Books (1969, 1946).

American Association of School Administrators. "School Climate, Curriculum Top Superintendents' Priorities," *School Administrator*, 44(6):36–37 (June 1987).

APPLE, M.W. *Ideology and Curriculum*. Boston, MA:Routledge and Kegan Paul (1979).

ARONOWITZ, S. and H. A. Giroux. *Education Under Siege*. South Hadley, MA:Bergin and Garvey Publishers, Inc. (1985).

Associated Press. "Math Curriculum in U.S. Blasted," *Burlington County Times*, p. 9 (January 12, 1987).

Associated Press. "Students Faulted on Global Issues," *New York Times*, p. B 10 (May 13, 1987).

Associated Press. "U.S. Doubles Foreign Debt in a Year," *Philadelphia Inquirer*, p. 1, 12-A (June 24, 1987).

BAUMOL, W. J. "A Modest Decline Isn't All That Bad," *New York Times*, p. B.1 (February 15, 1987).

BEAUCHAMPS, G. *Curriculum Theory*. Wilmette, IL:The Kagg Press (1975).

BELLACK, A. A., H. M. Kliebard, R. T. Hyman, and F. L. Smith, Jr. *The Language of the Classroom*, New York:Teachers College Press (1966).

BELLAH, R. N. *Beyond Belief* (1970). New York, as cited in O'Neil, W. F. *Educational Ideologies*. Santa Monica, CA:Goodyear Publishing Company, Inc., p. 119 (1981).

BERTALANFFY, L. V. *General System Theory*, New York:George Braziller (1968).

BURRUP, P. E. and B. Brimley, Jr. *Financing Education in a Climate of Change*. Boston, MA:Allyn and Bacon, Inc. (1982).

CRONIN, J. M. *Big City School Bankruptcy* (Policy Paper No. 80-C3) Washington, D.C.: National Institute of Education (Grant No. OB-NIE-G-80-0111) (1980).

DARLING-HAMMOND, L. "We Need Schools Able and Willing to Use Carnegie's Teachers for the 21st Century," *Chronicle of Higher Education*, p. 76 (July 16, 1986).

DAVIDSON, J. W. and M. H. Lytle. *After the Fact* (2nd ed.). New York:Alfred A. Knopf (1986).

DENZIN, N. K. *The Research Act*. New York:McGraw-Hill Book Company (1978).

DICKERSON, J. W. Bedford County, *Report of the Superintendent of Common Schools of the Commonwealth of Pennsylvania*. Harrisburg:Singerly and Myers, State Printers, pp. 52–59 (1867).

DRAIN, S. C. "A Mechanic Gave the World a Lift," *American History Illustrated*, pp. 42–46, 50 (November 1987).

EDWARDS, S. and W. Richardson. *A Survey of MCPS Withdrawals to Attend Private School*. Rockville, MD:Montgomery County Public Schools (1981).

EISNER, E. W. *The Educational Imagination: On the Design and Evaluation of School Programs*. New York:MacMillan Publishing Co. (1985).

ELLIS, T. "Schools Should Teach Values Based on Bible," *USA Today*, p. 10 A (April 7, 1987).

ENGLISH, F. W. *Critical Audit Process (CAP) for Schools Requiring Review beyond CAR/CSIP Process*. Albany, NY:New York State Education Department (1987).

ENGLISH, F. W. *An Educational Performance Audit of the Mt. Pleasant Public Schools*. Unpublished final audit report (1985).

ENGLISH, F. W. "It's Time to Abolish Conventional Curriculum Guides," *Educational Leadership*, 44(4):50–52 (December–January, 1986–1987).

ENGLISH, F. W. *Quality Control in Curriculum Development*. Arlington, VA:American Association of School Administrators (1978).

ENGLISH, F. W. and B. E. Steffy. *Educational Consulting*. Englewood Cliffs, NJ:Educational Technology Publications (1984).

EVANS, G. "A Black University Makes Money-Raising Look Easy. It's Anything But," *Chronicle for Higher Education*, 32(1):16 (September 3, 1986).

FIELDS, C. M. "Need to Retrain People in Changing Fields Confronts Colleges with Creative Challenge," *Chronicle of Higher Education*, 32(3):37–39 (September 17, 1986).

FLINDERS, D. J., N. Noddings, and S. J. Thornton. "The Null Curriculum: Its Theoretical Basis and Practical Implications," *Curriculum Inquiry*, 16(1):33–42 (Spring 1986).

FRECHTLING, J. A. and S. M. Frankel. A Survey of Montgomery County Parents Who Transferred Their Children between Public and Private Schools in 1980–81. Rockville, MD:Montgomery County Public Schools (June, 1982).

GARMS, W. I., J. W. Guthrie, and L. C. Pierce. *School Finance*. Englewood Cliffs, NJ: Prentice-Hall, Inc. (1978).

GIROUX, H. A. *Theory and Resistance in Education*. MA:Bergin and Garvey Publishers, Inc. (1983).

GRATIOT, M. H. "Why Parents Choose Non-Public Schools: Comparative Attitudes and Characteristics of Public and Private School Consumers," *Dissertation Abstracts International*, 40, 4825-A (University Microfilms No. 8006315) (1980).

GRIESEMER, J. L. and C. Butler. *Education under Study*. Chelmsford, MA:Northeast Regional Exchange, Inc.

HASENFELD, Y. *Human Service Organizations*. Englewood-Cliffs, NJ:Prentice-Hall (1983).

HOYLE, J. R., F. W. English, and B. E. Steffy. *Skills for Successful School Leaders*. Arlington, VA:American Association of School Administrators (1985).

HOYT, E. P. *America's Wars and Military Excursions*. New York:McGraw-Hill (1987).

JASCHIK, S. "A Governor Pours Millions More into Education," *Chronicle of Higher Education*, 32(1):25 (September 3, 1986).

JASCHIK, S. "Somehow, Higher-Education Budget Officers Must Reconcile Politics, Reality," *Chronicle of Higher Education*, 32(41):17, 22 (June 24, 1987).

JOHNS, R. L., E. L. Morphet, and K. Alexander. *The Economics and Financing of Education*. Englewood Cliffs, NJ:Prentice-Hall, Inc. (1983).

KAPPAN. "U.S. Math Curriculum Needs Overhaul, New Study Says," pp. 558–559 (March 1987).

KIRST, M. W. *Who Controls Our Schools?* New York:W. H. Freeman and Company (1984).

KOEPP, S. and A. Constable. "Placing the Blame at E. F. Hutton," *Time*, p. 54 (September 16, 1985).

KUHN, A. and R. D. Beam. *The Logic of Organization*. San Francisco:Jossey-Bass, Publishers (1982).

LESSINGER, L. *Every Kid a Winner.* New York:Simon and Schuster (1970).

LINCOLN, Y. S. and E. G. Guba. *Naturalistic Inquiry.* Beverly Hills, CA:SAGE Publications (1985).

MANCHESTER, W. *The Death of a President*. New York:Harper and Row Publishers (1967).

McCOY, C. R. "A School Takeover Bill OKd," *Philadelphia Inquirer*, p. 1 and 5-B (June 9, 1987).

MILLER, J. P. and W. Seller. *Curriculum*. New York:Longman (1985).

MINTZBERG, H. *The Structuring of Organizations*. Englewood Cliffs, NJ:Prentice-Hall, Inc. (1979).

MIRGA, T. "Creationism Law in La. is Rejected by Supreme Court," *Education Week*, 6(39):1, 6 (June 24, 1987).

Mt. Pleasant Public Schools Newsletter, "Audit Keys Curriculum Change," p. 1, 7 (March, 1985).

National Education Association, *Inquiry Report Kanawha County West Virginia a Textbook Study in Cultural Conflict*. Washington, D.C.:Teacher Rights Division (February 1975).

OLSON, L. "State Comparisons Will Be Difficult, Experts Predict," *Education Week*, 5(39):1, 14 (June 18, 1986).

OTTAVIANO, D. M. "Palmyra Votes No on Bond," *Philadelphia Inquirer*, p. B. 1 (June 24, 1987).

PARENTI, M. *Power and the Powerless*. New York:St. Martin's Press (1978).

PASCHAL, J. "Accountants Clean House," *The Cincinnati Inquirer*, Section H: 1, 8 (September 6, 1987).

PERLEZ, J. "Removal of School Board Members in District Seen," *New York Times* (February 1, 1987).

POPHAM, W. J. "The Merits of Measurement-Driven Instruction," *Phi Delta Kappan*, 68(9):679–682 (May 1987).

PRIAL, F. J. "Grand Jury Study Faults Bronx School System," *New York Times*, p. L 33 (February 1, 1987).

RECER, P. "Investigation Began Immediately," *Burlington County Times*, p. 5 (January 29, 1986).

RIIS, J. A. *The Battle with the Slum*. New York:The MacMillan Company (1902).

RIIS, J. A. *How the Other Half Lives*. New York:C. Scribner's Sons (1890).

ROTHMAN, R. "Using Pupil Scores to Assess Teachers Criticized as Unfair," *Education Week*, 6(36):1, 18 (June 3, 1987).

ROWAN, B., S. T. Bossart, and D. C. Dwyer. "Research on Effective Schools: A Cautionary Note," *Educational Researcher*, 12(4):24 (1983).

Sarasota, Florida, "Mission Statement of the School Board of Sarasota County, Florida," memorandum from the superintendent (August 21, 1987).

SAYLE, A. J. *Management Audits*. London:McGraw-Hill Book Company (UK) Limited (1981).

SECCOMBE, V. A. "The Impact of Tuition Tax Credit Legislation on Public Schools," Unpublished doctoral dissertation. Lehigh University, Bethlehem, PA (1987).

SEGLEM, L. "Governors Differ on School Takeover Proposal," *New Jersey Courier-Post*, p. 9A (December 10, 1986).

SELLTIZ, C., L. S. Wrightsman, and S. W. Cook. *Research Methods in Social Relations*. New York:Holt, Rinehart, Winston (1976).

SHOR, I. *Culture Wars*. Boston, MA:Routledge and Kegan Paul (1986).

SILVER, P. *Educational Administration*. New York:Harper and Row (1983).

SONTAG, S. *On Photography*. New York:Farrar, Straus, and Giroux (1977).

SORGE, M. "Worker Absences Plague Carmaker," *The Detroit News*, p. E.1, 3 (March 26, 1987).

Special Task Force on Education, *Chicago School System Recommended Actions*, Chicago, IL (March, 1981).

SPRING, J. *The American School 1642–1985*. New York:Longman (1986).

STEVENS, M. *The Big Eight*. New York:MacMillan Publishing Company (1981).

STROHMEYER, J. "Crisis in Bethlehem," *Lehigh Alumni Bulletin*, pp. 20–29 (Spring 1987).

TOWER, J., E. Muskie, and B. Scowcroft. *The Tower Commission Report*. New York:The New York Times (February 1987).

United States Chamber of Commerce, *The Neglected Imperatives of Education*, Washington, D.C. (1971).

United States Department of Education, *A Nation at Risk: The Imperative for Educational Reform*, Washington, D.C. (April 1983).

WAGNER, J. *Images of Information*. Beverly Hills, CA:SAGE Publications (1979).

WALBERG, H. J. *Improving Educational Standards and Productivity*. Berkeley, CA: McCutchan Publishing Corporation (1982).

WEICK, K. "Educational Organizations as Loosely Coupled Systems," *Administrative Science Quarterly*, 21:1–19 (December, 1976).

WEICK, K. "Sources of Order in Underorganized Systems: Themes in Recent Organizational Theory," in *Organizational Theory and Inquiry*. Y. S. Lincoln, ed. Beverly Hills, CA:SAGE Publications, pp. 106–136 (1985).

WHARTON, B. "Principal, Teacher Convicted," *Burlington County Times*, p. 1, 6 (June 5, 1987).

WHELLER, D. L. "Two Universities Chastised on Fraud Investigations," *Chronicle of Higher Education*, 33(38):1, 7 (June 3, 1987).

WHITE, P. E. "Resources as Determinants of Organizational Behavior," *Administrative Science Quarterly*, 19:366–76 (1974).

WISE, A. E. *Legislated Learning*. Berkeley, CA:University of California Press (1979).

/ INDEX

/ ABOUT THE AUTHOR

Fenwick W. English is Professor and Head, Educational Administration, Teachers College, University of Cincinnati, Ohio. Dr. English has been a superintendent of schools for five years in New York State for two school districts, an associate director of the American Association of School Administrators, and a partner in the internal accounting and consulting firm, Peat, Marwick, Main. At Peat, Marwick, Dr. English directed that firm's North American consulting practice in elementary and secondary education in Washington, D.C.

In 1979 Dr. English managed the first curriculum audit (a.k.a educational performance audit) for Peat, Marwick of the Columbus, Ohio, Public Schools. Since that time he has directed twenty other audits in seven states, for school districts in rural, suburban, and urban settings. In 1986 he conducted a number of curriculum audits for the New Jersey Attorney General's Office in the seven-year school finance litigation, Abbott v. Burke. He is the author or coauthor of eight previous books in education and over seventy articles in a broad spectrum of professional journals. He received his B.S. and M.S. from the University of Southern California and his Ph.D. from Arizona State University.